Lecture Notes in Artificia

Subseries of Lecture Notes in Com

Edited by J. G. Carbonell and J. Sie

Lecture Notes in Computer Science

Edited by G. Goos, J. Hartmanis, and J. van Leeuwen

Springer
Berlin
Heidelberg
New York
Barcelona
Hong Kong
London
Milan
Paris
Tokyo

Mark d'Inverno   Michael Luck
Michael Fisher   Chris Preist (Eds.)

Foundations and Applications of Multi-Agent Systems

UKMAS Workshops 1996-2000
Selected Papers

 Springer

Series Editors

Jaime G. Carbonell, Carnegie Mellon University, Pittsburgh, PA, USA
Jörg Siekmann, University of Saarland, Saarbrücken, Germany

Volume Editors

Mark d'Inverno
University of Westminster, Cavendish School of Computer Science
9-18 Euston Centre, London NW1 3ET, UK
E-mail: dinverm@wmin.ac.uk

Michael Luck
Southampton University, Department of Computer Science
Southampton SO17 1BJ, UK
E-mail: mml@ecs.soton.ac.uk

Michael Fisher
University of Liverpool, Department of Computer Science
Liverpool L69 7ZF, UK
E-mail: M.Fisher@csc.liv.ac.uk

Chris Preist
Hewlett-Packard laboratories Bristol
Filton Road, Stoke Gifford, Bristol BS12 6QZ, UK
E-mail: cwp@hplb.hpl.hp.com

Cataloging-in-Publication Data applied for

Die Deutsche Bibliothek - CIP-Einheitsaufnahme

Foundations and applications of multi agent systems : selected papers /
UKMAS Workshops 1996 - 2000. Mark d'Inverno ... (ed.). - Berlin ;
Heidelberg ; New York ; Barcelona ; Hong Kong ; London ; Milan ;
Paris ; Tokyo : Springer, 2002
  (Lecture notes in computer science ; Vol. 2403 : Lecture notes in
artificial intelligence)
  ISBN 3-540-43962-5
CR Subject Classification (1998): I.2.11, I.2, C.2.4

ISSN 0302-9743
ISBN 3-540-43962-5 Springer-Verlag Berlin Heidelberg New York

Springer-Verlag Berlin Heidelberg New York
a member of BertelsmannSpringer Science+Business Media GmbH

http://www.springer.de

© Springer-Verlag Berlin Heidelberg 2002
Printed in Germany

Typesetting: Camera-ready by author, data conversion by Steingräber Satztechnik GmbH, Heidelberg
Printed on acid-free paper   SPIN: 10873633   06/3142   5 4 3 2 1 0

Preface

Though the field of multi-agent systems has been growing rapidly and markedly over a number of years, it perhaps became especially established with the first International Conference on Multi-Agent Systems in San Francisco in 1995. That was also where the idea for a UK Special Interest Group was formed, and shortly afterwards, in the late summer of 1995, Mark d'Inverno, Michael Fisher, Nick Jennings, Michael Luck, and Mike Wooldridge met for a research meeting at the University of Westminster, and began a series of meetings that eventually became the UK Workshops on Multi-Agent Systems (UKMAS).

The UKMAS workshops have now been running for five years, in 1996 and 1997 under the heading of FoMAS (Foundations of Multi-Agent Systems) both organized by Michael Luck at University of Warwick and then subsequently in its current incantation, UKMAS, first by Michael Fisher at Manchester Metropolitan University, then by Chris Preist at Hewlett Packard Laboratories, Bristol, and finally by Mark d'Inverno at St. Catherine's College, Oxford in 2000.

The UK has been particularly strong in this area, and the MAS community's strength has been reflected by high rates of participation, high quality presentations and discussions, and by an impressive range of invited speakers. Though the workshops were always intended to provide a forum for discussion rather than more formal presentation or publication, we have sought to represent the discussions through summary papers that have been published in the Knowledge Engineering Review each year. After five years of very successful workshops, however, it seemed appropriate to provide a record of the more detailed and specific contributions from some of the speakers who have contributed over this time.

In consequence, we decided to produce an edited volume of selected papers representing the best of the first five years of UKMAS. As should be clear from the author list, we have been fortunate to welcome some of the most prestigious names in the field. Others who have contributed to the workshops include Aaron Sloman, Stan Franklin, Cristiano Caste!franchi, Ken Binmore, Ian Dickinson, and Craig Boutilier, and we thank them all for their input.

Over the years, numerous individuals have also contributed to the success of the workshops, most importantly the participants and speakers, but others must also be mentioned including Loretta Pletti, Serena Raffin, Chris Havill, Sam Akhtar, Ursula Brown, Anna Hemmings and Caroline Carpenter. We have been sponsored by BT Labs, FIPA, HP Labs, and more regularly by the UK's Engineering and Physical Sciences Research Council and AgentLink II, the European Commission's IST-funded Network of Excellence for Agent-Based Computing. We are immensely grateful to all for their support, which has enabled us to create a truly accessible and successful event.

Mark d'Inverno
May 2002   Michael Luck

Organization

UKMAS is organized by the UKMAS steering committee and runs effectively only through the contribution of the program committees.

Steering Committee

Mark d'Inverno	University of Westminster
Michael Fisher	University of Liverpool
Nick Jennings	University of Southampton
Michael Luck (Chair)	University of Southampton
Michael Wooldridge	University of Liverpool

Program Committee

Ruth Aylett	University of Salford
Rachel Bourne	Queen Mary, University of London
Alex Coddington	University of Durham
Kerstin Dautenhahn	University of Hertfordshire
Jürgen Dix	University of Manchester
Jim Doran	University of Essex
Peter Edwards	University of Aberdeen
Michael Fisher	University of Liverpool
Nick Jennings	University of Southampton
Luc Moreau	University of Southampton
Tim Norman	University of Aberdeen
Simon Parsons	Massachusetts Institute of Technology
Jeremy Pitt	Imperial College, London
Chris Preist	Hewlett Packard Laboratories, Bristol
Omer Rana	University of Wales, Cardiff
Chris Reed	University of Dundee
Nir Vulkan	University of Oxford
Michael Wooldridge	University of Liverpool

Sponsoring Institutions

AgentLink II, the European Network of Excellence for Agent-Based Computing
BT Laboratories, Ipswich
FIPA (The Foundation for Intelligent Physical Agents)
Hewlett Packard Laboratories, Bristol
EPSRC (The Engineering and Physical Sciences Research Council)

Table of Contents

Coordinating Intelligent Agents*

Keith Decker

Department of Computer and Information Sciences,
University of Delaware, Newark, DE 19716,
decker@udel.edu

Abstract. This chapter will focus on how to get organizations – multiple software agents and perhaps humans – to coordinate thier activities when they are working on shared, loosely coupled problems, such as engineering design or information gathering. It will describe some useful representations (including TÆMS [Task Analysis and Environment Modeling System]) for annotating an agent's representation of its activities, and some approaches (including GPGP [Generalized Partial Global Planning]) to designing coordination mechanisms that are adapted to some particular problem-solving environment. Examples will be drawn from various projects in distributed information gathering and distributed hospital patient scheduling.

1 Introduction

Our research program is involved in developing intelligent software agents (large, persistent, autonomous, communicative, goal- and data- driven computer programs) and *organizations* of these agents (sometimes including humans) that can operate in environments where there is a lot of uncertainty about what is happening and where there may be time pressures or deadlines. The agents will in general have many goals, some partially overlapping or conflicting. We are not (and can not) realistically look for optimal solutions, but instead must satisfice – try to find a solution that is "good enough" in the time and resources that are available. No agent can work completely alone.

This research program can be divided into three areas. First, how to formally represent and reason about these sorts of problems, both externally as a human software engineer and internally as a software agent. To this end we developed the TÆMS task structure description language (representing what we think are the important concepts) and the GPGP approach to coordination (a way to reason about TÆMS descriptions within each software agent so that a team of them acts coherently together). Secondly, we actually build software and tools for building actual software agents. This includes the RETSINA project that started with Dr. Katia Sycara at CMU, and the current DE-CAF project at the University of Delaware that combines features of RETSINA and those from TÆMS and GPGP. Finally, we are also interested in understanding, modeling, and even imitating human organizational structures in the context of software agents (both organizations of ALL software agents, and mixed human/software agent hybrid organizations). This is very important both because complex problems often need more

---

* This work was supported by the National Science Foundation under grant IIS-9733004.

M. d' Inverno et al. (Eds.): UKMAS 1996–2000, LNAI 2403, pp. 1–18, 2002.

than trivial organizaitonal solutions, and because most real systems are embedding in existing human organizations (so they had darn well respect the boundaries of those organizations and the roles of the people with whom they interact). This chapter, then, serves as a brief overview of the work in these three general areas.

2   Representing Coordination Problems: TAEMS

Coordination has been abstractly defined by Malone as the act of managing the inter-dependancies between activities [22]. A percieved difficulty with writing about coordination problems was that most approaches either sacrificed realistic complexity for precise specification (e.g. game theoretic models that assumed agent choice from static, well-known alternatives [27]), or sacrificed any rigorous specification for the sake of realistic complexity (e.g. text-based descriptions of domains like the DVMT [Distributed Vehicle monitoring Testbed] [20]). TÆMS (Task Analysis and Environment Modeling System) was developed to bring some rigor to the specification of complex environments by carefully representing the structure of the tasks in those environments. By "complex" we mean environments where there are alternative tasks, uncertainty in task outcomes, and timing considerations with respect to task completion and the effect of any task interdepedencies.

The TÆMS language is used to formally define what a task strucure is, what parts are known by what different agents, and what happens when agents execute these parts. TÆMS is often used as an annotation language on top of HTN (Hierarchical Task Network [16]) plans, based on careful, functional descriptions and an underlying state-based model of computation. The basic idea is that each agent is trying to maximize performance, as described by some set of utility characteristics (summarized as "quality" for good characteristics, and "cost" for bad characteristics). Since the time that something gets done often affects these things a lot, we also track the "duration" of various activities. TÆMS task structure annotations describe how the actions of any agent effect the perfomance of that agent or others (by changing quality, cost, or duration). Thus it extends HTN ideas toward specifying "worth-oriented" domains [27]. The basic relationship here is the "subtask" relationship; but more important are various hard and soft relationships that might exist between tasks (i.e. "enables" where A must come before B, or "facilitates", where doing A will cause B to be done better, cheaper, or quicker). All relationships have a formal, quantitative mathematial definition. TÆMS agents can reason about these task structures, and even use them as a language for communicating about coordination problems (see the next section on GPGP). Recent extensions to TÆMS have included multiple outcome specifications (contingencies) [33, 31].

In utility theory, agents have preferences over possible final states (action or plan outcomes), and preference-relevant features of an outcome are called *attributes*. A substantial body of work exists on relating attribute values to overall utilities [32]. At its core, TÆMS is about specifying these attributes and the processes by which they change – what we call a model of the task environment. In the following example we will stick to two attributes, *quality* and *duration*; typically a third *cost* attribute is also used.

Actions. A TÆMS *action* (or *executable method*) represents the smallest unit of analysis. In an implementation such as DECAF (see later), this corresponds to a Java procedure or procedures over whose internals we do not wish to reason. $d_0(M)$ is the *initial duration* of action M, and $q_0(M)$ is the *initial maximum quality* of action M. $d(M, t)$ is the *current duration*, and $q(M, t)$ is the *current maximum quality* of action M at time t. $Q(M, t)$ is the *current quality* of action M. $Q(M, t) = 0$ at times t before the execution of M. If an agent begins to execute M at time t (written $\text{Start}(M)$) and continues until time $t + d(M, t)$ (written $\text{Finish}(M)$), then $Q(M, \text{Finish}(M)) = q(M, \text{Finish}(M))$ (i.e. the current actual quality becomes the maximum possible quality). For the purposes of this example, the amount of work done on an action M here is simply $\text{Work}(M) = \text{Finish}(M) - \text{Start}(M)$. If there were no interrelationships (*non-local effects*, NLEs) between M and anything else, then $q(M, t) = q_0(M)$ and $d(M, t) = d_0(M)$. The execution of other actions and tasks effect an action *precisely by changing the current duration and current maximum quality of the action* (that is, $d(M, t)$ and $q(M, t)$, as specified below). For the purposes of this chapter, we will also assume that $Q(M, t) = 0$ for $Start(M) \leq t < Finish(M)$; other definitions of Q are possible to represent anytime algorithms, etc. Action pre-emption and resumption may also be modeled by extending these simple definitions [6].

Tasks. A TÆMS *task* (or *subtask*) represents a set of related subtasks or actions, joined by a common *quality accumulation function*. For example, in an AND/OR tree, an AND task indicates that all subtasks must be accomplished to accomplish the task, while an OR task indicates that only one subtask needs to be accomplished. Since TÆMS is about worth-oriented environment modeling, we use continuous rather than logical quality accumulation functions (for example min instead of AND, max instead of OR[1]). Given a subtask relationship subtask$(T_1, \mathbf{T})$ where $\mathbf{T}$ is the set of all direct subtasks or actions of T_1, then if T_1 is an AND task we may recursively define $Q(T_1, t) = Q_{\min}(T_1, t) = \min_{T \in \mathbf{T}} Q(T, t)$. For the purposes of evaluation, the amount of work done on a task is the sum of all the work done on its subtasks, and the finish time of a task is the latest (max) finish time of any subtask.

Non-local Effects (NLEs). Any TÆMS action/method, or a task T containing such a method, may potentially affect some other method M through a *non-local effect e*. We write this relation (a labeled arc in the task structure graph) as $\text{nle}(T, M, e, p_1, p_2, \ldots)$, where the p's are parameters specific to a class of effects. For this chapter, there are three possible outcomes of the application of a non-local effect on M under our model: $d(M, t)$ (current duration) is changed, $q(M, t)$ (current maximum quality) is changed, or both. An effect class e is thus a function $e(T, M, t, d, q, p_1, p_2, \ldots)$: [task × method × time × duration × quality × parameter 1 × parameter 2 × ...] $\mapsto$ [duration × quality]. For the purposes of this example, we will ignore the details regarding *where* information is available, i.e. non-local effects that depend on the transmission of information. Let us consider the two most popular NLEs: enables and facilitates.

Enables. If task T_a enables action M, then the maximum quality $q(M, t) = 0$ until T_a is "completed", at which time the current maximum quality will change to the initial maximum quality $q(M, t) = q_0(M)$. Another way to view this effect is that it changes the "earliest start time" of *enabled* method, because a rational scheduler will not execute the method before it is enabled.

---

[1] The full set of quality accumulation functions, including alternate definitions for AND and OR, is discussed in [6].

$$\text{enables}(T_a, M, t, d, q, \theta) = \begin{cases} [d, 0] & t < \Theta(T_a, \theta) \\ [d, \mathbf{q}_0(M)] & t \geq \Theta(T_a, \theta) \end{cases} \tag{1}$$

The term $\Theta(T_a, \theta)$ computes the earliest time at which task T_a reaches quality θ.

Facilitates. Computationally, facilitation occurs when information from one task, often in the form of constraints, is provided that either reduces or changes the search space to make some other task easier to solve. A simple to understand example of this relationship in computation is the relationship between sorting and searching. It is faster to retrieve an item from a sorted data structure, but sorting is not *necessary* for retrieval. Hence the sorting task facilitates the retrieval task.

In our framework, one task may provide results to another task that facilitates the second task by decreasing the duration or increasing the quality of its partial result. Therefore the facilitates effect has two constant parameters (called *power* parameters) $0 \leq \phi_d \leq 1$ and $0 \leq \phi_q \leq 1$, that indicate the effect on duration and quality, respectively. The effect varies not only through the power parameters, but also through the quality of the *facilitating* task available when work on the *facilitated* task starts (the ratio R, defined below).

$$R(T_a, s) = \frac{\mathrm{Q}_{\mathrm{avail}}(T_a, s)}{\mathbf{q}(T_a, s)}$$
$$\text{facilitates}(T_a, M, t, d, q, \phi_d, \phi_q) = [d(1 - \phi_d R(T_a, \text{Start}(M))),$$
$$q(1 + \phi_q R(T_a, \text{Start}(M)))] \tag{2}$$

So if T_a is completed with maximal quality, and the result is received before M is started, then the duration $\mathbf{d}(M, t)$ will be decreased by a percentage equal to the duration power ϕ_d of the facilitates effect. The second clause of the definition indicates that communication after the start of processing has no effect. In this paper we will only use the duration effect power ϕ_d. Negative values for power parameters produce "hindering" or "inhibition" effects.

Computing $\mathbf{d}(M, t)$ and $\mathbf{q}(M, t)$. Underlying a TÆMS model is a simple state-based computation. Each method has an initial maximum quality $\mathbf{q}_0(M)$ and duration $\mathbf{d}_0(M)$ so we define $\mathbf{q}(M, 0) = \mathbf{q}_0(M)$ and $\mathbf{d}(M, 0) = \mathbf{d}_0(M)$. If there are no non-local effects, then $\mathbf{d}(M, t) = \mathbf{d}(M, t-1)$ and $\mathbf{q}(M, t) = \mathbf{q}(M, t-1)$. If there is only one non-local effect with M as a consequent $\text{nle}(T, M, e, p_1, p_2, \ldots)$, then $[\mathbf{d}(M, t), \mathbf{q}(M, t)] \leftarrow e(T, M, t, \mathbf{d}(M, t-1), \mathbf{q}(M, t-1), p_1, p_2, \ldots)$. If there is more than one non-local effect, then the effects are applied in the order enables, then facilitates.

TÆMS has been extended quite a bit since its original definition. Most importantly, the number of quality accumulation functions has risen from 4 to 11 [19], resource usage can be modeled [5], and contingency plans can be represented [31]. In particular, contingencies are represented by indicating that tasks have more than one *outcome*, with some probability. Each outcome may then differentially express non-local effects (e.g. a "successful" outcome may enable downstream actions, while an "error" outcome does not).

2.1 Using TÆMS

A TÆMS model of environmental and task characteristics has three levels: *generative*, *objective*, and *subjective*. The *generative* level describes the statistical characteristics of objective problem instances (called *episodes*) in a domain. A generative level model consists of a description of the generative processes or distributions from which the range of alternative problem instances can be derived, and is used to study performance over a range of problems in an environment. The *objective* level describes the essential, 'real' task structure of a particular problem-solving situation or instance over time. Typically no agent ever has access to this complete and total information in the model or simulation. Finally, the *subjective* level describes the agents' view of the situation. A subjective level model is essential for evaluating coordination algorithms, because while individual behavior and system performance can be measured objectively, agents must make decisions with only subjective information.

An objective coordination problem instance (usually called an *episode*) is defined as a set of root tasks, each with a deadline. The root tasks may arrive at different times. For the purposes of abstract evaluation, a *solution* S to an episode can be represented abstractly as a set of after-the-fact *schedules* for each agent, indicating the Start and Finish times for each action. We can then calculate the finish time of S, Finish(S), as the latest action finish time, the amount of work done as the sum of the work done in each action, the total quality as the sum of the root task qualities at the finish time (or at the task deadlines), or other performace functions. This abstract problem formulation and evaluation has been instantiated for several particular multi-agent problem-solving environments, such as randomly generated problems [11], the distributed vehicle monitoring problem [8, 9], distributed data processing [25], and hospital patient scheduling [5].

For example, one of the first applications of the approach was to explain the results of Durfee, Corkill, and Lesser [15] that showed that no single coordination algorithm uniformly outperformed the others. In [8, 9] we went on to predict the performance effects of changing:

- the number of agents
- the physical organization of agents (i.e., the range of their sensors and how much the sensed regions overlap)
- the average number of vehicles in an episode
- the agents' coordination algorithm
- the relative cost of communication and computation

By building a TÆMS model of the DVMT problem and then describing a physical organization and coordination algorithm, we can derive and verify an expression for the time of termination of a set of agents in any arbitrary simple DVMT-like environment.

A particular episode in this environment can be described by the tuple $D = <A, r, o, T_1, \ldots, T_n>$ where n is a random variable drawn from an unknown distribution representing the number of vehicles.

Each root task Ti is associated with a vehicle track of length l_i and has the same basic objective task structure, based on the DVMT:

- l_i Vehicle Location Methods (VLM's) that represent processing raw signal data at a single location to a single vehicle location hypothesis.

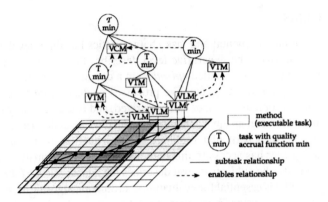

Fig. 1. Objective task structure associated with a single vehicle track.

- $l_i - 1$ Vehicle Tracking Methods (VTM's) that represent short tracks connecting the results of the VLM at time t with the results of the VLM at time $t + 1$.
- 1 Vehicle Track Completion Method (VCM) that represents merging all the VTM's together into a complete vehicle track hypothesis.

Non-local enables effects exist between each method at one level and the appropriate method at the next level as shown in Figure 1 – two VLMs enable each VTM, and all VTM'S enable the lone VCM.

With appropriate analysis, one can derive estimates for how much low-level (VLM) data is seen at the most highly loaded agent (under some coordination scheme for distributing the load), $\hat{S}$; the number of root tasks seen at this agent, $\hat{N}$; and the average number of agents that see a single root task, a. The total time until termination in such an episode is the time to do local work at the busiest agent, combine results from $(a - 1)$ other agents, and build the completed results, plus two communication and information gathering actions:

$$\hat{S}d_1 + (\hat{S} - \hat{N})d_2 + (a - 1)\hat{N}d_2 + \hat{N}d_3 + 2I + 2C \tag{3}$$

We can use Eq. 3 as a predictor by combining it with the probabilities for the values of $\hat{S}$ and $\hat{N}$ (see Figure 2). Our analysis also explained another observation that has been made about the DVMT – that the extra overhead of meta-level communication is not always balanced by better performance. These analytical models are validated by statistical methods on detailed simulations and/or application systems.

3   An Abstract Approach to Coordination: GPGP

Now that we have talked about "representation", let us move onto *designing coordination mechanisms* (using these representations). GPGP is a domain independent *scheduling* approach. The term "planning" in the name is historical, from Durfee's PGP. In the modern AI view of a continuum between planning and scheduling, both GPGP and PGP focus on the scheduling side. The GPGP approach makes several architectural assump-

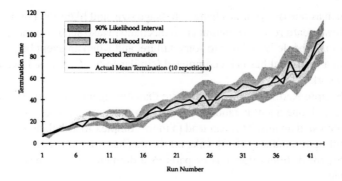

Fig. 2. Actual system termination versus analytic expected value and analytically determined 50% and 90% likelihood intervals. Runs arbitrarily ordered by expected termination time.

tions. Most important of these is that the agent represents its current set of intended tasks using the TÆMS task structure representation language.

An agent using the GPGP approach provides a planner or plan retriever to create task structures that attempt to achieve agent goals, and a scheduler that attempts to maximize utility via choice, serialization, and absolute temporal location of basic actions in the task structure. Each GPGP *mechanism* examines the changing task structure for certain situations, such as the appearance of a particular class of task relationship, and responds by making local and non-local *commitments* to tasks, possibly creating new communication actions to transmit commitments or partial task structure information to other agents. The set of coordination mechanisms is extendible, and any subset or all of which can be used in response to a particular task environment situation. By defining them in TÆMS terms, they can (and have been) applied to domains quite different from vehicle monitoring, such as hospital scheduling and software process management. Initially, GPGP defined the following five coordination mechanisms based on Durfee's PGP:

Updating Non-local Viewpoints. Each agent detects the possible coordination relationships and then communicates the related task structures. A *coordination relationship* is simply a task interrelationship (e.g. enables, facilitates, etc.) that extends between the task networks of two different agents. Detecting the existence of such relationships is domain dependent. In a domain such as distributed sensor networks, possible coordination relationships are detected geographically with respect to physical sensor locations[10]. In an application such as financial information gathering[14] possible relationships are recorded before a partial plan is distributed to multiple agents. In the hospital scheduling problem, the set of "possible relationships" are well-known medical domain knowledge, and are based on the particular set of tests ordered by the examining doctor and recorded by the nursing unit.

Communicate Results when They Will Be Used by Others. For example, if the results of task A at agent A will enable the execution of task B at agent B, then actually send those results when they become available. In our previous GPGP studies, we modeled the performance of communicating whenever it seemed advantageous versus only when tasks had been committed to, with respect to environmental features such as rate of dynamic change, message size, and likelihood of distraction [9, 11]. The standard result communication mechanism also sends notifications when a result *cannot* be delivered due to some failure, and when an agent believes all of its work on a joint goal has been completed (similar to the Cohen & Levesque model of teamwork [21]).

Handling Simple Redundancy. When more than one agent wants to execute a redundant method, one agent is randomly chosen to execute it and send the result to the other interested agents. This can lead to more complex load-balancing mechanisms for handling redundancy [8, 6]. Like all the mechanisms, this one can be switched on or off for different domains or parts of a domain – sometimes redundancy is *desirable*.

Handling Hard Relationships from the Predecessor Side. Here, A is required to come before B. A is the "predecessor" task, B is the "successor". The idea used in PGP and generalized in GPGP is that the agent with the predecessor task will commit to a completion time locally, and then transmit the commitment to the agent responsible for B. Note that this is *not* the only way to handle this relationship (see below).

Handling Soft Relationships from the Predecessor Side. A "soft" relationship exists between A and B if when A is executed before B, the execution of B will be perhaps faster or will return better results, but it is not strictly necessary. A simple example is sorting versus searching: sorting facilitates searching, but sorting is not strictly necessary before searching. In this PGP generalization, again the agent with the predecessor task commits to a completion time and transmits the commitment to the successor.

The most important thing about the GPGP approach is that it assures the generality of the mechanisms, because each mechanism is specified as a response to some pattern in a TÆMS task structure. Although the specific task structure differs from task instance to task instance and domain to domain, these coordination relationship show up over and over again in different locations in each new domain. Thus the GPGP approach allows us to apply the five Durfee mechanisms to domains other than distributed vehicle monitoring (such as randomly generated problems, distributed data processing[24], choosing organizational forms[7], local area network diagnosis [28], or hospital patient scheduling and information gathering as discussed in this paper). The only limitation is the reliance on a TÆMS specification of the underlying task.

3.1   Task-Structure-Based Coordination

To achieve its desires, an agent must build appropriate structures outlining possible paths to achievement (traditional AI planning or simple plan retrieval) and has to select appropriate actions at suitable times with the right sequence (task/action scheduling). Task structures might be created in agent architectures by various means: table lookup, reactive planning, task reduction, classical HTN planning, etc. We assume the result is a TÆMS -style HTN. An agent scheduler can be implemented with any number of algorithms (cf. comparisons in [17]). However, because of the inevitability of non-local dependencies, and the associated uncertainty of the action characteristics, the ability of the scheduler is severely limited if it can not acquire information about when and how the non-local dependencies are to be handled. It is this information that is provided by coordination mechanisms.

Previous work on GPGP coordination mechanisms [12] had described them in an abstract way, which made implementation and analysis difficult. Our more recent observation is that we can specify a specific coordination mechanism generally as a set of protocols (i.e., more task structures) specific to the mechanism, and a pattern-directed re-writing of the HTN. For example, if Act2 at Agent 2 enables Act1 at Agent 1, then one coordination mechanism (out of many) might be for Agent 1 to ask Agent 2 to do Act2, and to commit ahead of time to a deadline by which Act2 will be completed. Here the protocols are a reservation and a deadline commitment protocol, and the re-writing changes "Act2 enables Act1" into "reserve-act enables deadline-commitment enables Act2 enables Act1". To support this activity, an agent architecture must provide a facility for examining patterns of relationships in the current task structures between local tasks and *non-local* tasks, and re-writing them as required by the mechanism. This approach enables the cataloging of potential coordination mechanisms for a relationship, much more clear comparisions, and the real possibility of supporting automated coordination in an agent architecture such as DECAF (leaving aside for the moment the important question of *which* coordination mechanism to use for any particular relationship and context).

For example, we have catalogued at least seventeen coordination mechanisms for enablement relationships. Many of these are subtle variations, while some are quite different. For example, if a task TB at agent B enables task TA at agent A, one could:

- Have B commit to a deadline for TB (the original PGP-inspired mechanism [12]);
- Have B send the result of TB ("out of the blue", as it were) to A when available;
- Have A request that B complete TA by some deadline;
- Have A poll for the completion of TB (Our model of current hospital practice [13]);
- Have B commit (once and for all) to a timetable for carrying out instances such as TB without commiting to this specific instance individually)
- ...etc.

The seventeen mechanisms are not an exhaustive list, and many are simply variations on a theme. They include avoidance (with or without some sacrifice), reservation schemes, simple predecessor-side commitments (to do a task sometime, to do it by a deadline, to an earliest-start-time, to notify or send result directly when complete), simple successor-side commitments (to do a task with or without a specific EST), polling approaches (busy querying, timetabling, or constant headway), shifting task dependencies by learning or mobile code (promotion or demotion), various third-party mechanisms, or more complex multi-stage negotiation strategies.

In order that these mechanisms be applicable across task structures from any domain, the result of the mechanism is some alteration of the task structure. This might be a structural alteration (i.e. removing or adding tasks) or an alteration of the annotations on the task structure. As an example of the latter, consider the scheduling problem imposed by a task structure that includes a non-local task. In general the local agent may have no knowledge about the characteristics of that non-local task. Thus even though the agent may have perfect knowledge about all of its local tasks, it cannot know the combined characteristics of the complete task structure. Coordination mechanisms that rely on commitments from other agents to remove this uncertainty and allow the local agent to make better scheduling decisions.

3.2   Using GPGP

Probably the most well-studied use of the GPGP approach in an application was our study of the hospital patient scheduling problem [5]. Our model was drawn from a case study of an actual hospital [23, 18]:

> *Patients in General Hospital reside in* units *that are organized by branches of medicine, such as orthopedics or neurosurgery. Each day, physicians request certain tests and/or therapy to be performed as a part of the diagnosis and treatment of a patient. [. . .] Tests are performed by separate, independent, and distally located* ancillary departments *in the hospital. The radiology department, for example, provides X-ray services and may receive requests from a number of different units in the hospital.*

Furthermore, each test may interact with other tests in relationships such as enables, requires−delay (a slight variation on enables where the second task must be both af-ter and delayed), and inhibits (a negative variation of the soft facilitates relationship where the performance of some test within some timeframe invalidates the results of another). These task relationships indicate when the execution of one task changes the characteristics (here, primarily duration) of another task [10].

Experiments simulating the hospital's current coordination structure showed a mis-match between the structure and the current hospital environment. Although the modern hospital task environment is quite complex and interrelated (see Figure 3), the coordina-tion structure actually used by the hospital assumes that there are no interrelationships! Each ancillary acts independently, without communication with either nursing units or other ancillaries (except for the initial patient order from the nursing unit). Unit nurses try to make sure the proper prerequisite tests (represented here by enablement constraints) are done first. While this structure seems sorely lacking when compared to the current environment, it may historically have been a reasonable, low overhead arrangement.

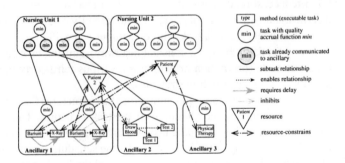

Fig. 3. High-level, objective task structure and subjective agent views for a typical hospital patient scheduling episode.

In this environment, the GPGP mechanisms to communicate task structures, partial results, and handling hard and soft relationships were demonstrated to be useful (even though they were originally developed for the DVMT environment). However, we also developed a new GPGP coordination mechanism oriented toward handling *mutually exclusive resource* constraint relationships between tasks at different agents (here, the patients are the mutex resources). The approach was that of a simple single stage, multi round cooperative negotiation, which has good flow properties and low overhead, which is important in an environment where the task mix may change dynamically with new patients, and where there is uncertainty over exactly how long procedures will take. The experimental results showed that the new mechanism increases the performance of agents by both decreasing patient stays and increasing throughput when there are many inter-ancillary relationships.

4   Building Real Software Agents: DECAF

Finally, we may discuss using these ideas to build real software agents. DECAF (Distributed, Environment-Centered Agent Framework) is an agent toolkit which provides a platform to design, develop, and execute agents to achieve solutions in complex software systems. DECAF provides the necessary architectural services of a large-grained intelligent agent [14, 29]: communication, planning, scheduling, execution monitoring, and coordination. This is essentially, the internal "operating system" of a software agent, to which application programmers have strictly limited access.

Functionally, DECAF is based on RETSINA [29, 4, 14, 34, 33] and TÆMS[10, 31]. TÆMS provides the framework for defining action alternatives, tradeoffs, and agent coordination information. RETSINA provides the idea of adaptability by allowing multiple outcomes, and reactive data flow constructs. The information provided by the TÆMS modeling language is not enough to actually be used to program an agent (via a simple task-reduction planner or more complex HTN planner). This is because TÆMS abstracts away the *specific* inputs ("provisions") and outputs ("results") associated with each action or task. In the RETSINA project, a data-flow based method was used to record this information. By combining these two ideas, a fully useful agent programming language is created. Both RETSINA and TÆMS (and thus DECAF) allow multiple *outcomes* from a task for representing contingency plans, branches, or loops.

Figure 4 represents the high level structure of the DECAF architecture. Structures inside the heavy black line are internal to the architecture and the items outside the line are user-written or provided from some other outside source (such as incoming KQML messages). There are five internal execution modules (square boxes) in the current DECAF implementation, and seven associated data structure queues (rounded boxes).

4.1   Agent Initialization

The execution modules control the flow of a task through its life time. After initialization, each module runs continuously and concurrently in its own Java thread. When an agent is started, the agent initialization module will run. The *Agent Initialization* module will read

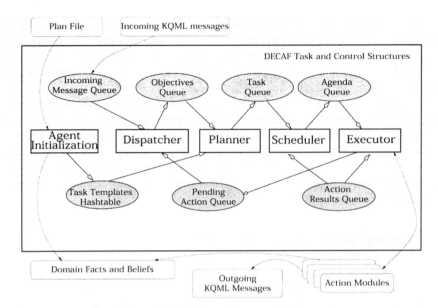

Fig. 4. DECAF Architecture Overview

plan file(s) containing the TÆMS task structure templates. Each task reduction specified in the plan file will be added to the *Task Templates Hash table* (plan library).

Next, the Agent Initialization Module registers with an ANS (Agent Name Server, or FIPA Directory Service) and sets up all socket and network communication. Finally, the agent may make use of a *Startup* root task. The Startup task is special since no message will be received to begin its execution. If such a Startup root task is part of the plan file, the initialization module will add it to the *Task Queue* for immediate execution. Agent initialization is done once and then control is passed to the other four main agent threads, described next.

4.2 Dispatcher

The *Dispatcher* waits for incoming messages which are placed on the *Incoming Message Queue*. An incoming message contains a KQML *performative* (or FIPA *communicative act*). An incoming message can result in one of three actions by the dispatcher:

- The message is attempting to communicate as part of an ongoing conversation. The Dispatcher makes this distinction mostly by recognizing the :in-reply-to field designator, which indicates the message is part of an existing conversation. In this case the dispatcher will find the corresponding action in the *Pending Action Queue* and set up the tasks to continue the agent action.
- The message indicates that it is part of a new conversation. This will be the case whenever the message does not use the :in-reply-to field. If so a new *objective* is created (equivalent to the BDI "desires" concept[26]) and placed on the *Objectives Queue* for the Planner. The dispatcher assign a unique identifier to this message which is used to distinguish all messages that are part of the new conversation.

– The dispatcher is responsible for is the handling of error messages. If an incoming message is improperly formatted or if another internal module needs to sends an error message the Dispatcher is responsible for formatting and send the message.

4.3 Planner

The Planner monitors the Objectives Queue and matches new goals to an existing task template as stored in the Plan Library. The initial, top-level objectives are roughly equivalent to the BDI "desires" concept[26], while the expansion into plans is only part of the traditional notion of BDI "intentions", which for DECAF is divided into three reasoning levels, planning, scheduling, and execution. A copy of the instantiated plan, in the form of an HTN corresponding to that goal is placed in the *Task Queue* area, along with a unique identifier and any provisions that were passed to the agent via the incoming message. If a subsequent message comes in requesting the same goal be accomplished, then another instantiation of the same plan template will be placed in the task queue with a new unique identifier. The Task Queue at any given moment will contain the instantiated plans/task structures (including all actions and subgoals) that should be completed in response to an incoming request.

4.4 Scheduler

The *Scheduler* waits until the Task Queue is non-empty. The scheduling functions are actually divided into two separate modules; the *Task Scheduler* and the *Agenda Manager*.

The purpose of the Task Scheduler is to evaluate the HTN task structure to determine a set of actions which will "best" suit the users goals. The input is a task HTN will all possible actions, and the output is a task HTN pruned to reflect the desired set of actions.

Once the set of actions have been determined, the Agenda Manager (AM) is responsible for setting the actions into execution. This determination is based on whether all of the provisions for a particular module are available. Some provisions come from the incoming message and some provisions come as a result of other actions being completed. This means the Tasks Queue Structures are checked any time a provision becomes available to see which actions can be executed now.

The other responsibility of the AM is to reschedule actions when a new task is requested. Every task has a window of time that is used for execution. If subsequent tasks can be completed while currently scheduled are running then a commitment is made to running the task on time. Otherwise the AM will respond with an error message to the requester that the task cannot be completed in the desired time frame.

4.5 Executor

The *Executor* is set into operation when the Agenda Queue is non-empty. Once an action is placed on the queue the Executor immediately places the task into execution. One of two things can occur at this point: The action can complete normally. (Note that "normal" completion may be returning an error or any other outcome) and the result is placed on the *Action Result Queue*. The framework distributes the result as provisions to downstream actions that may be waiting in the Task Queue. Once this is accomplished the Executor examines the Agenda queue to see if there is further work to be done.

The other case is when the action partially completes and returns with an indication that further actions will take place later. This is a typical result when an action sends a message to another agent requesting information, but could also happen for other blocking reasons (i.e. user or Internet I/O). The remainder of the task will be completed when the resulting KQML message is returned. To indicate that this task will complete later it is placed on the *Pending Action Queue*. Actions on this queue are keyed with a *reply-to* field in the outgoing KQML message. When an incoming message arrives, the Dispatcher will check to see if an *in-reply-to* field exists. If so, the Dispatcher will check the Pending action queue for a corresponding message. If one exists, that action will be returned to the Agenda queue for completion. If no such action exists on the Pending action queue, an error message is returned to the sender.

4.6   Using DECAF

While DECAF has been used as a platform for experimenting with soft-realtime action scheduling and GPGP, it has also been used for education and information-gathering applications, with about 90 registered users [http://www.cis.udel.edu/~decaf/]. One of the most complete applications is an bioinformatics information-gathering system for genomic annotation, BioMAS [3, 2].

One part of the annotation problem for biologists is that there is a large set of heterogeneous and dynamically changing databases, all of which have information to bring to bear on the biological problem of determining genomic function. There are biologists producing thousands of possible genes, for which functions must be hypothesized. Historically, for all but the largest sequencing projects, this must be done by hand by a single researcher and their students.

Multi-agent information gathering systems have a lot to contribute to these efforts. Several features make a multi-agent approach to this problem particularly attractive: information is available from many distinct locations; information content is heterogeneous; information content is constantly changing; much of the annotation work for each gene can be done independently; biologists wish to both make their findings widely available, yet retain control over the data; new types of analysis and sources of data are appearing constantly.

BioMAS is a prototype multi-agent system for automated annotation and database storage of sequencing data using DECAF. The resulting system eliminates tedious and always out-of-date hand analyses, makes the data and annotations available for other researchers (or agent systems), and provides a level of query processing beyond even some high-profile web sites. Figure 5 shows an overview of the system as four overlapping multi-agent organizations. The first, *Basic Sequence Annotation*, is charged with integrating remote gene sequence annotations from various sources with the gene sequences at the Local KnowledgeBase Management Agent (LKBMA). The second, *Query*, allows complex queries on the LKBMAs via a web interface. The third, *Functional Annotation* is responsible for collecting information needed to make an informed guess as to the function of a gene, specifically using the three-part Gene Ontology [30]. The fourth

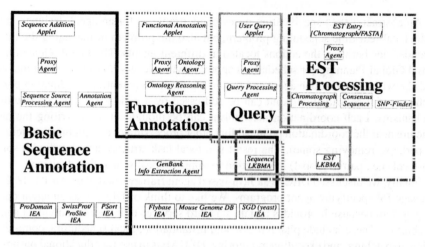

Fig. 5. Overview of DECAF Multi-Agent System for Genomic Analysis

organization, *EST Processing* enables the analysis of expressed sequence tags (ESTs) to produce gene sequences that can be annotated by the other organizations.

An important feature to note is that we are focusing on annotation and analysis services that are not organism specific. In this way, the resulting system can be used to build and query knowledgebases from several different organisms. The original subsystems (basic annotation and the simple query system) were built to annotate the newly sequenced Herpesvirus of Turkey (the bird), and then to compare it to the other known sequenced herpesviruses[2]. Work is well underway to build a new knowledgebase from chicken ESTs, using the same set of agents.

Such an information gathering system is actually a very straightforward application of DECAF. It requires no sophisticated coordination, for example. However, even in such a simple system the use of TÆMS -style representations can help. For example, we are working on providing alternative task structures for queries that allow a user to specify that they would prefer a high quality answer over a quick one (perhaps, because they are preparing for publication). This would allow certain analyses and external annotation queries to be re-run at query time, instead of relying on locally cached data.

5   Conclusions

This chapter has discussed the study of coordination in multi-agent systems. We began with a discussion of how to represent the problem or task structures at hand in the environment. The TÆMS language was an attempt to formalize features of complex multi-agent task environments – that is, environments with alternative actions, various types of uncertainty, deadlines, and so on. We discussed using TÆMS purely as an abstract representation that is amenable to analysis, usually coupled with simulation. Thus one can examine the linkages between features of a task environment and the mechanisms that the agents use to deal with those features.

---

[2] See http://udgenome.ags.udel.edu/herpes/.

An abstract TÆMS specification poses many problems for an agent designer, such as the local real-time scheduling problem, but also the problem of managing the inter-dependencies between the actions located at different agents. The GPGP Generalized Partial Global Planning (or scheduling) approach views every non-local-effect that extends between a task at one agent and that of another as a potential coordination point. Each potential coordination point can be addressed by a wide variety of coordiantion mechanisms. Each coordination mechanism can be thought of as re-writing the task structure near the coordination point, adding other processing or communication actions (or perhaps, removing some). The result is a local task strucure annotated with some non-local (i.e., partial global) information to improve local scheduling decisions.

Finally, we discussed DECAF, a Java-based agent framework that uses a TÆMS -like language for specifying agent programs. We like to think of DECAF as an agent operating system because it provides certain standard services to integrate individual agent capabilities. These include plan retrieval and instantiation, local scheduling, communication dispatching, and execution monitoring. DECAF is in use for educational purposes and also for building information gathering applications such as the BioMAS genomic annotation system. Currently, DECAF is being fitted with a GPGP coordination service to provide automated coordination of multi-agent tasks [1].

References

[1] W. Chen and K. Decker. Coordination mechanisms for dependency relationships among multiple agents (poster). In *Proceedings of the 1st Intl. Joint Conf. on Autonomous Agents and Mult-Agent Systems*, Bologna, 2002.

[2] K. Decker, S. Khan, C. Schmidt, and D. Michaud. Extending a multi-agent system for genomic annotation. In M. Klusch and F. Zambonelli, editors, *Cooperative Information Agents IV*, pages 106–117. Springer-Verlag, 2001.

[3] K. Decker, X. Zheng, and C. Schmidt. A multi-agent system for automated genomic annotation. In *Proceedings of the 5th Intl. Conf. on Autonomous Agents*, Montreal, 2001.

[4] K. S. Decker, A. Pannu, K. Sycara, and M. Williamson. Designing behaviors for information agents. In *Proceedings of the 1st Intl. Conf. on Autonomous Agents*, pages 404–413, Marina del Rey, February 1997.

[5] Keith Decker and Jinjiang Li. Coordinating mutually exclusive resources using gpgp. *Autonomous Agents and Multi-Agent Systems*, 3(2):133–157, 2000.

[6] Keith S. Decker. *Environment Centered Analysis and Design of Coordination Mechanisms*. PhD thesis, University of Massachusetts, 1995.
    `http://dis.cs.umass.edu/~decker/thesis.html`.

[7] Keith S. Decker. Task environment centered simulation. In M. Prietula, K. Carley, and L. Gasser, editors, *Simulating Organizations: Computational Models of Institutions and Groups*, pages 105–131. AAAI Press/MIT Press, 1997.

[8] Keith S. Decker and Victor R. Lesser. An approach to analyzing the need for meta-level communication. In *Proceedings of the Thirteenth International Joint Conference on Artificial Intelligence*, pages 360–366, Chambéry, France, August 1993.

[9] Keith S. Decker and Victor R. Lesser. A one-shot dynamic coordination algorithm for distributed sensor networks. In *Proceedings of the Eleventh National Conference on Artificial Intelligence*, pages 210–216, Washington, July 1993.

[10] Keith S. Decker and Victor R. Lesser. Quantitative modeling of complex computational task environments. In *Proceedings of the Eleventh National Conference on Artificial Intelligence*, pages 217–224, Washington, July 1993.

[11] Keith S. Decker and Victor R. Lesser. Designing a family of coordination algorithms. In *Proceedings of the First International Conference on Multi-Agent Systems*, pages 73–80, San Francisco, June 1995. AAAI Press. Longer version available as UMass CS-TR 94–14.

[12] Keith S. Decker and Victor R. Lesser. Designing a family of coordination algorithms. In *Proceedings of the First International Conference on Multi-Agent Systems(ICMAS-95)*, San Francisco, 1995.

[13] Keith S. Decker and J. Li. Coordinating mutually exclusive resources using gpgp. *Autonomous Agents and Multi-Agent Systems*, 3, 2000.

[14] Keith S. Decker and Katia Sycara. Intelligent adaptive information agents. *Journal of Intelligent Information Systems*, 9(3):239–260, 1997.

[15] Edmund H. Durfee, Victor R. Lesser, and Daniel D. Corkill. Coherent cooperation among communicating problem solvers. *IEEE Transactions on Computers*, 36(11):1275–1291, November 1987.

[16] K. Erol, D. Nau, and J. Hendler. Semantics for hierarchical task-network planning. Technical report CS-TR-3239, UMIACS-TR-94-31, Computer Science Dept., University of Maryland, 1994.

[17] J.Graham and K.Decker. Towards a distributed, environment-centered agent framework. In *Intelligent Agents IV, Agent Theories, Architectures, and Languages*. Springer-Verlag, 2000.

[18] A. Kumar and P.S. Ow. A study of distributed problem solving for patient scheduling. In *Proc. ORSA/TIMS*, Washington, D.C., 1988.

[19] V. Lesser, B. Horling, R. Vincent, A. Raja, and S. Zhang. The taems white paper. http://mas.cs.umass.edu/research/taems/white/, 1999.

[20] Victor R. Lesser and Daniel D. Corkill. The distributed vehicle monitoring testbed. *AI Magazine*, 4(3):63–109, Fall 1983.

[21] Hector J. Levesque, Philip R. Cohen, and José H. T. Nunes. On acting together. In *Proceedings of the Eighth National Conference on Artificial Intelligence*, pages 94–99, July 1990.

[22] Thomas W. Malone. Modeling coordination in organizations and markets. *Management Science*, 33:1317–1332, 1987.

[23] P. S. Ow, M. J. Prietula, and W. Hsu. Configuring knowledge-based systems to organizational structures: Issues and examples in multiple agent support. In L. F. Pau, J. Motiwalla, Y. H. Pao, and H. H. Teh, editors, *Expert Systems in Economics, Banking, and Management*, pages 309–318. North-Holland, Amsterdam, 1989.

[24] M.V. Nagendra Prasad, K. S. Decker, A. Garvey, and V.R. Lesser. Exploring organizational designs with TÆMS: A case study of distributed data processing. In *Proceedings of the Second International Conference on Multi-agent Systems*, Kyoto, Japan, December 1996.

[25] M.V. Nagendra Prasad and V.R. Lesser. Learning situation-specific coordination in generalized partial global planning. In *AAAI Spring Symposium on Adaptation, Co-evolution and Learning in Multiagent Systems*, Stanford, March 1996.

[26] A.S. Rao and M.P. Georgeff. BDI agents: From theory to practice. In *Proceedings of the First International Conference on Multi-Agent Systems*, pages 312–319, San Francisco, June 1995. AAAI Press.

[27] J. S. Rosenschein and G. Zlotkin. *Rules of Encounter: Designing Conventions for Automated Negotiation among Computers*. MIT Press, Cambridge, Mass., 1994.

[28] Toshiharu Sugawara and Victor R. Lesser. On-line learning of coordination plans. Computer Science Technical Report 93–27, University of Massachusetts, 1993.

[29] K. Sycara, K. S. Decker, A. Pannu, M. Williamson, and D. Zeng. Distributed intelligent agents. *IEEE Expert*, 11(6):36–46, December 1996.

[30] The Gene Ontology Consortium. Gene ontolgy: tool for the unification of biology. *Nature Genetics*, 25(1):25–29, May 2000.

[31] T. Wagner, A. Garvey, and V. Lesser. Complex goal criteria and its application in design-to-criteria scheduling. In *Proceedings of the Fourteenth National Conference on Artificial Intelligence*, Providence, July 1997.

[32] M.P. Wellman and J. Doyle. Modular utility representation for decision-theoretic planning. In *Proc. fo the First Intl. Conf. on Artificial Intelligence Planning Systems*, pages 236–242, June 1992.

[33] M. Williamson, K. S. Decker, and K. Sycara. Executing decision-theoretic plans in multi-agent environments. In *AAAI Fall Symposium on Plan Execution*, November 1996. AAAI Report FS-96-01.

[34] M. Williamson, K. S. Decker, and K. Sycara. Unified information and control flow in hierarchical task networks. In *Proceedings of the AAAI-96 workshop on Theories of Planning, Action, and Control*, 1996.

Strategies for Discovering Coordination Needs in MultiAgent Systems[1]

Edmund H. Durfee

Computer Science and Engineering Division,
EECS Department, University of Michigan,
Ann Arbor, MI 48109,
durfee@umich.edu

Abstract. While numerous techniques have been developed by which agents can coordinate over the allocation of scarce resources or the pursuit of interdependent goals, less is understood about how agents discover, in the first place, with whom they should worry about coordinating and about what. We have studied several strategies for making such discoveries, ranging from communicating abstract information to anticipate potential interactions ahead of time, to learning from interactions as they occur to anticipate future interactions. In this paper, we briefly summarize some of the strategies we have been investigating, and opportunities for further exploration.

1 Introduction

When multiple computational agents share a task environment, interactions between the agents generally arise. An agent might make a change to some feature of the environment that in turn impacts other agents, for example, or might commandeer a non-sharable resource that another agent desires. When the decisions that an agent makes might affect what other agents can or should decide to do, agents will typically be better off if they coordinate their decisions.

Numerous techniques exist for coordinating decisions about potential interactions. These include appealing to a higher authority agent in an organizational structure, instituting social laws that avoid dangerous interactions, using computational markets to converge on allocations, explicitly modeling teamwork concepts, using contracting protocols to strike bargains, and iteratively exchanging tentative plans until all constraints are satisfied. There is a rich literature on these and other mechanisms for coordinating agents; the interested reader can see [6].

However, each of these mechanisms takes as its starting point that the agents requiring coordination know, at the outset, either with whom they should coordinate, or what issues they should coordinate about. As examples, an organizational structure

---

[1] This article was originally published in the DoD Software Tech News, Volume 5, Number 1,
www.dacs.dtic.mil

M. d' Inverno et al. (Eds.): UKMAS 1996–2000, LNAI 2403, pp. 19–26, 2002.
© Springer-Verlag Berlin Heidelberg 2002

inherently defines how agents are related to each other, and a computational market corresponds to some resource or "good" that was somehow known to be contentious.

A central thrust of our research is in pushing back the boundaries of what is assumed known in a multiagent setting in order to bootstrap the coordination process. That is, we want to develop techniques by which agents can discover whom they should coordinate with, or what they should coordinate about, so that the rich variety of coordination techniques can then be employed. This paper briefly summarizes some of our progress, results, and plans on this front.

2 Unintended Conflicts

An important case in which agents need to discover coordination needs is the following. Agents occupy an open, dynamic environment, and each agent has its own independent objectives. Yet, in pursuing its objective, an agent can unintentionally interfere with others, sometimes catastrophically. Therefore, it is important for each agent to discover whether something it is doing needs to be coordinated with others.

We have been studying coalition operations as an example application domain where this kind of problem arises. In a coalition, objectives and responsibilities are distributed among multiple functional teams, where operational choices by one team can infrequently and unintentionally affect another team. The repercussions of unintended interactions can range from merely delaying the accomplishment of objectives (such as waiting for assets that were unexpectedly borrowed by someone else) to more catastrophic outcomes (such as so-called friendly fire). We have been developing computational techniques in which each team is represented by a computational agent, and these agents predict the unintended interactions and resolve them before they occur. The resulting coordinated plans of the agents should be efficient (e.g., agents should not have to wait unnecessarily for others), flexible (e.g., agents should retain room in their plans to improvise around changing local circumstances), and realizable (e.g., agents should not have to message each other at runtime in a manner that outstrips communication capabilities).

Conceptually, our techniques begin by assuming that each agent can represent its plans in a hierarchical task network (HTN), capturing the possible decompositions of abstract plan steps into more detailed plans. As a simple example, consider the case of agent A moving through a grid world to reach a destination (Figure 1). The HTN for this agent is in Figure 2. At the most abstract level (wide upper arrow in Figure 1, top node in the HTN), the plan is simply to go from the initial location to the destination. This is in turn composed of the three sequential steps of going to the door, through the door, and beyond the door (the other solid arrows in Figure 1, the second tier of nodes in Figure 2). The ordering constraints are captured in the HTN (Figure 2) by the arrows labeled "B" for "before." For both the first and last step at this level, there are two ways of accomplishing the step. For example, for getting to the door, the upper route or the lower route could be chosen. Each of these in turn can be decomposed into a sequence of two movements; the upper, for example, is to the right and then down.

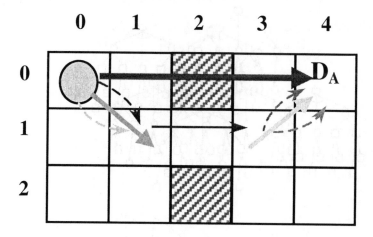

Fig. 1. Example Movement Task

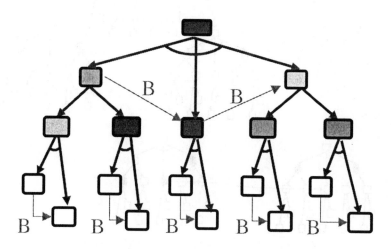

Fig. 2. Example Hierarchical Task Network (HTN)

An advantage of using the hierarchical representation is that each agent has, simultaneously, a model of itself at multiple levels of detail. In an open environment populated by numerous agents, being able to communicate about and exchange abstract information can enable agents to quickly determine which (small) subset of agents in the world they actually could potentially interact with (Figure 3a to Figure 3b). In the simple movement task example, for instance, the grid might be much larger, and the subset of agents is small whose planned movements, even abstractly defined, indicate a potential collision with agent A. For those agents, it might even be possible to impose constraints at the abstract level to ensure against unintended collisions, such as sequentializing the overall plans so that only one of the affected

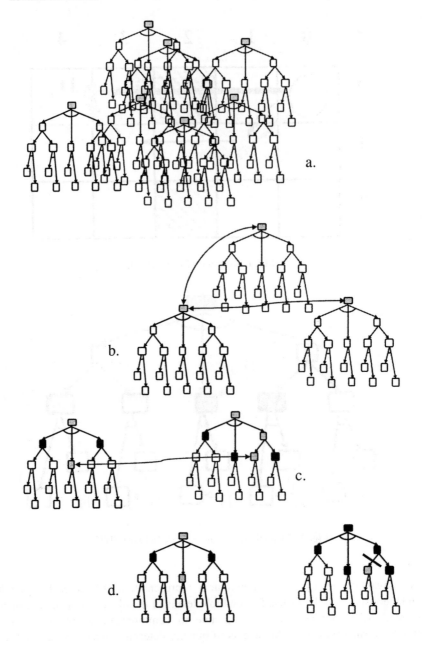

Fig. 3. Example Hierarchical Task Network (HTN)

agents moves at a time. Or, for the remaining agents, additional details of the HTNs can be exchanged. As a result, agents that were potentially interacting might be determined to not interact at all, reducing the number of agents further and introducing constraints between only substeps of plans leaving agents to do their other substeps as they wish (Figure 3c). Finally, further investigation might indicate that the potential conflict can be isolated to a particular choice that an agent might make; a commitment by the agent to forbid that choice leaves the plans coordinated without imposing any ordering constraints between the agents' plans at all (Figure 3d).

This example illustrates that, by working from the top down, agents can more efficiently identify and zoom in on the problematic interactions. By digging down deeply, they might be able to impose commitments (on relative timing or on choices of ways in which they will accomplish their tasks) that lead to very crisp coordination. However, in dynamic environments, sometimes it is better to impose constraints at more abstract levels: while this might require more sequential operation than desired, it also allows agents to avoid commitments to details that they might regret. As is intuitive in human coordination, each agent retains more flexibility for improvising

when it makes more vague commitments to others. Moreover, digging down deeply requires more rounds of communication and analysis, so coordinating at abstract levels incurs less overhead. Among our ongoing research activities are developing methods for quantitatively evaluating tradeoffs between coordination "crispness", overhead, and flexibility.

We have developed techniques for formulating summaries in HTNs that permit the kind of top-down reasoning that we have just described, and have shown that such techniques can indeed much more efficiently coordinate agents [3]. These techniques have been shown to be sound and complete. At the cost of completeness, we have also developed a version of these techniques that can be used on-line [5]. The on-line techniques allow agents to postpone decisions about which of the alternative ways they will use to accomplish a task until that task is the next to be done. This in turn provides increased flexibility to the agents, leading to more reliable agent operation in dynamic domains than methods that require agents to make selections before execution begins.

3   Dealing with Centralization

The techniques just outlined have the feature that, to ensure that all possible interactions are detected and dealt with, some agent or agents need to compare all agents' most abstract plans. This implies that, at some point, information about all agents needs to be known in one place, which is antithetical to decentralized multiagent systems. Certainly, our current implementations rely on a central coordinator to discover potential agent interactions, although in principle once these are discovered the job of working with the agents to resolve the interactions can be delegated to multiple sub-agents, where each handles a different partition of the agent population.

How can we get around the need for centralization? Well, first of all, it should be noted that our use of centralization for detecting interactions does not imply that authority, or even knowledge about agent preferences, is centralized. In our model, the coordination process merely detects potential interactions and finds possible resolutions (more detailed resolutions as time goes on). To agree upon which resolution to use, the affected agents can employ any of the various coordination mechanisms mentioned at the beginning of this paper. That is, these are appropriate once the agents know about the interactions and who is involved.

In turn, this suggests that one way of eliminating the centralization of the detection process requires that agents are initialized with some knowledge. For example, the organizational structure in which they reside might inherently partition the agents, such that coordination can be carried out in parallel in different partitions. Or agents might be initialized with knowledge of the possible actions of other agents that can be used to anticipate interactions. For example, our research is using these ideas to coordinate resource-limited agents in a multiagent world [4]. In the simplest sense, a resource-limited agent needs to decide how to allocate its limited capabilities in order to meet its performance goals across the scope of worlds that it might encounter. By employing knowledge about what actions other agents might take in particular situations, it can better predict what worlds it might encounter, and can even use its uncertainty to focus communication with those other agents to ask them which of the alternative actions they plan to take for a critical situation. Such communications could also permit agents to avoid taking redundant actions in situations where they would react the same way. In the long run, agents can even engage in negotiation to convince others to favorably change how they react to particular circumstances.

4 Congregating over Mutual Concerns

An alternative means of determining coordination needs, instead of centralizing information or inherently distributing key coordination knowledge, is to instead permit coordination needs to be discovered through interactions. While this would be inappropriate in applications where uncoordinated interactions could be catastrophic (such as when friendly fire arises in coalition operations), there are many applications where the consequences of poor coordination are not so dire.

Consider, for example, interactions among groups of people with similar interests, such as in an electronic newsgroup. A well-defined group permits an efficient exchange of relevant information among interested people, with a minimum of tangential communications that waste readers' time. A poorly-defined group, on the other hand, wastes readers' time and might lose readership quickly, but with no significant lasting effects on the participants. In this case, then, it is possible that people might congregate around newsgroup topics in an emergent way, through experimentation and exploration in the space, until they converge on relatively stable newsgroups that lead to productive interactions.

We have been conducting research in understanding the dynamic processes of congregating in open environments [2]. In our model, agents move among congregations until they find places where they are satisfied, where satisfaction depends on the other members of their congregation. Since these other agents are also moving around to find satisfactory congregations, agents are engaged in non-stationary ("moving target") search. In general, convergence in such systems is slow if it happens at all, and we have been studying mechanisms that enhance convergence such as: varying the movement costs of agents so that some "hold still" while others move; allowing like-minded agents to move as a coalition; giving agents the ability to remember and return to previously-experienced congregations; and allowing agents in a congregation to summarize their common interests and advertise this information to other agents.

As a specific form of congregating, we have been particularly interested in information economies, where competing producers of information goods must bundle and price their goods so as to attract (a subset of) the information consumers. Where a producer ends up in the product-and-price space is influenced not only by the consumer preferences, but also by the positioning decisions of other producers. Among our research results are that we have defined some of the conditions that promote the discovery of niche markets in the information economy, such that producers engage in stable relationships with an interested subset of the consumer population, and avoid mutually-harmful interactions (price wars) with other producers [1]. As suggested above, the price paid for this decentralized technique for discovering which agents should coordinate (interact) with each other is that, on the way to the ultimate mutually-profitable result, producers will sometimes compete with each other and do poorly temporarily as a result.

5   Summary and Future Directions

In this paper, we have claimed that, while powerful techniques exist for coordinating agents that already know whom or about what to coordinate, there are still many issues that need to be explored in designing efficient mechanisms by which to determine what needs to be coordinated in the first place. We briefly described some mechanisms that we are exploring for this purpose. One of these involves agents iteratively exchanging plan information at increasingly detailed levels to isolate potential interactions and impose effective commitments to resolve conflicts. Another, on the other hand, permits suboptimal interactions to occur, and allows the agent population to self-organize, over time, into congregations that emphasize beneficial interactions.

There are many directions in which we are, or are considering, extending these research activities. We need to develop heuristic means by which agents can decide on the level of detail at which they should coordinate, and metrics for comparing alternative coordination decisions in uncertain environments. We need to extend the soundness and completeness proofs, as well as the complexity analyses, of the techniques as we continue to augment and improve them. Coordination commitments that are derived between agents should be generalized and remembered to form the core of a suite of team plans, and the processes by which coordination needs are discovered should apply not only between agents but also between agent teams. Finally, these techniques need to be implemented and evaluated in the context of challenging applications, such as in the domain of coordinating coalition operations.

References

1. Christopher H. Brooks, Edmund H. Durfee and Aaron Armstrong. "An Introduction to Congregating in Multiagent Systems." In *Proceedings of the Fourth International Conference on MultiAgent Systems* (ICMAS-2000), pages 79-86, July 2000.
2. Christopher H. Brooks, Edmund H. Durfee and Rajarshi Das. "Price Wars and Niche Discovery in an Information Economy." In *Proceedings of the ACM Conference on Electronic Commerce 2000 (EC-00)*, October 2000.
3. Bradley J. Clement and Edmund H. Durfee. "Theory for Coordinating Concurrent Hierarchical Planning Agents Using Summary Information." In *Proceedings of the National Conference on Artificial Intelligence* (AAAI-99), pages 495-502, July 1999.
4. Haksun Li, Edmund H. Durfee, and Kang G. Shin "Multiagent planning with internal resource constraints." To appear in *Proceedings of the AAAI 2002 Workshop on Planning With and For MultiAgent Systems*, July, 2002.
5. Pradeep M. Pappachan and Edmund H. Durfee. "A satisficing multiagent plan coordination algorithm for dynamic domains." (abstract) *Proceedings of the ACM Conference on Autonomous Agents (Agents-01)*, June 2001.
6. Gerhard Weiss (editor). Multiagent Systems: A Modern Approach to Distributed Artificial Intelligence. MIT Press: Cambridge Massachusetts, 1999.

Acknowledgements

The ideas and results described in this paper were developed with numerous collaborators. In particular, I'd like to thank my students, including Brad Clement, Pradeep Pappachan, Chris Brooks, Haksun Li, and Jeff Cox. The work was supported, in part, by DARPA under the Control of Agent-Based Systems Initiative (F30602-98-2-0142), by DARPA under the Automated Negotiating Teams Initiative (subcontract to Honeywell on F30602-00-C-0017), and by NSF grant IIS-9872057.

Agent-Mediated Interaction. From Auctions to Negotiation and Argumentation

Carles Sierra and Pablo Noriega

Artificial Intelligence Research Institute – IIIA,
Spanish Council for Scientific Research – CSIC,
08193 Bellaterra, Barcelona, Catalonia, Spain,
sierra@iiia.csic.es, pablo@iiia.csic.es

Abstract. Most approaches to modelling agent interactions tend to focus just on the mechanism: the protocol and language used for the interaction, and forget the context where that interaction takes place. We hold that although the complexity of the problem to be solved is associated to the complexity of the mechanism, modelling the mechanism alone is insufficient. We argue that an appropriate representation of the context and pragmatics associated to the interaction, as well as a practical way of enforcing the accepted interaction conventions are essential for the design of successful MAS applications. The concept of Electronic Institution is presented both as a way to reconcile mechanisms with their corresponding pragmatic and contextual aspects, and a way of extending familiar notions of mediation to MAS.

1 Introduction

In this paper we explore two dimensions that we believe should be present in the design of multi-agent systems. One is the relationship between the complexity of the problem that participating agents attempt to solve, and the complexity of the interactions among them; more specifically, the complexity of the language these agents use to communicate. The other dimension has to do with the use of some sort of mediation among participating agents in order to achieve, or facilitate, successful interactions. By exploring these two dimensions in three familiar examples of agent interactions – auctions, structured negotiation and persuasive argumentation – we will argue in favour of the notion of an Electronic Institution as a powerful device to handle complex agent interactions. We will show that electronic institutions are a natural device to make explicit not only the interaction mechanisms required in MAS, but also the contextual and pragmatic features that are needed for adequate MAS modelling of complex problem solving tasks.

M. d' Inverno et al. (Eds.): UKMAS 1996–2000, LNAI 2403, pp. 27–48, 2002.

2   Interaction Mechanisms. The Myopic View

In this section three increasingly complex interaction mechanisms are briefly overviewed. We will see how the increasing complexity of the mechanisms leads to the solution of more complex problems, and we will argue that ignoring the pragmatics of the interaction makes the mechanisms almost inapplicable in real settings.

2.1   Auctions

When participating in auctions, buying agents use a rather simple language to communicate, both in terms of the illocutionary particles they hear or utter – basically *offer* goods and *accept* prices – and of the content language: in most auctions, the buyer simply accepts a posted price, the auctioneer, hence, needs to communicate buyers only those elements that characterize the item that is being auctioned and the current bidding-price. Overall an extremely simple ontology. In fact, quite similar to the language of ants in an ant algorithm! The problem to be solved is the allocation of the good to the buyer that values the good most, or more precisely, to the buyer that is ready to pay more for the good. A simple language for an, in principle, simple *unidimensional search problem.*

To more accurately illustrate this simple communication language here is a brief description of a real auction house.

A Fish Auction House in the Catalonian Seashore. Twice a day the fishing fleet of the town of Blanes (Costa Brava) sells its catch in the local market place. The market is managed by the fishermen's guild under a lease from the government. Fishermen get their revenues from the auctioning of their catches using the traditional *Dutch*[1] auction protocol (see Figure 1). The Blanes market is nowadays mechanised to a certain extent: it has a panel showing the high pace decreasing prices of the auctioned item, and information about the boat and the boxes being auctioned; infra-red sensors permit buyers wandering around to stop the decreasing pace by pointing with a personal infra-red bidder to the ceiling of the room; a complete information system to support registering, payment, credits and so on, is maintained by the auction house. However, although the Blanes fish market has evolved to a certain degree, its main features are the traditional ones (documents on this specific market date back to the XVth Century). For a complete account of the details of this example of an auction house refer to [13].

There are three types of participants in this auction house: *sellers, buyers* and different types of *market intermediaries.* They interact in order to perform a series of activities:

– **Sellers and Buyers Admission.** This activity is performed by a market intermediary (that is usually different for buyers and sellers) that authenticates, manages the credit of buyers and sellers, and is responsible for the

---

[1] This downward bidding protocol is called *Dutch* because it is similar to the one used in Holland to sell flowers.

agentMediated

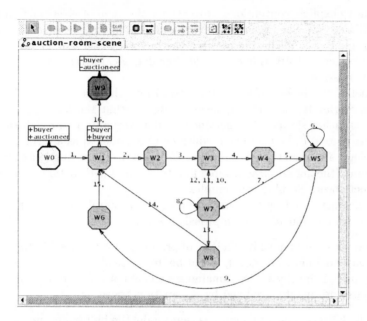

Fig. 1. Dutch Auction Bidding Protocol Diagram. It involves the roles of an *auctioneer* and *buyer* agents. Numbers denote illocution schemata as explained in the text of the paper; for instance, label 1 corresponds to *inform*(?x : *auctioneer*, all : *buyer*, *open_auction*(?n)). As in other figures, boxes represent conversation states, arrows represent transitions triggered by the utterance of the illocutions matching the corresponding label, and rectangles denote access (+) and exit (-) states for participating roles.

assignment of bidding devices to the buyers. The sellers' admitter is responsible for the registration process of the goods on sale (assignment of initial auctioning prices and quality of fish) and on the sequencing of the boxes to be auctioned.

– **Sellers and Buyers Settlements.** This activity is mediated by another type of staff members who are responsible for invoicing and payment procedures to and from sellers and buyers.
– **Auctioning.** Again, a scene mediated by a staff auctioneer. This activity involves the actual assignment of boxes to buyers according to the Dutch protocol. The auctioneer takes care of incidents like collisions (more than one buyer bid at the same price), invalid bids (someone made a bid before the auction clock was started), or cancellation due to unforeseen circumstances (malfunctioning of a device, erroneous bid, ...).

These activities are dialogical in the sense that all observable interactions are tagged with an illocution, an interaction has social consequences only if tagged by an illocution, and only admissible illocutions are uttered and uttered according to explicit conventions. Notice that the type of electronic auctioning used in Blanes could be argued not to be dialogical in *stricto-senso* since there is an electronic device mediating between the buyer and the auctioneer, although its role is a mere substitution of the old time dialogical utterances by equivalent infra-red emissions.

As mentioned before, if we look in detail into the auctioning activity – or, more appropriately, the bidding *scene*[2] – we see that the language needed to model it is rather simple: the auctioneer (either verbally or through the panel) announces a good to be auctioned, which can be modelled as a term in a simple fish ontology, and then there is a sequence of prices from the auctioneer to buyers and a signal (the actual *mine* uttered in a traditional live auction) from a buyer to the auctioneer. Nothing too complex.

The language used by the interacting agents is simple because the problem to solve is simple, but *also* for empirical reasons:

- Fish must be sold quickly. The use of protocols not bounded in time, like for instance an English protocol, would be impractical.
- Only price is involved. The remaining elements of the transaction: weight of the box and quality, are fixed by the auction house.

Here is the actual list of illocutions that model the bidding rounds in a Dutch auction, as labelled in Figure 1:

$$1 \quad inform(?x : auctioneer, all : buyer, open\_auction(?n))$$
$$2 \quad inform(!x, all : buyer, open\_round(?r))$$
$$3 \quad inform(!x, all : buyer, to\_sell(?good\_id))$$
$$4 \quad inform(!x, all : buyer, buyers(?b))$$
$$5 \quad inform(!x, all : buyer, offer(!good\_id, ?price))$$
$$6 \quad inform(!x, all : buyer, offer(!good\_id, ?price))$$
$$7 \quad commit(?y : buyer, !x : auctioneer, bid(!good\_id, ?price))$$
$$8 \quad commit(?y : buyer, !x : auctioneer, bid(!good\_id, ?price))$$
$$9 \quad inform(!x, all : buyer, withdrawn(!good\_id, ?price))$$
$$10 \quad inform(!x, all : buyer, collision(?price))$$
$$11 \quad inform(!x, all : buyer, sanction(?buyer\_id))$$
$$12 \quad inform(!x, all : buyer, expulsion(?buyer\_id))$$
$$13 \quad inform(!x, all : buyer, sold(!good\_id, ?price, ?buyer\_id))$$
$$14 \quad inform(!x, all : buyer, end\_round(?r))$$
$$15 \quad inform(!x, all : buyer, end\_round(!r))$$
$$16 \quad inform(!x, all : buyer, end\_auction(!n))$$

---

[2] We'll refer to these dialogical activities as *scenes* because they are performed or *enacted* much like scenes in the script of a theater play are performed: agents (actors) engage in dialogues according to their pre-assigned role (character).

It should be noted that although this list of illocutions – and their pragmatic impact – may adequately model the auction scene, it is by no means sufficient to properly model a complete *auction house,* as we shall show below.

2.2 Negotiation

Other negotiation protocols are used to solve more complex problems: service agreements, selection of products and their associated payment conditions, or to agree on a co-ordinated action to perform a task. Such protocols are defined in order to facilitate agents the exploration of the space of potential agreements. Mathematically speaking, this means a set of points in a multidimensional space defined by the attributes of the negotiation object, such as, for instance, conditions of the service, characteristics of products, or responsible agents for given actions. Auctions are, in a sense, degenerated negotiation dialogues where the only negotiable dimension is price. This is the reason why dialogues in auctions tend to be rather simple. To illustrate a slightly more complex type of negotiation, specially in terms of content of the illocutions, see in Figure 2 a standard negotiation protocol – the one we propose for supply chain negotiations – and compare it with the auction protocol in Figure 1.

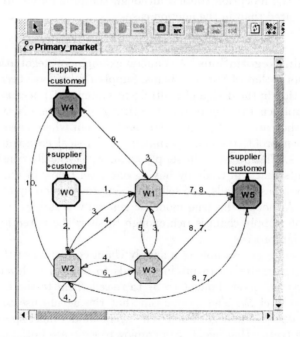

Fig. 2. Negotiation Protocol diagram.

The fact that we move from a one-dimensional space into a multi-dimensional one makes the agent interaction language change substantially. The dialogue, although pragmatically remains almost identical – *offers* and *acceptance* of offers – is now open to new strategic possibilities like making trade-offs between attributes, deciding to concede less on important attributes and more on the less important ones, using time as a relevant element in defending a deal, ... The language gets more complex for a more complex problem: *distributed search for an agreement in multidimensional spaces.*

While in auctions it can be argued that the proper strategy of a buyer is to simply bid the perceived value of an item, the strategic decisions are far more involved for participants in the type of structured negotiation we are mentioning[23]. Negotiating agents need to decide not only if an offer is acceptable, but what counteroffer to respond with, and what criteria are more relevant to consider in the computation of counteroffers in a given environment: remaining negotiation time?, available resources? Also, the guessing of the opponent preferences (or the assumption of some default preferences as explored in [5]), or past experiences, may be of critical importance in order to develop successful negotiation strategies.

Summarizing, in terms of the problem to be solved negotiation can be viewed as a distributed search through a space of potential agreements [7, 10]. The dimensionality and topology of this space is determined by the structure of the negotiation object. In terms of language complexity we observe an increase in the complexity of the illocution content although the pragmatics are not specially more sophisticated than in the auction case.

Supply Chain Negotiations. A common example for negotiation interaction between agents is that of Supply Chains. Supply chains have been a traditional focus of attention in the design of multi-agent systems [21] because of the significant role supply chains play in the structuring of the manufacturing economy and because they are a naturally distributed system where agents try to maximise their own profit, therefore permitting a classical economical analysis of their strategies. Thus, a MAS in supply chain will typically consist of a group of selfish agents that will trade by buying one level below in the chain, adding value to the purchased goods, and selling the improved good up to the next level in the chain. Although the true model is generally a supply tree or a supply graph, a simple supply chain is rich enough to show the potential complexities of a MAS design process.

Let us consider an example of a supply chain consisting of three levels: S_1, processing rough materials to produce goods to be sold to level S_2 which, in turn, processes the goods bought to S_1 to re-sell them to the final consumers represented as level S_3. The mechanism that the agents use to buy and sell products is a one-to-one negotiation. The agent model must specify a range of strategies and tactics that agents can employ to generate initial offers, evaluate proposals and offer counter proposals. Figure 2 shows a protocol that could be used to model this sort of negotiation, where the buyers play the *customer* role and sellers play the role of *supplier*. The following list contains the illocutions associated to the labels in figure 2:

1 *offer(?s : supplier, ?c : customer, sign(?d : deal, ?date), ?date)*

2 *offer(?c : customer, ?s : supplier, sign(?d : deal, ?date), ?date)*

3 *offer(!s : supplier, !c : customer, sign(?d : deal, ?date), ?date)*

4 *offer(!c : customer, !s : supplier, sign(?d : deal, ?date), ?date)*

5   *reject(!ccustomer, !s : supplier, sign(!d : deal, !date))*

6   *reject(!s : supplier, !ccustomer, sign(!d : deal, !date))*

7   *withdraw(!c : customer, !s : supplier)*

8   *withdraw(!s : supplier, !c : customer)*

9   *accept(!c : customer, !s : supplier, sign(!d : deal, !date))*

10   *accept(!s : supplier, !c : customer, sign(!d : deal, !date))*

2.3 Argumentation

Argumentation is a key form of interaction in multi-agent systems where independent agents behave autonomously. Since under those conditions agents have no direct control on one another, the only way they can influence one another's behaviour is through persuasion. In this situation, agents are not, as in negotiation, looking for a point in a multidimensional space that is acceptable to both parties, but rather trying to change the opponent's mind in order to change his/her preferences, beliefs or goals. The pragmatics of the dialogues thus are far richer than in negotiation or auctions. Here agents try to persuade by threatening, by appealing to authority or by promising a reward in the future, just to mention a few possibilities. Figure 2.3 shows a protocol for argumentative dialogues.

Again, in this case, the language gets more complex. Not only the set of illocutionary particles needs to be expanded to include the likes of *threaten*, *reward* or *appeal* [24], but the content of the illocutions has to contain arguments to try and convince our opponent of, for instance, the impossibility of accepting a proposal or the preferability of certain attribute values over others, as well as permitting the critique of certain aspects of a proposal. Broadly speaking agents need to use a language rich enough to build arguments. Propositional logic, or even better first order logic seems necessary for this purpose. The language gets more complex for a more complex problem: *distributed search for an agreement (in multidimensional spaces) with dynamically changing preference sets.*

The decision procedures to be used by agents are again, in this case, more complex. On top of the action choices that an agent already has in negotiation – such as, for example: "how much do I concede", "do I wait?", "should I trade-off issues a and b, or do I better concede?" – there is a complete new set of possible decisions to consider: "should I trade-off or should I argue?", "what argument should I send?", "should I argue in favour of my last proposal?", "should I attack my opponent's last argument or should I send a new argument in favour of my last proposal?". The decisions are more complex because we have the possibility of using the current search space to proceed on the search (as in negotiation) and we have the new possibility of *changing* the search space by arguing, so that offers become interesting to the opponent.

In terms of language complexity, in argumentation we observe a richer set of illocutionary particles, and richer pragmatics as well. Also, the content language gets necessarily enriched by the fact that the some of the new illocutionary acts involve arguments or explanations, that in several cases will have reflexive capabilities to refer to previous arguments or previous offers. A much more complex language scenario for a far more complex problem to be solved.

In all these three cases, even in the simplest one, the underlying context of the negotiation is far more complex than we have been able to describe in terms of the negotiation mechanisms, and the agent interactions involved require some sort of social structure to properly support the interaction conventions, as we will argue next.

BT Quoting. We shall exemplify argumentative dialogues with an illustrative scenario motivated by work in the ADEPT project [8] which developed negotiating agents for business process management applications. In particular, the researchers considered a multi-agent system for managing a British Telecom

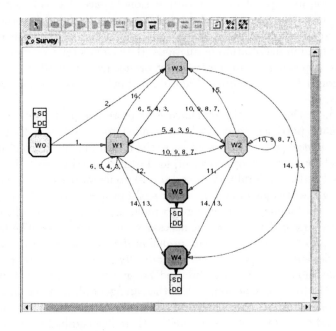

Fig. 3. Argumentation protocol example. The protocol corresponds to an argumentative protocol between agents DD and SD.

(BT) business process – namely, providing a quotation for designing a telecommunications network which offers particular services to a commercial customer. The overall process receives a customer service request as its input and generates as its output a quote specifying how much it would cost to build a network to realise that service. Here we consider a subset of the agents involved in this activity: the customer service division (CSD) agent, the design division (DD) agent, the surveyor department (SD) agent, and the various agents who provide the out-sourced service of vetting customers (VC agents). A full account of all the agents and their negotiations is given in [23].

In order to properly model this problem domain, we found that agents would need to exchange, at least, three types of argument. These are: *threats* (failure to accept this proposal means something negative will happen to you), *rewards* (acceptance of this proposal means something positive will happen to you), and *appeals* (you should prefer this option over that alternative for some reason). Not surprisingly, these argument types are also amongst the most common in the general argumentation literature [9, 26].

Figure 3 illustrates the argumentative dialogue between DD and SD agents. The following list enumerates the arc labels.

$$1 \quad offer(?a:DD,?b:SD,?wff)$$
$$2 \ request(?a:DD,?b:SD,?wff)$$
$$3 \quad offer(!a:DD,!b:SD,?wff)$$
$$4 \ threaten(!a:DD,!b:SD,?wff)$$
$$5 \ reward(!a:DD,!b:SD,?wff)$$
$$6 \ appeal(!a:DD,!b:SD,?wff)$$
$$7 \quad offer(!b:SD,!a:DD,?wff)$$
$$8 \ threaten(!b:SD,!a:DD,?wff)$$
$$9 \ reward(!b:SD,!a:DD,?wff)$$
$$10 \ appeal(!b:SD,!a:DD,?wff)$$
$$11 \ accept(!a:DD,!b:SD,?wff)$$
$$12 \ accept(!b:SD,!a:DD,?wff)$$
$$13 \quad withdraw(!a:DD,!b:SD)$$
$$14 \quad withdraw(!b:SD,!a:DD)$$
$$15 \ reject(!a:DD,!b:SD,?wff)$$
$$16 \ reject(!b:SD,!a:DD,?wff)$$

3 Electronic Institutions

3.1 Intuitive Notions

Human interactions very often follow *conventions*; that is, general agreements on language, meaning, and behaviour. By following conventions, humans attempt to make their interactions more effective by decreasing uncertainties in the behaviour of others, removing conflicts on meaning, having clearer expectations on the possible outcomes of the interaction and, in general, simplifying the decision process by restricting the potential actions that may be undertaken to a limited set. These benefits explain why conventions – of different sorts – have been so widely used in various domains of human interaction such as trading, public service, games, and the like.

In some situations, conventions become foundational and, in a sense, those conventions become *norms* [2] that establish how interactions of a certain sort will and *must* be structured within an organisation. Such is the essence of what is commonly understood as a human institutions [15]. Human institutions not only structure human interactions, but they are also supposed to enforce individual and social behaviour by obliging every one involved to act according to its norms [20]. This is the case of, for instance, auction houses, courts of law, parliaments or stock exchanges where, in order to achieve a goal, participants – be they staff members of the institution or external participants – must behave within the institution according to the explicit conventions of that institution.

The benefits derived in human organisations by establishing and following conventions become even more apparent when we move into an electronic world where human interactions are mediated or carried out by software agents [12]. In such cases, conventions are necessary to avoid conflicts in meaning, to structure interaction protocols, and to limit the action repertoire of participants, much in the same way that human institutions work; however, the electronic world is a setting where participants may be software entities endowed with limited rationality. The notion of *electronic institution* thus becomes a natural extension of human institutions by permitting not only humans, but also autonomous agents, to interact with one another.

Considering the computer realisation of an institution, we take the stance that *all* interactions among agents are realised by means of message interchanges. We take a strong dialogical stance in the sense that we view multi-agent systems as a type of *dialogical system* [17, 13]. The interaction between agents within an electronic institution therefore becomes an exchange of illocutions. In accordance with the classic understanding of illocutions (e.g. Austin [1] or Searle [22]), illocutions "change the world" by establishing or modifying the commitments or obligations of the participants. Therefore, formally speaking, an agent in an electronic institution is any entity capable of establishing commitments. In other words, an entity not capable of establishing commitments should not (must not) speak in an institution. The notion of being capable of establishing commitments is the cornerstone of the construction of institutions because otherwise no notion of enforcement or penalty could arguably be used. In a sense, institutions exist because they are the warrants of the satisfaction of the commitments established by the participants.

In the next subsection we describe the various types of convention that, we think, need to be established in order to properly specify an electronic institution [13, 19].

3.2 Electronic Institutions Basic Concepts

Electronic institutions, as well as human institutions deal with two complementary aspects of the conventions that articulate interactions. On one hand, they need to make explicit for participating agents what is significant (or pertinent) in such interactions and therefore institutions need to address *ontological* (and contextual) issues that are to be used by participating agents in their illocutory exchanges, with a shared meaning and with specific intended effects. On the other hand, institutions need to make explicit those *deontological* aspects that govern the accepted behaviour of participants and may in the end warrant the satisfaction of commitments made within the institution. In order to address these aspects, we have found useful to organize the conventions that govern electronic institutions into three types: ontological and communication conventions, social conventions that govern collective interactions, and rules that normalise (mostly) individual behavior. Each of these three types of conventions are discussed immediately below in a separate section (for a formal account of these components see [13, 19, 18]).

Ontological and Communicational Conventions: The Dialogical Framework

These conventions help to clarify the meaning of the illocutions exchanged among participants. In order to do so, one needs to make explicit what are the entities the institution deals with, that is, the goods, participants, roles, locations, time intervals, and so on [13]. Likewise, the precise language for interaction should become explicit as part of these conventions. To this end, we propose that communicating agents must share a *dialogical framework* [14]. This is composed of a communication language, a representation language for domain content and an ontology. By sharing a dialogical framework, heterogeneous agents can exchange knowledge and co-ordinate actions with one another.

Definition 1. *A dialogical framework DF is a tuple $\langle R, SS, O, L, I, CL, Time \rangle$ where*

- R *stands for a role set (or a set of accepted roles);*
- $SS \subseteq R \times SR \times R$ *stands for a social structure with SR a set of social relations identifiers;*
- O *stands for an ontology (vocabulary);*
- L *stands for a representation language for domain content;*
- I *is the set of illocutionary particles;*
- CL *is the (agent) communication language;*
- $Time$ *is a discrete and partially ordered set of instants.*

The role set provides an abstract characterization of the functioning of the different agents in the system [16]. The representation language (e.g., KIF [6] or first-order logic) allows the encoding of the knowledge to be exchanged among agents using the vocabulary offered by the ontology O. The ontology contains constants and terms relative to the domain, including predicate identifiers like *sold, withdrawn, collision,* or *startingprice,* and constants like *cod, 20USD,* or

Titanic. Propositions built with the aid of L, the "inner" language, are embedded into an "outer language", CL, which expresses the intentions of the utterance by means of the illocutionary particles in I. A possible set of illocutions could be {assert, not_assert, request, declare, offer, deny, accept, command }. We take this approach in accordance with speech act theory which postulates that utterances are not simply propositions that are true or false, but attempts on the part of the speaker that succeed or fail [22]. We consider that CL expressions are constructed (like in KQML) as formulae of the type $\iota(\alpha_i : \rho_i, \alpha_j : \rho_j, \varphi, \tau)$ where $\iota \in I$, α_i and α_j are terms which can be either agent variables or agent identifiers, ρ_i and ρ_j are terms which can be either role variables or role identifiers, $\varphi \in L$ and τ is a term which can be either a time variable or a value in *Time*.

To illustrate these concepts consider the following dialogical framework for a bidding round of a Dutch auction in a fish market (previously described in 2.1). The set of roles is

$$R = \{ boss, auctioneer, buyer\ manager, buyer\ admitter, seller\ manager,$$
$$seller\ admitter, buyer, seller \}$$
$$SS = \{ (boss, has\_power, auctioneer),$$
$$(boss, has\_power, buyer\ manager),$$
$$(boss, has\_power, buyer\ admitter),$$
$$(boss, has\_power, seller\ manager),$$
$$(boss, has\_power, seller\ admitter),$$
$$(auctioneer, has\_authority, buyer),$$
$$(auctioneer, has\_authority, seller) \}$$

The chief staff agent of the auction house plays the role of *boss*. It exerts power over all agents playing the other staff roles of the institution: *auctioneer* responsible of the actual fish auctioning and the different buyer and seller *managers* and *admitters* responsible of payments to and from sellers and buyers and of the admittance of participants respectively. Auctioneers have authority over sellers and buyers because the boss delegates power to them about decisions on winner determination and on modification of auction conditions (order of auctioning, withdrawal of products, etc.).

Social Conventions: Scenes and Performative Structure

These conventions regulate the interactions among participants. They contain agreements on protocols and on the sequence of activities in the institution. *Scenes* regulate the protocol to follow for each individual activity and the *Performative Structure* establishes the links and traversal paths between the scenes.

The overall activity within an electronic institution is a composition of multiple, well-separated, and possibly concurrent, dialogical activities, each one involving different groups of agents playing different roles. For each such activity, which we will call a scene, interactions between agents are articulated through the meeting of various groups of agents that follow well-defined communication protocols. Thus, for example, in the context of an auction house, there are the following scenes involving the following agents and the following protocols: buyer and seller admission scenes subject to an information seeking protocol (staff members acquire information concerning the goods to be auctioned and the credit of buyers), an auction scene subject to the corresponding auction protocol (for instance, English or Dutch), and scenes corresponding to the buyer and seller settlements that correspond to contract signing protocols (buyers get the goods in return for money and sellers get money in return for the goods that have been sold). In fact, with this model no agent interaction can take place outside of the context of a scene. We consider the protocol of each scene to model the possible dialogical interactions between the group of agents playing specific roles. In other words, scene protocols are patterns of multi-role conversation [13].

A scene protocol is specified by a graph whose nodes represent the different states of the conversation and the arcs connecting the nodes are labelled with illocutions that make the scene state change (see Figure 3). The graph has a single initial state (non-reachable once left) and a set of final states representing the different acceptable endings of the conversation. There is no arc connecting a final state to some other state.

Figure 3 shows an example of a scene protocol specified with the ISLANDER toolbox [3]. This scene corresponds to the Survey scene of the institution presented in Figure 6. Normally, the correct evolution of a conversation protocol requires a certain number of agents for each of the various roles involved in it, in the example in Figure 3 we have two roles a Surveyor Department agent (SD) and a Design Division agent (DD). The set of roles will be denoted by the symbol R. Then a minimum and maximum number of agents per role is defined and the number of agents playing each role has to be in this interval – in this example, it happens to be one agent both as minimum and maximum – (denoted by two functions min and Max). Because we need to model multi-agent conversations in which the set of participants may dynamically vary, scenes need to be specified such that agents can either join in or leave at particular moments during an ongoing conversation. For this purpose, we differentiate the sets of *entrance* (denoted by WA) and the *exit* states (denoted by WE) for different roles. The entrance or exit of agents has to satisfy the restriction mentioned above about the number of agents for each role. Obviously, the final states ought to have exit states for each role, in order to allow all the agents to leave when the scene is finished. In contrast, the initial state has to be an access state for the roles whose minimum is greater than zero, in order to start the scene.

Definition 2. *Formally, a scene is a tuple[3] where:*

$$S = \langle R, W, w_0, W_f, (WA_r)_{r \in R}, (WE_r)_{r \in R}, \Theta, \lambda, min, Max \rangle$$

- R *is the set of roles of the scene, a subset of R in Definition 1;*
- W *is a finite, non-empty set of scene states;*
- $w_0 \in W$ *is the initial state;*

---

[3] When we need to differentiate the elements of two scenes s and s' we will use a superindex s or s'.

- $W_f \subseteq W$ *is the non-empty set of final states;*
- $(WA_r)_{r \in R} \subseteq W$ *is a family of non-empty sets such that* WA_r *stands for the set of access states for the role* $r \in R$;
- $(WE_r)_{r \in R} \subseteq W$ *is a family of non-empty sets such that* WE_r *stands for the set of exit states for the role* $r \in R$;
- $\Theta \subseteq W \times W$ *is a set of directed edges;*
- $\lambda : \Theta \longrightarrow CL$ *is a labelling function relating each transition with an illocution schema expressed in the language CL.*
- $min, max : R \longrightarrow \mathbb{N}$ $min(r)$ *and* $max(r)$ *return respectively the minimum and maximum number of agents that must and can play the role* $r \in R$;

Notice that not every illocution scheme is valid to label an arc. In general, a *CL* expression $\iota(\alpha_i : \rho_i, \alpha_j : \rho_j, \varphi, \tau)$ from Definition 1 can label an arc if:

- α_i and α_j are agent variables;
- ρ_i and ρ_j are either role variables or role identifiers in R_s; and
- τ is a time variable;

These variables will be bound to concrete values during the execution of the scene. For example, agent variables in an illocution scheme will be bound, respectively, to the identifier of the agent that has uttered the illocution and to the identifier of the agent who has received the illocution. Then at each moment, the bindings of the variables will be the context of the scene execution. These variables have a local scope within a scene execution that, as said, represents an actual activity undertaken by a group of agents. There are several such activities within any possible institution, so there must be a way of modelling their interconnections. The notion of a *performative structure* is the most complex and interesting of the proposed formalism, since it precisely models the relationships among scenes.

Notice that although conversations (scenes) are currently admitted as the unit of communication between agents, limited work has been done concerning the modelling of the relationships between different scenes. This issue is particularly significant when conversations are embedded in a broader context, such as, for instance, organisations and a hierarchy of institutions. If this is the case, it is important to capture the relationships between scenes. Our argument is that this is precisely the main difference with classic Mechanism Design, understood with the narrow view of the description of the central activity of an interaction. We believe that for MAS specification, a specification model that has a holistic view of the pragmatics and the web of activities (central and peripheral) is essential. Electronic Institutions aim at playing this role.

In general, the activity represented by a performative structure can be depicted as a collection of multiple, concurrent scenes. Agents navigate from scene to scene constrained by the rules defining the relationships between scenes. Moreover, the same agent can potentially participate in multiple scenes at the same time. From a structural point of view, performative structures' specifications must be regarded as networks of scenes. At execution time, a performative structure becomes populated by agents that make it evolve whenever these comply with the rules encoded by the specification. Concretely, an agent participating in the execution of a performative structure devotes its time to jointly start new scene executions, to enter active scenes where the agent interacts with other agents, to leave active scenes to possibly enter other scenes, and finally to abandon the performative structure.

At this point it should be noted that the way agents move from scene to scene depends on the type of relationship holding between the source and target scenes. Sometimes we might be interested in forcing agents to synchronise before jumping into either new or existing scene executions, or offering choice points so that an agent can decide which target scene to incorporate itself into, and so on. Summarizing, in order to capture the type of relationships listed above, we consider that any performative structure can contain special elements (that we call *transitions*) whose function is to mediate different types of connections among scenes. Each scene may be connected to multiple transitions, and in turn each transition may be connected to multiple scenes. In both cases, the connection between a scene and a transition is made by means of a directed arc. Then we can refer to the source and target of each arc. And given either a scene or a transition, we shall distinguish between its incoming and outgoing arcs. Notice that there is no direct connection between two scenes (i.e., all connections between scenes are mediated by transitions). Also we do not allow the connection of transitions. Each arc connecting a scene with a transition is labelled with the roles played by the agents that traverse it and a set of constraints that must be satisfied by the agents. Any agent playing a different role from those marked on the arc or not satisfying the constraints will not be authorised to abandon the scene at the beginning of the arc. Similarly, arcs connecting a transition with a scene are labelled with the roles that the agents traversing it will play in the target scene. See an example of performative structure in Figure 6.

Agents move from a scene instance (execution) to another by traversing the transition connecting the scenes and following the arcs that connect transitions and scenes. Transitions should therefore be regarded as a kind of router that contains local information about the scene instances that they connect. Therefore, instead of modelling some activity, they are intended to route agents towards their destinations in different ways, depending on the type of transition. The arcs connecting transitions to scenes also play a fundamental role. Notice that as there might be multiple (or perhaps no) scene executions of a target scene, it should be specified whether the agents following the arcs are allowed to start a new scene execution, whether they can choose a single or a subset of scenes to incorporate into, or whether they must enter all the available scene executions. Formally:

Definition 3. *A performative structure is a tuple*

$$PS = \langle S, T, s_0, s_\Omega, E, f_L, f_T, f_E, C, \mu, ML \rangle$$

where

– *S is a finite, non-empty set of scenes; defined according to Definition 2.*

- T is a finite and non-empty set of transitions;
- $s_0 \in S$ is the root scene;
- $s_\Omega \in S$ is the output scene;
- $E = E^I \cup E^O$ is a set of arc identifiers where $E^I \subseteq S \times T$ is a set of edges from scenes to transitions, and $E^O \subseteq T \times S$ is a set of edges from transitions to scenes;
- $f_L : E \to 2^{V_A \times R}$ is the labelling function associating each arc with pairs of agent variables and roles;
- $f_T : T \to \tau$ maps each transition to its type – where $\tau = \{sync/parallel, choice/choice, sync/choice, choice/parallel\}$ corresponds to the behaviour of the transition with respect to the incoming and outgoing arcs;
- $f_E : E^O \to \epsilon$ maps each arc from transition to scene to its type - where $\epsilon = \{1, some, all, new\}$ correspond to one, several, all, or a newly created running execution of the target scene respectively;
- $C : E \to ML$ maps each arc to a meta-language expression representing the arc's constraints that agents must satisfy to follow the arc;
- $\mu : S \to \mathbb{N}$ sets an upper bound to the number of allowed simultaneous running executions of a given scene; and
- ML is a meta-language over CL and L as defined in Definition 1.

Behaviour Conventions: Normative Rules

These conventions determine the socially pertinent commitments for the participating agents and describe their various obligations and rights. As discussed so far, a performative structure can be seen to constrain an agent's behaviour at two levels:

1. *intra-scene:* Scene protocols dictate, for each agent role within a scene, what can be said, by whom, to whom, and when.
2. *inter-scene:* The connections among the scenes, given by the performative structure, define the possible paths that agents may follow depending on their roles. Furthermore, the constraints over output arcs impose additional limitations on the agents when attempting to reach a target scene.

Although these may appear distinct, an agent's actions within a scene may have non-local consequences in that it may either limit or enlarge its acting possibilities in subsequent scenes. Such consequences may have effect along two different directions. On the one hand, some actions will introduce subsequent acting commitments that have to be interpreted as acting obligations. While on the other hand, consequences occurring locally within a scene may vary the paths that an agent can follow in the performative structure because they affect the satisfaction and contravention of the constraints labelling the paths. Both types of consequences need to be kept by an institution on a per agent basis so that the different obligations and restrictions may be subsequently enforced.

In order to represent the deontic notion of obligation (see [27] for background details) we set out the predicate *Obl* as follows:

$$Obl(x, \psi, s) = \text{agent } x \text{ is obliged to do (in fact, to 'say')} \psi \text{ in scene } s. \quad (1)$$

where ψ is taken to be an illocution scheme. We will note by Obl the set of obligations and by $obl_i \in$ Obl any concrete obligation.

Behaviour conventions of an Electronic Institution are specified as a special type of rule, called a *normative rule*, that captures which agent actions (illocutions) have consequences that need to be kept in its context. Given a performative structure, the normative rules are written in its meta-language according to the following schema:

$$(s_1, \gamma_1) \wedge \ldots \wedge (s_m \gamma_m) \wedge \neg(s_{m+1}, \gamma_{m+1}) \wedge \ldots \wedge \neg(s_{m+n}\gamma_{m+n}) \rightarrow obl_1 \wedge \ldots \wedge obl_p$$

where $(s_1, \gamma_1), \ldots, (s_{m+n}, \gamma_{m+n})$ are pairs of scenes and illocution schemes, $\neg$ is a defeasible negation, and $obl_1 \wedge \ldots \wedge obl_p$ are obligations. The meaning of these rules is that if the illocutions $(s_1, \gamma_1) \wedge \ldots \wedge (s_m, \gamma_m)$ have been uttered, and the illocutions $(s_{m+1}, \gamma_{m+1}) \wedge \ldots \wedge (s_{m+n}, \gamma_{m+n})$ have *not* been uttered, the obligations $obl_1 \wedge \ldots \wedge obl_p$ hold. Therefore, the rules have two components, the first one is causing the obligations to be activated (for instance winning an auction round by saying 'mine' in a downwards bidding protocol, generates the obligation to pay) and the second is the part that removes the obligations (for instance, paying the amount of money at which the round was won).

We can now show how these ideas are put to work to extend the three examples of agent interaction mechanisms we discussed earlier.

4   Revisiting the Mechanisms. The Big Picture

4.1   Auctions

Although Auction houses can be seen as a very simple co-ordination mechanism (in a sense as simple as an ant algorithm), some economists (such as Smith [25] or McAfee and McMillan[11]), however, refer to them as *institutions* [15] and are careful to point out that, in addition to the bidding conventions, other equally relevant conventions and elements are used in an auction house to achieve a proper co-ordination of buyers and sellers: conventions for the registration of participants and goods, conventions on guarantees and payment, commissions, starting prices, etc.

The actual auctioning of goods (what we would call the auctioning scene) can certainly be understood as governed by a simple language and protocol, according to the point of view introduced in Section 2. It is when looking at the global picture of all the activities that take place around that kernel dialogue that we can appreciate that even auctions involve many more and more complex interactions, and are hence supported by complex institutions. Any model that concentrates just on the auction mechanism and ignores the full picture will lead to systems difficult to use in the real world and difficult to integrate with the existing legacy systems. An auction does not end when the auctioneer has the last standing bid in an English auction and assigns the good after the sequence 'going-going-gone' is finished. A process of credit checking, payment procedures, document generation starts that is essential for the successful completion of the transaction.

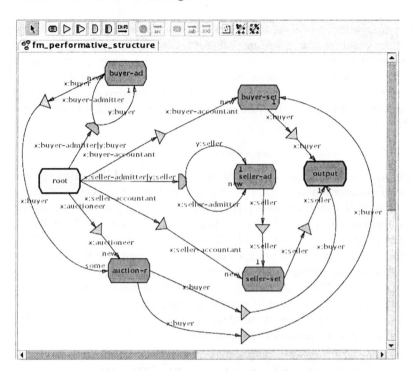

Fig. 4. Performative structure of the FishMarket Institution. Each rectangle represents a scene and the labelled links correspond to the movements of agents between scenes. Transitions are represented as triangles. *root* is the initial scene to enter the institution, and *output* is the scene through which all agents leave the institution.

When analyzing the example of the fish market as introduced in this paper from this broader perspective, we observe a series of activities that complement and modify the simple auction protocol: the buyers' and sellers' registration and settlements. Also, many pragmatic elements have to be modelled (even for this simple mechanism). For instance, the fact that buyers have an associated credit in the auction house changes the winner determination protocol by introducing the fact that the bid of a buyer has to be supported by its current credit, and therefore the auctioneer has to check that. As argued in this paper, even simple mechanisms have complex societal restrictions that require elaborated specification languages. See in Figure 4 the performative structure of the FishMarket.

4.2 Negotiation

In the supply chain example, we have to realise that each chain level is a global view of a reality consisting of many individual agents, and that the transactions modelled as those flows are the result of the social interaction of the agents following particularly well established conventions. For instance, the interaction between the agents at levels S_1 and S_2 is modelled as negotiation. The interac-

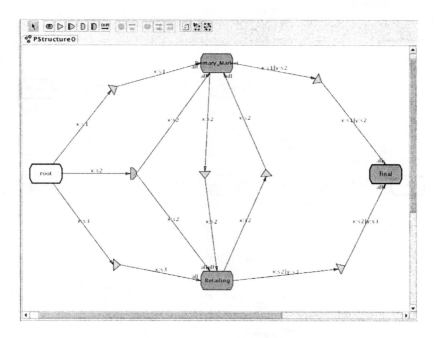

Fig. 5. Performative structure of the Supply Chain Institution.

tion between levels S_2 and S_3 could probably be better modelled by fixed-price mechanisms. Electronic Institutions offer the necessary principled way to model such interactions. In our Institution specification for the example we consider two scenes: One, *primary_market*, for the interaction between agents of S_1 and S_2 and another, *retailing*, for the interaction between S_2 and S_3. Scene *primary_market* is endowed with a protocol as the one in Figure 2.

4.3   Argumentation

In the case of the argumentation example, its electronic institution has to account for many complex activities a part from the scenes where the argumentation takes place. The first stages of the Provide_Customer_Quote service involve the CSD agent capturing basic information about the customer and vetting the customer in terms of their credit worthiness. The latter service is performed by one of the VC agents and negotiation is used to determine which one is selected. If the customer fails the vetting procedure, then the quote process terminates. Assuming the customer is satisfactory, the CSD agent maps their requirements against a service portfolio. If the requirements can be met by a standard off-the-shelf portfolio item then an immediate quote can be offered based on previous examples. In the case of bespoke services the process is more complex. The CSD agent negotiates with the DD agent for the service of costing and designing the desired network service. To prepare a network design it is usually necessary to have a detailed plan of the existing equipment at the customer's premises.

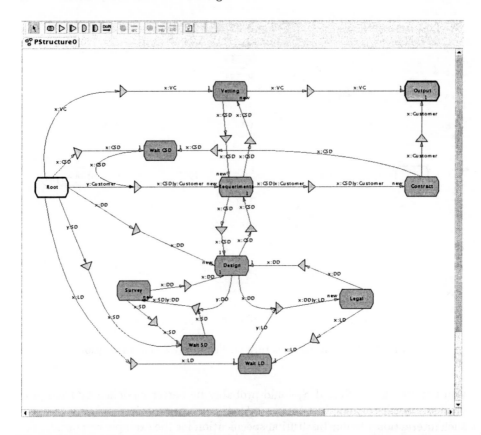

Fig. 6. Performative structure of the BT Institution. As before, each rectangle represents a scene and the labelled links correspond to the movements of agents between scenes. Transitions are represented as triangles.

Sometimes such plans might not exist and sometimes they may be out of date. In either case, the DD agent determines whether the customer site(s) should be surveyed. If such a survey is warranted, the DD agent negotiates with the SD agent for the Survey_Customer_Site service. This negotiation differs from the others present in this scenario in that the two agents are part of the same department. Moreover, the DD agent has a degree of authority over SD. Agent negotiation is still required to set the timings of the service, but the SD agent cannot simply refuse to perform the service. On completion of the network design and costing, the DD agent informs the CSD agent which informs the customer of the service quote. The business process then terminates. Figure 6 summarises this institution.

5   Conclusions

In this paper we argued for the concept of Electronic Institutions as a methodological tool to specify multi-agent systems, as they permit a view that is broader than that offered by the usual mechanism design approach. Electronic Institutions give a handle to designers of multi-agent systems to address the difficult problem of specifying the many inter-related activities required for successful complex agent interactions.

We also explored the correspondence between the complexity of the problem to be solved and the complexity of the communication language of participating agents. We used three interaction examples – of growing complexity – to illustrate this point, as summarized in the following table:

Interaction	Pragmatics	Content
Auctions	Offer, Accept	simple terms, integers
Negotiation	Offer, accept	complex terms
Argumentation	Offer, Critique, Appeal, Threaten	complex terms, FOL formulae

Acknowledgements

Most of the material of this paper is the result of collaborative work with different researchers among which we'd like to mention Nick Jennings, Simon Parsons, Julian Padget, Juan Antonio Rodriguez, and Peyman Faratin. This line of research is currently being supported by the MCYT research project eINSTITUTOR (TIC2000-1414) and the IST project SLIE (IST-1999-10948). The graphics in the paper have been produced with the help of Marc Esteva using the Electronic Institution specification tool ISLANDER [4].

References

1. J. L. Austin. *How to Do Things With Words*. Oxford University Press, 1962.
2. C. Castelfranchi, F. Dignum, C. Jonker, and J. Treur. *Deliberate Normative Agents: Principles and Architectures*, pages 364–378. Intelligent Agents VI (LNAI-1757). N. Jennings and Y. Lesperance (eds.). Springer-Verlag, 2000.
3. M. Esteva and C. Sierra. ISLANDER1.0 Language Definition. Technical report, IIIA-CSIC, 2001.
4. Marc Esteva, David de la Cruz, and Carles Sierra. ISLANDER: an electronic institutions editor. In *AAMAS'02*, page in press. ACM Press, 2002.
5. P. Faratin, C. Sierra, and N. R. Jennings. Using similarity criteria to make negotiation trade-offs. In *Proc. Fourth Int. Conf. on Multi-Agent Systems, ICMAS'00*, pages 119–126, 2000.
6. Michael R. Genesereth and Richard E. Fikes. Knowldege interchange format version 3.0 reference manual. Technical Report Report Logic–92–1, Logic Group, Computer Science Department, Standford University, June 1992.
7. N. R. Jennings, P. Faratin, A. R. Lomuscio, S. Parsons, M. Wooldridge, and C. Sierra. Automated negotiation: Prospects, methods and challenges. *Group Decision and Negotiation*, 10:199–215, 2001.

8. N. R. Jennings, P. Faratin, T. J. Norman, P. O'Brien, and B. Odgers. Autonomous agents for business process management. *Int. Journal of Applied Artificial Intelligence.*, 14(2):145–189, 2000.
9. M. Karlins and H. I. Abelson. *Persuasion.* Crosby Lockwood & Son, London, UK, 1970.
10. B. Laasri, H. Laasri, S. Lander, and V. Lesser. A generic model for negotiating agents. *International journal of Intelligent and Cooperative Information Systems*, 1(2):291–317, 1992.
11. R. P. McAfee and J. McMillan. Auctions and bidding. *Journal of Economic Literature*, XXV:699–738, 1987.
12. P. Noriega and C. Sierra. Auctions and multi-agent systems. In Matthias Klusch, editor, *Intelligent Information Agents*, pages 153–175. Springer, 1999.
13. Pablo Noriega. *Agent-Mediated Auctions: The Fishmarket Metaphor.* Number 8 in IIIA Monograph Series. Institut d'Investigació en Intel.ligència Artificial (IIIA), 1997. PhD Thesis.
14. Pablo Noriega and Carles Sierra. Towards layered dialogical agents. In *Third International Workshop on Agent Theories, Architectures, and Languages, ATAL-96*, 1996.
15. Douglas C. North. *Institutions, Institutional Change and Economics Perfomance.* Cambridge U. P., 1990.
16. P. Panzarasa, T. J. Norman, and N. R. Jennings. Social mental shaping: modelling the impact of sociality on autonomous agents' mental states. *Computational Intelligence*, 2001.
17. N. Rescher. *Dialectics: A controversy-oriented approach to the theory of knowledge.* SUNY, 1977.
18. Juan A. Rodríguez-Aguilar, Francisco J. Martín, Pablo Noriega, Pere Garcia, and Carles Sierra. Towards a test-bed for trading agents in electronic auction markets. *AI Communications*, 11(1):5–19, 1998.
19. Juan Antonio Rodriguez-Aguilar. *On the design and construction of Agent-mediated Institutions.* Number 14 in Monografies de l'IIIA. IIIA-CSIC, 2002.
20. L. Royakkers and F. Dignum. Organisations and collective obligations. In *11th International Conference on Databases & Expert Systems Applications (LNCS-1873)*, pages 302–311. Springer-Verlag, 2000.
21. N. Sadeh-Koniecpol, D. Hildum, D. Kjensta, and A. Tseng. Mascot: An agent-based architecture for coordinated mixed-initiative supply chain planning and scheduling. In *Workshop notes, Agent-Based Decision Support for Managing the Internet-Enabled Supply Chain, Third International Conference on Autonomous Agents (Agents '99)*, 1999.
22. J. R. Searle. *Speech acts.* Cambridge U.P., 1969.
23. C. Sierra, P. Faratin, and N. R. Jennings. A service-oriented negotiation model between autonomous agents. In *MAAMAW'97*, number 1237 in LNAI, pages 17–35, Ronneby, Sweden, 1997.
24. C. Sierra, N. R. Jennings, P. Noriega, and S. Parsons. A framework for argumentation–based negotiation. In *Intelligent Agents IV*, pages 177–192, 1997.
25. Vernon L. Smith. *Auctions*, pages 39–53. The new Palgrave: a dictionary of Economics. John Eatwell, Murray Milgate and Peter Newman (eds). McMillan, London, 1987.
26. K. P. Sycara. Persuasive argumentation in negotiation. *Theory and Decision*, 28:203–242, 1990.
27. G. H. von Wright. Deontic logic. *Mind*, (60):1–15, 1951.

Game Theory and Artificial Intelligence

Moshe Tennenholtz

Faculty of Industrial Engineering and Management,
Technion – Israel Institute of Technology, Haifa 32000, Israel

Abstract. Game Theory and Artificial Intelligence are two mature areas of research, originating from similar roots, which have taken different research directions in the last 50 years. Recent research however shows that the connections between these areas are deep, and that the time had come for bridging the gap between these research disciplines. In this paper we concentrate on basic issues in representation, reasoning, and learning, and discuss work that lies in the intersection of Artificial Intelligence and Game Theory, for each of these subjects.

1 Introduction

The early 50's at Princeton university were very fruitful. Many new ideas have been generated, and many brave attempts of extending classical mathematical and economic reasoning, as well as embodying these new types of reasoning in "computing machines" have been suggested. Many of the founders of Game Theory and Artificial Intelligence were there at that time, as students or professors, initiating new lines of research. Now, fifty years later, we realize that these fields have taken different directions, but the connections between them are fundamental and deep. Exploring and expanding upon these connections may yield significant contributions to both fields.

This article presents a biased perspective about the Game Theory and Artificial Intelligence connections. I will concentrate on three fundamental topics in computer science and game theory: representation, reasoning, and learning. I will introduce basic problems associated with these topics, and discuss the way they are addressed in my own work.

2 Representation, Reasoning, and Learning

Both game theory and Artificial Intelligence deal with "intelligent" agents, who are embodied in a complex world. These agents may interact with other agents, and try to optimize their behavior, while employing various reasoning and learning techniques. The following issues are fundamental both to economics/game theory and to CS/AI:

1. **Reasoning about Distributed Systems.** Work in CS discusses protocols for distributed environments, emphasizing computational constraints, such as communication complexity, and distributed systems features such

M. d' Inverno et al. (Eds.): UKMAS 1996–2000, LNAI 2403, pp. 49–58, 2002.

as network topology. Work in game theory discusses agent interactions that are subject to rational constraints, i.e. agents will follow their own interests. Needless to say that reasoning about distributed systems, incorporating both communication constraints as well as rationality constraints, is of basic importance to both disciplines. Indeed, the Internet setup is an instance of a non-cooperative distributed system. In this environment, different users may have different objectives, while interacting in a computational environment.

2. **Learning.** Learning, and in particular reinforcement learning, is a fundamental topic in both CS/AI and game theory/economics. Work in game theory emphasizes learning as a descriptive tool, explaining the emergence of Nash equilibrium or predicting agents' behavior[8]. Work on reinforcement learning in AI [18] emphasizes a normative approach, and deals with algorithms for obtaining high payoffs in uncertain environments based on observed feedback. Effective reinforcement learning schemes for adaptive behavior in hostile environments, are fundamental for both disciplines. Efficient algorithms that deal with optimal agent's behavior in adversarial environments will enable to introduce a normative approach to reinforcement learning in non-cooperative environments.

3. **Representation.** Work in game theory and in economics is centered around modelling agents as expected utility maximizers. Work in CS/AI has considered, in addition to that classical decision criterion, other forms of decision making. This includes, for example, competitive analysis (aka the competitive ratio decision criterion) [1], and the safety-level (worst case) maximization approaches. The understanding of the conditions under which an agent can be viewed as using these decision-theoretic approaches is fundamental to these disciplines. The foundations of expected utility maximization have been provided by the "crowing achievement of the theory of choice": Savage axiomatization [16]. Savage has shown several conditions on an agent's choice among actions under which it can be viewed *as if* it were an expected utility maximizer. However, similar foundations are required for the other decision criteria.

In the following sections we discuss some of our previous work on these three fundamental problems.

3   Reasoning

Consider a distributed system where resources are to be allocated among a set of agents. Each agent associates any subset of the resources with a particular (private) value. One way of interpreting an agent's valuation for a set of resources is as the agent's maximal willingness to pay for that set. A useful approach for dealing with resource allocation in a general non-cooperative multi-agent setup, is by using an auction. Economists use auctions in order to try and obtain economic efficiency. In an economically efficient allocation a center chooses an allocation in which the sum of agents' valuations is maximized. However, in order to implement such desired behavior one should overcome two major obstacles:

1. Rationality: agents may cheat about their valuations.
2. Communication bounds: the number of possible bundles (subsets) of resources might be very big, and therefore communicating an agent's valuation for each possible subset of the resources might become infeasible.

The first problem is addressed using the famous Clarke mechanism [5]. This mechanism is central to the economic mechanism design literature, and deals with general resource allocation problems in non-cooperative environments.

Given a set of resources $R = \{R_1, \ldots, R_m\}$, and a set of agents $\{1, 2, \ldots, n\}$, we conduct the following procedure:

1. Agent i $(1 \leq i \leq n)$ is asked to report its valuation for any $b \subseteq 2^R$. Let us denote agent i's report for the bundle b by $v_i(b)$.
2. Each allocation σ of the resources to the agents is associated with a value $\Sigma_{i=1}^{n} v_i(R^{\sigma_i})$ where R^{σ_i} is the set of resources assigned to i by σ and $v_i(R^{\sigma_i})$ is the value reported for that bundle by agent i. The center will choose an allocation of maximal value. We denote this allocation by σ^*.
3. Given the above reports, the center can similarly compute an optimal allocation σ_i^* that ignores the reports of agent i, and does not allocate resources to that agent.
4. Agent i will pay the center $A_i - B_i$, where A_i is the value of σ_i^*, and B_i is the sum of the other agents' (reported) valuations in σ^*.

The above protocol has a desired property: it is dominant strategy for each agent to be honest about its valuations. Regardless of the other agents' actions, the optimal action for an agent is to truthfully report its valuations. As a result, the protocol is economically efficient. Typically, economists are interested in equilibrium strategies: a strategy profile (one for each agent) is in equilibrium, if it is irrational for each (single) agent to deviate from its strategy in that profile, assuming that the others stick to their strategies. In particular, truth revealing is an equilibrium of the game generated by the above protocol.

The above basic result can (and is) viewed as "very good news". However, given the second obstacle that we have mentioned before, one may need to consider the case where agents can not report their valuations for every bundle. In the following we assume that each agent assigns valuation 0 for obtaining no resource. Assume that agent i explicitly reports valuations only for bundles in the set $B \subseteq 2^R$, and provide the following program for the computation of their reported valuations for any bundle: $v_i(d) = max_{b \in B, b \subseteq d} v_i(b)$. The first question is whether we can get an equilibrium where the agents report their (true) valuations only for a small number of bundles, and provide the above-mentioned program for computing the reported valuations for the rest of the bundles. The answer for this is positive. Consider the case where $B = \{R\}$. In this case we get that truth revealing is in equilibrium, while the agents report on their valuations for a single bundle!

The above observation is fundamental to the game theory/CS interaction. Given the non-cooperative resource allocation setting, there exists an equilibrium with small communication complexity for the game associated with the most famous protocol in that setting. However, in this equilibrium the sum of agents' valuations for the selected allocation, termed the social surplus, will be typically lower than in the more "standard" equilibrium (where agents report their valuations on every possible bundle of resources). This observation leads to a challenging line of research dealing with the tradeoff between communication efficiency and economic efficiency. In this article we share with the reader one of the basic results about that tradeoff (see Theorem 2 below).

Consider the case where the set B is a partition of the set R, i.e. the bundles in B are mutually disjoint and their union covers the set R. The following result has been obtained by Holzman, Kfir-Dahav, Monderer, and Tennenholtz [13]:

Theorem 1. *When B is a partition of R, truth revealing (for the valuations of the bundles in B, where $v_i(d) = max_{b \in B, b \subseteq d} v_i(b)$) is an equilibrium of the Clarke mechanism.*

Let us denote by r_B the ratio between the optimal social surplus that can be obtained by allocating R to the agents (using the Clarke mechanism with no communication constraints; i.e. the social surplus obtained in the "standard" equilibrium), to the social surplus obtained in the equilibrium of the Clarke mechanism where agents report their valuations only for the bundles in B, as above. The value of r_B measures the amount of "economic loss" that we have if the agents will be bidding only for bundles in B. The communication gain in this case will be proportional to the size of B (i.e. the valuations for only $|B|$ bundles, instead of $2^{|R|}$ bundles will need to be communicated). Notice that the center will not need to re-construct the agents' full valuation functions, and compute optimal allocations considering only allocations of bundles in B.

We can show [13]:

Theorem 2. *Let $B = \{A_1, ..., A_k\}$ be a partition of R into k non empty sets of maximum size $\beta(B)$. (That is, $\beta(B) = \max\{|A_1|, ..., |A_k|\}$.) Then*

$$r_B \leq \beta(B) \cdot \varphi(k),$$

where

$$\varphi(k) = \max_{j=1,...,k} \min\{j, \frac{k}{j}\}.$$

Notice that $\varphi(k) \leq \sqrt{(k)}$. The above theorem gives an upper bound on "how bad" r_B might be. Many other results are presented in [13].

4   Learning

Learning is a major issue in both Artificial Intelligence and Game Theory. In particular, work on reinforcement learning got a lot of attention by both CS/AI researchers and game-theorists/economists in the recent years. We will illustrate the connections between the related lines of research using the model of repeated games. Results regarding more general models will be mentioned following that.

Work on learning in game theory [8] has concentrated for long time on the attempt for providing a justification for the Nash equilibrium concept. For simplicity, consider two-person games. In a (static) two person game, we have two players, each one of them can select from a finite set of strategies. The pair of strategies selected, one by each player, determine the payoffs to be obtained by the players. More generally, a player may select a mixed strategy which is a probability distribution on the set of (pure) strategies. A Nash equilibrium is a pair of (possibly mixed) strategies, one for each player, such that a deviation by one of the players is irrational (i.e. a deviation will not increase the agent's expected payoff) assuming that the other player sticks to its strategy (the above should hold for any deviation by each single player). In the learning literature, researchers have considered the case where the game is repeatedly played, and each player adapts its behavior based on the feedback it receives, i.e. a player's selected strategy at a particular stage depends on its observed history of the previous stages. The idea is to look for "natural learning rules" that will lead to (and hence justify) playing a Nash equilibrium. Another, perhaps even more challenging perspective, adopted by game-theorists is to build such adaptive (reinforcement learning) rules that will mimic the way humans behave in such repeated games [6].

The AI perspective on learning is mainly a normative one. The objective is, roughly speaking, to provide the agent with a learning rule that will guarantee it (with high probability) a high accumulated payoff after a short time [18, 9]. Consider the repeated game model discussed above, and consider the payoff of one player, who we term the "agent", when interacting in a repeated game with another (malicious) player, who we term the "adversary". If the agent would have known the game that is played, then the best that it could have done is to choose the probabilistic maximin strategy of the game, i.e. a (potentially mixed) strategy that its worst case payoff is maximal. More technically, for every mixed strategy of the agent and a strategy of the adversary one can compute the expected payoff for the agent. Given that, one can compute the expected payoff that can be guaranteed for the agent by choosing that mixed strategy. The mixed strategy for which this (worst case) value is maximal is the probabilistic maximin strategy. However, when the game is unknown, it is unclear how the agent should behave. Assuming that the agent can observe its payoffs and the other player's behavior in previous stages, then it can use that information to select a strategy in a given stage. This is yet again a reinforcement learning problem, but it has also a computational aspect: given $\epsilon > 0, 0 < \delta < 1$, and a game G, which is of size $|G|$, we are interested in constructing an algorithm (to be adopted by the agent), A, for which there exists a T, polynomial in $\frac{1}{\epsilon}, \frac{1}{\delta}, |G|$, such that A has the property that for every $t \geq T$ the average payoff obtained by the agent is ϵ close to the probabilistic maximin value of G with probability of failure of at most δ. Such a result will complement the game-theoretic perspective, and provide a useful normative approach to reinforcement learning in hostile environments. Fortunately, in a recent work, Brafman and Tennenholtz [3] have shown that such an algorithm exists. Their algorithm, called R_{max}, is applicable to general stochastic games (to be discussed below), and as a result it is applicable to repeated games as mentioned above.

The idea of the R_{max} algorithm when applied to repeated games is simple. Assume that the maximal payoff that can be obtained by the agent is R. The agent will initially assume that its payoff is R for every strategy profile. When the agent observes the payoff obtained using a certain strategy profile then it modifies its model of the game (i.e. the agent assigns the observed payoff to the corresponding strategy profile in its model of the game; the payoffs for entries that have not been visited yet remain R, the maximal possible payoff). At each stage, the agent selects a probabilistic maximin strategy of the corresponding (fictitious) game where the payoffs for all unknown entries are taken to be R (notice that the payoffs assumed for the adversary are irrelevant here).

Theorem 3. *Given a game G, and $\epsilon > 0, 0 < \delta < 1$, there exists a number T, polynomial in $\frac{1}{\epsilon}, \frac{1}{\delta}, |G|$, after which R_{max} will have the property that for every $t \geq T$, the average payoff obtained by the agent is ϵ close to the probabilistic maximin value of G, with a probability of failure of at most δ.*

In the recent years, Markov Decision Processes (MDPs) [12] had become a model of great interest to AI researchers (see e.g. [2]). In an MDP, the agent is in one of finitely many states, and can select one of finitely many actions. The action selected in a given state will lead to a certain payoff, and to a new state. The identity of the new state to be reached is based on a given probabilistic transition function. Reinforcement learning in the context of MDPs deals with the situation where the payoffs and transition probabilities are initially unknown. MDPs do not model multi-agent activity. However, one can consider a model where each state of the MDP corresponds to a game, where two players need to select their actions. The actions selected by both players will determine their payoffs as well as the probability of moving to another state (where another game is played). This general model is called a stochastic game [17], and it is a very rich and expressive model. As we mentioned, the general result presented by Brafman and Tennenholtz holds for general stochastic games. This requires the introduction of the (so called) mixing time of the optimal policy in a stochastic game. The R_{max} algorithm is polynomial also in the mixing time of the optimal policy. The discussion of these are omitted from this paper.

5   Representation

The previous sections adopted the perspective of modelling agents as decision makers, who try to optimize their payoffs. This is the typical approach in economics/game theory, and a popular approach in the recent AI/CS literature (see the discussion in [15]).

In economics and game theory an agent is viewed as an expected utility maximizer, i.e. it assigns probabilities to the states of the environment, and utilities to various outcomes or consequences, and chooses the action, protocol, strategy or policy that maximizes its expected utility. A fundamental problem faced

by economists is the adequacy of expected utility maximization for agent mod-
elling/representation. This problem has been addressed by the fundamental work
of Savage [16]. Savage presents several properties of an agent's choice function
(i.e. postulates regarding the way it chooses among alternatives and ranks them)
under which it can be viewed *as if* it were an excepted utility maximizer. Savage's result provides foundations to the expected utility maximization decision
criterion.

Decision-theoretic approaches in computer science are not restricted to expected utility maximization. For example, in this section we discuss another
decision criterion, which is most popular in the theoretical computer science literature: the competitive ratio decision criterion [1]. Consider an agent who needs
to choose an action/protocol/strategy/policy from a finite set A. The environment may be in one of finitely many states, selected from a set S. The agent's
payoff when selecting $a \in A$ in state $s \in S$ is $u(a, s) > 0$. The agent does not know
the state of the environment and needs to choose an action. Let a_s be an optimal
action for the state s and denote its payoff (when the state is indeed s) by r_s. The
regret of action a is defined as $Reg(a) = max_{s \in S} \frac{r_s}{u(a,s)}$. The competitive ratio
decision criterion tells the agent to choose an action $a_{opt} \in argmin_{a \in A} Reg(a)$.
We will refer to a_{opt} as a competitive action, and to $Reg(a_{opt})$ as the competitive
ratio of the related problem.

The competitive ratio approach may be quite powerful. For example, if the
competitive ratio is 2, then by choosing a competitive action we are guaranteed
to obtain a payoff that is at least half of the optimal payoff that could have been
obtained had we known the actual environment state/behavior.

Given the importance of competitive analysis, a natural and fundamental
question that should be answered, is under which conditions on the agent's
choice among actions the agent can be viewed as if it adopts the competitive ratio
decision criterion. This will provide foundations, similar to the ones provided for
the use of expected utility maximization, to the representation of agents, as used
in the recent CS literature.

The above challenge has been addressed in the work by Brafman and Tennenholtz [4]. In that work the authors provide two choice axioms that serve as
sound and complete axiomatization for the competitive ratio decision criterion.
In the binary case, one of these choice axioms suffices. The second condition is
more technical, and less controversial, so the discussion of it (as well as of the
general case) is omitted from this paper.

In the case of binary decisions, an agent selects from among two actions: a
and b. The world can be in one of several states. The information available to
the agent when taking its decision is represented by its *information state*. An
information state $l \in 2^S$ is the set of states (or "possible worlds") that the agent
considers possible: one of the states in l is the actual one, but the agent does not
know which state in l is indeed the "real world". For ease of exposition, we assume
that any subset of the states in S corresponds to some information state the agent
may reach. Let $L = 2^S$ be the set of possible information states the agent may
reach. Then, a policy for the agent is a function $P : L \rightarrow \{a, b\}$. Notice that

an explicit representation of P might be exponential in $|S|$. Consider however a decision theoretic representation, using a payoff function $U : S \times \{a, b\} \to R_+$. This representation is polynomial in the number of states. Given such function U, and an information state $l \in L$, consider the projection $U^l : l \times \{a, b\} \to R_+$. We can now apply the competitive ratio decision criterion to U^l. If the competitive action is uniquely determined then we can check and see whether it coincides with the action selected by P in l.

Given a set of states S, with a corresponding set of information states $L = 2^S$, we will say that a protocol $P : L \to \{a, b\}$ is competitive-ratio representable if there exists a function $U : S \times \{a, b\} \to R_+$, such that for every $l \in L$ we have that the (only) competitive action given U^l is $P(l)$.

Notice that the existence of a competitive-ratio representation has very useful properties. First, it will imply a polynomial representation of the protocol, rather than an exponential explicit representation. In addition, if we could find sound and complete conditions on the agent's protocol under which a protocol is competitive-ratio representable then we would provide foundations to this fundamental decision-theoretic approach for agent modelling.

Given a protocol P, we will say that P is *closed under unions* if for every $l_1, l_2 \in L$, such that $P(l_1) = P(l_2)$, we also have that $P(l_1 \cup l_2) = P(l_1) = P(l_2)$. Intuitively, closure under unions tells us that if an agent prefers action c upon action d, where the information state is l_1, and also when the information state is l_2, then it will still prefer c to d if it is told that the information state is either l_1 or l_2. The following theorem [4] provides the desired axiomatization:

Theorem 4. *Given a binary choice problem, closure under unions is a sound and complete axiomatization for the competitive-ratio decision criterion.*

The above implies that any protocol that has a competitive-ratio representation satisfies the closure under union property (soundness). While one can easily check this property, the other direction (completeness) is less straightforward: if an agent's protocol satisfies the closure under union property, one can construct a payoff function U, such that when applying the competitive ratio decision criterion to U^l, the (only) competitive action obtained is $P(l)$, for every $l \in L$.

The construction algorithm for the payoff function U, used by Brafman and Tennenholtz, is polynomial in the number of states and actions, and the computed payoffs are integers. Hence, the process is constructive and practical. Closure under union tells us the exact power of the competitive ratio approach for agent modelling and representation.

6   Discussion

Game Theory and Artificial Intelligence are mature communities. Moreover, Game Theory has considered in the past CS-like representations (e.g. when players are modelled as automata [11]), and work in AI has considered the use of game-theoretic mechanisms [14, 10]. However, as we have tried to illustrate in this paper, these are only tips of the iceberg, and fundamental connections among the fields do exist. In particular, the areas of general resource allocation, learning, and agent modelling, suggest fundamental challenges for both CS/AI and economics/game theory. We have chosen to explore these topics by presenting concrete results, that establish tight connections between AI and game theory. Needless to say that the connections between the areas are not restricted to the subjects covered in this paper. For example, the whole field of knowledge theory [7] lies in the intersection of game theory and AI, as well the whole art of transforming mechanisms into working protocols (see the discussion at [19]).

I see the connections between the AI and game theory as consisting of three parts:

1. Re-visiting economic and game-theoretic approaches, in view of their use in computational settings.
2. Deal with computational issues in the context of game-theoretic approaches.
3. Integrate game-theoretic approaches and CS approaches in order to yield new theories for non-cooperative multi-agent systems

These tasks can not be tackled by one community is isolation from the other ones, and call for real collaboration between computer scientists and AI researchers, to game theorists and economists. I strongly believe that this collaboration will lead to significant scientific and technological contributions.

References

1. Allan Borodin and Ran El-Yaniv. *On-Line Computation and Competitive Analysis.* Cambridge University Press, 1998.
2. C. Boutilier, T. Dean, and S. Hanks. Decision Theoretic Planning: Structural Assumptions and Computational Leverage. *Journal of Artificial Intelligence Research*, 11:1–94, 1999.
3. R. Brafman and M. Tennenholtz. R-max – A General Polynomial Time Algorithm for Near-Optimal Reinforcement Learning. In *Proc. of the 17th International Joint Conference on Artificial Intelligence*, pages 953–958, 2001.
4. R. I. Brafman and M. Tennenholtz. An axiomatic treatment of three qualitative decision criteria. *Journal of the ACM*, 47(3), March 2000.
5. E. Clarke. Multipart pricing of public goods. *Public Choice*, 18:19–33, 1971.
6. I. Erev and A.E. Roth. Predicting how people play games: Reinforcement learning in games with unique strategy equilibrium. *American Economic Review*, 88:848–881, 1998.
7. R. Fagin, J. Y. Halpern, Y. Moses, and M. Y. Vardi. *Reasoning about Knowledge.* MIT Press, 1995.
8. D. Fudenberg and D. Levine. *The theory of learning in games.* MIT Press, 1998.
9. L. P. Kaelbling, M. L. Littman, and A. W. Moore. Reinforcement learning: A survey. *Journal of AI Research*, 4:237–285, 1996.
10. S. Kraus. Negotiation and cooperation in multi-agent environments. *Artificial Intelligence*, 94:79–97, 1997.
11. A. Neyman. Bounded complexity justifies cooperation in the infinitely repeated prisoner's dilemma. *Econ. Lett.*, 19:227–229, 1985.
12. M.L. Puterman. *Markov Decision Processes: Discrete Stochastic Dynamic Programming.* Wiley, 1994.

13. Holzman R, Noa Kfir-Dahav, Dov Monderer, and Moshe Tennenholtz. Bundling Equilibrium in Combinatorial Auctions. Working paper Technion http://ie.technion.ac.il/ dov/rndm6.pdf, 2001.
14. Jeffrey S. Rosenschein and Gilad Zlotkin. *Rules of Encounter*. MIT Press, 1994.
15. S. Russell and P. Norvig. *Artificial Intelligence: A Modern Approach*. Prentice Hall, 1995.
16. L.J. Savage. *The Foundations of Statistics*. John Wiley and Sons, New York, 1954. Revised and enlarged edition, Dover, New York, 1972.
17. L.S. Shapley. Stochastic Games. In *Proc. Nat. Acad. Scie. USA*, volume 39, pages 1095–1100, 1953.
18. R. S. Sutton and A. G. Barto. *Reinforcement Learning: An Introduction*. MIT Press, 1998.
19. M. Tennenholtz. Electronic commerce: From game-theoretic and economic models to working protocols. In *IJCAI-99*, 1999.

Rights for Multi-agent Systems

Eduardo Alonso

Department of Computing, City University,
London EC1V 0HB, United Kingdom, eduardo@soi.city.ac.uk

Abstract. As utility calculus cannot account for an important part of
agents' behaviour in Multi-Agent Systems, researchers have progressively
adopted a more normative approach. Unfortunately, social laws have
turned out to be too restrictive in real-life domains where autonomous
agents' activity cannot be completely specified in advance. It seems that
a halfway concept between anarchic and off-line constrained interaction is
needed. We think that the concept of right suits this idea. Rights improve
coordination and facilitate social action in multi-agent domains. Rights
allow the agents enough freedom, and at the same time constrain them
(prohibiting specific actions). Therefore, rights can be understood as
the basic concept underneath open normative systems where the agents
reason about the code they must abide by.

1 Introduction

So far, the Rational Choice Theory (RCT) has been the most influential theory
for designing agents in Artificial Intelligence and Distributed Artificial Intelligence. According to this approach to rationality, agents with complete knowledge
make their decisions in order to maximise their own utilities. In this traditional,
non-constrained approach agents have been assumed 'free': They act of their
own accord and are not subject to any set of (social) rules. However fruitful this
approach has been, there have been pointed out (e.g., [17]) several drawbacks in
RCT, namely:

1. In real dynamic domains agents do not have enough information or time
   to perform complex, optimal utility calculus. An agent does not know all
   the alternatives, does not know the exact outcome of each, and does not
   have a complete preference order for those outcomes. This problem becomes
   particularly grave in Multi-Agent Systems (MAS) due to the presence of
   various agents, each with their own beliefs, goals and intentions.
2. On the other hand, the utilitarian approach has failed in explaining cooperation and social action. As illustarted in the *Prisoner's Dilemma*, agents can
   choose dominant, but socially irrational strategies. In the example depicted
   in **Table 1**, the equilibrium point is (2,5), even though (4,8), the Pareto
   solution, is more attractive. RCT says, however, that this solution is not
   stable, because the agents have an incentive to deviate from this strategy.
   Agents face a 'trust dilemma': They can take a position that, if rational, at
   least one of them may be tempted not to implement.

M. d' Inverno et al. (Eds.): UKMAS 1996–2000, LNAI 2403, pp. 59–72, 2002.

Table 1. Cooperation? Social action?

Agent 1

		A	B	C
	L	3,4	**2,5**	1,3
Agent 2				
	R	**4,8**	1,2	0,9

Following this line of argumentation, we cannot explain either collective action or cooperation. There is no notion of social action as a jointly planned course of action: Agents calculate individually and separately their best options. Moreover, communication or negotiation would not help, for agents cannot trust each other and will back down on the agreed commitments. In a word, cooperation is futile.

In order to cope with these problems, the MAS community has adopted a more constrained approach to rationality including conventions, norms and/or social laws. It is well-known that agents working under norms do not need to calculate continuously their utilities and, consequently, do not need complete information. Agents are supposed to act in a somehow predetermined way according to the principle of 'mutual expectation'. Besides, norms imply that the agents respect certain social constraints that deter them from breaking agreements. Unfortunately, research in this field has fallen into two extreme positions: Shoham and Tennenholtz [19] have studied off-line social laws, which agents must comply with automatically. Agents are assumed to follow rules just because they are designed to do so. Following this line of argumentation agents are not seen as autonomous any more. Proposals so formulated are thus closer to Distributed Problem Solving than to MAS.

Alternatively, conventions (e.g., [25]) have been introduced as rules emerging during repeated encounters in open normative systems. The problem here is that no notion of sanction is considered. Consequently, if the agents have the chance to calculate their utility each time they interact, conventions are continually under consideration. In other words, following a convention is not always a stable strategy.

It seems, therefore, that we need a concept that allows agents to reason and make decisions, but that implies enforcement at the same time. That is, we need a halfway concept (neither off-line nor strictly on-line) that guides, but does not control, the behaviour of autonomous agents. Our contention is that the concept of 'right' suits these requirements.

The remainder of the paper is structured as follows. In the second section, we present the concept of rights as liberties; in the third section, we characterise a simple theory of rights; in the fourth section, we consider what we can gain by introducing rights in the coordination process in terms of complexity, efficiency, stability, and flexibility; in the fifth section, the relationships between constrained and unrestricted behaviour in the coordination process are studied; we shall finish with some conclusions and further research.

2 Rights

Roughly stated, a right is considered as a set of restrictions on the agents' activities which allow them enough freedom, but at the same time constrain them. Not surprisingly, some authors (e.g., [24]) have expressed the same idea from a RCT perspective, by introducing some constraints in the set of strategies available to the agents. In so doing, agents are free to converge on 'stable social laws' (qualitative equilibria). However interesting this approach may be, it presents a serious handicap: To make sure that the agents choose a stable and efficient strategy, the designer decides beforehand which strategies should be eliminated. The designer, therefore, manipulates the process and creates an 'illusion of freedom'.

We understand this concept from a more social approach, as was advanced in [2]: To explain social behaviour we need to think of the agent as a *homo sociologicus* rather than as a *homo economicus*.

Generally speaking, if an agent has the right to execute a set of actions then (a) he is permitted to perform it (under certain constraints or obligations), (b) the rest of the group is not allowed to execute any action inhibiting the agent from exercising his right, and (c) the group is obliged to prevent this inhibitory action.

We can illustrate this idea with a simple traffic-world example that will be used throughout the paper. In **Figure 1**, x has the right to drive along the main A road under certain constraints (to have the corresponding licence, to respect the speed limit, to drive on the left, etc.); y is not allowed to take this road from the B road at that junction at the same time, because this action inhibits x's right[1]; finally, the rest of the group must stop y from breaking the law and, if needed, punish the offence. In large organizations, the group can delegate these responsibilities to expert agents, police-traffic agents in this case.

This third point follows from Castelfranchi's *right to claim* [6], according to which any agent has the right to ask for help if his counterpart in the interaction (a short term deal or a long term socially established pattern of behaviour) does not abide by the terms of the contract.

We extend, nonetheless, this notion and talk about the *right to be protected*: Agents have the right to be aided even when they themselves do not know that their rights are under threat (and therefore do not make any claim). So, even if x doesn't know that y has the intention of breaking the law and does not claim the group for help (right to claim), the group is obliged to assist him (right to be protected).

---

[1] We assume that x has priority according to the current traffic code.

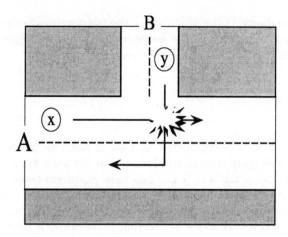

Fig. 1. A traffic example.

2.1 Three Facts about Rights

We are introducing now three distinctive facts about rights. These rights are related very closely to, but are not reducible to permissions or the right to claim. They are very basic rights, represent universal interests and form systems.

1. **Liberties:** Unlike in [15], rights are not considered in this paper as permissions. We are interested in basic rights, in what N.P. Barry called liberties [4]. Of course, once a right is adopted, it works like a permission. The main difference between rights and permissions lies in the fact that rights are universal statements: (a) the entire group agrees on them; (b) they establish equality; (c) they apply for the long-term. Nobody can delegate or trade with rights. Permissions, on the other hand, are relative.

   Let's illustrate these differences with an example. In many countries, drivers must pay a fixed amount of money to have the permission to drive along a motorway. Once a driver has paid, he has the right to drive along the motorway. We can think of such a condition as the need for a permission: There is an agreement saying that if an agent pays, say, £5 then he gets the permission to use the road. However, this agreement is quite special, because it is applicable to any agent anytime. Agents do not have to ask for permission to drive along the motorway, but only to abide by certain constraints (to pay £5).

   That is not the case with mere premissions. A driver can reach an agreement with the owner of a private parking place: To pay £30 per night. That's a bilateral one-shot agreement. If another driver wants to use the parking, he has no rights until he reaches another agreement with the parking owner. The previous agreement does not set up a precedent. Renegotiation is required.

   Rights are essentially social concepts: the notion of group is a guarantee that agents' rights (and their corresponding obligations) are observed through sanctions and compensations. Moreover, rights mean that all the agents in a group are closely related: Those agents exercising a right (active agents) are constrained by the obligations linked to that right, whereas the others (passive agents) are constrained by prohibitions (it is forbidden to violate others' rights).

2. **Hierarchies:** Rights form systems. Permissions do not. As a consequence, rights cannot be adopted individually, one by one. For example, I am not allowed to accept the right to drive on the left (because it is instrumental in satisfying my goal of driving work on time) and reject at the same time the right to live (which may turn out to be in conflict with my goal, so I could be tempted to run over any pedestrian crossing the road in my way).

    Ideally, rights are totally ordered in a hierarchy according to the interests they represent. The higher a right is in the hierarchy, the more important the interest it represents. Therefore, a right is only overruled by another in a higher position. In theory, conflicts between rights are automatically solved according to this order, because higher rights act as constraints for lower rights. As driving along A has precedence over driving from B to A, one of the constraints for exercising this second right is that there is no agent exercising the first.

3. **Interests vs Utilities:** The main purpose of recognising rights is to protect certain interests of individuals against additive calculations of utilities. Utilitarians can reply that the disutility of frustrating expectations and the utilities of honouring them should be introduced in the utility equations[2]. On the contrary, rights are beyond utility calculus: They represent values or interests. The point of speaking of rights is precisely that we do not want such utilities calculated. Quoting Nielsen and Shiner [14]

    > "For the sake of security and psychological stability we want interests of individuals (...) protected against such calculations, and hence we grant them rights. (...) And where rights exist, they are not to be overridden by mere utilities." (Nielsen and Shiner (1977), p. 127)

    An agent is entitled to exercise a right (in a way legitimised in the stipulation of the right) despite the greater utility realised by breaking this right. In the traffic example, it doesn't matter if there are three agents y, w, and z intending to drive from B to A, so that the addition of the utilities that these three agents would get by breaking the law would be greater than the utility that x gets by driving along A. This kind of calculations are out of the question, precisely because of x's right to drive along A.

    A direct implication of defining rights over utilities is that agents can exercise their rights even though their behaviour is considered wrong. It is important to differentiate between 'legally' right and 'morally' right. It can be 'morally' wrong to exercise a 'legal' right: Nobody is allowed to prevent a Sunday driver from driving as long as he is abiding by the traffic code. He just drives badly.

---

[2] This idea finds philosophical support in the Theory of Social Exchange, according to which every social interaction is rooted in the 'reciprocity principle' [5, 21].

3   A Language for Describing Rights

This section presents a formal characterisation of the concept of right. Apart from different axioms for characterising rights and permissions respectively, our model follows Norman's *et al.* [15]. Readers are referred to that paper for a complete description of the syntax and semantics of the proposed language.

3.1   Syntax

The language $\mathcal{L}$ is based on dynamic logic, because we want to talk about agents performing actions, action sequences, etc. We will have three basic sets: propositional variables, P, agents, Agents, and actions, Actions. The symbols for our language of rights, $\mathcal{L}$, are as follows: x and y denote agents. The group, an agent after all, will be represented by the symbol g. α, β, γ, and δ denote individual actions.

The main predicates in our language refer to agents' mental attitudes, action expressions and normative expressions. Unlike in [12, 22] we are not using deontic logic to express deontic notions. This is because non-forbidden actions are not necessarily allowed actions. In our model (as in [15]) rights must be explicitly established.

The fact that an agent x has the intention to execute action α, is represented as $I(x, \alpha)$. $Done(x, \alpha)$ is used to denote that agent x has just performed action α. $Happens(\alpha)$ means that α does occur.

As for normative notions, that x is allowed to execute α is represented as $A(x, \alpha)$; if x is forbidden to execute α, we will use $F(x, \alpha)$; finally, if there is an obligation, $O(x, \alpha)$ will be used. The most important predicate refers to the concept of right: $R(x, \alpha)$ means that agent x has the right to execute α. The set of potential rigths, Right, is completely ordered according to their social relevance, $(Right, \leq)$.

Atomic propositions and compound formulae of $\mathcal{L}$ are defined as usual. $Inh(\alpha, \beta)$ means that α inhibits β: If α happens then β does not happen. Formally, $Inh(\alpha, \beta)$ iff $Happens(\alpha) \rightarrow \neg Happens(\alpha; \beta?)$, where $\alpha; \beta$ means 'do α followed by β', and ϕ? means 'proceed if ϕ is true'.

3.2   Semantics

The semantics for the language of rights, $\mathcal{L}$, is based on a possible worlds model [9], *à la* Norman *et al.* [15]. The class of models of $\mathcal{L}$ that we are interested in are those satisfying the constraints introduced by the following axioms.

3.3   Axiomatics

It remains to provide the axiomatics for $\mathcal{L}$.

- **Permission:** Firstly, to have a right does not automatically allow the right-holder to exercise its content. There are some conditions with which the agents have to comply. That is, that an agent has the right to execute an action does not mean that it is legal for him to execute such an action.

$$\neg \exists y (R(x, \alpha) \wedge R(y, \beta) \wedge I(y, \beta) \wedge \alpha < \beta \wedge \text{Inh}(\beta, \alpha)) \rightarrow A(x, \alpha) \qquad (1)$$

It is one thing to be allowed to exercise a right; it is another to have the intention of exercising it. Rights do not elicit actions. Social commitments do [10]. If the agent is allowed to execute an action, he has the chance to choose whether or not to proceed. So, rights provide the agents with freedom, for they depend on their own motivation to make a decision and act. On the other hand, having an intention does not entitle the agent to execute the corresponding action in normative systems: In normative scenarios, the agent must have the legal capability (he has to be allowed) to do so.

- **Prohibition:** If an agent is allowed to execute an action and has the intention to do so, then no other agent is allowed to exercise a lower inhibiting right. In the traffic example, y is allowed to exercise the right of taking the junction $A\text{-}B$, as long as x does not have the intention to drive along the main road.

$$(A(x, \alpha) \wedge I(x, \alpha) \wedge \text{Inh}(\beta, \alpha)) \rightarrow F(y, \beta) \qquad (2)$$

For simplicity, we have adopted in this paper a relativistic approach in which for an action to be forbidden it has to inhibit someone's rights. We could, however, introduce a more general notion of illegality: It is forbidden to drive at more than 50mph in town, regardless an agent driving at, say, 60mph is inhibiting someone else's rights. In such a case, nobody has to be protected. Nevertheless, the group has still the obligation to stop the offender.

- **Obligation:** To prevent and/or to sanction.
Prevention If an agent has the intention of executing a banned action, β, then the group is obliged to accomplish an inhibitory action and prevent the crime before β is done.

$$(F(y, \beta) \wedge I(y, \beta)) \rightarrow O(g, \gamma) \qquad (3)$$

where $\text{Inh}(\gamma, \beta)$.
Sanction: Finally, if that action has been executed, then the group has to sanction the offender by inhibiting some of his rights (e.g. suspending his licence).

$$(F(y, \beta) \wedge \text{Done}(y, \beta) \wedge R(y, \delta)) \rightarrow O(g, \gamma) \qquad (4)$$

where $\text{Inh}(\gamma, \delta)$. Obviously, (3) and (4) refer to x's right to be protected. If the group has to prevent the offence, it has to be endowed with an efficient mechanism to recognise intentions. On the other hand, if the crime is eventually committed, the group has to know if it was intentional. Different sanctions correspond to different degrees of intentionality (for instance, murder is more severely punished than manslaughter). It is true that justice is concerned about the legality of actions. But it is also true that when

Table 2. Sample right.

CONDITIONS

- $R(x, \alpha)$, $R(y, \beta)$ and $R(y, \delta)$
- $Inh(\beta, \alpha)$, $Inh(\gamma, \beta)$, and $Inh(\gamma, \delta)$
- $\alpha > \beta$

RULES

R1 $A(x, \alpha)$
R2 IF $I(x, \alpha)$ **THEN** $F(y, \beta)$
R3 IF $I(y, \beta)$ **THEN** $O(g, \gamma)$ *Prevention*
R4 IF $Done(y, \beta)$ **THEN** $O(g, \gamma)$ *Sanction*

---

it comes to do justice, agents' intentions and beliefs have to be taken into account. If I drive over a pedestrian, no doubt I have executed an illegal action. However, if the pedestrian was jaywalking and run unexpectedly into my car, then it would be unfair to blame me for the accident. We will issue intention recognition in future papers.

More specifically, we can explain what to exercise a right means following the sample displayed in **Table 2**. We have omitted a few features in this figure:

- firstly, x has to observe some constraints if it decides to execute α. If it does not do so, then y has the right to claim;
- secondly, when an agent has performed a forbidden action, the offended agent is usually more concerned about compensations than about sanctioning the offender. Therefore, actions restoring (part of) their rights have to be added to the algorithm;
- finally, sanctions should be introduced in preventive cases (like in attempted murder), not only if the prohibited action is eventually done.

In the next section we will study how rights help us reduce coordination complexity and gain in efficiency.

4   What Do We Gain by Using Rights?

We contend that the idea of using rights is worthy of consideration because it makes easier to have agents coordinated. In seeking for argue this hypothesis we present a qualitative (rather than quantitative) analysis. As it has been repeatedly pointed out (e.g., [16, 23, 26]), coordination is mainly concerned with complexity, efficiency, stability, and flexibility. Roughly speaking, complexity refers to how difficult it is to find a solution, and depends on the amount of information and/or time required to represent and solve the problem; efficiency

Table 3. Coordination in different MAS approaches.

	RCT	Norms	Rights
Complexity	High	Medium	Low
Efficiency	Low	High	High
Stability	High	High	High
Flexibility	High	Low	High

speaks about the quality of the outcome, how good it is; then, the solution must be stable, that is, agents should have no reason to diverge from it; and finally, for a MAS to be flexible means that the agents are able to respond by themselves to the changing environment. In dynamic MAS, we want autonomous agents to obtain the best stable results using as few resources as possible. We illustrate in **Table 3** how different approaches work to get agents coordinated, and what we gain by using rights:

1. Complexity: We can see rights as social conditions to execute actions. An agent must have the legal capability to perform an action. Consequently,

- the representational complexity is reduced. Theoretically, x does not need to know from, to where, when or how other agents are driving in **Figure 1**. Agents do not have to anticipate all possible course of events;
- performance itself is also improved: The conditions for success are partially assured through prohibitions and obligations. Rights restrict potentially harmful interactions, and avoid conflict by cutting some paths;
- moreover, rights reduce negotiation and communication costs. Obviously, x and y do not negotiate each time they meet in the A-B junction [3].

We depict the traffic problem decision tree in **Figure 2**, where a means that x is driving along A and b that y is driving from B to A. The first agent has priority, so the first and the third branches are pruned. Agents do not have to reflect on these branches and reckon what they would individually gain or lose by trying an alternative path. The second branch is executed directly.

If compared with other approaches, we maintain low levels of complexity by using rights. RCT is highly complex when it comes to find a solution: Agents have to take into consideration all possible options. As for norms, it may seem that they cope with complexity as rights do: They, too, cut different paths, create safety areas, and reduce communication after all. However, it is worth noticing that it is the designer who establishes off-line the strategy to be followed. So, even though the overall performance is satisfactory, it requires lots of representational work.

---

[3] It is also true that communication can be required even if rights are fully specified. Typically, when one's rights affect others'. For example, if x decides to park just before the junction, he will have to communicate his intention to y, as this second agent can then exercise his right of driving from B to A without delay.

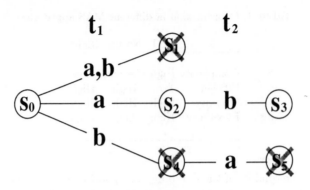

Fig. 2. Rights and complexity.

2. Efficiency and stability: Rights are essentially social notions. The group guarantees through sanctions that agents' rights (and their corresponding obligations) are observed.

In RCT, agents must sacrifice efficiency to preserve stability. When norms are involved, stability and efficiency (usually in terms of global utility) are assured, but only because agents obey orders. In our approach, autonomous agents are free to adopt efficient solutions, for the group is responsible for stability. Stability is now a social concept, not a strategic nor a normative one. The 'trust dilemma' is, therefore, solved: Agents do not have to watch each other; they can cooperate and make joint decisions.

The right to be protected is the main responsible for this dramatic change. With this meta-right at hand, agents would choose (4,8) in **Table 1**: If *Agent 1* does not abide by this agreement and finally executes *C*, then *Agent 2* is entitled to ask the group to sanction the first agent and force him to restore his rights. In order to assure that the agents will abide by the rules, 'Draconian laws' can be introduced.

In the long term, rights introduce fairness. As agents do not know beforehand which role they are going to play in the future, they assess the situation as 'Kantian' impartial judges. In the traffic world, agents have to answer this question: Is it instrumental to drive on the left to avoid conflict? The obvious answer is 'yes'. No individual parameters are taken into account at this level.

3. Flexibility: Rights give the agents the chance to decide to execute a set of actions. Right-holders are not committed to any specific action. However, if an agent exercises a right then he is committed to do so under certain constraints. Rights are not procedural, but they create attitudes in the agents. These agents are not mere vehicles of established norms, but they can decide to abide by or break their obligations. That is the reason why sanctions are indispensable. This property is very valuable, because it puts the accent on agents' autonomy, unlike social laws or 'ad hoc' binding agreements (*e.g.*, [11, 18]).

In so doing, we can establish a clear distinction between rights and social commitments: Social commitments elicit actions, rights do not.

5   Rights in the Coordination Process

To sum up: Rights protect interests, reduce representational as well as procedural complexity, provide the agents with control mechanisms (the right to be protected) to assure stability and efficiency both in short and long term encounters, and preserve autonomy and flexibility.

Yet, a theory of rights alone cannot account for coordination in MAS. Not all interactions are ruled by rights. As is shown in **Figure 3**, coordination can be achieved through negotiation (or other non-normative coordination mechanism) and/or following rights.

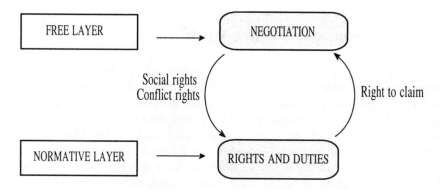

Fig. 3. The coordination cycle.

The first method rules the agent's 'free layer', and the second the 'normative layer'. The free layer governs unconstrained short term behaviour according to agents' preferences and dependence relationships [1, 3, 7, 20, 27], whereas the normative layer guides the long term activity.

All in all, coordination results from the bidirectional interaction between these two layers: Unconstrained behaviour and negotiation (its solver) are supervised by the right to be protected, and negotiation is sometimes necessary to complement the normative layer.

– **From rights to negotiation:** As it has already been mentioned, the right to be protected does not apply only to the execution of rights (when an agent does not abide by the constraints or obligations linked to the right in progress, or when someone tries to inhibit others' rights by executing forbidden actions). It is also applied to one-shot deals: When an agent does not fulfil his commitments, then the right to be protected is exercised by the other part. This right compels the group to force the offender to comply with the agreement.

- **From negotiation to rights:**[4] Conflicts can arise in the normative layer given underspecification. Usually, agents cannot be referred to a complete, unambiguous traffic code. Imagine that two drivers are trying to park in the same place, one backwards, the other forwards. As the right to park does not specify which agent has precedence, conflict follows.

  Experimentation can help to detect and avoid conflict cases (in the parking example, we can introduce a constraint on the right to park saying 'it is forbidden to park forwards' or give priority to the right of 'parking backwards'). However, the dynamic nature of social interaction makes it impossible to write down a perfect system of rights. Moreover, it is very difficult for (informationally) limited agents to know exactly how legal systems work.

6   Conclusions and Further Work[5]

In this paper, we have introduced a preliminary study of the concept of rights. There have been other approaches to rights in the MAS literature: Castelfranchi [6] explained how social commitments generate rights (to claim), and Norman *et al.* [15] have presented rights (permissions) as arguments in agreements. We have focused our work on more basic rights, called liberties, which represent and protect universal interests. No doubt all these rights are closely related. However, we understand that liberties play a very special role in a theory of coordination and social action. They endow autonomous agents with enough freedom and groups with enough power to assure stable and efficient solutions in uncertain domains.

The most obvious issue to be addressed in future work is the refinement of the model, both theoretically and formally. Specifically, some discussion must be undertaken about the dynamic aspects of rights (already treated in [8]): Their genesis, acceptance and abandonment.

Besides, it is obvious that the relationships between normative and social attitudes (joint intentions, mutual beliefs, etc.) must be studied in depth.

Finally, even though the traffic-world is quite natural to explain and to understand the intuitive meaning of rights, it is also true that a more elaborated

---

[4] In [2], we identified other cases in which normative agents have to negotiate, for example, when they exercise 'social rights'. Exercising our rights does not necessarily result in achieving our goals since others' cooperation may be required.

Since benevolence is not assumed, one's right does not automatically trigger others' actions. Leaving aside physical capacity, this is specially true in the case of 'social rights'. We can use Levesque's *et al.* 'Convoy example' [13] to illustrate this concept: An agent x can have the right to drive together with another agent y as a convoy. However, x needs y to exercise his right to drive, and to do it in a coordinated way. That means that x will likely have to convince y to adopt that goal, and then they will have to arrange how to drive the convoy (who drives in front, when to stop, etc...).

[5] Agents have been addressed as male because they are, undoubtedly, worse drivers than female agents.

domain problem (for example, electronic commerce) would show better how useful the framework here described may be.

References

1. E. Alonso. How individuals negotiate protocols. In *Proc. ICMAS-98*, pages 18–25, Los Alamitos, CA, 1998. IEEE Computer Science Press.
2. E. Alonso. Rights and coordination in multi-agent systems. In *Proc. UKMAS-98*, 1998.
3. E. Alonso. An individualistic approach to social action in Multi-Agent Systems. *Journal of Experimental and Theoretical Artificial Intelligence*, 11:519–530, 1999.
4. N.P. Barry. *An Introduction to Modern Political Theory*. Macmillan, London, 1989.
5. P.M. Blau. Interaction: social exchange. In D.L. Sills, editor, *The International Encyclopedia of Social Sciences*, New York, 1968. Macmillan.
6. C. Castelfranchi. Commitments: from individual intentions to groups and organisations. In *Proc. ICMAS-95*, pages 41–48, Cambridge, MA, 1995. MIT Press.
7. C. Castelfranchi, M. Miceli, and A. Cesta. Dependence relations among autonomous agents. In E. Werner and Y. Demazeau, editors, *Decentralized A.I. 3, Proc. MAAMAW-91*, pages 215–227, Amsterdam, The Netherlands, 1992. Elsevier Science Publishers.
8. R. Conte, C. Castelfranchi, and F. Dignum. Autonomous norm-acceptance. In Muller J.P., M.P. Singh, and A. Rao, editors, *Proc. ATAL-98*, pages 319–333, Berlin, 1998. Springer-Verlag.
9. J. Hintikka. *Knowledge and Belief*. Cornell University Press, 1962.
10. N.R. Jennings. Commitments and conventions: The foundation of coordination in Multi-Agent Systems. *The Knowledge Engineering Review*, 8:223–250, 1993.
11. S. Kraus, J. Wilkenfeld, and J. Zlotkin. Multiagent negotiation under time constraints. *Artificial Intelligence*, 75:297–345, 1995.
12. C. Krogh. The rights of agents. In M.J. Wooldridge, J.P. Mulle, and M. Tambe, editors, *Intelligent Agents II: Agent Theories, Architectures, and Languages:=20 Proc. IJCAI-95 Workshop*, pages 1–16, Berlin, 1996. Springer-Verlag.
13. H.J. Levesque, P.R. Cohen, and H.T. Nunes. On acting together. In T. Dietterich and W. Swartout, editors, *Proc. AAAI-90*, pages 94–99, Cambridge, MA, 1990. MIT Press.
14. K. Nielsen and R.A. Shiner. *New Essays on Contract Theory*. Canadian Association for Publishing in Philosophy, 1977.
15. T.J. Norman, C. Sierra, and N.R. Jennings. Rights and commitment in multi-agent agreements. In *Proc. ICMAS-98*, pages 222–229, Los Alamitos, CA, 1998. IEEE Computer Society.
16. G.M.P. O'Hare and N.R. Jenning (Eds.). *Foundations of Distributed Artificial Intelligence*. John Wiley and Sons, New York, 1996.
17. R. Reiner. Arguments against the possibility of perfect rationality. *Minds and Machines*, 5:373–389, 1995.
18. J.S. Rosenschein and G. Zlotkin. *Rules of Encounter*. The MIT Press, Cambridge, MA, 1994.
19. Y. Shoham and M. Tennenhlotz. On the synthesis of useful social laws for artificial agents societies. In *Proc. AAAI-92*, pages 276–281, Menlo Park, CA, 1992. AAAI Press.

20. J.S. Sichman, R. Conte, Y. Demazeau, and C. Castelfranchi. A social reasoning mechanism based on dependence networks. In A. Cohn, editor, *Proc. ECAI-94*, pages 173–177. John Wiley and Sons, 1994.
21. G. Simmel. *The Sociology of Georg Simmel*. Free Press, New York, 1908.
22. G. Staniford. Multi-agent system design: using human societal metaphors and normative logic. In M.J. Wooldridge and N.R. Jennings, editors, *Proc. ECAI-94 Workshop on Agent Theories, Architectures and Languages*, pages 289–293, Berlin, 1994. Springer-Verlag.
23. K.P. Sycara. Multiagent Systems. *AI Magazine*, 19:79–92, 1998.
24. M. Tennenhlotz. On stable social laws and qualitative equilibria. *Artificial Intelligence*, 102:1–20, 1998.
25. A. Walker and M. Wooldridge. Understanding the emergence of conventions in multi-agent systems. In *Proc. ICMAS-95*, pages 384–389, Cambridge, MA, 1995. MIT Press.
26. G. Weiss. *Multiagent Systems: A Modern Approach to Distributed Artificial Intelligence*. MIT Press, Cambridge, MA, 1999.
27. M. Wooldridge and N.R. Jennings. Towards a theory of cooperative problem solving. In J.W. Perram and J-P. Müller, editors, *Proc. MAAMAW-94, Workshop on Distributed Software Agents and Applications*, pages 40–53, Berlin, Germany, 1994. Springer-Verlag.

Infrastructure Support for Agent-Based Development

Ronald Ashri[1], Michael Luck[1], and Mark d'Inverno[2]

[1] Department of Electronics and Computer Science, University of Southampton,
Southampton SO17 1BJ, UK,
{R.Ashri,mml}@ecs.soton.ac.uk
[2] Cavendish School of Computer Science, Westminster University,
London W1W 6UW, UK, dinverm@westminster.ac.uk

Abstract. As the field of agent-based computing has continued to develop, there have been several contributions to its theoretical underpinnings, and several others to supporting the efforts of practical systems development. Yet the connection between the two has been limited at best. In this paper we aim to address these limitations through a consideration of appropriate agent infrastructure that can support *principled development* of agent systems based on a strong conceptual framework. As well as a general discussion of infrastructure requirements in this context, we also describe the PARADIGMA implementation environment, based on the SMART agent framework, which represents our initial efforts in this direction.

1 Introduction

Increasingly, the distinguishing quality of current computing environments is the union of loosely-coupled, heterogeneous, networked devices to form larger structures, such as local and wide area networks, which culminate in the Internet. Not surprisingly, this development mirrors the trend amongst organisations to increase the amount of cooperation between disparate units, irrespective of geographic locations. The move is towards a more decentralised, team-based and distributed structure [5], with the use of information technology tools over the Internet acting as the main enabling force. In addition, the personal lives of individuals have also been affected by the technological advances with the use of the Internet in the home increasing daily. Perhaps the most significant change in the use of personal computing devices is the spread, and rise in influence of, embedded and mobile devices with limited computational power, which have found favour in many aspects of everyday life, from mobile phones to personal digital assistants (PDAs), providing a counterpoint to the tradition of desktop computing.

In line with this profile, there is an increasing demand for *integrating* the various different kinds of such devices in order to provide an environment where access to information and services is available in a seamless manner, while transcending physical location and computing platform. The decentralised collaboration structures of organisations need to be supported by appropriate new solutions, whilst remaining integrated with pre-existing applications, often termed *legacy applications*. Furthermore, the simple administration and effective use of existing resources has become a significant issue. Agent-based systems, by virtue of their defining characteristics of autonomy, reactivity, proactiveness, and social ability, have been suggested as a means of providing solutions

M. d' Inverno et al. (Eds.): UKMAS 1996–2000, LNAI 2403, pp. 73–88, 2002.

to some of these problems [10]. The power of this paradigm stems from the fact that the dynamics of social interaction, such as communication and cooperation, can be used to effectively model such heterogeneous, decentralised and loosely-coupled domains through the interaction of agents.

Nevertheless, for the agent-based systems paradigm to gain widespread use (especially in industrial settings) there are several issues that need to be resolved, a good review of which can be found in [3]. These range from low-level networking concerns such as robust network protocols (e.g. the IPv6 protocol), to appropriate middleware solutions (e.g. CORBA and Jini) and higher level agent communication language standardisation efforts (eg. FIPA ACL [4], KQML [8], etc.). All these efforts are geared towards achieving the primary aim which is, undoubtedly, application development in order to address the needs outlined above. Underpinning the success of these attempts, however, is perhaps a better understanding of the theoretical aspects of multi-agent systems. This will enable the development of applications in a principled manner leading to more robust and extensible solutions.

Theoretical research is useful because it can provide, typically through formal methods, clear concepts and definitions by tackling the ontological and epistemological issues in a research field. In the case of agent-based systems, a good theory could provide definitions of agents as well as explicate the relationships between them and other entities in the world. An appropriate, common theory also makes the comparison, evaluation and sharing of research results easier and can expedite progress in the field.

One of the problems of adopting theoretical work is that it does not easily lend itself to implementation. The reasons for this are twofold. Firstly, the theory might not take into account complications that may arise due to the limitations of the platform on which a program is to be developed. Secondly, the theory may be too abstract for a developer to see a direct connection to an implementation, or the theory might lend itself to many different interpretations at the implementation level. In a development environment where the culture of rapid application development is overpowering, theories are often seen as a hindering rather than facilitating factor. The result of this lack of reconciliation between theoretical approaches on the one hand and development and deployment on the other is that we now have a large variety of alternative concepts of what an agent is, and few means to practically evaluate the various claims made [12].

There are several ways to address this gap between theory and practice. For example, more detail could be added to a theory in order to bring it closer to implementation or, alternatively, software engineering methodologies could be developed providing a path from theoretical specification to practical implementation. In this paper, however, we propose to address the issue through the provision of appropriate infrastructure tools that interpret theoretical approaches and allow for the rapid development of applications. Through the methodical *translation* of a theory into infrastructure, developers can more readily access the overarching concepts, allowing for a more principled use of the theory, without radically changing their methods of application development. Such infrastructure tools can form the basic buildings blocks required for the development and deployment of an application. Furthermore, they can serve to verify the theory's applicability in real world situations, possibly leading to refinements or even rejection of a theory. We adopt this approach in order to address two concerns. On the one hand there is the need to evaluate, refine and make theory more accessible, and on the other we wish to answer the question of what appropriate infrastructure for agent-based systems actually is.

Applications development support through the provision of appropriate *infrastructure* typically needs to address two important issues. Firstly, we need to identify the significant re-usable and domain independent components that can form part of the infrastructure. Secondly, an appropriate framework through which to allow the application designer to manipulate these elements must be constructed. Both of these tasks are made easier if there is good theoretical work to underpin them. Such a theory can provide suggestions as to the entities that should exist in an agent-based system and their relationship (ontological issues) as well as what can be done with those entities (epistemological issues). Conversely, through this principled application development using the derived infrastructure, we can gain a better understanding of the theory, which can enable its refinement and extension as necessary.

The challenge of developing a usable infrastructure for agent-based systems is to produce a system at the right level of generality. For example, infrastructure that provides support only for network communication is inadequate for any substantial system, while infrastructure that forces a developer to employ, for example, a certain planning algorithm, may be overly specific and consequently constraining. While it is important to realise that infrastructure support goes beyond support for general distributed systems it is equally important to recognise that it cannot be a direct translation of a theory of agent-based systems to a programming language. That can only be one component of a larger structure that attempts to relate that theory to implementation concerns such as networking communication tools, host platform operating possibilities and limitations. This suggests that an agent infrastructure should touch upon high-level issues concerning the structure of individual agents and their interaction as well as lower-level issues.

In this paper, we consider exactly these concerns, and offer an analysis of the requirements for infrastructure to support the development and operation of agent-based systems, informed through experience in developing an agent implementation environment based on a conceptual agent framework. We begin by grounding the discussion through a short description of the environments that we are considering for the application of agent-based systems and elaborate on the kind of modularity that agent infrastructure for such environments should support. We then move on to outline our initial efforts in attempting to realise this set of requirements in the development of the PARADIGMA agent implementation environment by using appropriate conceptual and technical tools. Finally, we review related work and suggest ways to proceed further.

2   Heterogeneous Environments

Increasingly, the range of devices used to access networks is diversifying. This, coupled with the increase in the numbers of users accessing such networks, creates the need for a different approach to distributed computing. While until recently the methodologies and tools for developing distributed applications called for abstracting beyond location issues, since assumptions could be made about the reliability and performance of networks, we are now forced to take into account both physical and virtual boundaries. The former is necessary due to the latency in information transmission, and the latter due to the partitioning of networks according to the organisational needs of network ownership and administration. In addition, solutions also need to deal with constant change in such environments, which comes about due to the fluctuating nature of organisational hierarchies, changes in needs, replacement of components and the underlying infrastructure, as well as limitations of that infrastructure. More specifically, the following salient characteristics of such environments need to be considered by any attempt to develop practical agent systems in these emerging computing environments.

- The devices used to access information and services vary greatly in capability. At one end of the spectrum, powerful desktop computers typically have much better network support, while at the other end mobile devices have limited computational power, poor display capabilities and uncertain network support. In addition, a whole host of devices occupy the points in between.
- There is a multitude of operating environments and network access protocols.
- As mobile users change geographical locations, they very often also have to change service providers, raising problems of interoperability and security.
- Devices and supporting infrastructure are continuously changed and also upgraded through efforts to offer better support and increased capabilities.

Mobile devices and, more importantly, the need to support mobile users, mean that applications should be able to provide a consistent method of accessing information and services as a user changes both her geographical position and her operating platform for accessing these services. This may entail a need for agents to migrate between devices, such as from a desktop computer to a PDA, or between service providers in order to continue offering support to users. It may also be beneficial, in terms of efficient use of computational power and bandwidth conservation, for agents to migrate to more powerful platforms in order to perform more demanding tasks before returning to a user's device with results.

The main challenge in providing support for agent applications within such extremely heterogeneous environments is finding an effective means of enabling agents to adapt to the environment. This adaptive behaviour should allow the use of different execution mechanisms based on the computational platform, different channels of communication with the user and other entities in the environment (based on network and display capabilities) and, finally, the reconfiguration of agents to enhance their operational capability based on changes in user needs and upgrades to devices.

Agents must thus be able to adapt and improve through the addition or removal of the particular characteristics relating to the adoption and creation of goals to achieve on the one hand, and the ways in which they achieve these goals on the other. For example, an autonomous agent responsible for kitchen appliances might be modified to deal with new devices in the kitchen by adding new goals and (*values* of goals), with plans to achieve the goals, as well as new capabilities for the specific appliance control and interaction. Alternatively, a personal assistant agent residing on a desktop computer might reduce its normal set of actions (or capabilities) to a minimal set of those that are essential in order to migrate to a mobile PDA while maximising the retained information relating to user preferences, profile, and other relevant and important information.

3 Decoupling Agent Behaviour and Description

3.1 Decoupling for Flexibility and Evaluation

One way to achieve this kind of functionality is to ensure a complete separation of architectural issues on the one hand, relating to the *behaviour* of agents, and the manner in which agents are *described* on the other. Agent descriptions provide an enumeration of the different components that make up an agent, almost in jigsaw-puzzle fashion, including attributes, goals and capabilities, for example. By contrast, agent behaviour is determined through the way in which these components come together inside an agent architecture on a particular execution platform, with a range of complex concerns such as how goals are activated, and capabilities selected. (We will say more about the details of agent description in Section 4.) Separating the *description* of an agent from concerns of control, execution environments, etc., not only makes for good software engineering in terms of modular design, which enables reuse and wide-scale development, but also enables agents to cope in the kinds of environments that we are considering.

In particular, this decoupling is crucial for the flexibility required of agents in heterogeneous and dynamically changing environments; because agent description is independent of agent behaviour, we are free to develop different types of execution platform on which to operate essentially the same agent, but using alternative architectural organisation.

The approach offers benefits to both those with a research-based focus and those with a more practical perspective aimed at real systems development. From the research side, it allows the effective comparison of different agent behaviour algorithms applied to the same agent description, providing a sensible and calibrated means of evaluation. From the development side, it allows the development of execution platforms that are tailored to their specific computing environments. For example, an agent execution platform on a mobile device is naturally more limited in available capacity and features, and might therefore use simpler or less sophisticated behavioural mechanisms than an execution platform on a powerful workstation. In both cases, the same agent description can be applied, but the resulting behaviour leveraging that description would be tailored to the environment within which the agent is executing. In principle, systems developers should eventually be able to access libraries of agent components which can be pieced together and coupled to appropriate execution platforms to achieve the desired effect.

3.2 Decoupling for Mobility

Additionally, decoupling enables agent *mobility* to be achieved in a more lightweight and secure manner. Mobile agents require packaging up through serialisation to be moved between execution platforms [2, 11]; typically this includes the state of the agent, and the agent *as is*. In the case of large agents, or those with many resources or capabilities, the transport costs can become significant, and since one of the key motivating principles behind mobile agents is to minimise transport by focusing on code rather than data, this can be a problem.

In a decoupled system, however, agents can be packaged as a set of descriptions coupled with specific implementation of capabilities thus minimising transport overheads. Moreover, one of the main problems of mobile execution platforms is effectively securing the underlying infrastructure from malicious agents [9, 16]. Traditionally, such platforms provide the agent with an execution thread, and have minimal control over what happens within that thread other than imposing access rights to the sensitive parts of the system [17]. By imposing constraints on the structure of capabilities through the definition of generic interfaces, we can enforce tighter control over what an agent can and cannot do within an execution platform.

3.3   Conceptual Infrastructure

We argue that a strong and clear conceptual underpinning is required at the level of infrastructure so as to guide its development as well as the subsequent development of agent superstructures. In a series of papers (e.g. [7, 13, 14]), Luck and d'Inverno have provided such a conceptual foundation through the development of a framework for agent systems that supports many of the features that we listed above. Their SMART agent framework provides an encompassing structure that clearly differentiates between agent and non-agent entities in the environment, and specifies agents in a compositional way. In essence, the framework proposes a four-tiered hierarchy that includes the generic and abstract notion of an entity from which objects, agents and autonomous agents are, in turn, derived. Figure 1 shows a Venn diagram that describes the different levels in the hierarchy, and outlines the ways in which they are related. Though we will not offer a detailed exposition of the framework, we review the key concepts below.

The essential ingredients of the SMART framework are the following four types:

– attributes, which are features of the world that can potentially be perceived in an omniscient sense;

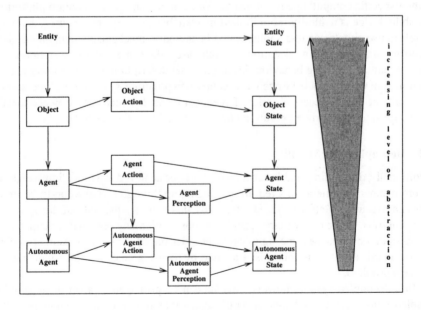

Fig. 1. Structure of the SMART Framework

- actions, which can change the state of the environment in which they are performed by either adding or removing attributes;
- goals, which are states of affairs to be achieved in the environment; and
- motivations, which are non-derivative high-level structures that lead to the generation and adoption of goals, and affect the outcome of any task intended to satisfy those goals.

We can then define the components of the four-tiered framework using these types. The *entity* serves as an *abstraction mechanism*; it provides a template from which objects, agents and autonomous agents can be defined. Anything that is considered to be a single component is represented as an *entity*. These entities may have complex descriptions, but at the very highest level they are just collections of attributes.

```
┌─ Entity ─────────────────────────────────────────────
│ attributes : ℙ Attribute
│ capabilities : ℙ Action
│ goals : ℙ Goal
│ motivations : ℙ Motivation
├──────────────────────────────────────────────────────
│ attributes ≠ {}
└──────────────────────────────────────────────────────
```

An entity must be situated in an environment and, conversely, an environment must include all the entities within it. There may well also be other attributes that are not associated with an entity and so the union of all the attributes from each entity will only be a subset (in general) of all the attributes that comprise the environment. In the following schema, the *environment* variable is the set of all environment attributes, and the *entities* variable the set of all entities in that environment.

```
┌─ Env ────────────────────────────────────────────────
│ environment : ℙ Attribute
│ entities : ℙ Entity
├──────────────────────────────────────────────────────
│ environment ≠ { }
│ ⋃{e : entities • e.attributes} ⊆ environment
└──────────────────────────────────────────────────────
```

Objects are then simply entities with sets of capabilities that can be performed to change the state of the environment.

```
┌─ Object ─────────────────────────────────────────────
│ Entity
├──────────────────────────────────────────────────────
│ capabilities ≠ { }
└──────────────────────────────────────────────────────
```

In turn, agents are objects with sets of goals, where goals are defined as desirable environmental states, and autonomous agents are those agents able to generate their own goals through the motivations that drive them. Here, motivations can be regarded as preferences or desires of an autonomous agent that cause it to produce goals and execute plans in an attempt to satisfy those desires.

```
┌─ Agent ──────────────────────────────────────────────────
│  Object
│  ────────────────────
│  goals ≠ { }
└──────────────────────────────────────────────────────────
```

```
┌─ AutonomousAgent ────────────────────────────────────────
│  Agent
│  ────────────────────
│  motivations ≠ { }
└──────────────────────────────────────────────────────────
```

For each of the four high-level components we also provide a skeletal architecture to describe its interaction. In order to show this let us consider the description of agent. In general, an agent is able to perceive its environment. An agent in an environment may have a set of percepts available, which are the possible attributes that it could perceive, subject to its capabilities and current state. We refer to these as the *possible percepts* of an agent. However, due to limited resources, an agent will not normally be able to perceive all those attributes possible, and will base its actions on a subset, which we call the *actual percepts* of an agent.

To distinguish between representations of mental models and representations of the *actual* environment, we introduce two types, *View* and *Environment*. The first of these is defined to be the perception of an environment by an agent. This has an equivalent type to that of *Environment*, but now physical and mental components of the same type can be distinguished.

$View == \mathbb{P}_1 \, Attribute$
$Environment == \mathbb{P}_1 \, Attribute$

```
┌─ AgentPerception ────────────────────────────────────────
│  Agent
│  perceivingactions : ℙ Action
│  canperceive : Environment → ℙ Action ⇸ View
│  willperceive : ℙ Goal → View → View
│  ─────────────────────────────────────────────────
│  perceivingactions ⊆ capabilities
│  ∀ env : Environment; as : ℙ Action •
│        as ∈ dom(canperceive env) ⇒ as = perceivingactions
│  dom willperceive = {goals}
└──────────────────────────────────────────────────────────
```

In addition, an agent will be able to perform actions determined by its goals, perceptions and the environment. This is specified by the *agentactions* function in the *AgentAction* schema below, which is dependent on the goals of the agent, the actual perceptions of the agent and the current environment. The first predicate requires that *agentactions* returns a set of actions within the agent's capabilities, while the last predicate constrains its application to the agent's goals.

```
┌─AgentAction ──────────────────────────────────────────────
│ Agent
│ ObjectAction
│ agentactions : ℙ Goal → View → Environment → ℙ Action
├───────────────────────────────────────────────────────────
│ ∀ gs : ℙ Goal;  v : View;  env : Environment •
│        (agentactions gs v env) ⊆ capabilities
│ dom agentactions = {goals}
└───────────────────────────────────────────────────────────
```

Now that these skeletal architectures have been described it is then possible to define the *state* of an agent or autonomous agent within an environment. Once an agent is placed in an environment, its attributes are accessible and it is possible to specify the *possible percepts* and *actual percepts* of the agent. These are denoted by the variables, *possiblepercepts* and *actualpercepts*, which are calculated using the *canperceive* and *willperceive* functions respectively. The action or actions the agent actually performs in the environment are a function of its goals, its percepts and the environment itself. The reader will notice that the schema below also includes a schema called *ObjectState* (not specified here) that defines the state of the higher-level SMART object component in an environment. This should provide an indication of how increasingly more refined and detailed concepts are built incrementally and systematically from higher level ones. The structure of the very basic framework and related model can be seen in Figure 1. An arrow here simply indicates schema inclusion.

```
┌─AgentState ───────────────────────────────────────────────
│ AgentPerception
│ AgentAction
│ ObjectState
│ posspercepts, actualpercepts : View
├───────────────────────────────────────────────────────────
│ actualpercepts ⊆ posspercepts
│ posspercepts = canperceive environment perceivingactions
│ actualpercepts = willperceive goals posspercepts
│ perceivingactions = { } ⇒ posspercepts = { }
│ willdo = agentactions goals actualpercepts environment
└───────────────────────────────────────────────────────────
```

In addition to these basic levels, and in order to further explicate the consequences of their framework, Luck and d'Inverno introduce two additional refinements: *neutral objects* are objects that are not agents, and *server agents* are agents that are not autonomous [14]. The relationship between neutral objects and server agents is complementary, since neutral objects give rise to server agents when they are ascribed goals by other agents in the environment. Once these goals are achieved or they are no longer feasible, server agents revert back to neutral objects.

In short, this conceptual framework provides a basis for us to use in reasoning about agent and non-agent entities within a coherent whole, while at the same time providing us with the requisite level of component differentiation to underpin the division between behaviour and description. We now move on to discuss how these concepts can be encapsulated within the technical framework that can provide an infrastructure for agent-based systems.

3.4   Technical Infrastructure

In line with the aims discussed above, and based on the conceptual infrastructure outlined, we have developed an agent system, PARADIGMA, that provides a technical infrastructure for the development of agent applications. PARADIGMA unites theory with practical implementation in an attempt to provide an accessible and grounded set of tools for agent development. Key to this is ease of understanding and simplicity of use, as well as an ability for elegant expansion and adaptation to change.

An overview of PARADIGMA is presented in Figure 2. At the top level, the agent framework provides the conceptual tools that guide the design of the agents and define the relationships between them. PARADIGMA can be considered as implementing the framework through the use of the standard technologies that appear at the lower level (and which we discuss later). We have opted for the use of standard technologies for the underlying functionality as opposed to a proprietary system not only because it provides a sensible and robust route for development, but also because it enables interaction and cross-development with others, and makes access to the overarching conceptual and theoretical issues easier. Indeed, one of the arguments advanced in justification of a certain degree of reticence on behalf of developers in relation to agent systems is, in many cases, a reliance on non-standard technologies. We seek to ensure that this is not the case here, and that recent convergence between the fields of autonomous agents, object-oriented systems and distributed systems contributes to our own efforts in the agent arena.

Decoupling Behaviour and Description.   In order to achieve the desired decoupling of description and behaviour at the implementation level we have made clear distinctions between the task of composing an agent by assembling the required building blocks,

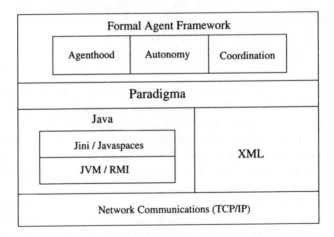

Fig. 2. Paradigma overview

such as attributes, capabilities and goals and relating these components via decision mechanisms.

A description of an entity in PARADIGMA is, in essence, a collection of XML documents. Each document contains within it a set of components of the same type. For example, an *attribute* document, which is the simplest structure, contains a series of type-value definitions that can be declared either constant or variable. A *capabilities* document, on the other hand, contains a description and type of the capability and also a link to the code that implements the capability (in the same spirit as dMARS plans [6], for example). This enables the implementations to vary in order to suit executing platforms, or so as to provide newer versions of capabilities. It is envisaged that eventually the developer will have access to libraries of capabilities that can be linked to the agent descriptions. Goals, plans and motivations are more elaborate structures and can vary according to the desired level of complexity required by the developer. For example, a simple plan structure may just define a series of capabilities that an entity should perform, while a more complicated structure may also include invocation conditions and postconditions, as well as elements that should remain true during the execution of the plan.

Once such a description has been pieced together based on the requirements of the application, the developer can insert it into an execution platform. At this stage, the XML documents will be interpreted and the appropriate capabilities will be retrieved. The executing environment then couples the entity to decision mechanisms in order to effect execution.

The complete process of agent creation and execution is illustrated in Figure 3, which is divided into two stages, initialization and operation. An agent is created by supplying the required building blocks of attributes, capabilities, goals, plans and motivations.

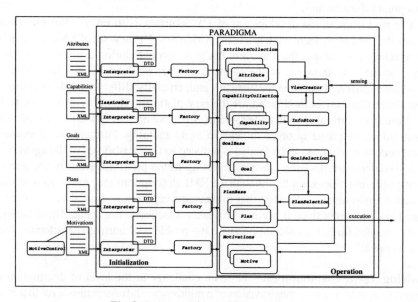

Fig. 3. Agent creation and agent operation

As mentioned earlier, capabilities require specific implementations, whose location is made part of their description. The last element required at this stage, especially for autonomous agents, is some form of control mechanism that will dictate, for example, how motivations change as the state of the environment changes. In the figure this is illustrated by the *MotiveControl* component, to enable it to adjust its motivations as the state of the environment changes. In the current implementation of PARADIGMA, motivations are seen as a tuple of three variables: an identifying name, a strength or salience rating and a boolean indicating whether the strength is variable. The control component could be as simple as a set of rules indicating the values motivation strengths should take as attributes of the environment change, though it could equally provide a more sophisticated set of constraints.

All this information is interpreted and checked before the agent is constructed by the *Factory* components, based on the requirements of the execution environment in question. Following a successful initialisation stage, the execution environment becomes responsible for executing the supplied agent description. In the figure, we show some of the essential components for these tasks, such as *ViewCreator* for collecting information about the environment, *InfoStore* for maintaining acquired information so that it may be shared with others if appropriate and, finally, plan and goal selection units.

As can be seen, by taking this approach we have a complete decoupling of all the components that comprise an agent from the agent development and execution platform. Furthermore, it becomes trivial to change platforms in order to suit particular situations, or in order to incorporate other desired changes and advances. For example, if we wish to provide different descriptions of *attributes*, all that is required is to develop a new DTD or XML Schema and replace the current *Factory* component with a new one. We can thus allow for the evaluation of different implementations of capabilities, decision mechanisms, etc, while still remaining within the environment that is provided by our conceptual infrastructure.

The next stage in the development of PARADIGMA is to reverse this process and capture the state of an agent back in a set of XML files. The new set of XML descriptions would reflect the changes that the agent has gone through during execution, and would allow for the easy transport of the agent to another platform. There, the agent may make use of different decision mechanisms and, crucially, different implementations of capabilities that may be optimized for the new platform. This provides an interesting departure from current mobile code systems, since we are not limited to any particular programming language in order to achieve agent mobility. Furthermore, because the actual code that will need to be loaded is reduced to the capabilities of the agent, while the integration with decision mechanisms is up to the platform, security concerns are slightly different. For example, although the XML descriptions may move from untrusted to trusted environments, the code that implements capabilities may always come from trusted environments since it is not inextricably attached to the agent. These issues, of course, require further consideration since the problem of untrusted platforms always remains open.

Enabling Agent Communities. The main challenge at the level of distribution and support of agents involves the provision of a middleware infrastructure layer that is able to support dynamic communities of entities where constant change is always part of the agenda. For the purposes of PARADIGMA, we have chosen Jini because of the features that come closest to fulfilling all the requirements discussed earlier. A more thorough review than is possible here of the Jini infrastructure to support implementation of Luck and d'Inverno's framework is given in [1], but we outline and illustrate the key points below.

Entities executing in a PARADIGMA platform can at any time make use of available facilities in order to announce their existence on the network. Note that this is not a requirement but an option, since it may not always be desired or even feasible to perform such announcements. This is important in terms of separating the issues related to cooperation with, and discovery of, other agents from issues related to the operation of a single agent. Nevertheless, if a decision to make an announcement has been taken, then PARADIGMA will attempt to discover the available registries, represented by Jini lookup services. Once such lookup services are discovered, the entity will guide the platform as to the information it wants to make known about itself. This information will be registered in the Jini lookup service along with a proxy that will allow interested parties to make direct contact with the entity. Lookup services are managed through a leasing mechanism that requires registered entities to renew their interest in retaining their information within the lookup service or have their information discarded. In essence, Jini provides the required network connectivity and administration infrastructure for the support of heterogeneous communities of entities, thus making it suitable as an environment for implementation of the conceptual framework described above.

By way of example, Figure 4 illustrates how neutral objects can be discovered and used by other agents in a Jini-supported environment, and in particular PARADIGMA. A device or software component, represent by a neutral object (drawn using a solid circle line), creates an appropriate description of itself and registers the required information relating to the attributes and capabilities in a Jini lookup service along with a proxy (drawn using a dotted circle) that can be used to access it. If an agent (represented by the stick figure) decides that the device is useful for its needs, it downloads the proxy and creates a server agent with the relevant goals, and which wraps around the proxy. Once the server agent has achieved its goals it is discarded and the neutral object is disengaged.

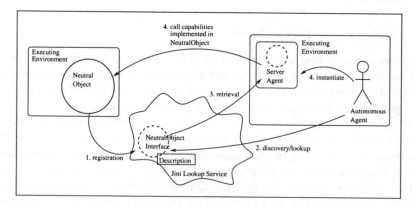

Fig. 4. Using neutral objects

In the case of autonomous agents, the registered proxy can be an interface that implements appropriate communication protocols. Other agents could then retrieve this implementation so as to communication with the agent. An interesting dynamic here is that the communication interfaces can act as *translators* from one communication protocol to another, and can vary according to the entities the autonomous agent wishes to communicate with. For example, in environments where bandwidth and reliability are important, the implemented interface could direct messages to appropriate messaging routes that would ensure the messages are not lost.

4   Discussion

4.1   Related Work

PARADIGMA attempts to address a wide range of issues starting with identifying the appropriate concepts to support agent-based systems infrastructure, and ranging to consider the appropriate technologies for implementing such concepts. In terms of the approach we have adopted, which clearly distinguishes the relationship between agent and non-agent entities, and separates issues of description from issues of behaviour, PARADIGMA can be thought of as a system that integrates several different strands of agent research. Similar work has been done with the DARPA-funded Control of Agent-Based Systems (CoABS) program [15], whose main goal is to provide the appropriate infrastructure to enable integration of heterogeneous agent-based systems. At the middleware layer it makes use of Jini network technology and, similar to PARADIGMA, it allows for the registration of agents to the Jini lookup service along with appropriate descriptions. CoABS also provides mechanisms for agent communication through RMI. In terms of the layers of required infrastructure discussed earlier, CoABS addresses the middleware layer by facilitating management and communication of agents, but it does not address the higher level issues of mobility and intelligent agents. As such, it takes a different approach to PARADIGMA by transferring the burden of addressing these concerns to application developers. CoABS could, therefore, act as an integrator of other infrastructures but, does not provide the required functionality to allow mainstream developers to use agent concepts directly.

4.2   Conclusions and Further Work

Agent-based systems have a vital role to play in the immediate development of applications and services across the distributed and increasingly pervasive computing fabric of our everyday environments. The convergence of related fields of distributed computing and object-oriented development also provides extra support and impetus for the adoption of agent technology into the mainstream. Yet this provides an opportunity that can only be taken if two conditions hold. First, mainstream technologies must be used for infrastructural underpinning of agent applications to enable accessibility, further development, and, importantly, *integration*. Second, the kinds of applications that we build must be constructed in ways that facilitate flexibility, evaluation, and the potential for secondary capabilities (that are still critical for many applications and environments) like mobility.

One of the main problems that have delayed the wide deployment of agent-based systems has been the lack of integration between different systems. The agreement on common infrastructure would enable that integration, especially if the infrastructure made use of other standards and systems that have already found a wider acceptance, such as Jini at the middleware level.

In constructing PARADIGMA, we have done just this, through our two-levels of technical infrastructure and conceptual infrastructure, which support the decoupling of agent behaviour from agent description to achieve exactly these aims. PARADIGMA is a fully functional execution and development platform with which to build real applications, and all the work described in this paper is fully implemented. The next stage in its development is, at one level to build a broad range of applications to demonstrate its suitability, and at another to examine the mechanisms required for dynamic self-modification of agent capabilities.

References

1. Ronald Ashri and Michael Luck. Paradigma: Agent implementation through Jini. In A. M. Tjoa, R.R. Wagner, and A. Al-Zobaidie, editors, *Eleventh International Workshop on Databases and Expert System Application*, pages 453–457. IEEE Computer Society, 2000.
2. J. Baumann, F. Hohl, K. Rothermel, and M. Straer. Mole - concepts of a mobile agent system. *World Wide Web*, 1(3):123–137, 1998.
3. J. Bradshaw. Agents for the masses. *IEEE Intelligent Systems*, 14(2):53–63, 1999.
4. Bernard Burg, Jonathan Dale, and Steven Willmott. Open standards and open source for agent-based systems. *Agentlink News*, (6):2–5, 2001.
5. D. DeSanctis and B. Jackson. Co-ordination of information technology management: Team based structures and computer-based communication systems. *Journal of Management Information Sciences*, 4(10):85–110, 1994.
6. M. d'Inverno, D. Kinny, M. Luck, and M. Wooldridge. A formal specification of dMARS. In *Intelligent Agents IV: Proceedings of the Fourth International Workshop on Agent Theories, Architectures and Languages*, pages 155–176. Springer-Verlag, 1365, 1998.
7. M. d'Inverno and M. Luck. A formal view of social dependence networks. In C. Zhang and D. Lukose, editors, *Distributed Artificial Intelligence Architecture and Modelling: Proceedings of the First Australian Workshop on Distributed Artificial Intelligence, Lecture Notes in Artificial Intelligence*, volume 1087, pages 115–129. Springer Verlag, 1996.
8. T. Finin, Y. Labrou, and J. Mayfield. Kqml as an agent communication language. In J. Bradshaw, editor, *Software Agents*. MIT Press, Cambridge, 1997.
9. Robert Gray, David Kotz, George Cybenko, and Daniela Rus. D'agents: Security in a multiple-language, mobile agent system. In Giovanni Vigna, editor, *Mobile Agents and Security*, volume 1419 of *Lecture Notes in Computer Science*, pages 154–187. Springer-Verlag, 1998.
10. Nicholas R. Jennings. On agent-based software engineering. *Artificial Intelligence*, 117:277–296, 2000.
11. Danny Lange and Mitsuru Oshima. *Programming and Deploying Java(tm) Mobile Agents with Aglets(tm)*. Addisson-Wesley, 1998.
12. M. Luck. From definition to development: What next for agent-based systems. *Knowledge Engineering Review*, 14(2):119–124, 1999.
13. M. Luck and M. d'Inverno. A formal framework for agency and autonomy. In *95*. 254–260, 1995.

14. M. Luck and M. d'Inverno. Engagement and cooperation in motivated agent modelling. In *Proceedings of the First Australian DAI Workshop*, volume 1087 of *Lecture Notes in Artificial Intelligence*, pages 70–84. Springer Verlag, 1996.
15. C. Thompson, T. Bannon, T. Pazandak, and V. Vasudevan. Agents for the masses. In *Workshop on Agent-based high Performance Computing: Problem Solving Applications and Practical Deployment*, 1999.
16. Christian F. Tschudin. Mobile agent security. In Matthias Klusch, editor, *Intelligent Information Agents*, pages 431–446. Springer-Verlag, 1999.
17. Tom Walsh, Noemi Paciorek, and David Wong. Security and reliability in concordia. In *31st Annual Hawai'i International Conference on System Sciences (HICSS31)*, 1998.

An Anthropological Approach to the Discovery of Ontologies in Multi-agent Societies

Rafael H. Bordini[1], Renata Vieira[2], and John A. Campbell[3]

[1] Instituto de Informática,
Universidade Federal do Rio Grande do Sul (UFRGS),
CP 15064, CEP 91501-970, Porto Alegre, RS, Brazil,
bordini@inf.ufrgs.br
[2] Centro de Ciências Exatas e Centro de Ciências da Comunicação,
Universidade do Vale do Rio dos Sinos (UNISINOS),
CP 275, CEP 93022-000, São Leopoldo, RS, Brazil,
renata@exatas.unisinos.br
[3] Department of Computer Science,
University College London,
Gower Street, London WC1E 6BT, U.K.,
J.Campbell@cs.ucl.ac.uk

Abstract. We presented our approach to ascription of intensional ontologies to societies of agents at UKMAS-99. The idea of an intensional ontologies is based on a pragmatic theory of intensionality. The work we presented included a mechanism for retrieving taxonomical relations from the intensional ontologies. Both the process of ascription of ontologies and the retrieval of taxonomical relations were inspired by work on cultural anthropology. These ideas were formalised using a framework for the specification of agent theories based on the Z language. This paper reviews the main ideas of that work and introduces a new application: extracting ontologies from text corpora.

1 Introduction

We have previously introduced the idea that an agent can ascribe ontological descriptions for the terms used in the communication language to a society being observed (Bordini, Campbell and Vieira 1997). For this particular problem, we have proposed the use of a pragmatic theory of intensionality, which is based on the work of Martin (1959), and has been revived and adapted to the MAS context by Vieira and da Rocha Costa (1993). The underlying intention (cf. Bordini 1999) is that certain individual agents should be able to interact in societies of agents which were designed using paradigms or theories of agents different from their own, or which have had different histories of autonomous evolution, with application to interoperability of Multi-Agent Systems (MAS).

We then extended our work on ascription of intensional ontologies to show how an agent can work out the taxonomical relations existing among the terms in the intensional ontology it has ascribed to a society of agents. (This was first introduced in (Bordini, Campbell and Vieira 1998) and presented at UKMAS-99 (Bordini, Campbell and Vieira 1999).) We have noted that some initial taxonomical relations can be recovered directly

M. d' Inverno et al. (Eds.): UKMAS 1996–2000, LNAI 2403, pp. 89–109, 2002.
© Springer-Verlag Berlin Heidelberg 2002

from an ascribed intensional ontology. This process too was inspired by the methods used by cultural anthropologists, as we shall discuss later. A taxonomy is clearly important from an agent's reasoning point of view; this has been a recurrent observation in artificial intelligence (AI) research since the early days. Furthermore, from experience in anthropology, it is known that a taxonomy can be quite revealing about the traits of a particular culture. The extension given in that paper was, thus, related to a fundamental aspect of the procedures of an anthropologist studying a particular society. We suggest that the same approach is of value for an "anthropologist agent" studying a MAS, to ease "agent migration" (Bordini 1999). All these ideas have been formalised in Z using Luck and d'Inverno's (1995) framework for the specification of agent theories. A complete account of that framework can be found in a recent book by d'Inverno and Luck (2001).

Ontologies have been discussed in, and instrumental to, a variety of domains ranging from philosophy to databases, including AI and natural language processing. They function as a reference source for either domain knowledge (special domain/application ontologies) or common knowledge (knowledge databases such as WordNet and CYC). Ontology engineering and maintenance is very complex and expensive; that is why much work on ontology extraction has appeared recently. One source of coded knowledge for automatic ontology engineering is texts such as scientific publications, or corporate documentation. Examples of proposed approaches to ontology extraction from texts are (Hahn and Schnattinger 1998; Aussenac-Gilles, Biébow and Szulman 2000; Mädche and Staab 2000; Nobécourt 2000).

This paper reviews the main ideas on ascription of intensional ontologies and gives a flavour of the Z specifications presented in (?). We have excluded the formalisation related to retrieval of taxonomical relations for the sake of space. We also mention in this paper an innovative formulation of the problem of ontology ascription which is based on the idea of "corpora as societies". That is to say, we are investigating the applicability of our approach to extraction of ontologies from corpora, where the role of "informant agents" in our previous work would be performed by texts.

This paper is structured into three main parts. The next section overviews the main concepts and definitions which are the basis of our approach to ontology discovery. We then give a flavour of the formal specifications we have previously produced (in Section 3). The third main part, given in Section 4, mentions an application of our approach to processing of text corpora. This is a recent ongoing work on which many experiments are envisaged.

2   Background

2.1   Subjective Intensionality

This section covers only the main concepts related to subjective intensionality which we shall use next. We have given a larger account of these concepts and some discussion of its advantages in (Bordini, Campbell and Vieira 1997); for further details it is necessary to refer to (Vieira and da Rocha Costa 1993), or even to their main source (Martin 1959).

The *intension* of an expression is what is known about it in order to identify the object/entity to which it refers. We can say that intension is related to notions of mental entities, properties, relations, and concepts, while *extension* is related to objective entities (i.e., objects, structures). Further, we have the concept of *subjective intensions*. These are associated with the intuitive notion of connotation of a term or name; that is, related to the properties that are associated with a term in an individual's mind in such a way that they are normally borne in mind when the individual uses that term at a certain time[1]. Further, *quasi-intensions* are linguistic reductions of the mental entities relative to intensions. Therefore, the terminology *subjective quasi-intensions* emphasises that the theory deals with virtual classes of expressions related to particular users of the language; in other words, it is a linguistic reduction of the cognitive notion of connotation.

Subjective quasi-intensions and related notions (defined below) are based on the acceptance relation between agents and expressions. The definition for the acceptance relation, based on Martin's original one (1959), follows.

Definition 1 (Acceptance Relation). *Acceptance is an empirical relation between users and sentences of a language, observed by an experimenter at a certain time who asks questions by means of a set of sentences forming a logical theory. Whenever an agent answers affirmatively to (has a positive attitude towards) one of these sentences we say that the agent* accepts *that sentence (which must belong to the set of sentences given by the experimenter) at that time.*

Definition 2 (Subjective Quasi-Intension). *The notion of* subjective quasi-intension *for an individual constant (term) is defined as the properties a language user associates with the term, as expressed in the sentences that the given user* accepts *at a certain time.*

Definition 3 (Intersubjective Quasi-Intension). *This concept regards groups of language users, rather than individuals, at a certain time. An* intersubjective quasi-intension *is the equivalence class of all the* subjective quasi-intensions *of a certain group of users of the language.*

Intertemporal Quasi-Intensions are relative to a particular language user at all times. *Objective Quasi-Intensions* can also be defined on the basis of acceptance. They are at the same time intertemporal and intersubjective quasi-intension of expressions, that is, a class whose members are members of the subjective quasi-intensions of all language users at all times. They are said to be essential properties, as they are universally accepted (within a specific community). One last type of quasi-intensions is that of *Societal Quasi-Intension* which relates to a particular group of agents. In Martin's theory, *Co-Intensiveness* is defined as a relation between terms that have the same subjective quasi-intension (or indeed for any of the types of quasi-intensions mentioned above).

In this theory, a proper "understanding" of a concept can be defined as the situation in which the subjective intension of a term relative to an agent is the same as the intersubjective intension of all agents, some expert group or a specialist.

---

[1] Since these are notions intrinsic to the users of the language, they can also be called *pragmatical intensions*.

2.2   The Process of Ascription of Intensional Ontologies of Terms

We take *ontology* to mean very much the same as proposed by Gruber (1993), i.e. the definition of a set of representational terms[2] (stated as a logical theory). However, it is important to bear in mind that the theory of intensionality presented here deals only with individual terms (that is, the equivalent of nouns in natural languages). The major contribution of this approach to description of ontologies is that its underlying theory allows us to work towards providing agents with mechanisms for dealing with ontologies themselves (i.e., ascribe possible ontological representations to societies in case they are not available, effect changes in ontologies without consequent interoperability problems, etc.).

The following definition expresses our conception of ontology:

Definition 4 (Intensional Ontology of Terms). *An* Intensional Ontology of Terms (IOT) *is a set of terms where each one is associated with the (minimal) set of predicates (properties) that is necessary and sufficient to distinguish (unequivocally) itself from every other term in the universe of discourse of a communicating society of agents.*

In our approach, the definition of a term is a set of predicates that are considered to hold for that term. It is important to appreciate that not all predicates that hold for the term are needed for its ontological description: there is a difference between knowledge representation and commitment to ontological conventions (Gruber 1993). Therefore, if some notion of order for the predicates is available (e.g., a hypernymy or hyponymy relation[3]), this can reflect on the minimal set of predicates: it would include only the most generic ones which are enough to distinguish the term unequivocally.

We have seen that based on intersubjective quasi-intensions (see Section 2.1), a definition for an expression can be given by a set of properties that are accepted by a group of agents as being related to the expression. This is the key point for allowing an anthropologist agent to ascribe an ontological description to a community of agents; it can do so by interviewing the group of *informant agents* that it takes from that particular community. Properties that are associated unanimously with a term's definition among the informant agents should be registered in the construction of an ontology for that community. It is important to note that the anthropologist agent itself needs a theory (i.e., a set of attributes for each term) with which to interview the informant agents. The sentences in such a theory will be submitted to the informant agents in order to check whether they accept the sentences or not. In general, the set of sentences to be used in an interview should be the result of observations of the use of language in that society, in the fashion of ethnographers.

2.3   Discovering Taxonomies in Social Anthropology

Our previous work was based on ethnographic studies of cognitive systems as seen by social anthropologists of the cognitive school, and the main concepts involved in the

---

[2] In our original formulation, the representational terms are those used in the communication language of a MAS.

[3] If x is a generalisation of y, one says that x is in a *hypernymy* relation to y; if x is a specification of y, one says that x is in a *hyponymy* relation to y.

elaboration of taxonomies by anthropologists. It relied heavily on the ideas presented by Frake (1969)—and more generally by Tyler (1969)—which have allowed us to see that our early approach to ontologies contained the necessary means to augment ascribed ontologies of terms with the specification of the taxonomical relations among those terms.

Anthropologists (or ethnographers) start their work by recording culturally significant noises and movements from what is heard or seen during observation of a particular community. Recording complementary names applied to the same objects (and eliminating referential synonyms) may yield a recorded sequence like[4]:

Object A is named: *something to eat, sandwich, ham sandwich.*
Object B is named: *something to eat, pie, apple pie.*
Object C is named: *something to eat, pie, cherry pie.*
Object D is named: *something to eat, ice-cream.*

The diagram of the sub-partitioning of the segregate[5] "something to eat," as revealed by the naming responses to the four objects above, is in Figure 1.

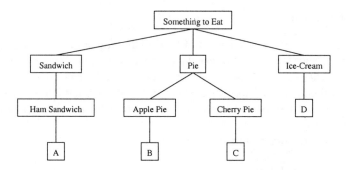

Fig. 1. Sub-partitioning of the segregate "Something to Eat" based on the naming responses of objects A–D (adapted from (Frake 1969)).

This resembles remarkably our conception of intensional ontologies. It therefore allowed us to realise that we already had all the information we needed for the generation of taxonomical relations. Instead of complementary names applied to each object, we have the properties (attributes) that characterise each term in the communication language. Accordingly, by retrieving properties in common and those that differ, we are able to do exactly the same as ethnographers do, and actually create taxonomies extended with the relevant attributes used to classify objects in one or other segregate.

---

[4] The example given by Frake (1969) concerns a conversation at a lunch counter, and has been abridged here.
[5] A *segregate* is a terminologically distinguished array of objects (Frake 1969). The notion of *contrast* is also important in taxonomies. Two categories contrast only when the difference between them is significant for defining their use; that is, they form a contrasting set if they are distinctive alternatives in a classifying context.

We formalised both those processes using the Z language, based on Luck and d'Inverno's (1995) framework for the specification of agent theories. A part of this formalisation, concerning ascription of intensional ontologies, is given next.

3   A Flavour of the Formal Specifications

We now illustrate how the formalisation of our approach was carried out (we exclude the schemas related to retrieval of taxonomical relations). The complete specification was given in full in (Bordini, Campbell and Vieira 1998; Bordini 1999) but also in (Bordini, Campbell and Vieira 1999); a case study on two taxonomies from a ontology of terms from the game of cricket can also be found on those papers. Our Z schemas make reference to the framework for formalisation of agent theories elaborated by Luck and d'Inverno (d'Inverno and Luck 2001; 1998; 1996; Luck and d'Inverno 1995; 1996) based on the Z formal specification language (Spivey 1992; Potter, Sinclair and Till 1996). Some familiarity with formal specification methods, in particular with the Z language, is assumed.

3.1   The Basic Setting

Before we introduce the formalisation of how an anthropologist agent can ascribe intensional ontologies to societies of agents, the basic setting in which it can occur must be presented. This section introduces the basic types used in the formalisation, and provides the specifications for informant agents, target societies, and some global functions needed in the rest of the specifications for access to available target societies and to deal with time instants.

We begin by introducing the basic types:

$[Term, Pred, TimeInstant]$

and the following abbreviation for the type *Sent*:

$Sent == (Pred \times Term)$

where *TimeInstant* is taken to be the set of constants representing time instants as it is intuitively understood. *Term* is the set of terms[6] (also called individual constants) of the Communication Language (CL) used by the agents in any Target Society (TS). *Pred* is the set of predicative constants (predicates) from CL. A sentence (*Sent*) of CL is a pair containing a predicate and a term, meaning that the term has the property (attribute) indicated by the predicate. We consider here only sentences of this sort; the consistent acceptance of sentences including the logical connectives by communicating agents within the quasi-intensional approach is given by Vieira and da Rocha Costa (1993).

We now present the definition of an *InformantAgent*, which is built on the definition of *AutonomousAgent* that is part of Luck and d'Inverno's framework (see, e.g., d'Inverno

---

[6] Note that *Term* (and *Pred*, mentioned next) are infinite domains; particular target societies will specify the subset of terms (and predicates) they use, as we shall see later.

and Luck 1996). The only requirement that we impose on the agents that will work as Informant Agents (IA) to the Anthropologist Agents (AA) (the specification of AA is in the next section) is that they make available an acceptance relation *accepts*, in the sense of acceptance we mentioned in Section 2.1. (Note that the relation *accepts* is used in the prefix notation.) This should be seen as the interface between IAs and the world, as it is how AAs access the information they need from these agents (for the particular purpose of ontological ascription). The type of the relation makes it clear that each individual IA may or may not accept a certain sentence *s* of its CL, given a set of sentences *S*, at one particular time instant *ti*.

InformantAgent

AutonomousAgent

$accepts\_ : \mathbb{P}(\textit{Sent} \times \mathbb{P}\,\textit{Sent} \times \textit{TimeInstant})$

$\forall s : \textit{Sent};\ S : \mathbb{P}\,\textit{Sent};\ ti : \textit{TimeInstant} \bullet$
$\quad accepts(s, S, ti) \Rightarrow s \in S$

The single explicit constraint in the predicate part of the schema above says that IAs only manifest their acceptance of sentences which have been presented to/inquired of them by an AA; this is how Martin (1959) conceived it in his theory of subjective intensionality. Clearly, this is not sufficient to specify whether an agent accepts a sentence or not. However, the definition of *accepts* is purposely left loose. A complete definition of that relation would need to refer to particular informant agents' mental states and their architectures (and this is of course not desirable in a project aiming at interoperability). For example, if the informant agent works as a theorem prover (Fisher 1995), accepting a sentence means simply trying to prove it, and accepting it if it is a theorem (given the agent's current set of beliefs). If the IA is a database system with an agent "wrapping" (Genesereth and Ketchpel 1994), all that is necessary is to check whether the information affirmed in a particular sentence is consistent with the information in the database or not. However agents work, it should always be quite straightforward for designers of agent systems to add this relation as an interface to some particular agents so that they can work as IAs. This is the only requirement that we impose to allow interoperation of agents as far as ontological ascription is concerned. It appears to be quite a reasonable one, especially when contrasted with the degree of constraint implied by the alternative approach of having everything standardised—which would no doubt be preferable from an engineering or a tidy administrative viewpoint if one could be in a position to enforce this *a priori* on all the components and the agent societies in a broader system, but the larger such a system may become in practice, the less likely it will be that this degree of control can be exercised.

Having defined the state space of informant agents, we can now show what designers of societies of agents need to add to their systems so that ascription of intensional ontologies can occur (i.e., the specification of *TargetSociety* below). Before that, we introduce two more basic types. These are the set of constants used as identifiers to TSs (*TSocId*) and to IAs (*InfAgId*). The anthropologist agents and the migrant agents (whose formal specifications are not given here for the sake of space) should be able to refer to all existing societies of agents (the former analyse them and the latter may need to migrate to them), and for each TS its set of IAs must be identified as well (by the AAs only; remember that AAs can only ascribe IOTs by relying on the IAs of each society). That is why we introduce the following basic type for the constants used for identification (of TSs and IAs).

$[TSocId, InfAgId]$

A *TargetSociety* is based on the schema *MASystem* defining what a MAS is (d'Inverno and Luck 2001, Section 3.2.3) to which we add all the necessary features for a society of agents to be a *target society* (i.e., agents can, in our approach, migrate to them). It has a partial injection *iag* from informant agents' identifiers to the actual informant agents in the society. This is used to access the IAs in that particular society (which is why a partial injection is used: two identifiers cannot correspond to the same IA). In order to make certain predicates to be introduced later easier to specify, we add a variable *ias* which is constrained to contain all members of the current domain of *iag* (in other words, it contains the set of all identifiers of the IAs that are available in that TS). It is necessarily a non-empty set ($\mathbb{P}_1$) because, as we have said, informant agents are fundamental in this context. Further, a TS has three non-empty sets related to the CL used in it. First, *clterms* is the specific set of terms used in that particular CL. Second, *clpreds* is the set of predicates (or predicative constants) of that CL. As one can see in the predicate part of the schema below, these sets are defined by checking all the terms and predicates that happen to exist in the acceptance relations of all IAs. Finally, *clsents* is the set of all possible sentences created from the particular terms and predicates of that CL.

__*TargetSociety*_____

MASystem
$ias : \mathbb{P}_1\ InfAgId$
$iag : InfAgId \rightarrowtail InformantAgent$
$clterms : \mathbb{P}_1\ Term$
$clpreds : \mathbb{P}_1\ Pred$
$clsents : \mathbb{P}_1(Pred \times Term)$

$ias = \text{dom } iag$
$\forall t : Term \bullet (\ t \in clterms \Leftrightarrow$
$\qquad \exists ia : InfAgId;\ p : Pred;\ S : \mathbb{P}\ Sent;\ ti : TimeInstant\ |$
$\qquad\qquad ia \in ias \bullet iag(ia).accepts((p, t), S, ti)\ )$
$\forall p : Pred \bullet (\ p \in clpreds \Leftrightarrow$
$\qquad \exists ia : InfAgId;\ t : Term;\ S : \mathbb{P}\ Sent;\ ti : TimeInstant\ |$
$\qquad\qquad ia \in ias \bullet iag(ia).accepts((p, t), S, ti)\ )$
$clsents = (clpreds \times clterms)$

We now introduce in the axiomatic description below some global variables and functions, which will be needed in the rest of the specifications. The bijection *tsoc* gives a mapping between target society identifiers and actual TSs (there should be a one-to-one correspondence between them, thus a bijection). This is to represent the idea that all existing societies of agents should have an identification, and that there is always a way to access the actual TSs through their identifiers[7]. Again for simplicity, we add a variable *tsocs* which contains the set of identifiers for all existing TSs (i.e., all members of the current domain of *tsoc*).

Because some of the concepts to be formalised are dependent on time, we need some definitions for handling it. An injective sequence over time instants *the_time* must be available. It is supposed to be the clock of the system: it defines the order in which each constant of type *TimeInstant* occurs. Being an injective sequence, it is assured that a constant denoting a time instant occurs no more than once over time, and we must add a predicate saying that all possible time instants are present in the range of the sequence *the_time*, thus giving a complete order for their occurrence. We then have a binary relation (in infix notation) *before_eq* stating whether a time instant t_1 either occurs before or is the same as a time instant t_2. It is defined by checking whether the natural number associated with t_1 in the sequence *the_time* (we do this by using the inverse relation denoted by "$\sim$" superscript) is less than or equal to the one associated with t_2. It will make our next definitions easier if we provide a global function *most_recent* which, given a non-empty set of time instants, returns the one that is most recent (i.e., the last to occur, the one with the largest number associated with it in the domain of *the_time*). This is easily defined in terms of the relation *before_eq*, by means of a μ-expression which gives the one *ti* in the provided set of time instants for which it is true that each time instant in the provided set either occurs before *ti* or is *ti* itself.

$$
\begin{array}{l}
tsocs : \mathbb{P}\ TSocId \\
tsoc : TSocId \rightarrowtail TargetSociety \\
the\_time : \mathrm{iseq}TimeInstant \\
\_\ before\_eq\ \_ : TimeInstant \leftrightarrow TimeInstant \\
most\_recent : \mathbb{P}_1\ TimeInstant \rightarrow TimeInstant \\
\hline
tsocs = \mathrm{dom}\ tsoc \\
\mathrm{ran}\ the\_time = TimeInstant \\
\forall\ t_1, t_2 : TimeInstant\ \bullet \\
\quad t_1\ before\_eq\ t_2 \Leftrightarrow the\_time^\sim(t_1) \leq the\_time^\sim(t_2) \\
\forall\ tis : \mathbb{P}_1\ TimeInstant\ \bullet \\
\quad most\_recent(tis) = (\mu\ ti : TimeInstant \mid ti \in tis\ \wedge \\
\qquad (\forall\ t : TimeInstant \mid t \in tis\ \bullet\ t\ before\_eq\ ti))
\end{array}
$$

Given these basic definitions, we are now ready to see how an anthropologist agent can ascribe an intensional ontology to a target society.

3.2   Formalisation of the Ascription of Intensional Ontologies

First we define abbreviations for some types which will be used later. Referring back to Section 2.2 makes it easy to understand that the signature *IntensionalOntologyOfTerms* is a partial function from terms to non-empty sets of predicates. It is a partial function because it is possible that the AA will not be able to find definitions for all terms used

---

[7] Given the present infrastructure of network services, this is not an unrealistic supposition.

in the TS (and TS itself uses only a subset of them), but if there is an entry for a term in the IOT, then there must be a non-empty set of predicates which defines it. Referring to Section 2.1 leads to the definition of the type *SubjectiveQuasiIntension*: the subjective quasi-intension of a term, for a particular IA, who is from a TS , given a set of sentences (informed by an AA), at a specific time, is a set of predicates which are the properties that the agent accepts as being related to that term. Note that this can be an empty set of predicates if it happens that the IA does not know the particular term in question. The type *IntersubjectiveQuasiIntension* is the same, except that it does not depend on a specific IA (recall that these are relative to the whole group of IAs from a particular TS).

$$IntensionalOntologyOfTerms == Term \twoheadrightarrow \mathbb{P}_1 \, Pred$$

$$SubjectiveQuasiIntension ==$$
$$(Term \times InfAgId \times TSocId \times \mathbb{P} \, Sent \times TimeInstant) \rightarrow \mathbb{P} \, Pred$$

$$IntersubjectiveQuasiIntension ==$$
$$(Term \times TSocId \times \mathbb{P} \, Sent \times TimeInstant) \rightarrow \mathbb{P} \, Pred$$

We now give axiomatic definitions for the functions *subjective_quasi_intension* and *intersubjective_quasi_intension*, which will be used later (when defining the ascription of IOTs), and the related definition of the *co_intensive* predicate. The intuition for the definitions below is given after them.

> $subjective\_quasi\_intension : SubjectiveQuasiIntension$
> $intersubjective\_quasi\_intension : IntersubjectiveQuasiIntension$
> $co\_intensive \_ : \mathbb{P}(Term \times Term \times IntensionalOntologyOfTerms)$
>
> ---
>
> $\forall t : Term;\; ia : InfAgId;\; ts : TSocId;\; S : \mathbb{P} \, Sent;$
> $\quad ti : TimeInstant \mid t \in tsoc(ts).clterms \wedge$
> $\quad\quad ia \in tsoc(ts).ias \wedge S \subseteq tsoc(ts).clsents \bullet$
> $\quad\quad\quad subjective\_quasi\_intension(t, ia, ts, S, ti) = \{p : Pred \mid$
> $\quad\quad\quad\quad tsoc(ts).iag(ia).accepts((p, t), S, ti)\}$
>
> $\forall t : Term;\; ts : TSocId;\; S : \mathbb{P} \, Sent;\; ti : TimeInstant \mid$
> $\quad t \in tsoc(ts).clterms \wedge S \subseteq tsoc(ts).clsents \bullet$
> $\quad\quad intersubjective\_quasi\_intension(t, ts, S, ti) =$
> $\quad\quad\quad \bigcap\{ia : InfAgId \mid ia \in tsoc(ts).ias \bullet$
> $\quad\quad\quad\quad subjective\_quasi\_intension(t, ia, ts, S, ti)\}$
>
> $\forall t_1, t_2 : Term;\; iot : IntensionalOntologyOfTerms \mid$
> $\quad t_1 \in dom \, iot \wedge t_2 \in dom \, iot \bullet$
> $\quad\quad co\_intensive(t_1, t_2, iot) \Leftrightarrow iot(t_1) = iot(t_2)$

For all terms *t* used in the CL of that TS, all *ia* that are informant agents of a target society *ts*, all sets of sentences *S* (which are necessarily from that TS's particular CL), and all time instants *ti*, the *subjective_quasi_intension* of *t*, for an *ia* from *ts*, given *S*, at time *ti*, is the set of predicates that *ia* accepts as being associated with term *t*, for the set of sentences *S*, at *ti*. The *intersubjective_quasi_intension* of *t* in the TS *ts*, given *S*, at *ti*, is the set of predicates accepted by all informant agents from *ts*: it is the intersection of the subjective quasi-intensions of all IAs from that TS for that term *t* (again given *S* and *ti*). Note that we need to make use of the *tsoc* function and of the TS's *iag* function to map from identifiers to actual TSs or IAs.

We have also given above the definition of *co_intensive*, which is a predicate that holds when two terms have the same set of predicates associated with them in a given intensional ontology of terms. (Note that in this case we refer to co-intensiveness on the notion of intersubjective quasi-intension, which is used in the ascription of ontologies, as we see later.)

The definition of *AnthropologistAgent* is given below. It is based, as for the definition of IA, upon the fact that it is an *AutonomousAgent* (provided in the framework) with some additional particular features.

We say first that an AA is able to generate the questions that are needed to interview the IAs (function *generate_sentences*). It is evident that this function is not properly defined in the predicate part of the schema below. The process of generating the necessary questions (i.e., the set of sentences that are submitted for IAs to accept or reject) was discussed by Bordini, Campbell and Vieira (1998) to some extent, but no formalisation is as yet available for this. However, it is known that the generation of sets of sentences is dependent on the target society and the particular time instant when the interview will take place, thus the signature of *generate_sentences* is as given below. Note that this function can return an empty set in situations where the AA does not have much experience with a particular TS at a particular time.

Next, there is the function *history_of_intensional_ontologies*. This is the most important part of AAs because it keeps track of all IOTs an AA has ascribed. Because a TS's IOT may vary over time (we shall comment further on this later), the function *history_of_intensional_ontologies* maps a pair stating a TS and a time instant to the IOT that was ascribed to that TS at that time.

The two items mentioned above are the important aspects of AAs, but we have included a few more variables in the schema in order to make the access to the information from the AA easier in later specifications. The set *known_societies* records all TSs that have been analysed by a particular AA so far; it is the set of all *TSocId* that appear as the first members of the pairs belonging to the domain of *history_of_intensional_ontologies*. There is also *all_versions*, which is a function that, given a target society identifier *ts*, provides all the time instants at which IOTs were ascribed to *ts*, provided, of course, that *ts* is in the set of *known_societies*. Finally, *current_ontology* maps *ts* (which is as before) to the time interval *ti* that is the *most_recent* of the time intervals associated with *all_versions* of IOTs existing for that *ts* in the *history_of_intensional_ontologies*.

In the schema below, we also provide a relation which may be useful for migrant agents' reference: it is *current_synonyms*, which is a (reflexive and transitive) relation over terms created with the help of the predicate *co_intensive* (defined above) with respect to the *current_ontology* from each particular target society *ts*.

```
  AnthropologistAgent
┌─────────────────────────────────────────────────────────────
│ AutonomousAgent
│ generate_sentences : (TSocId × TimeInstant) → ℙ Sent
│ history_of_intensional_ontologies :
│     (TSocId × TimeInstant) ⇸
│         IntensionalOntologyOfTerms
│ known_societies : ℙ TSocId
│ all_versions : TSocId ⇸ ℙ TimeInstant
│ current_ontology : TSocId ⇸ IntensionalOntologyOfTerms
│ current_synonyms : TSocId ⇸ Term ↔ Term
├─────────────────────────────────────────────────────────────
│ known_societies = {s : (TSocId × TimeInstant) |
│     s ∈ dom history_of_intensional_ontologies • first s}
│ ∀ ts : TSocId | ts ∈ known_societies • all_versions(ts) =
│     {ti : TimeInstant | (ts, ti) ∈
│         dom history_of_intensional_ontologies}
│ ∀ ts : TSocId; ti : TimeInstant | ts ∈ known_societies ∧
│     ti = most_recent(all_versions(ts)) • current_ontology(ts) =
│         history_of_intensional_ontologies(ts, ti)
│ current_synonyms = {ts : TSocId | ts ∈ known_societies •
│     ts ↦ {t₁, t₂ : Term | t₁ ≠ t₂ ∧
│         co_intensive(t₁, t₂, current_ontology(ts)) • (t₁, t₂)}}
└─────────────────────────────────────────────────────────────
```

Having defined the state space of *AnthropologistAgent*, we now need to say what are the initial values for the variables in it, so as to be precise with the Z method. The only relevant variable is *history_of_intensional_ontologies'*, and its initial value is evidently the empty set.

```
  InitialAnthropologistAgent
┌─────────────────────────────────────────────────────────────
│ AnthropologistAgent'
├─────────────────────────────────────────────────────────────
│ history_of_intensional_ontologies' = ∅
└─────────────────────────────────────────────────────────────
```

We can now specify the operation *AscribeIntensionalOntologyOfTerms*, which alters the state of an AA (Δ*AnthropologistAgent*). This operation is given two inputs: ts? is the target society for which an IOT should be ascribed and the time ti? when the ascription is taking place. The operation consist of asserting that *history_of_intensional_ontologies'* should be overridden from its previous definition to map the pair $(ts?, ti?)$ to the IOT which maps each of the terms of that TS to its intersubjective quasi-intension, provided this is not an empty set[8]. The set of sentences S that must be provided to the function *intersubjective_quasi_intension* as a parameter (alongside $ts?, ti?$ and, of course, the term t) is produced by the function *generate_sentences* for that particular $ts?$ at $ti?$.

---

[8] Note that in the present formalisation we do not constrain the ontological description of a term to have a minimal set of properties as we originally suggested in Definition 4.

```
┌─ AscribeIntensionalOntologyOfTerms ──────────────────────────
│ ΔAnthropologistAgent
│ ts? : TSocId
│ ti? : TimeInstant
├──────────────────────────────────────────────────────────────
│ history_of_intensional_ontologies' =
│     history_of_intensional_ontologies⊕
│     (let S == generate_sentences(ts?, ti?) •
│         {(ts?, ti?) ↦ {t : Term | t ∈ tsoc(ts?).clterms ∧
│         intersubjective_quasi_intension(t, ts?, S, ti?) ≠ ∅ •
│             t ↦ intersubjective_quasi_intension(t, ts?, S, ti?)}})
```

In brief, the non-empty intersubjective quasi-intension of a term is its definition, in our approach. When the intersubjective quasi-intension is an empty set, the AA cannot ascribe a definition to that term. Recall that by the type of the IOTs (i.e., a partial function) we express the fact that there may not be definitions for all existing terms.

Because agents only accept sentences that are in the set of sentences they were given by an AA (stated in *InformantAgent*), and the intersubjective quasi- intension of a term is based on accepted sentences (stated in the axiomatic descriptions), and an ascribed ontology only contains those terms whose intersubjective quasi-intensions are non-empty (in the schema above), we can derive the theorem below which concerns the state space of *AnthropologistAgent* (but only now are we able to introduce it). It says that if there is a term t in an ascribed IOT, it is guaranteed that there was at least one sentence concerning that term in the set of sentences generated by the *AnthropologistAgent*. (A corollary would be that if the set of generated sentences is empty, the ascribed IOT is an empty set too).

```
AnthropologistAgent;
t : Term; ts : TSocId; ti : TimeInstant |
    t ∈ tsoc(ts).clterms ∧
    (ts, ti) ∈ dom history_of_intensional_ontologies ⊢
        t ∈ dom history_of_intensional_ontologies(ts, ti) ⇒
            t ∈ {s : Sent | s ∈ generate_sentences(ts, ti) • second s}
```

We emphasise that, given that we use the notion of intersubjective quasi- intension, which is time-specific, for the definitions of the terms in the ontology (see *AscribeIntensionalOntologyOfTerms*), these definitions may not be valid *ad infinitum*. Thus, the anthropologist agent may need to review the ontology it has ascribed to a particular society from time to time, as autonomous evolution within societies takes place or the AA alters its set of IAs, or the AA's set of sentences to be given to the IAs is changed, etc. That is why we refer to this type of ontology as *evolutionary*, since we intend agents to be able to improve them with time. Since in our definitions we state that AAs keep track of the whole history of ontologies they have ascribed to each of the TSs, this allows one to analyse how that TS has evolved as far as ontology is concerned. Some agents may be able to analyse the historical evolution of ontologies provided by an AA: one could find it interesting in the future to consider *historian agents*, or *linguist agents* interested in *agent archaeology*, who might make use of that information.

However, based on the concept of objective quasi-intentions (see Section 2.1), some subset of the ontology may form an immutable part of it, composed of the terms universally accepted in that community. In order to deal with this point, we start by providing abbreviations for the types (as we did for subjective and intersubjective quasi-intension). One should note that *IntertemporalQuasiIntension* is the same as *SubjectiveQuasiIntension* except that it does not depend upon *TimeInstant*. Likewise, *ObjectiveQuasiIntension* is the same as *IntersubjectiveQuasiIntension* except for the dependence on time; alternatively, one can see *ObjectiveQuasiIntension* as based on *IntertemporalQuasiIntension* except that the former does not concern particular informant agents.

$$IntertemporalQuasiIntension ==$$
$$(Term \times InfAgId \times TSocId \times \mathbb{P}\,Sent) \rightarrow \mathbb{P}\,Pred$$

$$ObjectiveQuasiIntension ==$$
$$(Term \times TSocId \times \mathbb{P}\,Sent) \rightarrow \mathbb{P}\,Pred$$

The axiomatic description below states that the function *intertemporal_quasi_intension*, given a term t, informant agent ia, target society ts, and set of sentences S, yields a set of predicates which ia accepts as being associated with term t at all times, given the set of sentences S. The *objective_quasi_intension* of t in society ts, given S, is the set of predicates accepted by all IAs from ts, for that term, at all times: it is the intersection of the intertemporal quasi-intensions of all IAs in that TS for that term t (again, given S).

$\quad$ *intertemporal_quasi_intension* : *IntertemporalQuasiIntension*
$\quad$ *objective_quasi_intension* : *ObjectiveQuasiIntension*

$\quad \forall\, t : Term;\ ia : InfAgId;\ ts : TSocId;\ S : \mathbb{P}\,Sent \mid$
$\qquad t \in tsoc(ts).clterms \wedge ia \in tsoc(ts).ias \wedge$
$\qquad S \subseteq tsoc(ts).clsents \bullet$
$\qquad\qquad intertemporal\_quasi\_intension(t, ia, ts, S) =$
$\qquad\qquad\qquad \{p : Pred \mid (\forall\, ti : TimeInstant \bullet$
$\qquad\qquad\qquad\qquad tsoc(ts).iag(ia).accepts((p, t), S, ti))\}$
$\quad \forall\, t : Term;\ ts : TSocId;\ S : \mathbb{P}\,Sent \mid$
$\qquad t \in tsoc(ts).clterms \wedge S \subseteq tsoc(ts).clsents \bullet$
$\qquad\qquad objective\_quasi\_intension(t, ts, S) =$
$\qquad\qquad\qquad \bigcap\{ia : InfAgId \mid ia \in tsoc(ts).ias \bullet$
$\qquad\qquad\qquad\qquad intertemporal\_quasi\_intension(t, ia, ts, S)\}$

In order to say that AAs may also provide immutable intensional ontologies, based on the concepts specified above, we introduce the schema *ExperiencedAnthropologistAgent* which is built on the schema *AnthropologistAgent* and includes a function *immutable_intensional_ontology* which maps TSs to IOTs. (It does not depend on time as before, as these IOTs are the ones that are not supposed to change.) As in the case of *history_of_intensional_ontologies*, it only maps terms that have a non-empty set of predicates to define them, except that in this instance the set of predicates is given by *objective_quasi_intension* instead of *intersubjective_quasi_intension*. Note that the TS identified by *ts* must necessarily be in the set of *known_societies* of that AA, and the set of sentences *S* to be verified by informants is defined here as the union of all sentences that the AA generates for that society at all times. Evidently, the larger this set is the better, as the chances of finding which are the immutable terms in that society are increased.

$$
\begin{array}{|l}
\hline
\_\_ExperiencedAnthropologistAgent _____ \\
AnthropologistAgent \\
immutable\_intensional\_ontology : TSocId \nrightarrow \\
\quad IntensionalOntologyOfTerms \\
\hline
\forall\, ts : TSocId \mid ts \in known\_societies \bullet \\
\quad immutable\_intensional\_ontology(ts) = \\
\qquad (\textbf{let } S == \bigcup \{ti : TimeInstant \bullet generate\_sentences(ts, ti)\} \bullet \\
\qquad \{t : Term \mid objective\_quasi\_intension(t, ts, S) \neq \varnothing \bullet \\
\qquad\qquad t \mapsto objective\_quasi\_intension(t, ts, S)\}) \\
\hline
\end{array}
$$

Migrant agents may well find it useful to know which subset of the intensional ontology is immutable. Note that some societies may never keep immutable terms, or it may take a long time to arrive at a sound conclusion that there is a immutable subset of an intensional ontology. We have further discussed this point elsewhere (Bordini, Campbell and Vieira 1998).

We have found, as d'Inverno and Luck (2001) claim and demonstrate for other applications, that Z is an excellent basis for clear specification of agents with special properties. It has allowed a rapid and effective progression from the initial qualitative ideas on agency with an anthropological flavour to the precise form given above, and to theorems that they satisfy. Furthermore, it should allow us to formalise the missing parts (also mentioned in our previous work) incrementally. Building on definitions from Luck and d'Inverno's framework (i.e., *AutonomousAgent* and *MASystem*), makes it possible for us to integrate our approach with other agent theories specified in the same framework (see, e.g., d'Inverno and Luck 1996), besides the obvious advantage of exempting us from specifying those basic concepts. Also, as d'Inverno and Luck (1996) indicate, the framework can be used directly in the implementation of simulations of the agent theories that have been formalised. As a matter of fact, we have type-checked these specifications using ZTC (Jia 1995) and animated a simplified[9] version of them using PiZA (Hewitt 1997).

4   A Promising Application: Corpora as Societies

In the work reported above, we proposed ontological ascription as a means towards interoperability of multi-agent systems. We have also dealt with the recovery of taxonomical relations from intensional ontologies in our anthropological approach to interoperability. As we mentioned in Section 1, cognitive anthropologists emphasise the

---

[9] The simplifications concern mainly some of the global definitions for the basic setting (e.g. access to TSs), which are not directly implementable in the Z tools used. All main algorithms are shown to work as intended in the animated version.

importance of taxonomies in understanding cognitive systems. The importance of ontologies and taxonomies for information retrieval and extraction is also well known (Guarino, Masolo and Veter 1999; Welty and Ide 1999; Barros, Gonçalves and Santos 1998; Borgo *et al.* 1997). The representation of semantic relations can be used in the identification of relevant documents, yielding more accurate results. Besides information retrieval and extraction, there are many other applications where ontologies are necessary, such as "the semantic web", knowledge management, and natural language generation.

Our original proposal of an intensional ontology is based on the relation between a language user and terms of the language, more specifically the *acceptance relation*. In the context of multi-agent systems, this can be formulated on the basis of interviews with given (informant) agents. As we mentioned in Section 1, one present line of research proposes the use of vast sources of coded knowledge that are available in corpora for automatic ontology engineering (Hahn and Schnattinger 1998; Aussenac-Gilles, Biébow and Szulman 2000; Mädche and Staab 2000; Nobécourt 2000). In our ongoing work, we consider the application area of ontology extraction from written texts, revisiting our approach so that the role of an informant agent is fulfilled by a text. Texts can be regarded as agents, in the sense that each text corpus presents an individual discourse in which terms are used in a particular way. Some corpora, such as the ones maintained by the international Survey of English Usage at University College London, are both computer-based and extremely large.

The intensional ontology framework, described in the previous section, can therefore be reused having in mind texts as the subjects of the acceptance relation. The idea of subjective quasi-intension is related to the state of mind of a subject and is revealed through the process of an interview. Our current line of investigation is to check whether a corresponding notion of subjective quasi-intension can be revealed when a text is considered as such a source of information. The properties related to terms in a text can be retrieved through natural language processing, as outlined below.

In adjusting our previous framework to the current setting, we have to consider that quasi-intensions are related to language in use for communication among agents, whereas texts convey messages which refer to parts of the intensionality of terms. Closeness to the previous notion of subjective quasi-intensions could be achieved by the union of all properties found in a collection of texts. Similarly, properties that are accepted by all users might well be properties expressed in all texts, across corpora. Therefore, we would need to process a collection of corpora to extract the equivalent of intersubjective quasi- intentions.

In the original approach, properties of a term that are accepted by an agent were used in determining the term's quasi-intension. Here, properties expressed with respect to a term in a text are used instead. Such properties can be found through the identification of the syntactic contexts associated with a given term (i.e., a noun). These syntactic contexts can be extracted from a large collection of texts and then used to derive subjective and intersubjective quasi-intensions in the "corpus as an agent" or "corpora as societies of agents" metaphor. Just as an illustration, we give a simple example that should be easy to find in most corpora of ordinary texts having some reference to intellectual activities: the term *school* can be related to properties (stated as pre or post modifications) such as: *high*, *public*, *Romantic*, *primary*, *private*, and *Baroque*.

In our future experiments, we intend to extract concrete instances of all these contexts. We give a sample of such an extraction below. For this, we have used the corpora processing system presented by Gasperin *et al.* (2001). That system is intended for measuring similarity of words by using the syntactic contexts that they share. For the extraction of the syntactic contexts, which is of interest here, the system uses the "Palavras" parser (Bick 2000). The work by Gasperin *et al.* is based on Grefenstette's (1994) method for context extraction (also intended for similarity measure) and further details the information contained in the extracted contexts.

That detailed context information is used in our example, where they are characterised by the abbreviations given next. For any noun x, the code[10] snsp↑ y means that a prepositional phrase with noun y modifies x, where the preposition is given in brackets; snsp↓ y means that a prepositional phrase with x can modify a noun y, where the preposition is given in brackets; adj↑ y means that y is an adjective modifying x; subj↓ y means that y is a verb whose subject is x; dobj↓ y means that y is a verb whose direct object is x; sobj↑ y means that y is a noun which is the direct object of a verb whose subject is x; and sobj↓ y means that y is the subject of a verb whose direct object is x.

The example given below was obtained from the Corpus of the NILC (*Núcleo Interinstitucional de Lingüística Computacional*), maintained by USP São Carlos, UFS-Car, and UNESP. In fact, the corpus used in this experiment is a subset of the NILC corpus with Brazilian texts related to sports (not surprisingly, mainly on football) having some 1.4 million words. We have chosen a small set of terms to form the sample ontology below. The choice was based on the fact that there are taxonomical relations among those terms. This may be useful in verifying also the applicability of our approach for retrieving taxonomical relations from intensional ontologies, which was not presented in this paper but appears in (Bordini, Campbell and Vieira 1998; 1999).

For each chosen word, the corpus processing system returned a large number of syntactic contexts where they appeared. We sorted this list of contexts in decreasing order of frequency (i.e., the number of times they occurred). We then checked which contexts the chosen terms had in common and which were specific to each of them. The list given below is a manual selection of these results. Portuguese words are followed by their translation into English given in square brackets.

- Contexts found in common between terms *atleta* [athlete], *jogador* [player], *atacante* [forward], *zagueiro* [defender], and *goleiro* [goalkeeper] (out of 17 contexts):
  - subj ↓ *fazer* [to make]
  - subj ↓ *dizer* [to say]
  - adj ↑ *bom* [good]
  - snsp↑ *(de) seleção* [(from) squad]
- Contexts found in common between terms *jogador* [player], *atacante* [forward], *zagueiro* [defender], and *goleiro* [goalkeeper] (out of 26 contexts):
  - sobj ↑ *gol* [goal]
  - sobj ↑ *bola* [ball]
  - sobj ↑ *partida* [match]

---

[10] Available types of contexts that do not appear in the example given here are: adj↓, subj↑, dobj↑, iobj↑, and iobj↓, whose meanings can be inferred.

- • sobj ↑ *time* [team]
- Contexts specific to *jogador* [player] (out of the first 10 in a list of 479 contexts):
  - • snsp↑ *(de) futebol* [(of) football]
  - • sobj ↑ *falta* [fault]
  - • sobj ↓ *clube* [club]
- Contexts specific to *atacante* [forward] (out of the first 56 in a list of 93 contexts):
  - • adj ↑ *meio* [centre, or inside]
  - • subj ↓ *atingir* [to reach, or get to]
  - • snsp↑ *(de) ponta* [(in) winger (position)]
- Contexts specific to *zagueiro* [defender] (out of the first 6 in a list of 24 contexts):
  - • adj ↑ *central* [central (full back)]
  - • snsp↓ *retorno (de)* [return, or coming back (of)]
  - • snsp↑ *(de) área* [(of) area[11]]
- Contexts specific to *goleiro* [goalkeeper] (out of the first 16 in a list of 37 contexts):
  - • snsp↓ *(de) saída* [leaving, or advancing (of)]
  - • dobj ↓ *encobrir* [to chip over]
  - • subj ↓ *espalmar* [to deflect away (with one's hands)]

The contexts in the first item above are common to all terms we have considered in this sample, including the most general term in the associated taxonomy, which would be "athlete". It is more general than (football) "player", so in the context we do not see contexts such as "ball" and "goal" (which appear in the second item, where "athlete" was not included). In our approach to retrieving taxonomical relations from intensional ontologies, properties that terms have in common (in their quasi-intensions) relate to partitioning segregates, and properties that are specific to certain terms are used to identify contrasting sets (refer to Section 2.3 for the meaning of these concepts in Cultural Anthropology).

In the future, we plan to conduct a series of experiments to evaluate our approach to intensional ontologies of terms when adapted to guide ontology extraction from corpora.

5 Conclusion

In our previous work, presented at UKMAS-99, we have reported on a way of discovering ontologies used in societies of agents. It was based on a theory of intensionality, and connected with our anthropological approach to interoperability of multi-agent systems. Further, inspired by work on ethnography, we have provided a means for an anthropologist agent to recover taxonomical relations (augmented with the attributes defining each term in the taxonomy) from the intensional ontologies it has ascribed to societies of agents, and we have formalised it along with the ascription process using a Z framework for the formalisation of agent theories.

In this paper we have presented the main ideas of that work, and have given a flavour of the formal specification (for ascription of ontologies, in particular). We have also mentioned here a new and promising potential application for our previous more formal work: that of corpora processing for ontology extraction. The idea is to extract

---

[11] This is a more complete reference to *defender* in Portuguese.

the instersubjective quasi-intention from properties related to terms in the texts. In the present paper, we have set out the ground for a series of future experiments associating our approach with natural language processing for the extraction of ontologies from corpora.

Acknowledgements

We are grateful to Antônio Carlos da Rocha Costa for his contributions to earlier stages of this work, to Caroline V. Gasperin for extracting the contexts from the corpus for the sample experiment in Section 4, and to Luis C. Lamb for translating those Brazilian football terms into English. This work was partially supported by CNPq and FAPERGS.

References

Aussenac-Gilles, N., Biébow, B. and Szulman, S. 2000. Corpus analysis for conceptual modelling. In *Workshop on Ontologies and Texts, Knowledge Engineering and Knowledge Management: Methods, Models and Tools, held as part of the 12th International Conference on Knowledge Engineering and Knowledge Management (EKAW'2000), Juan-les-Pins, French Riviera, 2nd of October*. Springer-Verlag.

Barros, F. A., Gonçalves, P. F. and Santos, T. L. 1998. Providing context to web searches: The use of ontologies to enhance search engine's accuracy. *Journal of the Brazilian Computer Society* 5(2). ISSN 0104-6500.

Bick, E. 2000. *The Parsing System "Palavras": Automatic Grammatical Analysis of Portuguese in a Constraint Grammar Framework*. Ph.D. Dissertation, Århus University, Århus.

Bordini, R. H., Campbell, J. A. and Vieira, R. 1997. Ascription of intensional ontologies in anthropological descriptions of multi-agent systems. In Kandzia, P. and Klusch, M., eds., *Proceedings of the First International Workshop on Cooperative Information Agents (CIA'97), 26–28 February, Kiel, Germany*, volume 1202 of *Lecture Notes in Artificial Intelligence*, 235–247. Berlin: Springer-Verlag. UCL-CS [RN/97/1].

Bordini, R. H., Campbell, J. A. and Vieira, R. 1998. Extending ascribed intensional ontologies with taxonomical relations in anthropological descriptions of multi-agent systems. *Journal of Artificial Societies and Social Simulation* 1(4). <http://www.soc.surrey.ac.uk/JASSS/1/4/3.html>.

Bordini, R. H., Campbell, J. A. and Vieira, R. 1999. Extending ascribed intensional ontologies with taxonomical relations in anthropological descriptions of multi-agent systems. In Preist, C., ed., *Proceedings of the Second Workshop of the UK Special Interest Group on Multi-Agent Systems*, 179–201. Hewlett-Packard Laboratories, Bristol, 6th–7th of December, 1999. Reprinted abridged version of the JASSS paper.

Bordini, R. H. 1999. *Contributions to an Anthropological Approach to the Cultural Adaptation of Migrant Agents*. Ph.D. Dissertation, University of London.

Borgo, S. et al. 1997. Using a large linguistic ontology for internet-based retrieval of object-oriented components. In *Proceedings of the Ninth International Conference on Software Engineering and Knowledge Engineering (SEKE'97), June 18-20*. Madrid.

d'Inverno, M. and Luck, M. 1996. A formal view of social dependence networks. In Zhang, C. and Lukose, D., eds., *Distributed Artificial Intelligence: Architecture and Modelling—Proceedgins of the First Australian Workshop on DAI, in conjunction with the Eighth Australian Joint Conference on Artificial Intelligence (AI'95), November 1995, Canberra, Australia*, number 1087 in Lecture Notes in Artificial Intelligence. Berlin: Springer-Verlag. 115–129.

d'Inverno, M. and Luck, M. 1998. Engineering AgentSpeak(L): A formal computational model. *Journal of Logic and Computation* 8(3):1–27.

d'Inverno, M. and Luck, M. 2001. *Understanding Agent Systems*. Springer Series on Agent Technology. Berlin: Springer-Verlag.

Fisher, M. 1995. Representing and executing agent-based systems. In Wooldridge, M. J. and Jennings, N. R., eds., *Intelligent Agents—Proceedings of the International Workshop on Agent Theories, Architectures, and Languages (ATAL-94), held as part of ECAI-94, Amsterdam, 8–12 August, 1994*, number 890 in Lecture Notes in Computer Science, 307–323. Berlin: Springer.

Frake, C. O. 1969. The ethnographic study of cognitive systems. In Tyler, S. A., ed., *Cognitive Anthropology*. New York: Holt, Rinehart and Winston Inc. 28–41.

Gasperin, C., Gamallo, P., Agustini, A., Lopes, G. and Lima, V. 2001. Using syntactic contexts for measuring word similarity. In *Proceedings of the Workshop on Semantic Knowledge Acquisition and Categorisation*. Helsinque.

Genesereth, M. R. and Ketchpel, S. P. 1994. Software agents. *Communications of the ACM* 37(7):48–53. URL: http://logic.stanford.edu/sharing/papers/.

Grefenstette, G. 1994. *Explorations in Automatic Thesaurus Discovery*. Kluwer Academic Publishers.

Gruber, T. R. 1993. Toward principles for the design of ontologies used for knowledge sharing. In Guarino, N. and Poli, R., eds., *Formal Ontology in Conceptual Analysis and Knowledge Representation*. Kluwer Academic Publishers. URL: http://www-ksl.stanford.edu/knowledge-sharing/papers/.

Guarino, N., Masolo, C. and Veter, G. 1999. Ontoseek: Content-based access to the web. *IEEE Inteligent Systems* 70–79.

Hahn, U. and Schnattinger, K. 1998. Towards text knowledge engineering. In *Proceedings of the 15th National Conference on Artificial Intelligence (AAAU-98) and 10th Conference on Innovative Applications of Artificial Intelligence (IAAI-98), Madison, WI, 26–30 July*, 524–531. Menlo Park, CA / Cambridge, MA: AAAI Press / MIT Press.

Hewitt, M. A. 1997. *PiZA: Prolog Z Animator, User Guide, version 1.0.9*. URL: http://www.noodles.demon.co.uk/PiZA/PiZADocs.html.

Jia, X. 1995. *ZTC: A Z Type Checker, User's Guide, version 2.01*. Division of Software Engineering, School of Computer Science, Telecommunication, and Information Systems, DePaul University, Chicago, Illinois. Available on anonymous ftp at ise.cs.depaul.edu.

Luck, M. and d'Inverno, M. 1995. A formal framework for agency and autonomy. In Lesser, V. and Gasser, L., eds., *Proceedings of the First International Conference on Multi-Agent Systems (ICMAS'95), 12–14 June, San Francisco, CA*, 254–260. Menlo Park, CA: AAAI Press / MIT Press.

Luck, M. and d'Inverno, M. 1996. Formalising the contract net as a goal-directed system. In Van de Velde, W. and Perram, J., eds., *Agents Breaking Away: Proceedings of the Seventh European Workshop on Modelling Autonomous Agents in a Multi-Agent World*, number 1038 in Lecture Notes in Artificial Intelligence. Eindhoven: Springer-Verlag. 72–85.

Mädche, A. and Staab, S. 2000. Discovering conceptual relations from text. In Horn, W., ed., *Proceedings of the 14th European Conference on Artificial Intelligence (ECAI-2000), Berlin, 20–25 August*. Amsterdam: IOS Press.

Martin, R. M. 1959. *Toward a Systematic Pragmatics*. Amsterdam: North-Holland.

Nobécourt, J. 2000. A method to build formal ontologies from texts. In *Workshop on Ontologies and Texts, Knowledge Engineering and Knowledge Management: Methods, Models and Tools, held as part of the 12th International Conference on Knowledge Engineering and Knowledge Management (EKAW'2000), Juan-les-Pins, French Riviera, 2nd of October*. Springer-Verlag.

Potter, B., Sinclair, J. and Till, D. 1996. *An Introduction to Formal Specification and Z*. Hemel Hempstead: Prentice Hall, second edition.

Spivey, J. M. 1992. *The Z Notation: A Reference Manual*. Hemel Hempstead: Prentice Hall, second edition.

Tyler, S. A., ed. 1969. *Cognitive Anthropology*. New York: Holt, Rinehart and Winston Inc.

Vieira, R. and da Rocha Costa, A. C. 1993. The acceptance relation and the specification of communicating agents. In Schlageter, G., Huhns, M. and Papazoglou, M., eds., *Proceedings of the First International Conference on Intelligent and Cooperative Information Systems – Special Track in Issues on Cooperating Heterogeneous Intelligent Agents*, 247–255. Rotterdam, The Netherlands: IEEE Computer Society Press, May, 1993.

Welty, C. and Ide, N. 1999. Using the right tools: Enhacing retrieval from marked-up documents. *Computers in the Humanities* 33(10):183–216.

Scalability in Multi-agent Systems:
The FIPA-OS Perspective

Phil Buckle[1], Tom Moore[1], Steve Robertshaw[1], Alan Treadway[1],
Sasu Tarkoma[2], and Stefan Poslad[3]

[1]Emorphia Ltd., Mill House, Station Approach,
Harlow Mill, Harlow, Essex, CM20 2EL, UK
{phil.buckle,tom.moore,steve.robertshaw,alan.treadway}
@emorphia.com
[2]Department of Computer Science, P.O.Box 26 (Teollisuuskatu 23),
00014 University of Helsinki, Finland
sasu.tarkoma@cs.helsinki.fi
[3]Department of Electronic Engineering, Queen Mary University of London,
Mile End Road, London, E4 1NS, UK
stefan.poslad@elec.qmul.ac.uk

Abstract. As agent systems move out of the research laboratories towards commercial application environments it is becoming increasingly apparent that scalability issues have to be investigated. A revision of what scalability means is proposed; especially regarding its application in the description of attributes of agent systems. A new model of scalability is described, and investigated through discussing qualitative as well as quantitative issues. A case study of a current project is provided to demonstrate how measures that determine how agent scalability might eventually be measured is presented.

1   Introduction

Intelligent agent technology is still a relatively young technology but one that is having to grow up fast due to its inherent suitability for deploying in environments that current technologies are proving to be unable to provide solutions for. Such environments range from managing resources in the radio environment of 3G mobile telephone networks to holonic manufacturing systems.

Within such environments, moreover, it is almost certain that agent systems will be deployed on a scale not yet seen in experimental systems. The discussion contained below will examine the scalability of agent systems; however, we will define an extension to current views of "scalability" to reflect more accurately how agents and agent systems might be recognised as having scaled. Before we do this we introduce the origins of the development toolkit that we have based our measurements upon: FIPA-OS. In recording this evolution we provide, for the reader new to agent technology, a brief introduction to the development of agent theory and describe efforts of international standards organisations to provide a stable and standardised environment within which developers can work. Finally we introduce the central

M. d'Inverno et al. (Eds.): UKMAS 1996–2000, LNAI 2403, pp. 110–130, 2002.
© Springer-Verlag Berlin Heidelberg 2002

concepts of the FIPA-OS agent toolkit, which implements the specifications of the main international agent standards body: FIPA[1].

In the next section we begin to examine what scalability means within the context of agent systems and discuss qualitative issues related to messaging, service discovery and behavioural attributes. We pay particular attention to the aspects of service discovery where some particularly useful findings have arisen out of recent work carried out on simulated large-scale network deployments using the FIPA-OS platform. This work is then discussed within the context of a real deployment of a network of heterogeneous FIPA compliant platforms in the AgentCities project.

Finally, we pay attention to the special requirements of deploying agent systems in constrained physical devices, such as those that are expected to be deployed in future mobile telecommunications networks. An evolution of the FIPA-OS agent toolkit, μFIPA-OS, has been developed to meet these needs and is discussed in a context where agent scalability on small devices is addressed from many perspectives; in terms of functionality, the partitioning of functionality, and coping with heterogeneous hardware availability. We discuss μFIPA-OS, which is able to deploy a number of FIPA compliant agents on any nomadic terminal. μFIPA-OS has support for FIPA-OS tasks and conversations and agents that are programmed for FIPA-OS can be executed in μFIPA-OS, with certain limitations. Finally we examine the measures taken to promote yet further footprint reductions in the μFIPA-OS extensions to support minimal agents that further enhance the scalability of the deployed agents.

We conclude with some observations and recommendations based on the current work reported here as well as proposals for future work.

2   Agents

Agents have arisen as a combination of different disciplines. The major contributing disciplines are peer-to-peer computing, distributed artificial intelligence, human-computer interaction and artificial life. Agents evolved in the mid 1980s when Brooks, considering whether a logic based system was viable, spawned a new branch of distributed artificial intelligence (DAI). The basis of DAI is that intelligence is an observed rational behavior found in the interactions between an agent and its environment [1]. The reactive, subsumption based, multi-agent system (MAS) architectures followed which were organised through a pyramidal hierarchy of abstractions to deliver system level intelligence in the application of the MAS. In the early 1990s hybrid MAS evolved where agents retained the social abstraction hierarchy but encapsulated individual intelligence characteristics. Such hybrid MAS were able to support complex interactions and when the practical reasoning ability of deliberative agents became possible with the Kripkesque BDI (Belief, Desire, Intentions) logics, agents evolved into the current, deliberative, state of the art.

---

[1] Foundation for Intelligent Physical Agents: http://www.fipa.org/ .

2.1   Agent Definition

Any definition of an agent is open to contradiction, even the term "agent" is seen as contentious by some, so perhaps it is better to start with what an agent is not. An agent is not dependent upon a particular design methodology or implementation mechanism, neither is it dependent upon any programming language, target operating system or physicality. An agent, therefore, can only be classified through its apparent actions and intelligence. An agent can be either a physical or virtual entity, one that embodies one or more of the following characteristics [2,3]:

- Perception of an incomplete world model. A world model is internally held conceptualisation of an environment that embodies the qualitative and quantitative.
- A peer communication capability within the MAS in a common format and structure.
- Individual goals towards which an agent will work, through modifying its world model and intentions.
- Interaction with an environment, external to the MAS, if appropriate i.e. some agents may be exclusively communicative.
- Skills and services that may be offered to, or traded, with other agents.
- Autonomy. An agent acts independently of peers, supervisory applications and users; however, agent behaviour can be constrained to ensure that an agent acts on behalf of users.
- Mobility. Some agents are able move around an electronic network.
- An agent will act rationally in order to achieve its goals and will not act in such a way as to prevent its goals being achieved insofar as its beliefs permit.
- Collaboration. An agent does not assume omnipotence in others; it will query a user to determine appropriate actions under conflicting instructions. An agent can refuse to execute certain tasks, if it determines the requested task would cause damage to other users.

2.1.1   The FIPA Agent Model

In order to build an interoperable MAS, all aspects of the MAS first require clear definition. For a MAS to be scaleable, interoperability and communications issues must be standardised in some way. FIPA is, arguably, the leading MAS standardisation body, it was founded in 1996 in order to produce software standards for heterogeneous and interacting agents and agent-based systems. Since 1996, FIPA has produced standards that define, amongst other things, agent communication, management, resources and mobility. The viability of these standards has been proven through independent implementations of the standards in disparate environments that have been proven to successfully interoperate.

To allow agents to locate and communicate with one another, the FIPA MAS architecture was defined. The FIPA MAS architecture specifies: in the directory facilitator (DF), a yellow-pages functionality to support service discovery; in the agent management system (AMS), a white-pages functionality to enforce proper agent lifecycle management; and in the agent communications channel (ACC), a message routing functionality that abstracts the issues of agent level communication above that imposed by the message transport protocol (MTP) implementations. See Fig. 1, below.

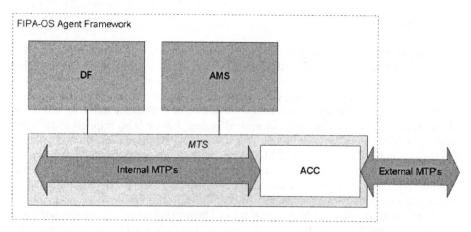

Fig. 1. The FIPA MAS Architecture

2.1.2   The FIPA-OS Implementation

FIPA-OS[2] is a component-based toolkit, enabling rapid development of FIPA compliant agents. The FIPA-OS agent platform is designed to supply the platform resources specified by FIPA, along with added functionality for assisting in the development of agents. The components of the FIPA-OS package provide standard components at both the platform and individual agent level; both components of the MAS architecture exactly implement the FIPA specifications.

The FIPA-OS agent shell allows an agent developer to manage the behaviour and communication of agents, without having to directly invoke message-sending methods or study low-level functions such as protocol management. The FIPA-OS agent shell uses a series of interfaces through which the agent kernel may access suitable components. This restricts access, at the agent level, only to the appropriate functions within the different components. Furthermore, this approach allows different implementations of the core components to be developed and used independently, providing flexibility in specific applications. The FIPA-OS agent shell augments the FIPA specifications with functionality to assist the developer in managing conversations and agent behaviour.

The platform components of FIPA-OS allow the transport and location of specified components of the FIPA framework. The internal MTPs of the FIPA-OS agent platform are implemented using the Sun JAVA Remote Method Invocation (RMI) system. The topology of this system is a client-server system through which the client may invoke methods on the server. A Naming Service is used to list and update references to different clients and servers. In the FIPA-OS platform, agents act as both servers and clients, allowing two-way communication between them. The role they take is dependent on the direction of communication between agents. To support this and to make it simpler for the user, a MTS object is included in the FIPA-OS agent shell, which handles the binding and unbinding to the NS.

---

[2] Available from: http://fipa-os.sf.net/ .

2.2   Issues

"How big is big" and "what does scaleable mean" in terms of defining the bounds of agent systems are commonly asked questions regarding MAS that are only just starting to be addressed. One view, being explored in the DIET project[4], is that MAS exist within [information] ecosystems and that the environmental constraints extant in the ecosystem acts to determine the degree of scalability inherent within any MAS. This view shows that, as in biological systems, there is an implicit relationship between a MAS and the environment that it exists within; however, this relationship largely constrains the definition of MAS scalability to the perception of considering it as an issue of canonical enumeration. Such quantitative discussions, whilst crucially important in many respects (particularly so with respect to devices capable of supporting only small footprint MAS), restrict the definition of what agent scalability *should* mean to an allegory of the problem of "how many angels fit on the head of a pin" that so entertained mediaeval philosophers. We define a broader scalability that considers other, qualitative, issues that relate to what it is that the agent, or the MAS that it exists within, is able to do and, moreover, how proficient they are in achieving what they are able to do.

2.2.1   Definitions Employed
All agents in the discussion presented here are virtual physical software entities that exist exclusively in computer networks; no consideration is given to actual physical agents, such as robots, or corporeal physical agents such, as human/animal delegates. Furthermore, these virtual physical software entities are static, not mobile entities. Static agents bring about remote change through influencing each other in exploiting their ability to communicate in a semantic language. The agents discussed exist only as part of a MAS and comply with the specifications laid down by FIPA, as implemented in the FIPA-OS agent toolkit.

2.2.2   Scope of Discussion
Scalability is regarded here in two contexts: where footprint is an issue, quantitative factors relating to the μFIPA-OS implementation are discussed, showing that where "size" is a crucial consideration in determining scalability within tightly constrained physical environments, novel tactics can be employed that ensure that behavioural, qualitative, aspects are diminished as little as possible. Where footprint is not an issue, the focus will be entirely upon the qualitative, behavioural aspects of agent scalability. In this discussion, relating to the full version of FIPA-OS, we will consider issues such as: communication propagation, service discovery and resource management. Furthermore, as collaboration between agents in a MAS is one of the key points in determining its success in delivering appropriate services, particular attention is paid to discussing the issues associated with service discovery. A case study follows that demonstrates how we propose to test the principles set down below, within the framework of the AgentCities project[3].

---

[3] Available at: http://www.agentcities.org/EUNET/index.php?target=welcome .

3   Communication Propagation

The paramount behaviour of an agent that exists within a MAS is that of semantic communication. In order to complete any but the most simple of tasks agents must rely on their abilities to "persuade" other agents to assist them. The semantics of agent communications are derived from the formal definitions of the communicative act that defines the type of message that the agent determines is appropriate

FIPA specifies a semantic model of communicative acts[5] that grounds the stated meanings of communicative acts and protocols in order that agents may attempt bring about changes in the belief states of other agents that will assist them in the tasks they have to complete. The abstract model that enables this type of interaction can be briefly described as: Agent i has amongst its *mental attitudes* some goal or objective *G* and some intention *I*. Deciding to satisfy *G*, the agent adopts a specific intention, *I*. If the agent is unable to achieve the goal itself, intention *I* manifests itself in the choice of an appropriate speech act and the construction of a message to another agent. The express purpose of this message is to achieve the intention of Agent i, through enlisting the help of Agent j. See Fig. 2.

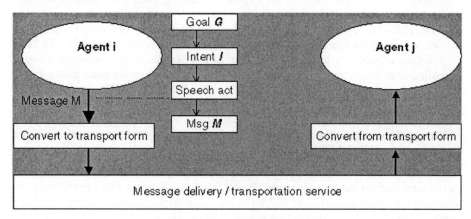

Fig. 2. Agent Message Passing

Typically agents possess incomplete knowledge within any particular problem domain and collaborate with each other to solve problems. Therefore, the communications within a typical MAS can be very intensive, especially when agents compete to deliver optimal services. Scalability issues associated with agent message handling can be addressed from two perspectives: the individual agent and the platform that supports the agent.

3.1   Agent Message Handling

FIPA classifies the following entities within the scope of message handling [5][6]:
- ACLMessage: A communication between two agents.
- Envelope: Every ACLMessage has an associated Envelope that contains message delivery information

☐ Conversation: A series of ACLMessages between two agents that are related (by either the conversation-id or reply-with/in-reply-to fields).

☐ Message Transport Service: Entity that provides ACLMessage delivery services based upon the properties defined by the ACLMessage's associated Envelope.

☐ Message Transport Protocol: Entity used by the MTS to transfer a message from one place to another.

☐ Agent Communication Channel: Entity that provides the MTS and acts as a gateway between FIPA platforms.

FIPA-OS provides the following components to handle these FIPA concepts [7]:

☐ ConversationManager: Provides conversation grouping and message protocol enforcement. At the expense of extra over-head in terms of message processing, this simplifies the development and debugging process for FIPA-OS agents.

☐ MTS (Message Transport Service): Provides ACLMessage delivery services. This is implemented as a stack containing multiple entities which modify/adjust the Envelope and ACLMessage (normally only to change encoding) as they pass through them. This stack arrangement allows different facets of the FIPA-defined MTS behaviour to be decomposed into individual entities, as well as simplifying addition of new behaviours, at the expense of adding extra over-head to message processing.

☐ MTPs (Message Transport Protocols): There are several implementations of MTPs, some of which are specified by FIPA, others are proprietary to FIPA-OS. An MTP generally consists of a mini-server that listens for incoming messages using a particular protocol, and a client that can send messages using the same protocol.

☐ ACC (Agent Communication Channel): The FIPA-OS ACC implementation assumes that the ACC exists on one physical host, and primarily acts as a gateway between platforms or agents on the same platform using mutually exclusive MTPs. Inter-platform messaging is already catered for within the MTS instance each agent encapsulates via the MTPs it contains.

In order for agents on the same platform to communicate with each other, naming services for each of the proprietary MTPs are used, this assumes that agents know the location of the naming services. FIPA-OS allows multiple naming-services per MTP type to be used. Ensuring there is no single point of failure at this level reinforces the robustness of the agent location mechanism. An agent will be registered with each naming service it knows about, and will search each in turn to locate an agent on the local platform. This process is recognised as potentially posing a scalability issue in terms of the time taken to resolve the entity that is to receive a particular message. FIPA-OS MTPs automatically cache name-service resolution results however, so only the initial message/response in a conversation or set of conversations might require either of the agents to perform a lookup.

3.2   FIPA-OS Platform Agents

A FIPA-compliant system such as FIPA-OS provides supporting services to an agent in the form of the mandatory agent management functions specified by FIPA [8] which are provided by the:

☐ AMS which manages agent lifecycles on a platform, and provides a white-pages directory service.

☐ DF which provides a yellow pages directory service.

Although FIPA caters for the provision of multiple instances of these types of Agents, it is implicit that there is only a single instance of the AMS and the DF with a reserved name on a platform, simplifying the process of resolving the names of these Agents. As a consequence FIPA-OS provides a single instance of the AMS and DF on a platform by default but does not limit the number of instances to a single occurrence of each type of agent.

This simplification diminishes the robustness and scalability of the FIPA model due to the fact that a single point of failure is introduced within a platform for AMS and DF services. Despite the fact that scalability is catered for through delegation to other AMS and DF instances, this remains an issue since the reserved agent names used for these agents are used as an initial contact point to locate the delegated AMS and DF instances. Therefore, these agents can still be considered as single points of failure.

3.3   Proposed Solutions

To remove the AMS and DF as central points of failure, FIPA-OS might be enhanced to avoid this issue by providing a fallback mechanism to automatically attempt to locate and use the services of other AMS/DF agents on the platform, not merely those with the reserved name for AMS or DF. This might involve the use of well-known secondary DF and AMS names that can be defined as part of the policy for the platform in order to remove this single point of failure.

To remove the ACC as a central point of failure, multiple distributed ACCs offering identical services could be introduced to the implementation to provide the same functionality as the single centralised entity, but for a sub-set of the agent platform (i.e. localised agents – on the same host/LAN). Alternatively additional distributed ACCs could be introduced to serve the entire agent platform. In either scenario the ability to have multiple ACC instances with configurable deployment locations and access mechanisms would resolve this bottleneck issue. An agent platform would simply publicise the MTP addresses of all ACCs to ensure that the handling of incoming messages is given the same level of redundancy as outgoing messages, where an ACC is necessary for inter-platform communication.

4.   Service Discovery

FIPA-OS agents advertise and discover service offerings, in accordance with the FIPA specifications, on the yellow pages service offered by the directory facilitator (DF) [8]. A local DF, when attempting to satisfy a service request made by an agent, can search federations of remote DFs. Search algorithms must be carefully chosen in order that MAS searching algorithms do not place constraints upon the scalability of the DF federation. It is anticipated that, as agent systems become more pervasive, a power-law degree distribution will evolve between elements in these large-scale networks and, moreover, that it will be between the platform DFs where any service level conflicts will emerge between platform implementations. The p2p nature of the FIPA-OS platform is important, and the ability of any platform to provide any service must remain implicit within the overall MAS concept. In its present form, FIPA-OS efficiently implements a simple broadcast search algorithm, which is acceptable in normal Poisson distribution networks and which we explore below.

4.1   Broadcast Search Method

The agents (DF) used in the propagation of a search may be represented as the nodes of a graph and categorised as follows[9]:
☐ Source node: a node from which a search is being instigated, or from which a current search is being propagated.
☐ Destination node: a vertex, which satisfies the constraints of the propagating search.
☐ Relay node: a node which is neither a source nor destination node, but through which the search propagates from source to destination.

Consider a single search starting from the source node, s; the search destination nodes, D, form a subset of the total network, V;

$$D \in . \{ V - s \} ,\tag{1}$$

as do the relay vertices, R,

$$R \in . \{ V - D - s \} .\tag{2}$$

Therefore, it must be the case that:

$$D \cap R = 0, s \notin . D, s \notin . R .\tag{3}$$

For any successful search, the proportion, P_v, of the network, V, searched is provided by the equation:

$$P_v = \frac{|R| + |D|}{|V|} .\tag{4}$$

For iterative searches, discrete time steps must be introduced to the calculations. The number of active vertices, A, at any time, t, in a broadcast search can be characterised as:

$$A[t+1] = \sum_{A[t]} k .\tag{5}$$

Assuming that the re-searching of a node is considered as a new search, the proportion of the network searched at any step of the broadcast search is:

$$P[t+1] = \frac{|A[t+1]|}{|V|} + P[t], \quad A[0] = s. \tag{6}$$

The significance of this is that for a deep search it is possible to search more than 100% of the network before reaching all destinations. The broadcast mechanism used in the FIPA-OS search allows for this possibility but it is clearly inefficient and not a scalable solution.

4.2   The Highest Degree Alternative

It is expected that networks will evolve away from Poisson distribution to Power-law distribution of the nodes as Agent systems become more pervasive. So we need to discover other more scalable solutions to the service discovery problem if the task of searching for services is going to be maintained within bounds that ensure acceptable degrees of success without consuming vastly disproportionate quantities of system resources.

If a node in a model (thought of as an agent in the FIPA-OS context) possesses a degree that is a measure of the possible connections (message load) that the node supports at any one time, then it should follow that some nodes in an agent system have higher degree than others due to the popularity of the services they offer. A number of studies [9] of real, large-scale networks show that the distribution of degrees is asymmetric across large-scale networks, and that the Poisson distribution represented in the broadcast algorithm is inaccurate. The trend towards there being a large number of low-degree nodes has been observed in the Gnutella network and the Internet [9]. The asymmetric degree distribution reflects the use of the network as a marketplace where services are sought for consumption. Most nodes of the network are interested in the consumption of services rather than the provision of resources and services, hence the consuming nodes do not have as many outgoing connections along which to provide services or to link with other service providers. A more realistic mathematical model for large-scale networks is a power-law degree probability distribution, which exponentially decays as degree increases.

The highest degree algorithm is a search algorithm that converges on the few high degree nodes within the network in order to distribute a search more efficiently [10]. The highest degree search mechanism allows searches to be routed through the small percentage of the network nodes, which have a large number of registrations and connections. The advantages of using the highest degree mechanism are the reduced network resources used in the search and the reduction of the probability of flooding the network on a search request. It should be made clear that the searches which result from this algorithm can take considerably more steps than the broadcast algorithm currently being used in the FIPA-OS platform, and that the search algorithm is less robust than the broadcast algorithm, since its propagation is dependent on up-to-date network information. The highest degree algorithm is represented thus:

$$p_k = C * k^{-\tau} * e^{-\frac{k}{K}}. \tag{7}$$

Where p_k is the degree probability, C is a normalisation constant [see (8)], k is the degree of outgoing connections at that node, • is a constant which determines the decay of the graph and $e^{-k/K}$ is the exponential cutoff term. n.b. K determines the size of the largest component in the network, and assures that the degree will not exceed the size of this giant component. Results from the analysis of real large-scale networks show values of • ~ 2.1→3 [9]. The exponential cutoff term is observed in real large-scale networks such as the Gnutella file-share network. The normalisation constant is derived by:

$$C = \frac{1}{\sum_{k=1}^{N} k^{-\tau} * e^{-\frac{k}{K}}} \tag{8}$$

The normalisation constant is introduced to ensure that results generated during scaling tests on limited test suites reflect the conditions likely to pertain in large-scale industrial deployments of FIPA-OS agent communities.

4.3   A Comparison of the Two Search Algorithms

Simulated testing of FIPA-OS platforms have been conducted with networks of platforms, search connected at the default DF node. These nodes were configured in a network of 1000 nodes with a maximum degree of 100. The Poisson distribution, for the broadcast algorithm, is shown in the top pane of Fig. 3 and the power-law distribution, for the highest degree algorithm, is shown in the bottom pane. The highest degree algorithm uses values of • = 2.1 and K = 0.5, both of which have been measured in current large scale peer networks [9].

Comparing the two elements of Figure 3 it can be seen that the probability of conducting successful searches is significantly increased when implementing highest degree searching algorithms. Moreover, that success is achieved with a much-reduced impact in terms of the search degree. The highest degree searching algorithms can, therefore, be shown to be considerably more tolerant in terms of MAS scalability than simple broadcast searches.

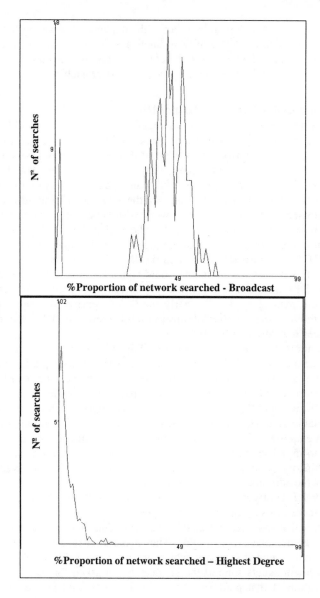

Fig. 3. Network proportions searched for broadcast (Top) and highest degree (Bottom)

4.3   Local Broadcast Search

A simpler alternative to implementing the non-scalable broadcast search in a power-law distribution environment is to define a decay function to the life expectancy of the search. This function will constrain the number of hops that the search can propagate over and, thus limit the network impact of the search to just the local domain. A Random Walk function applied to such a technique would further reduce the resource consumption associated with searching but at the expense of retaining local awareness of neighbour node degree. Scalability in such a system would be ensured through restraining the likelihood of unwanted network conditions extant in local network domains but at the cost of reducing the success factors of each search.

4.4   Belief Based Selection of Partner DF

The capability to "know" which DF to request services from would dramatically reduce the time and messaging overheads associated with any search. However, MAS are p2p communities and apriori knowledge of this type is just not possible due to the dynamic nature of such communities. Any such capability would require the maintenance of local knowledge regarding an agent's observations of other DF interactions with service agents, alternatively the DFs could form ad-hoc hierarchies to support knowledge based service discovery with super-DFs maintaining databases of information regarding which DFs, in its sphere of influence, have which services registered with them. In such a solution agents would make a service discovery request to a DF in the normal manner and the DF, if it were unable to find a service agent that satisfies the request by itself, would contact a super-DF to determine which of the nearby DFs have suitable services registered with them. Although this does introduce extra messaging in the early parts of service finding algorithms, it dramatically reduces the number of unsuccessful queries to DFs that do not have suitable services registered with them.

To allow automatic registration between DFs a system is required which will provide the needful DF with information for registration with platforms that are of interest. There is currently no mechanism for this employed within FIPA-OS. The simplest solution to this involves a service that will provide information on the available platforms and DFs within the network. To supply such information requires a series of reliable platforms and services, which will run 24:7 and provide non-biased listings for an enquiring DF. A system employing super-DFs will employ profiles that may be used to initialise the DFs in the system, some of which will be predefined as defaults within the community, while other entries could be configured and determined by the administrator of the platform.

If the super DF configuration is not chosen then limits should be imposed on the number of remote registrations a DF may perform, in order to limit the number of remote searches that may be sent to the platform. This will decrease the number of unnecessary searches that are serviced. The registration of a DF with a remote DF that will frequently send it searches which are not serviceable by the platform (i.e. none of the resident agents support the services being asked for) is a hindrance to the optimum operation of that platform. The local DF will need to use its resources to service a search request and all its ensuing communications for which there is no real advantage for the platform. In a competitive market, where there are a number of different commercial services in the market at different prices, time spent servicing a search request that will *definitely* not lead to a contract is a waste of resources (unless the search service itself is charged for). It would be useful to have a mechanism by which the local DF can identify the DFs it will get the most from being registered with and retain them within its registry. However, this facility could also be easily grounded at a Super-DF, as an enhanced composite solution, through the classification of its entries and the classification of a search. The Super-DF matches a list of entries to the search, and returns a shortlist (depending on how many results are requested) to the requesting local DF. This requires that each end DF has a description of itself with which to register, that will describe the services that are available to it. Through this type of classification, groups are formed naturally by the DFs as they register with other relevant platforms, thus alleviating the search propagation problem.

This solution may seem similar to the concept of index-serving databases for network information, which is already commonplace in the Internet, and is not in keeping with the p2p nature of the agent paradigm. However, the application of indexes and centralised search engines has already been applied to other p2p technologies such as the Napster music fileshare system. Moreover, the central service in an agent system is *not* being used as a server or as a hierarchical gateway to resources. The service is only used to find platforms that offer the services required, and any communication after the initial search is performed directly between the two platforms or agents.

5   Resource Management Scalability

In this short section we discuss one of the fundamental and most intractable of all of the issues regarding MAS scalability: that of quantity versus quality in a MAS's characteristics. Moreover, we examine the issues concerning how best to distribute a MAS across a network environment.

5.1   Behavioural Enhancement Costs

In terms of defining the benefits of deploying agent systems the main feature is that agents autonomously solve complex problems on behalf of a user. This implies that agents act in an environment and perform tasks that bring about desirable changes for the benefit of other entities. Therefore, at a minimum, an agent within a community must be able to do something: ideally, something useful. To think of deploying an agent in a MAS that does nothing other than hold conversations but not act upon them is depriving the system of valuable resources. At the other extreme, an agent capable performing any task required of it would be very likely to require the support of hardware systems that are no longer affordable to most potential consumers of a MAS. The costs associated with the behavioural enhancement of an agent, versus the cost associated with host resources must always be considered… is the gain worth the pain? In the worst cases an agent that does everything required of it may not be deployable on the target host and techniques such as those discussed in section 7, may be required to be deployed in designing a suitable MAS. In other even more constrained situations, sub optimality may be the only solution.

However, what is also very clear is the fact that an agent that does nothing is useless and does not deserve to consume the resources of its host. So the conundrum is this; how do we measure the relationship between the utility of the agent and the resources it is likely to consume? Agents existing at or near the extremes are easy to discriminate between; however, agents falling in the middle ground are much more difficult to deal with. A methodology for determining the cost/value relationship between resource consumption and agent ability must be designed; one that can weigh qualitative, behavioural issues against quantitative resource consumption issues.

5.2   Size of Platform

How do we best distribute agents within a MAS, on one large platform or on several smaller scale platforms? Before we discuss this further it is worth noting that we should consider the activity levels of agents as also being a factor in determining the scalability of agent systems. During protracted periods of system tests of the FIPA-OS platform it has been noticed that during periods of intense activity (periods of aggressive n-to-n negotiations for instance) memory consumption rises rapidly. Investigation has revealed that this is caused by garbage collection dependencies in the VM. Therefore, when measuring the optimality of a MAS community, not only is the number and behavioural capability of the agents to be considered but also the current degree to which they are meeting the extent of that behavioural capability. In other words, whilst it may be possible to launch four agents in a community on a device, when working hard in their respective roles it might be possible that only two could actually act at any one time due to the resource consumption of the other agents. The additional overhead associated with this feature is related to the messaging activities required to achieve any required result. The cost of an agent is not just measured in terms of its memory footprint but also in terms of its messaging activity and the resulting garbage collection activity required in freeing memory consumed by dead conversations.

In a FIPA compliant agent system all external communications are routed through the ACC; therefore, one big platform could be considered to be a better architectural solution to MAS design. However, it is most unlikely that only one platform would exist on its own; therefore, external communications are still required even in the single very large platform situation. As a result of the number of agents likely to be present on a very large platform, we must consider the effects of the ACC bottleneck problem. The ACC "bottleneck" has already been discussed in section 3 where it was suggested that a distribution of the ACC functionality was required within a MAS to overcome this problem. It was suggested that the level of distribution might become as high as 1 – 1 with each agent; however, if this was the case (at any level of ACC distribution) incomplete knowledge of message routing would result. Therefore, in the distributed ACC solution a higher degree of collaboration is required in order to route messages (forwarding, etc) and messaging overhead increases.

In the case of small MAS communities on a platform much of the issues regarding ACC bottlenecks are overcome but the reliance on slow interoperability protocols (such as IIOP) being used in routine transactions now become a feature of the problem. The optimality of agent communities in terms of size (agent and MAS), ability and activity levels, is an area of recommended investigation in the AgentCities project. The evolution from a small scale MAS, developed in one research project, into an element in a large scale MAS, is discussed as a case study in section 6, below.

6   The AgentCities Project

The CRUMPET[4] project is developing a service environment that will generically integrate the traditional Internet and wireless services to provide information and services for a heterogeneous, modern tourist population. CRUMPET provides information and services accessible from any location by different devices and different network connectivity allowing the user to prepare a journey and plan activities during that journey, or at the destination. To achieve these goals CRUMPET applies a multi-agent system based on FIPA-OS with agents that provide content, adapt content based on terminal or network constraints and enable value-add services such as planning a tour of a town. The CRUMPET service aims to provide a service for users roaming between London, Heidelberg and Helsinki and thus implements what could be seen as a subset of the AgentCities network of agent platform nodes.

The goal of the AgentCities project is to establish a network of agents running on different platform implementations, owned by different organisations from around the world. On each platform node a variety of agents can be supported, such as the fundamental agent management service agents as specified by FIPA (white and yellow pages), ontology services and domain specific application agents (such as the service agents produced by the CRUMPET project to enable personalised, localised tourism solutions). The basis for interoperability between all these distributed agents will be the FIPA agent standards [11].

Currently there are 26 individual platform nodes in the AgentCities network spanning US, Europe, Japan, Australia and New Zealand. Each platform supports the FIPA defined AMS and DF, plus a Ping Agent that is able to validate the communication channel between platform nodes. At present the DFs for each platform node are not federated as described earlier in this text, instead the MAS relies on a single global DF.

Although the number of nodes in the AgentCities network is unlikely to grow to the size simulated in the work described in this text, it still provides an excellent testbed for validating these initial experiments and the scalability of the CRUMPET project.

7.   μFIPA-OS Scalability

Personal Digital Assistants (PDAs) and other small devices have become popular in recent years and currently have enough processing power to support middleware solutions, such as Java-based solutions. This progress in hardware motivates the use of high-level processes on small devices, processes such as those enabled by software agent technology. This section examines μFIPA-OS developed by the University of Helsinki, which is a toolkit and platform for small devices derived from the FIPA-OS system.

Agent software scalability on small devices can be addressed from many directions; in terms of functionality, the partitioning of functionality, and coping with

---

[4] For further details on the IST project CRUMPET (IST-1999-20147) see http://www.ist-crumpet.org/ .

the heterogeneous hardware available. We present the Java-based µFIPA-OS, which is able to host a number of FIPA agents and executing AMS and DF on the terminal. It has support for FIPA-OS tasks and conversations and agents that are programmed for FIPA-OS can be executed on µFIPA-OS with certain limitations. To promote scalability the system has support for minimal agents that do not use FIPA-OS tasks and conversations.

7.1 Scalability Issues

The term scalability encompasses several meanings depending on the context where it is used. Generally, in distributed systems scalability means that a system can cope with the addition of sites and users without excess cost, loss of performance or complexity. However, in the context of small devices we are interested in scaling down a system, providing the existing services in a new different environment. By scalability, in the context of µFIPA-OS, we mean the ability of the system to adapt to environments of different sizes and intensities, of physical or software resources.

Increasing and decreasing functionality based on user, agent and terminal requirements can improve agent scalability. For example, application programmers might require full FIPA-OS functionality on a high-end PDA, but require only the core-messaging capability on a lower-end device and place the computationally heavy parts on the network. Moreover, developers may want to write their own task and conversation management routines to improve performance and garbage collection.

Interoperability between agent systems can improve scalability by allowing network access to standards-compliant resources. This allows the distribution of functionality across the agent domain; it is not necessary for the local device or platform to host all the services. The same approach can be used in intra-platform operation as well; closed solutions may offer more performance, for example an internal communication protocol may be tuned for more optimal use of bandwidth or system resources than, for example, a FIPA-specified message transport protocol[5].

Scalability down to very limited environments can be achieved by implementing a minimal user interface component that communicates with a more advanced component on the network that translates requests and mediates services to end clients. This kind of solution places the burden on the network rather than the client.

Various middleware solutions can be employed to increase the scalability of software. The Java language is currently being introduced into the embedded world, and different development environments and deployment solutions have become available both from companies such as Sun Microsystems, and open source initiatives such as Kaffe [12]. The key benefits of Java are portability of the interpreted byte code and ease of development, with the expense of performance and memory requirements. Although Java promises to reduce development costs when developing software for heterogeneous hardware, it is not suitable for all purposes [13], [14], because of issues in performance and memory consumption. Although the Java virtual machine promotes portability across a wide variety of devices, it introduces an extra memory overhead and the problems of indeterminist garbage collection. C and

---

[5] FIPA specifies only interoperability standards for external platform protocols.

C++ offer much better performance and memory handling albeit with the cost of being less portable.

There are several Java virtual machine specifications targeting different requirements. The choice of the Java specification affects performance, memory footprint, portability and reuse of code. The older PersonalJava-specification aimed at PDA devices has both open-source and commercial implementations available [15]. The newer Java 2 Micro Edition (J2ME) introduces several configurations targeted at PDA-devices and mobile phones. The Connected Device Configuration (CDC) is aimed at PDAs with good connectivity and is complemented by different profiles. PersonalJava is supported in J2ME through the use of CDC and PersonalProfile. Moreover, the Connected Limited Device Configuration (CLDC) has been designed for lower-end devices such as smart phones [14] that are characterized with sporadic connections. The performance and operation of software agents on small devices can be improved by supporting:

• Scalability through compile-time or startup-time configuration; what modules and what functionality is required by the agent or agents. Unnecessary classes and unnecessary processing should be avoided.
• Scalability through placing functionality on the network by using either internal or standards-compliant means. At extreme this means that there is only a user interface running on the terminal and the functionality is on the network.
• Portability, scalability supported by a virtual machine and virtual machine specification.

7.2   Design and Implementation

μFIPA-OS is a scaled down version of FIPA-OS and simplifies the implementation of the FIPA-OS interfaces. FIPA-OS employs software-engineering techniques that do not scale well to resource-constrained environments [13]. From the resource management viewpoint issues such as parsing, the use of threads, object creation, and the use of the Java reflection API [14] create overhead. The use of heavy communication standards such as CORBA and RMI add to the overhead, RMI for example is not efficient in wireless environments.

Basically, μFIPA-OS uses the same interfaces with the exception of the transport mechanism, which has been optimized for the embedded environment. Each FIPA-OS agent has its own transport stack and transport service objects, which is not sensible in resource-constrained environments. A new component called the multiplexer maintains the μFIPA-OS transports and encapsulates services. Thus, the μFIPA-OS transports are not compatible with FIPA-OS transports without modifications. μFIPA-OS does not support RMI or CORBA, but by default uses either an internal HTTP transport or the FIPA specified HTTP protocol for interoperability.

PersonalJava was chosen as the Java programming environment and as the virtual machine. In addition to PersonalJava and proprietary lightweight Java implementations, it is also possible to execute μFIPA-OS on CDC, and standard Java 1.1 and 1.3 on Linux. CLDC was found to be too limiting for the requirements of the FIPA-OS API and since the PersonalProfile for CDC was not available at the time.

μFIPA-OS agents are programmed in the same way as FIPA-OS agents, using tasks and conversations. μFIPA-OS supports a number of agents on the small devices, the sharing of transports and resource pools, and the possibility for local communication. However, tasks, conversations and local messaging present an extra layer of overhead.

μFIPA-OS addresses the scalability of agent implementations by supporting two APIs for creating agents; first there is the FIPA-OS API and then the minimal API, which supports only plain messaging and each agent needs to explicitly implement the management of messages. Although task and conversation management components have been optimised in μFIPA-OS, each layer adds to the overhead. Fig. 4. presents examples of the FIPA-OS agent stack and the μFIPA-OS agent stack. A factory object is responsible for the configuration of an agent and the initialisation of correct management components.

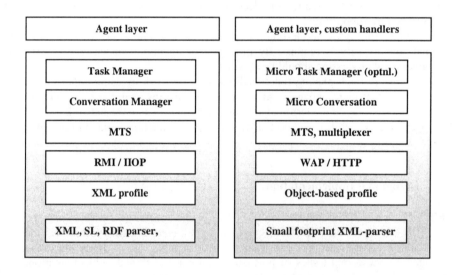

Fig. 4. Two concrete realisations using pluggable components.   The left stack represents a traditional FIPA-OS agent and the right stack depicts the μFIPA-OS equivalent.

Minimal agents use the same parsers and messaging features of the μFIPA-OS, including transports, but they do not use conversations or tasks. Messages are directly delivered to the corresponding callback methods and agent programmers have to implement the necessary behaviour. This enables the programmer to create thinner agents and custom functionality.

μFIPA-OS agents can be deployed using two different scenarios.   In the first scenario, μFIPA-OS is a part of a greater platform and the FIPA platform agents AMS and DF are running on the fixed network. In the second scenario, μFIPA-OS is running an independent agent platform and hosts the AMS and DF. The first scenario necessitates that μFIPA-OS and the agent platform are using the same internal transport (which can be also a FIPA specified protocol) and that the agent platform is able to forward messages to the mobile node. The latter scenario requires that the μFIPA-OS is running a FIPA compatible transport and able to receive messages and forward them to the proper agents.

8 Conclusions

Scalability in MAS is not just a factor determined through counting the number of agents resident on a platform within in any particular hardware environment. Other qualitative issues are also crucially important and we have suggested that a methodology should be developed, or extended, to identify benefits and losses associated with enhancing agent behaviour against deploying larger numbers of agents within a MAS. We, furthermore, identified the need for this methodology to take into account the potential states of an agent during its entire lifecycle: running agents consume more resources than resting agents.

In terms of scaling up a FIPA compliant MAS it will become necessary to remove the AMS and DF as central points of failure. The provision of a fallback mechanism to automatically locate the services of other AMS/DF agents on the platform rather than merely those with the reserved name for AMS or DF will ensure this and could involve use of well-known secondary DF and AMS names which are defined as platform policy. Decentralised communication mechanisms remove "server-like" dependencies from ACC. Removing the ACC as a central point of failure would be enabled through introducing multiple distributed ACCs that offer identical services. To ensure the continued interoperability of platforms, an agent platform would simply publicise the MTP addresses of all ACCs to ensure that the handling of incoming messages is given the same level of redundancy as outgoing messages.

Service discovery issues related to MAS scalability could be overcome through deploying sophisticated, knowledge based routing of search requests between DFs. Peer classification of agents should be considered, in order to alleviate the effects of power-law distribution, as the number of consumers in the network becomes disproportionately larger than the number of service providers, this will lead to ad-hoc hierarchies of DFs relieving searching issues in peered environments. Knowledge based routing using highest degree searches in power law distribution networks offers the most effective long term solution; however, random walk may offer the same benefits in localised network domains, during the migration from normal Poisson to power law distributions.

Within constrained devices, design considerations should take into account the potential for the provision of remote behaviours, relieving the performance bottleneck of the device. Such a small, inexpensive, nomadic device could appear to offer the same degree of ability, in terms of service offerings, as a more expensive device by exploiting services hosted in less constrained regions of a network. This would be achieved through using different agent configurations based on the environment, placing part of the functionality or all of the functionality on the fixed network and taking advantage of the emerging middleware solutions that enable the execution of high-level languages across heterogeneous platforms. μFIPA-OS supports, with minor modifications, the execution of FIPA-OS agents in such environments. However, the price of this portability is an increased demand for network resources, particularly in wireless environments, and reduced performance.

References

1. Jennings, NR., Nicholas, R., Sycara, K., Wooldridge, M.: A Roadmap To Agent Research and Development. Kluwer Academic Publishers, Norwell and Dordrecht.
2. Ferber, J.: Multi-Agent Systems: An Introduction to Distributed Artificial Intelligence. Addison Wesley, Reading and Harlow.
3. Hermans, B.: Intelligent Software Agents on the Internet. Tilburg University Press, Tilburg.
4. Marrow, P.: Scalability in Mutli-Agent Systems: The DIET Project. Available online at: http://www.cs.cf.ac.uk/User/O.F.Rana/agents2001/papers/17_marrow.pdf
5. FIPA.: Communicative Acts Specifications. FIPA, Available online at: http://209.61.157.155/specs/fipa00023/XC00023H.html
6. FIPA.: Agent Message Transport Specifications. FIPA, Available online at: http://209.61.157.155/repository/transportspecs.html
7. Emorphia.: FIPA-OS Developers Guide. Emorphia, Available online at: http://fipa-os.sourceforge.net/docs/Developers_Guide.pdf
8. FIPA.: Agent Management Specifications. FIPA, Available online at: http://209.61.157.155/specs/fipa00037/XC00037H.html
9. Lada A. Adamic, Rajan M. Lukose, Amit R. Puniyani and Bernardo A. Huberman: Search in Power Law Networks. , Physical Review E, The American Physical Society, Volume 64, 26 September 2001, Available online at: http://www.hpl.hp.com/shl/papers/plsearch/PRE46135.pdf
10. Moore, T.: Large-Scale Multi-Agent Systems an Analysis and Proposal. Available on request from: Dept of Electronics, University of York.
11. Willmott, et al. "Agentcities: A Worldwide Open Agent Network", Agentlink News. Issue 8, November 2001.
12. Transvirtual Technologies: Kaffe virtual machine. Available online at: http://www.kaffe.org
13. Laukkanen, M., Tarkoma, S., Leinonen, J.: FIPA-OS Agent Platform for Small-footprint Devices. In: John-Jules Meyer and Milind Tambe, editors, Pre-proceedings of the Eighth International Workshop on Agent Theories, Architectures, and Languages (ATAL-2001), pages 314-325, August 2001
14. Sun Microsystems: Java 2 Micro Edition homepage, 2001. Available online at: http://java.sun.com/j2me/
15. Sun Microsystems: PersonalJava technology White Paper, version 1.2, 2000

Agents and MAS in STaMs

Jim Doran

Department of Computer Science, University of Essex,
Colchester, UK, CO4 3SL,
doraj@essex.ac.uk

Abstract. We propose an abstract mathematical model of space and time within which to study agents, multi-agent systems and their environments. The model is unusual in three ways: an attempt is made to reduce the structure and behaviour of agents and their environment to the properties of the "matter" of which they are composed, a "block time" perspective is taken rather than a "past/present/future" perspective, and the emphasis is placed on discovering agents within the model, rather than on designing agents into it. The model is developed in a little semi-formal detail, some relevant experimental computational results are reported, and questions prompted by the model are discussed.

1 Introduction

The attempt to design intelligent machines has long been dominated by two broad approaches: the *symbolic* and the *connectionist* (e.g. [12,13]). The symbolic approach is high-level and emphasises rationality and thus mathematical logic, with the digital computer as the natural tool. Its little brother is theoretically disreputable, but sometimes effective, *ad hoc programming*: "let's just try to write a program that does X". The connectionist approach is low level and concentrates on building and analysing artificial neural networks with certain functionalities akin to those of the brain, particularly those of control, learning and generalisation. Although research within these paradigms over the past 50 years has been very extensive, many feel that less of substance has been achieved than has often been hoped or predicted. However, a new and promising paradigm has recently emerged in the literature, with an emphasis on complexity theory, and on a particular class of *dynamic systems* and associated concepts (state space, attractors, interdependence expressed by differential equations) as the key to understanding intelligence and cognition [2,4]. Furthermore, the idea of *evolutionary* learning and development has become very influential.

Against this background, we propose and develop in this paper a line of attack on the problem of understanding intelligence, agenthood and multiple agent systems (MAS) that has linkage with all of the "paradigms" just mentioned but does not fall neatly within any one of them. This line of attack embodies three main ideas. The first is to seek to understand agents (including "intelligent" agents) and multiple agent

M. d'Inverno et al. (Eds.): UKMAS 1996–2000, LNAI 2403, pp. 131–151, 2002.

systems not in terms of their formal abilities to manipulate meaningful symbols, or in terms of networks of simple computing elements with supposed similarities to the neural structure of the brain, but rather in terms of their underlying material structure and its properties. The approach is therefore strongly reductionist. The advantage of adopting such an approach is that the approach is natural (existing agents, after all, are material), that it enables a rich array of questions to be addressed in an integrated way, and that it prevents the intervention of intermediate high-level concepts with their confusing propensity both to be ambiguous and to take on a controversial intellectual life of their own. In particular, it tends to guard against the confusions that, we suggest, frequently flow from anthropocentrism and from matter/mind dualism.

Secondly, we employ the concept of "block" space-time. Familiar enough in space-time physics where as Minkowski space-time it is a foundation stone of the theory of general relativity, this concept has rarely seemed relevant in artificial intelligence work. However, in the model to be presented we seek an objective perspective, and "block-time" avoids the anthropocentrism inherent in the notion of "now", with its confusing connotation of a fixed past and an open future.

Finally, we seek not to design agents, but to *recognise* them. The aim is to observe and understand what can be there, rather than to specify what must be there. This is an unusual focus and its advantage is that it opens a door to aspects of agenthood that would not be encountered by using current agent design ideas. In particular, it makes it easier to recognise possibilities intermediate between conceptually distinct extremes, and to avoid our being "locked into" agents that are either useful or lifelike.

All three of these ideas tend to make the investigation simpler and more precise, avoiding a multitude of higher-level analytic concepts, and thus limiting the impact of misleading habitual preconceptions.

Much of the analysis of the model will be in terms of *condition-consequence rules* that will be derived from its particular structure. At first sight the use of rules in this form may seem an arbitrary limitation, but it should be noted that such rules are central elements of Turing Machines and are computationally very powerful. Furthermore, in the way that we shall use them, these rules also generalise important types of artificial neurone, so that the model to be presented is much more closely related to artificial neural networks, and indeed to cellular automata and to Boolean and multi-state networks, than may at first appear.

1.1 The Research Programme

Consider the following multi-stage investigation:
1. Select an abstract mathematical structure for use as a model of a space-time-matter continuum.
2. Examine how to detect and describe regularities within the structure.
3. Give a precise definition of an agent, consistent with our intuitions of agenthood, and examine how agents may be algorithmically detected within the structure.
4. Consider how particular agents within the structure may be examined algorithmically to establish whether or not they are in a defined sense "deliberative".

5. Consider multi-agent interaction and communication, including complexities that flow from adopting a block-time perspective.
6. Seek a coherent definition of an atemporal agent.

In the remainder of this paper this research programme will be taken through each of its six stages in a little detail. From the outset it seems important to recognise that although the technical development of the model is in principle quite precise -- a mathematical structure is specified and its properties investigated – its significance, if any, as a model of the actual space-time we inhabit is clearly a matter for assessment and even, in principle, empirical test. We shall return briefly to these issues in the final discussion.

2   A Simple Model of Space, Time and Matter

We work in terms of a simple, discrete model of a space, time and matter manifold that we call a "STaM" (for "Space, Time and Matter").

Definition. A *STaM* is an N-dimensional finitely bounded integer vector space, S, with a mapping from its elements to elements of a set M. For our purposes it is sufficient to assume a suitable inner product defined over S so that it is (at least) locally Euclidean. The elements of the set M correspond notionally to a finite enumeration of different possible states of matter.[1]

Intuitively a STaM is a space-time region, with (discrete) locations identified by integer N-tuples (Cartesian coordinates), and with a matter state associated with each location. In computational terms, a STaM could be a regular multi-dimensional array of fixed values over an arbitrary enumerated type (the matter states).

One dimension of the STaM is naturally taken to be temporal and directed, past to future, and the remaining dimensions to be spatial (but see Section 7). This straightforwardly gives a temporal sequence of spatial *STaM states*. Thus a physically intuitive example of a STaM is a 4D rectangular cuboid or "block", with one dimension interpreted as time. In this case, the STaM states are 3D "spatial" cuboids. However, it is sometimes simpler to think in terms merely of a two spatial dimensions, with time as a third dimension – a 3D cuboid. And then, to avoid uninteresting complications associated with boundaries, we may even "join up" the boundaries of the 3D cuboids so that it becomes finite but unbounded – a ring of tori.

We shall refer to the *locations*[2] of the STaM and their *(location-) states (of matter)*. Note also that by a *spatial location* we shall mean not one specific location in the STaM, but rather a sequence of successive locations with the same spatial coordinates

---

[1] A STaM can be seen as a special and very simple case of the space-time manifold, with a distribution of matter-energy-momentum over it, which lies at the heart of general relativity theory (see, for example, [7]). We are, in effect, assuming a "flat", discrete, matter-containing space-time. However, our reasons for wishing to consider space and time as a whole have nothing to do with relativity theory.

[2] We avoid the commonly used term "event" as liable to confuse in this context.

and extended in the temporal dimension. For brevity we shall usually refer to a spatial location as an *S-location*.

2.1 Regularities and Rules in STaMs

If we consider an arbitrary STaM, it may or may not have regularities within it, and any regularities there are may be of many different kinds. There are two contrasting views we may take of a STaM and of any regularities within it. We may (a) take the STaM as the primary given, and inspect it to see what regularities we can discover within it, or we may (b) regard the STaM as *generated* by some known or unknown prior process, for example, a set of generative rules, so that regularities within the STaM flow from the nature of the generating process. Alternative (a) invites the discovery of regularities within the given STaM, and a natural question is: what rule sets or other process could generate this STaM? Alternative (b), typically presumes that generative rules are given, as is the case with cellular automata, binary networks, and multi-state networks, and the natural question is: what are the properties of the generator and what STaMs could it generate? Contrary to our subjective experience suggesting that space-time is generated and, furthermore, generated "in" a temporal direction as we experience it, *we shall focus upon alternative (a)*.

We assume that regularities, however discovered, are to be expressed in the form of *condition* ➔ *consequence* rules that specify the matter state of a particular location by reference to certain earlier (i.e. temporally preceding) location states, without use of spatial variables. We allow conjunctions, but not disjunctions, on both the LHS and the RHS. Thus a typical rule might be

$$<4,4,t>:p \ \& \ <4,3,t>:q \ \& \ <4,2,t>:r \ ➔ \ <4,4,t+1>:y \ \& \ <4,3,t+1>:z$$

where the first two coordinates in a 3-tuple are spatial and the third is temporal and p, q, r, y and z are matter states. The set of locations referenced by the LHS of a rule we call the rule's *neighbourhood*.

It is apparent that these rules are analogous to the update tables of a Boolean or multi-state network. Furthermore, an artificial neurone that computes its (discrete) output by reference to (discrete) inputs (typically the prior outputs of neurones possibly including itself), (fixed) weights, and some activation function, may also be implemented as an update table or rule set.

We define a *complete* set of rules for a STaM as a set of rules sufficient to specify the entire STaM given its temporally earliest STaM state. There is always at least one complete rule set for a STaM, namely the set of all rules that conjoin *all* the STaM states up to and including that at a time t (LHS) and then specify the STaM state at time $t+1$ (RHS). It is clear that in general there may be many complete rules sets for a STaM, some intuitively much simpler than others.

Rule sets may or may not have either or both of the following additional properties. They may be

- homogeneous in space i.e. the rules are the same for all S-locations
- Markovian in the sense that the LHS and RHS of the rules refer only to successive STaM states. The example rule just given is Markovian.

Different rules sets for the same STaM may differ in these properties.

2.2 Influence

We shall say that one S-location X *influences* another Y, with respect to a rule set, if there exists a rule R within the rule set that determines a state of Y wholly or partially by reference to the state of X (that is, the LHS of the R references the state of X and the RHS of R specifies the state of Y). As will appear, this definition is an important building block for what follows.

2.3 Fitting a STaM Rule Set

The following outline algorithm indicates how a complete set of rules may be fitted to any given StaM

```
Initialise the set of rules to empty

For every S-location of the STaM,
   enumerate every distinct location-state, LS, that
       occurs in that S-location, and
     for each LS find a minimal temporally prior
       location-state combination (relative to LS)
       that   correctly   predicts   LS   (i.e.   all
       occurrences of LS are preceded by the location-
       state combination, and the combination never
       occur without LS following), and
     add the corresponding rule to the set of rules
```

In general there will be many different sets of rules that may be fitted to a given STaM depending upon the detailed form this algorithm takes.[3] Notice that since the rules are fitted to the *entire* STaM, they will not be inconsistent one with another.

2.4 The Interpretation of STaM Rules

A rule set associated with a STaM is somewhat analogous to physical laws in that they determine the dynamics within the model of the space-time manifold (i.e. the STaM). Although this analogy may seem remote, it does perhaps guide our intuition in a useful direction. However, it is important to realise that, in the perspective of an outside

---

[3] An *optimal* rule set may be defined in various ways e.g. by minimal rule complexity.

observer, the rules merely *predict* their consequence state(s). They do not generate them or otherwise bring them into being for, by assumption, the entire STaM already exists as a prior structure.

Are STaM rules causal? That is, is it reasonable to say that a rule condition *causes* its consequences? In what follows we shall take the view that an instance of a rule is indeed causal, whilst recognising that not all will agree and that the concept of causality is fraught with difficulty especially in the context of block time.

3   Agents in StaMs

Given the notion of a STaM and its associated rule sets, we now ask if there can be sets of locations and/or states within a STaM that may reasonably be regarded as agents.[4] Of course, and crucially, this requires us to decide just what "an agent" is. The agent definitions found in the literature of agent technology often refer to such complex and ambiguous notions as "autonomy", "pro-activity", "communication", and "sociability", and thus offer rather little help in this context. However, the standard AI textbook by Russell and Norvig [9, p. 31] describes an agent a little more usefully as "anything that can be viewed as perceiving its environment through sensors, and acting upon that environment through effectors, and Weiss [14, p. 584] gives as one definition of an agent "an active object or a bounded process with the ability to perceive, reason and act". Very different, and still quite imprecise, is the notion that when seeing an agent "an Augustinian god just sees a nexus for a complicated structure of correlations" [8, p.169]. However, this last remark does give us the important idea of an agent as some kind of locus of complexity in space-time.

Now we define two classes of agents that may occur within STaMs: those without and those with something akin to "physical structure". We shall suggest that both these types of agent may display cognition. It will be apparent that these two definitions are merely two of many that could reasonably be formulated.

3.1   Agents without Physical Structure (A-Agents)

Definition: An *agent without physical structure (A-agent)* is a fixed non-empty set of S-locations, each S-location extended over the same non-empty time interval, the A-agent's *temporal extension*, that meets the following requirements:

> Two disjoint non-empty subsets of the agent S-locations are *input* and *output* S-locations respectively. The remaining S-locations of the agent are *internal*. Input, output and internal S-locations have the following properties:

---

[4]   Notice that this question is never asked in space-time physics, although there is relatively frequent reference to "observers" and their "time lines".

- An *input* S-location is influenced only by S-locations external to the agent and influences only output S-locations and/or S-locations internal to the agent.
- An *output* S-location is influenced only by input S-locations and/or internal S-locations of the agent and influences only S-locations external to the agent.
- An *internal* S-location is influenced by, or influences, only other S-locations of the agent i.e. internal, input or output S-locations.

All other S-locations in the STaM are said to be *external* to the agent.

Notice that this definition of an A-agent rests directly on the definition of what it means for one S-location to influence another, and therefore rests in turn on a set of rules associated with the STaM.

The S-locations that comprise an A-agent need not necessarily be spatially contiguous (in term of the spatial structure of the STaM), although intuitively we tend to assume that they are. Furthermore, the temporal extension of an A-agent need not be large compared with its spatial extension, though again we tend to assume that it is.

Not any set of S-locations is an A-agent. In particular, a single S-location cannot be an A-agent (the input and output sets must be non-empty and disjoint) and a pair of locations (L1, L2) is an A-agent, with L1 as input and L2 as output, if and only if:

> L1 influences at most L2
> L2 does not influence L1
> L2 is only influenced by L1

An entire STaM is an A-agent if and only if there exists (at least) one S-location within it that no other S-location influences, and at least one other S-location within it that influences no other S-location.

Our definition of an agent permits some though-provoking special cases. For example, if a STaM is temporally circular, and therefore temporally finite but unbounded, then clearly an A-agent within it may also be. Should this possibility lead us to reject this definition of an agent? Our intuition is troubled by the notion of an agent that can potentially remember its own future! But if the agent in question has only limited memory, which seems natural enough, then the difficulty may be avoided.

3.2   Agents with Physical Structure (P-Agents)

We now offer a definition of agents with a property analogous to persistent *physical structure*. It is an attempt to meet our intuitive notions of agents as physically situated.

Definition: an *agent with physical structure (P-agent)* is a *pattern of locations* whose relative spatial positions are fixed over time, and that:

may be differently located in successive states of a sequence of spatial states of the STaM, the P-agent's *temporal extension*, and

has a non-null sub-pattern whose location states are fixed

In this definition the pattern of locations is analogous to physical structure and is (necessarily) emergent from the STaM regularities. In two-dimensional space, it might be, for example, a 10x10 square of locations. By contrast with A-agents, the rules of a P-agent are not those of the STaM itself. Rather, they are derived from the regularities detectable in the pattern locations of the agent whose location states are not fixed. Note that A-agents are *not* a special case of P-agents.

Interesting though they are, we shall say nothing more of P-agents in this paper. We conjecture that most interesting properties of A-agents hold also for P-agents.

3.3 The Capabilities of A-Agents

An A-agent meets some of the most often cited requirements of an agent: it "senses" (via its input S-location(s)), "decides" (via its internal S-location(s)), and "acts" (via its output S-location(s)), provided that we allow these words to be given a simple interpretation in terms of information flow.

A-agents are, in effect, traces of (recurrent) multi-state networks. Equivalently they receive input, have state (the combination of the location states of their internal S-locations), and use "if-then" rules to select actions. Thus their internal processing and complexity is akin to that of many of the agents discussed in the literature.

It may be objected, however, that an A-agent lacks a fundamental property: it does not learn or adapt. After all, it might be argued, STaMs are fixed so how can agents within them learn? There are two major flaws in this argument. Since a STaM includes time, it includes change although it is itself fixed. Perhaps less obviously, a network constituting an A-agent may learn not by changing its structure (its set of S-locations and the rule set) but by changing its state, that is, by changing its set of location-states and hence the dynamics of its interaction with its environment (compare [17]). Thus A-agents can indeed learn and adapt.

4   Creating STaMs and Finding Agents

How may particular STaMs be created? It is clearly quite possible to generate a STaM at random, but it seems most unlikely that a STaM obtained in this way will contain structures (for example, agents) of any significant interest. We therefore now describe computer experiments in which non-trivial A-agents have been created to meet particular requirements, as a stepping-stone to the construction of interesting STaMs for further study. It will turn out that we are also interested in just *how* the agents generated perform the task set for them.

4.1 SABN Problems

We first focus attention on a particular way of creating an A-agent as it might occur in a STaM. Assume a two-dimensional, binary STaM. One dimension is temporal, and each location is in one of just two states. Assume a partially specified A-agent comprising N S-locations of the STaM including just one input S-location and one output location. The successive states of the input and output S-locations (both therefore binary sequences) are specified. We seek a rule set for the N S-locations of the agent that satisfies the definition of agenthood, and that so determines the agent's "internal dynamics" that it meets the imposed boundary conditions, that is, the given input and output sequences, possibly together with a given set of initial location states at the commencement of the its temporal extension in the STaM.

We call an agent creation task of this type a *sensory action Boolean network* (SABN) problem, and refer to the task of meeting the boundary conditions as that of *supporting the history*. As is usual in work on Boolean networks [16], we assume Markovian but spatially heterogeneous rules, whose neighbourhoods are constrained to be of a specified size and the same for all the states of a particular S-location. These assumptions are not essential. It is important to keep in mind that that, in accordance with our definition of an A-agent, *it is not the rule set that constitutes the agent, but the Boolean "trace" that the rules generate.*

4.2 The COUNT Problem

The COUNT problem is a quite challenging example of a SABN problem. It requires an agent to "count" how many '1's there are in each of a set of strings of '1's and to respond accordingly. The sensory input is (conceptually) structured as a series of episodes. In each episode a '1' string of a different length is presented to the agent. During an episode the network agent must "count" the length of the string presented to it and return as its corresponding "action" output string four bits in which the first bit is always '1' and the following 3 bits a binary encoding of the length of the string. For example, the sensory input '11111' must lead to the action output '1101'. In our specific version of the problem seven episodes in all are presented, covering the string lengths 1 to 7 in a random order. The entire input and output sequences, each of length 93, are given in Table 1.

4.3 The Algorithm and Program

To solve a SABN problem, a consistent rule set must be found for each S-location specifying the conditions in which each distinct location state of the S-location occurs. Collectively these rules must support the specified history.

The conceptually simplest way to obtain a suitable set of update tables is by systematic enumeration and test. Of course, this is impossibly slow. We have therefore implemented (in the C language) a program that uses an *ad hoc* version of hill-climbing search with random restart that obtains solutions in a feasible amount of time[5].

Table 1. The sensory input (S) and action output (A) sequences for the COUNT Problem, presented episode by episode. There are seven episodes plus an initial "null" episode. The total length of each sequence is 93. The episodic structure is conceptual, and is not marked in the input and output sequences as presented to the agent.

```
Episode 0    S  000000
             A  000000

Episode 1    S     1111111000000000
             A     0000000011110000 0

Episode 2    S     111000000
             A     000010110

Episode 3    S     100000000
             A     001001000

Episode 4    S     110000000000
             A     000101000000 0

Episode 5    S     111110000000
             A     000000110100

Episode 6    S     11111100000000000
             A     00000001110000000

Episode 7    S     1111000000
             A     0000011000
```

4.4 Experimental Results

Sample experimental results obtained for the COUNT problem appear in Table 2. They demonstrate that the problem can indeed be solved, but that solution times depend greatly upon the number N of S-locations employed. The smaller is N, the longer it takes on average to find a solution. Actual times on a relatively fast PC (1.4 GHz) are from a few seconds up to several hours.

It is natural to ask whether these solutions are of any generality. Do they, for example, handle a string of any length? Do they handle an arbitrary sequence of strings, or just the given sequence? In fact, when tested the solutions have very little

---

[5] There is no reason to believe that use of a genetic algorithm, say, would obtain solutions any faster.

generality. Typically they do *exactly* the job required of them and no more.[6] For example, if the input and output sequences are repeated, without the network being re-initialised, then the network fails to handle the second presentation. This does not mean, of course, that more general solutions do not exist – merely that they are rare and have not been encountered in these trials.

Table 2. Effort expended to find three solutions to the COUNT problem for each of six specified sizes of Boolean network. Entries in the table are numbers of networks tested before success. The three searches for each size of network differ only in pseudo-random number stream. No solution network of size 8 could be found.

Network size	50	20	15	12	10	9
Neigh'd size	12	12	12	12	10	9
Solution 1	58	186	350	1894	21463	688363
Solution 2	79	44	238	10864	97990	4842134
Solution 3	43	60	1680	989	52245	3364584

Interestingly, and a little counter-intuitively, effective solutions to the COUNT problem may also be obtained by "fine tuning" the update tables of a randomly generated network provided that the network is relatively *large*. Since such a network is close to chaotic, in effect it never repeats its state, so that the desired output at a time in the history can often be obtained merely by making a single adjustment to the update table. Thus very regular external behaviour may be obtained from an internal structure that is close to chaotic.

4.5 Creating STaMS

A solution to the COUNT problem is an A-agent and furthermore may itself be regarded as a STaM – a STaM that is, in its entirety, a single A-agent. A small fragment of a COUNT solution STaM with 20 S-locations is shown in Table 3.

Thus we have now constructed a STaM that is of some interest because we know that *one interpretation* of it is as a single agent that handles the COUNT problem. But are there other interpretations of this STaM?

Table 3. A small fragment of a two-dimensional STaM derived from the COUNT problem. The states shown are of the first few times (left to right) of the first few S-locations (top to bottom) and of the last S-location. The first row is the "sensory input" and the last the "action output". In its entirety the STaM is a Boolean array of size 1880 (20 S-locations by 93 times).

---

[6] Compare [17, p. 243] "the networks evolve just enough plasticity to accomplish the particular tasks we have set for them".

00000011111110000000000011100000001000000..............
01100000000111001001000100101011...........
11001000111010100100111111010.........
10011110100010010000100001000....
11100010001101001110111....

....

...

.....

0000000000000001111000000000101100010010.............

4.6   Finding A-Agents in a STaM: Some Initial Results

In principle, it is not difficult to devise an algorithm to locate A-agents in a given STaM. All that is required is a scan of all subsets of the S-locations of the STaM, checking for those that meet the requirements of the definition. However, systematic enumeration is an extremely computationally intensive process even though we know that it will terminate since STaMs are by definition finite. Furthermore, application of the definition of an A-agent requires a rule set to have been associated with the STaM and influences determined, so that before seeking agents we first of all must apply a rule-fitting algorithm. We have therefore implemented two C programs, the first to fit rules to a given STaM (see Section 2.3), and the second to use the rules thus obtained to identify agents within the STaM. Importantly, both programs are heuristic. The rule-fitting program is heuristic in that it considers only certain relatively simple types of rules, those with a conjunction of at most three location states on the left hand side. No attempt is made to optimise *sets* of rules. The agent finding program ignores isolated instances of influence (see Section 2.2) concentrating rather on recurring influence instances, but then will find any A-agent that satisfies the definition.

In preliminary experiments these programs have been applied to the COUNT STaM of Table 3. It turns out that the original solution A-agent is *never* found but that, for each particular setting of the influence threshold, a set of other A-agents is. The A-agents found in a set can be both large and small, and are often substantially overlapping. One particular A-agent encountered comprises just the two input and output S-locations of the original A-agent.

We conjecture that the original agent is not found primarily because the rule-fitting program does not have the power to find rules of the complexity of those used to generate it. These, it will be recalled, have neighbourhoods of size 12. The agent-finding program is working with an effective but different set of rules and with patterns of *recurring* influence. It is not surprising that it finds other agents than those used to construct the STaM. But these "new" agents are just as real in the STaM. Our results may be summarised by saying that the agents detected in a STaM are strongly dependent upon the (essentially causal) interpretation placed upon it.

Are the agents that are discovered by the agent-finding program of any interest in themselves? Intuitively, it depends how complex they are, and this is a matter of their internal processing. To this issue we now turn.

5   Cognition in A-Agents

Finding A-agents by solving the COUNT problem, or by exploring a STaM, is one thing. Discovering just how an A-agent actually supports its corresponding history is quite another.[7] Is it purely "reactive", so that each input pattern is independently linked to its required output, or is there some definite process of counting within the agent? Or is there some "noisy" mixture of the two? Or is there something else? In a trivial sense what happens is clear. Rules "fire" successively and the required outcome is achieved. But what conceptual repertoire might support a more insightful analyse of the internal dynamics of an agent of this kind?

Dynamic systems theory is an established candidate [2,16,17], with analyses typically couched in terms of different types of attractor and of trajectories to and from them. Indeed, we can characterise many of the solutions we have obtained to the COUNT problem as follows: without significant input the system rests in a limit cycle attractor; in each episode the input moves the system away from the attractor in a manner specific to that input; and as the system returns to the attractor it generates the output corresponding to the input.

We suggest, however, that deliberative cognitive processes can occur in agents of this type (which potentially have the power of Turing Machines), and that therefore there is an effective *cognitive* language in which to discuss how these agents process internally. We briefly discuss this topic in the next section and address there the question of how to *recognise* deliberation.[8] We focus on predictive planning as an example of deliberative cognition.

5.1   What Is Predictive Planning?

We all have an understanding of predictive planning. Making use of its beliefs about the world and its current state, an agent, human or otherwise, uses internal representations of the external world to anticipate certain alternative courses of action and their consequences, and chooses between these alternatives in order to find the best, in some subjective sense, course of action – the plan. The choice may or may not be made "rationally". The agent then attempts to carry out the chosen course of action, which may or may not prove possible and which may or may not have the anticipated consequences. Thus planning involves the generation, examination and manipulation by the agent of representations of possible future states or properties of (its) world.

This notion of predictive planning has regularly been investigated in AI research, with many variations and simplifications, and there has been considerable progress in designing and implementing planning software and (to a lesser extent) hardware [9].

---

[7] Many authors have commented upon this difficulty, e.g. " ... it is common to achieve a perfectly competent network whose operation appears to be completely incomprehensible." [2, p. 470].

[8] We also conjecture that deliberation necessarily or typically occur in A-agents that are *minimal* in some important respect such as size, but more work is required before this can be confirmed or disproved.

In particular, most chess playing programs employ predictive planning. But there remain uncertainties about its essential nature and function. It is typically characterised, as above, using high level and ambiguous terms. As these terms are computationally grounded (for example, as a piece of planning software is designed and implemented) the ambiguity is removed, but with many essentially arbitrary decisions. Furthermore, consider the particular difficulties presented by an agent that has pervasively faulty planning processes and faulty beliefs about the nature and structure of its world and its possible actions – so that any "predictions" made by the agent are too thoroughly mistaken to reasonably merit the term "representations". Yet the agent does reach decisions about actions to perform. How could one determine that such an agent was (confusedly) planning rather than merely selecting actions "reactively" in a somewhat muddled way?

5.2 A-Agents That Plan

Predictive planning is not a matter of the external behaviour of an A-agent. Rather a consistent *interpretation* must be established that identifies certain patterns of agent "activity" as representations of certain sensory inputs, of possible action outputs, and of processing decisions. This interpretation can be based on consistencies between input and output and changes in the states of the A-agent's internal S-locations. But it is difficult to see exactly what the required consistencies should be. For example, what do representations represent: actions or plans? Furthermore, there is no reason to believe that the activity corresponding to a particular representation will be localised. This might be so in some of canonical form, but not in general.

   Planning programs in the artificial intelligence tradition construct and repeatedly modify plans until they satisfy conditions of coherence and effectiveness. We therefore conjecture that predictive planning is best viewed as a special case of the fundamental artificial intelligence method, *generate and test*. This implies that the key to the interpretation an agent's processing as planning is algorithmically to select a locus (possibly distributed) of repeated change in the compound state of the network and to construct an interpretation of that change as the development and testing of variant plans. Finding such an algorithm remains a challenge, which appears all the more daunting since it seems that a specific agent's processing may well be interpretable in terms of predictive planning in more than one way.[9]

---

[9] It is natural to ask whether this line of thought has anything to say about the symbol-grounding problem. If symbols are regarded as the objects of necessarily *conscious* thought, then maybe not. However, if we identify a symbol with the notion of a physical representation of a phenomenon external to the agent, that participates in internal processes in a defined way, then it may be that the "patterns of activity" mentioned above may be identified as symbols.

6 Multi-agent Systems (MAS)

We have already seen (in section 4.6) that a single STaM may contain many A-agents.[10] We define a Multi-Agent System, a MAS[11], in a STaM as a set of A-agents that:

- have disjoint location sets (we say that the A-agents are disjoint), and
- are such that any pair of A-agents within the MAS can directly or indirectly influence one another, that is, each A-agent of the pair has a location that directly or indirectly influences a location of the other.

It follows that a set of agents comprising a MAS exists within a set of collectively external locations that forms their common environment.

The first of these two requirements will be relaxed in section 6.3. The significance of the latter is that it seems unreasonable to include within a MAS A-agents that can never interact. The notion of "influencing" used here is that defined in section 2.2.

6.1 Interaction and Communication between A-Agents

Consider the following three ways in which one agent may causally impact another (expressed in terms of human interaction):

> *X accidentally makes a sound that Y hears and reacts to by turning towards X*

> *X deliberately make a sound intending that Y should hear it and react by turning towards X, and this is what happens*

> *X deliberately makes a sound intending that Y should hear it and react by interpreting it as a signal to, say, start an attack on their joint enemy Z, and this is what happens*

We may describe these three compound events as an *accidental causal impact*, an *intended causal impact*, and a *message*. Of course, there are other possibilities notably where an initiating agent's intention is not realised. To discuss such interactions between A-agents we return to the notion of causality introduced in section 2.4.

> **Definition.** A *causal connection* exists in a STaM from a set P of location states to a location state Q later than any of them if and only if there exists a set of rule instances that together specify Q from P. We say that P *grounds* the causal connection.
> **Definition.** An A-agent X in a STaM has a *causal impact* upon another A-agent Y if there is a state of one of the output S-locations of X (i.e. X performs

---

[10] We are currently experimenting with STaMs *constructed* from more than one A-agent.

[11] Given that we are considering A-agents, a better notation might be "A-MAS".

an action) that is a member of a set that grounds a causal connection to a state of an input S-location of Y.

A special case of the last definition occurs when the states constituting the set P are *entirely* within output S-locations of X, so that in some sense X is wholly responsible for the causal impact upon Y. It is clear that a causal impact can occur between A-agents only where one A-agent can influence another.

Intended causal impacts, including messages, require the initiating A-agent to have *planned* the causal impact and its consequences. This is a much stronger requirement (compare [10,15]), and cannot be addressed until the issue of planning within A-agents is clarified.

Can an A-agent in a STaM act upon its past? As our definition of causal connection is unidirectional in time, our answer is clearly "no", but see section 7.

6.2 Overlapping and Nested A-Agents

It is possible for A-agents within a STaM to overlap, and even be nested one within another. The overlapping may be in space or in time or in both. Of course, sections of the STaM shared between two or more A-agents must meet the requirements for all of them.

Can two overlapping or nested A-agents interact and/or communicate one with another in the sense of the last section? It is clear that they can, provided the underlying causal impact is into the future, as by definition it must be. Notice that this allows an A-agent to send a message to itself in the future, where its actual circumstances permit.

6.3 A-Agent Composition and Decomposition

Given our focus on multi-agent systems, it is appropriate to consider how two or more A-agents may be composed into a single A-agent, and vice versa. One possible definition is:

Definition. If it exists, the *composition* of a set of disjoint A-agents all with the same temporal extension is the A-agent comprising the union of their S-locations and with the same temporal extension. Input, output and internal S-locations must retain their prior classification, except that input or output S-locations may be internal in the composite A-agent.

Similarly

Definition. If one exists, a *decomposition* of an A-agent is a set of at least two disjoint A-agents, all with the temporal extension of the given agent, the union of whose S-locations (preserving the nature of input, output and internal S-locations except that input or output S-locations may become internal) is the set of S-locations of the given A-agent.

These definitions may be applied repeatedly, so that, for example, an A-agent may in principle be decomposed into a hierarchical set of sets of composing A-agents. Clearly, this process cannot continue indefinitely, as an A–agent with only two S-locations cannot be decomposed.

6.4 Understanding the Behaviour of MAS

We distinguish three approaches to the study of MAS. These are: by reference to existing social theory (e.g. [3,5]); in terms of controlling parameters (e.g. [6]); and from the theory of individual cognition. We comment briefly on the last of these possibilities.

If a MAS may be "read" as a single agent, then an understanding of the functioning of MAS may be based upon an understanding of the functioning of that single agent. Suppose, for example, that an A-agent that is a composition of a MAS is engaged in planning. Then the original set of A-agents must, it seems, be engaged in collective planning. Thus there is a direct linkage between the complex behaviour of the collective and of the individual. Furthermore, the collective planning process will be distributed over the A-agents of the MAS, but not in any particular way, nor in a way that is necessarily simple.

7 Temporal Orientation in Agents

Throughout the foregoing development, a particular temporal orientation in the STaM has been taken for granted. However, a moment's reflection makes clear that *any* well-defined dimension of a STaM may be taken to be temporal. Depending upon the choice made, different properties (and in particular, different agent sets) will be discovered in the STaM.[12]

We say that an A-agent is *individually temporally oriented with respect to direction D* if it meets the requirements of the usual A-agent definition with respect to the STaM rules associated with D (recall that rules are derived from a STaM by reference to a particular directed dimension of it).[13] It follows, of course, that for each discernable direction D in the STaM there will be zero, one or more A-agents that are individually temporally oriented to that direction. A particular STaM may contain many A-agents in a range of different temporal orientations. Indeed, rather than seeing a STaM as temporally oriented in some arbitrarily chosen direction, we may view *A-agents* as individually temporally oriented but *not* the STaM within which they reside.

---

[12] This has been experimentally verified using the COUNT solution STaM discussed above.

[13] Price [8] has discussed temporally oriented agents in some detail, but only with respect to a single fixed time dimension.

To explore the dependence of agenthood upon temporal orientation, we pose in the following sections two specific questions. Can A-agents in a STaM of differing temporal orientation interact and inter-communicate? Is there a coherent notion of an atemporal agent, that is, of an agent that has *no* temporal orientation?

7.1   Interaction between A-Agents of Differing Temporal Orientation

It is natural to say that an A-agent can be *aware* of anything that can causally impact upon it. Since anything[14] in an agents past can causally impact upon it, it follows that an A-agent, X, can be aware of another A-agent, Y, in its past, whatever Y's temporal orientation. For example, Y may be aligned in the reverse direction to X or may be aligned along what is to X a spatial direction.

Furthermore, an A-agent, X, may initiate a causal connection which later (with respect to X's temporal orientation) impacts upon a sensory (input) location of another A-agent, Y. As discussed previously, such an impact may or may not be intended. Intention requires, amongst other things, that X predicts the existence of Y in the future. In principle this seems possible. Notice that the temporal duration of Y, *from X's perspective*, is likely to be small.

7.2   Atemporal Agents in Atemporal STaMs

If the temporal orientation of a STaM, or of an agent within it, is essentially arbitrary, then it is natural to ask what can be said if there is *no* temporal orientation, if the STaM is atemporal (see Price [8, pp. 259-260] for a concept of "atemporal physics"). In particular, is there then no longer any possible notion of an agent? Or can there be an atemporal agent?

In an atemporal STaM the concept of condition-consequence rules based upon a particular direction is meaningless. However, we can instead deploy the concept of condition-consequence rules based upon pattern completion. Such a rule essentially states that wherever in the STaM a particular pattern of location states occurs (condition), then certain other location states will be found in a specified relationship to them (consequence). A *complete* set of such rules may then be defined (somewhat arbitrarily) as a minimal set such that every location state in the STaM occurs in the consequence of at least one rule.

Can we now, by analogy with an A-agent, define a notion of an atemporal agent? This is not straightforward, since we no longer have S-locations as building blocks for the definition. However, given a specific complete rule set it is possible, by extending our previous definition of causal[15] impact in terms of it, to define what it means for one location state to have a causal impact upon another. We may then define an *atemporal agent* as a set of locations (*not* S-locations!) that is partitioned into two

---

[14] We ignore the complications that arise from properties of the STaM rules analogous to the limited speed of light.

[15] But the use of the word "causality" is now no longer intuitive.

disjoint subsets one comprising *internal locations* of the agent and the other *boundary locations* in such a way that internal locations only causally impact one another and boundary locations but boundary locations can impact any locations including those external to the agent. It follows that, with these definitions, one atemporal agent may have a causal impact upon another.

What it might mean, if anything, for an atemporal agent to be interpreted as deliberative is difficult to say. It seems likely that a key step will be to set up an interpretation of the STaM in which certain features external to the agent are matched to internal features taken to be representations. But all the details of this remain to be worked out.

8 Discussion

The ideas and research programme outlined in this paper immediately prompt a number of questions. It is apparent that much more needs to be done to fill out the formal development of STaMs and their possible contents in precise mathematical detail. But what reason is there to believe that the ideas presented *can* be further elaborated consistently and precisely (assuming that what has been presented so far is indeed internally consistent)? Our reason to believe that they can is as simple as this. In mathematical terms, all that we are doing is to look at a range of mappings ("data structures") and to investigate the properties, of certain defined kinds, that they may or may not individually have. In itself this is not difficult. The real challenge lies not in carrying out such an investigation, but in how best to select interesting and productive definitions (e.g. a definition of an agent) to investigate.

Is the use of such terms as "agent" and "space-time" justified? We believe that, with due caution, it is. The model presented here is very abstract, in the sense of lacking specific structure, and is technically simple in that, for example, it is discrete, but it does interface both with agent technology and with the physics of space-time and a range of interesting questions may be posed in relation to it. The model unifies aspects of neural networks, cellular automata and agent theory. Furthermore, the notion that cognitive processes may be discernable within agents in STaMs is no more outlandish than suggesting that cognitive processes may be run on Turing Machines. So the model also enables more traditional and symbolic ideas of artificial intelligence to be addressed.

There is even a sense in which this model, or a similar model, could in principle be empirically tested. This is not because it makes explicit predictions that might or might not check out, but because it suggests certain empirical investigations that might or might not prove productive – for example, it suggests that there may be agents to be found in the world on time scales and in configurations (and even temporal orientations) different from those that we, in our anthropocentric way, tend to take for granted. Thus such models have the potential to break us free of habitual preconceptions.

9   Conclusions

We have proposed a multi-stage investigation into agents and multi-agent systems based on a model incorporating three unusual ideas: grounding agents and their environments in "matter", taking a block-time perspective, and focussing on the recognition rather than design of agents. We have taken the investigation forward in a little detail, shown that it is possible to study agents and multi-agent systems in this way, and shown that STaM agents correspond to Boolean and multi-state networks whose properties can be studied computationally. Our main conclusion is that the investigation is feasible, worthwhile and should be taken further. It potentially brings together a number of branches of artificial intelligence, has a not quite trivial linkage with space-time physics and the philosophy of time, and enables some interesting questions to be addressed from a new perspective.

References

1. Angeline, P. J., Saunders, G. M., Pollack, J. B.: An Evolutionary Algorithm that Constructs Recurrent Neural Networks. IEEE Transactions on Neural Networks, Vol. 5, No. 1 (1994) 54-65
2. Beer, R.: On the Dynamics of Small Continuous-Time Neural Networks. Adaptive Behavior, Vol. 3, No. 4, (1995) 469-509
3. Doran, J.E.: Trajectories to Complexity in Artificial Societies: Rationality, Belief and Emotions. In: Dynamics in Human and Primate Societies. Kohler, T.A., Gumerman, G.J., eds., Santa Fe Institute Studies in the Sciences of Complexity, Oxford University Press, Oxford and New York, (2000) 89-106
4. Eliasmith, C.: The Third Contender: a Critical Examination of the Dynamicist Theory of Cognition. Philosophical Psychology. Vol. 9(4), (1996) 441-463
5. Gilbert, N.: Modeling Sociality: The View from Europe. In: Dynamics in Human and Primate Societies. Kohler, T.A., Gumerman, G.J., eds., Santa Fe Institute Studies in the Sciences of Complexity, Oxford University Press, Oxford and New York, (2000) 355-371
6. Kluver, J., Schmidt, J.: Topology, Metric and Dynamics of Social Systems. Journal of Artificial Societies and Social Simulation, Vol. 2(3), (1999) <http://www.soc.surrey.ac.uk/JASSS/2/3/7.html>
7. Naber, G. L.: Spacetime and Singularities: An Introduction. Cambridge University Press, Cambridge (1988)
8. Price, H.: Time's Arrow & Archimedes' Point. Oxford University Press, Oxford and New York (1996)
9. Russell, S., and Norvig, P. (eds.): Artificial Intelligence: a Modern Approach. Prentice Hall (1995)
10. Saunders, G. M., Pollack, J. B.: The Evolution of Communication Schemes over Continuous Channels. In: From Animals to Animats 4. Proceedings of the Fourth International Conference on Simulation of Adaptive Behaviour (eds. P. Maes, M. J. Mataric, J-A. Meyer, J. Pollack and S. W. Wilson). September 9th-13th, 1996, Cape Cod, Massachusetts, (1996) 580
11. Teuscher, C.: Study, Implementation and Evolution of the Artificial Neural Networks Proposed by Alan M. Turing: A Revival of his "Schoolboy" Ideas. Swiss Federal Institute

of Technology, Lausanne, Logic Systems Laboratory, EPFL-DI-LSL, CH-1015, Lausanne (2000)

12. Turing, A. M.: Intelligent Machinery. Report Submitted to UK National Physical Laboratory, 1948. Reprinted in: Machine Intelligence 5. Meltzer, B., Michie, D., eds., Edinburgh University Press, Edinburgh (1969) 3-23

13. Turing, A. M.: Computing Machinery and Intelligence. MIND: a Quarterly Review of Psychology and Philosophy, Vol. LIX, No. 236, (1950) 433-460

14. Weiss, G. (ed.): Multiagent Systems. The MIT Press, Cambridge, Mass. and London, England (1999)

15. Werner, E.: Cooperating Agents: A Unified Theory of Communication and Social Structure. In: Distributed Artificial Intelligence, Volume II. Gasser, L., Huhns, M.N. eds., Pitman, London and Morgan Kaufmann, San Mateo, California (1989) 3-36

16. Wuensche, A.: Discrete Dynamical Networks and their Attractor Basins Complexity International, Volume 6, (online), and SFI Working Paper, 98-11-101 (1998)

17. Yamauchi, B.M., Beer, R. D.: Sequential Behavior and Learning in Evolved Dynamical Neural Networks. Adaptive Behavior, Vol. 2, No. 3 (1994) 219-246

Semantics of Agent Communication: An Introduction

Rogier M. van Eijk

Institute of Information and Computing Sciences, Utrecht University,
P.O. Box 80.089, 3508 TB Utrecht, The Netherlands,
rogier@cs.uu.nl

Abstract. Communication has been one of the salient issues in the research on concurrent and distributed systems. This holds no less for the research on multi-agent systems. Over the last few years the study of agent communication, and in particular the semantics of agent communication, has attracted increased interest. The present paper provides an introduction to this area. Since agent communication builds upon concepts and techniques from concurrency theory, we start by giving a short historical overview that covers shared-variable concurrency, message-passing, rendezvous, concurrent constraint programming and agent communication. Standard approaches of agent communication identify three different layers: a content layer, message layer and communication layer. To this model we add an extra level, namely the layer of the multi-agent system. Subsequently, we discern three approaches in developing the semantics of programming languages: the axiomatic, operational and denotational approach. Additionally, we discuss semantic aspects of agent communication, including communication histories, compositionality, observable behaviour, failure sets and full abstractness. We illustrate these issues by means of the framework ACPL (Agent Communication Programming Language). Finally, we briefly consider the specification and verification of agent communication.

1 Introduction

The introduction of novel application areas has urged the development of new programming concepts and techniques to assist both the programmer and end-user in managing the inherent complexity of computer software. A concept that plays a prominent role in the research of the late 1990s and the beginning of the third millennium is that of an *agent*. This concept has found its shape in the field of artificial intelligence and builds upon notions from other disciplines of research as philosophy, economics, sociology and psychology. Although in artificial intelligence, there is no real consensus on what exactly constitutes an agent, there are some generally accepted properties attributed to it. In fact, this can also be said about a related notion from computer science, namely that of an *object*, which over the years, despite a lack of consensus on its definition, nonetheless has proven to be a successful concept for the design of a new generation of programming languages.

In short, an *agent* is an autonomous entity that shows both a reactive and pro-active behaviour by perceiving and acting in the environment it inhabits [47]. Moreover, it has a social ability to interact with other agents in multi-agent systems, like the capability to share knowledge through communication, to coordinate its activities with those of

M. d' Inverno et al. (Eds.): UKMAS 1996–2000, LNAI 2403, pp. 152–168, 2002.

other agents, to cooperate with other agents or to compete with them. In the stronger conception of agency, an agent is additionally assumed to have a mental state consisting of *informational* attitudes, like knowledge and belief, as well as *motivational* attitudes, like goals, desires and intentions. In other words, rather than being thought of as a computational entity in the traditional sense, an agent is viewed upon as a more elaborate software entity that embodies particular human-like characteristics. For instance, an issue in the rapidly growing research area of electronic commerce, is the study whether agents can assist humans in their tedious tasks of localising, negotiating and purchasing goods [32]. In general, negotiation activities comprise the exchange of information of a highly complex nature, requiring the involved parties to employ high-level modalities as knowledge and belief about the knowledge and belief of the other parties. Moreover, more elaborate negotiations also involve aspects of argumentation to explain the reasons why particular offers are proposed.

We could say that emerging novel application areas require the development of new programming paradigms, since the emphasis of programming involves a shift from the traditional performance of *computations* towards the employment of the more involved concepts of *interaction* and *communication*. In particular, in the new paradigms, the central focus is on computer programs that interact and communicate at a higher level of abstraction. That is, rather than a mere exchange of low-level data, communication between agents can for instance involve propositions that are believed to be true or false, actions that are requested to be performed and goals that are to be achieved.

Over the last few years the study of agent communication, and in particular the semantics of agent communication, has attracted increased interest. The present paper provides an introduction to the area. It is organised as follows. In Section 2, we give a short historic overview of the research on communication in concurrent programming languages that covers shared-variable concurrency, message-passing, rendezvous, concurrent constraint programming and agent communication. We discuss the standard model of agent communication, which consists of a content layer, message layer and communication layer. To this model we add one extra level, namely the layer of the multi-agent system. Subsequently, in Section 3, we discern three approaches for developing the semantics of agent communication: the axiomatic, operational and denotational approach. Finally, in Section 4, we discuss compositionality, observability, specification and verification of agent communication.

2   From Shared Variables to Agent Communication

In our conception, the study of agent communication can be thought of as a next step in a long history of research on concurrent programming languages. Over the years the area of concurrency theory has produced many concepts, mechanisms and techniques for a clear understanding of the concurrency and communication aspects of programming languages. We give an overview.

2.1   Shared Variable Concurrency

In the early days, research on programming languages was concerned with languages for *sequential* programming. Characteristic of a sequential program is that its computation starts with the execution of the first action after which control moves along the subsequent actions of the program as dictated by the programming constructs. In other words, the execution of a sequential program is given by a single thread of control.

Later on, in the mid 1960s, people began to develop and study programming languages for computer systems in which execution is not a sequential process but where instead, different activities can occur concurrently. In particular, in a program of a *concurrent* programming language one cannot discern a single thread of control; there are multiple active processes each of which is governed by its individual thread. In comparison with sequential languages, programs in a concurrent programming language are far more complex. This is due to the fact that the concurrently operating processes of a program should be coordinated in such a way that they can cooperate with each other, but on the other hand their individual computations do not interfere.

Among the first programming languages for concurrent systems are the ones developed for *shared variable* concurrency [11]. According to this paradigm, a program is composed of a set of concurrent processes that communicate by means of a collection of shared variables. One of the key problems encountered for these languages is that it should be prohibited for different processes to have simultaneous access to the same variables. In other words, their activities need to be coordinated, for if they do have simultaneous access to a particular variable then unexpected behaviour can occur. This is illustrated in the following example.

Example 1. (*Simultaneous access*)
Suppose that the execution of an action $x := e$ consists of an evaluation of the expression e after which the computed value is assigned to the variable x. Consider a program that consists of two concurrently executing processes A and B, which are defined as follows:

$$A \equiv x := x + 1$$
$$B \equiv x := x + 2.$$

Process A increases the value of x by 1, while process B increases it with 2. If the initial value of the variable x is equal to 0, we would expect that its resulting value is 3. However, consider the following scenario. The process A computes the value of $x + 1$ and finds it to be equal to 1. Before it assigns this value to the variable x, the other process B executes the action $x := x + 2$. The evaluation of the expression $x + 2$ yields the value 2, which is subsequently assigned to the variable x. Meanwhile, the agent A finishes its execution by overwriting the current value 2 of x by the value 1. Thus, in this scenario, the final value of x is equal to 1 instead of the expected value 3.

In general, for each of the processes in a program for shared-variable concurrency, one can identify *critical sections* in which it is necessary that the process has exclusive access to particular shared data. Correspondingly, it should be ensured that only a restricted subset (typically, just *one* process) is executing its critical section at the same time. Many techniques have been developed for the synchronisation of processes that have shared data, among which the most prominent ones are *semaphores* [12] and *monitors* [27]. In real life, a semaphore allows only a restricted number of trains on a particular railroad track. In a computer, it allows only a restricted number of processes to be in their critical section. A monitor not only defines the procedures that can be invoked to operate on a particular set of shared variables, but also coordinates the execution of these procedures. Thus, a monitor can be thought of as implementing a screen around the shared procedures and data.

2.2 Distributed Programming

Next in the development of concurrent programming languages are the ones developed for computer systems in which processes do not operate on a shared memory but, instead, are distributed over multiple sites. Characteristic for a *distributed program* is that its computation is split up into smaller computations, each of which is delegated to one of the distributed processes. For these processes to be able to interact, they should have the possibility to exchange their computed results among each other. In the research on such *distributed programming languages*, which started in the 1970s, a prominent place is held by the languages of the Communicating Sequential Programming paradigm (CSP) [28], like OCCAM [29]. In CSP, interaction between the distributed processes is accomplished via an underlying communication network that connects the different sites, along which the processes can exchange messages with each other. Since there are no shared variables, the synchronisation issues for mutual exclusion, as sketched above, do not arise in a distributed environment. However, other problems remain, like, for instance, the problem that in a distributed program, processes can be waiting for particular data to arrive that however will never be supplied. In other words, it should be ensured that a distributed program is free from the possibility of *deadlock*. In a situation of deadlock, the execution of a program is blocked because none of its processes can proceed. A typical cause of deadlock is the fact that all processes are waiting for *another* process to make the next move, such that consequently no process can make a next step. This issue is illustrated in the following example.

Example 2. (Deadlock)
Let us consider a distributed programming language that comprises actions $c!e$ and $c?x$ for communication between processes. The execution of the former action consists of evaluating the expression e after which the computed value is sent along a communication channel c. The execution of the latter action consists of receiving a particular value along the communication channel c, which is subsequently assigned to the variable x. Consider a concurrent program that is comprised of the two processes A and B, which are defined as follows:

$$A \equiv c?x \cdot d!f(x)$$
$$B \equiv d?y \cdot c!g(y),$$

where $\cdot$ denotes sequential composition. The process A first receives a value along the communication channel c. After that, it applies the function f to this value, and subsequently sends it along the channel d. Concurrently, the process B first receives a value along the channel d that is assigned to the variable y. The function g is subsequently applied to the variable y, which yields a result that is sent along the channel c. However, the processes find themselves in a deadlock situation; that is, the first step of the execution of A is to receive a value along the channel c. This value can be supplied by process B, but not until this process has received a value along the communication channel d. The latter value can be provided by the agent A in turn, but only after it has received a value along *c*. Consequently, neither of the processes can proceed as each of them is waiting for the other process to make the first move.

Writing concurrent programs that are free from deadlock is by no way an easy task, since deadlock situations may not present themselves as obviously as in the above example. Therefore, various techniques have been developed to enable a profound analysis of the behaviour of concurrent programs.

There are two types of communication. The first one is called *synchronous* communication, like in CSP, which corresponds to a form of communication in which a process that wants to communicate a particular data item to another process, waits until the recipient is ready to receive it. The second kind of communication is referred to as *asynchronous* communication, which denotes a form of communication in which a process sends a particular data item irrespective of the current status of the recipient. That is, if at the moment of communication, the latter process is not ready to process the message, this message is, for instance, temporarily stored in a buffer from which it can be extracted as soon as the recipient is able to handle it.

2.3   Concurrent Object-Oriented Programming

In the practice of writing programs in the above distributed programming languages, an important pattern of interaction appeared to be that between a client and a server process: the client wants a particular task to be performed and the server is able to do this. The interaction pattern between these two processes comprises the communication of a message from the client to the server, followed by a suspension of the client and the execution of the corresponding task by the server. After completion of the task, the computed result is sent to the client that subsequently resumes its computation.

This two-way exchange of data between a client and a server can be implemented in CSP via two synchronous communication steps. In the first step, data is communicated from the client to the server, while the second step comprises the communication of data from the server to the client. In the meantime, the execution of the client is blocked. Normally, one server handles requests from multiple clients, each of which has its own communication channels that connect it to the server. Due to all these concurrent interactions, it can become quite hard for a programmer to keep understanding what is going on. This led to the introduction of the concept of a *rendezvous* [4], which collects the above steps of the interaction between a client and a server into one compound programming construct. This delivers the programmer from defining each individual step of the interaction.

The concept of a *remote procedure call* [7] is almost similar to that of a rendezvous. However, in a remote procedure call, an entirely new server process is created to handle the call. The client process can thus be viewed upon as performing the corresponding procedure itself; the execution only takes place at a remote site.

The rendezvous communication mechanism has been adopted in a new generation of distributed programming languages, which are the languages for *concurrent object-oriented programming* [2]. In this paradigm, a program consists of a collection of processes, which are called *objects*. These objects have their own set of variables and additionally are assigned a set of methods that can be invoked to operate on these variables. In fact, an object gives rise to a form of *data encapsulation*, since other objects can inspect and change the state of the object only through the invocation of one of its methods. Typical examples of this paradigm are the object-oriented languages of [1], which are inspired by the actor model of computation [25], and the language POOL [3]. The latter language has been designed to program populations of concurrently operating objects that dynamically evolve over time. That is, in this language, objects have the capability to create new objects, which causes the object population to increase. Communication between the objects takes place via method invocations, which are based on the rendezvous communication mechanism.

2.4   Concurrent Constraint Programming

In addition to the above paradigms for *procedural* programming, we consider the related research area of *declarative* programming. In essence, a declarative program specifies a particular problem that needs to be solved. The execution of the program then amounts to finding a solution for it. One class of concurrent declarative languages are the concurrent versions of the logic programming language PROLOG [21, 42], like for instance the language PARLOG [10].

At the end of the 1980s, the Concurrent Constraint Programming (CCP) [36] was developed, which presents a new perspective on the underlying philosphy of logic programming. In constraint programming, a problem is expressed declaratively by means of a set of constraints on variables; Any solution to the problem must satisfy all these constraints. The paradigm assumes as input a particular constraint system, which is an abstract model of information. A constraint system consists of a a set of basic pieces of information that are expressed in a constraint language (such as a decidable fragment of first-order logic), which can be combined by means of a conjunction operator. Moreover, the constraint system contains a particular ordering relation of the constraints. Examples of constraints are: $z - y = x$, $x + y \geq 4$ and $P(x,y) \wedge R(y,x)$.

The revolutionary starting point of CCP is that it abandons the traditional *memory-as-valuation* concept of von Neumann-computing, which underlies the traditional programming languages. In the traditional view, the memory of a computer is an assignment of values to variables. However, in CCP, computation is based upon a novel view, namely the view of the comuter memory as a *constraint* on the range of values that variables can take. The idea is that this constraint is refined over and over again, until it represents the final result of the computation.

The computational model of CCP is based upon a set of concurrently operating processes that communicate with each other by means of a global store. This store is represented by a conjunction of constraints that express partial information on the values of the variables that are involved in their computations. The idea is that the multiple processes refine the partial information by adding new constraints to the store, until ultimately, the store contains the final solution to the problem. An example of an implemented concurrent constraint programming language is the language Oz [41].

In CCP, the operation $\texttt{tell}(\varphi)$ is used to add a constraint φ to the store. In order for the processes to communicate and synchronise with each other, there is an additional operation $\texttt{ask}(\varphi)$ that is used to test if the store entails the constraint φ. If the test succeeds then the corresponding process resumes its execution, otherwise its execution is suspended until φ is indeed entailed by the store through updates by other processes. So, a process that executes $\mathtt{ask}(x \geq 1)$ to ask for the information $x \geq 1$, can can resume its execution after for instance, two other processes have executed $\mathtt{tell}(x + y \geq 4)$ and $\mathtt{tell}(y = 3)$, respectively.

The introduction of the CCP paradigm means an important step in the research on concurrent programming, because it yields a novel view on programming. Instead of the manipulation of variables, which is characteristic for the imperative languages, programming in this paradigm amounts to the computation with *information*.

2.5 Agent Communication

In our opinion, the study of programming languages for multi-agent systems can be thought of as a next step in the research on concurrent programming languages. An essential aspect of multi-agent systems is that communication between agents proceeds at a higher level of abstraction in comparison with for instance object-oriented systems. That is, in object-oriented programming, an object is an encapsulated unit of data, with which other objects can interact through an invocation of one of its methods. Communication between agents takes place at a higher level of abstraction, involving propositions that are believed to be true or false, actions that are requested to be executed and goals that are to be achieved. One of the first proposed agent-oriented programming languages is the language AGENT-0 [39] in which agents are directly programmed in terms of mental concepts as their beliefs, capabilities and commitments. Other programming languages followed, like the languages PLACA [44], CONCURRENT METATEM [20], DESIRE [9], AGENTSPEAK [35] and 3APL [26].

With respect to their communication aspects, there is a close connection between the paradigm of concurrent constraint programming and the field of multi-agent programming. In both paradigms, the communication of *information* plays a central role. However, whereas CCP is suited for processes that communicate with each other by means of a global store, in multi-agent systems, agents are typically *distributed* over multiple sites [8].

One of the topics of current research on agent communication is the development of standard *agent communication languages* that enable agents from different platforms to interact with each other on a high level of abstraction [31, 40]. The most prominent communication languages are the language KQML [18] and the language FIPA-ACL [19, 33]. In essence, an agent communication language provides a set of communication acts that agents in a multi-agent system can perform. The purpose of these acts is to convey information about an agents own mental state with the objective to effect the mental state of the communication partner.

Communication actions of agent communication languages are comprised of a number of distinct layers. Figure 1 depicts the three-layer model of KQML. The first layer of KQML consists of the informational content of the communication action. This content is expressed in some agreed-upon language, like a propositional, first-order or some other knowledge representation language. This correpsonds to the constraint language of CCP. The second layer of the communication action expresses a particular attitude towards the informational content in the form of a speech act. Examples of speech acts are $\mathtt{tell}$ to express that the content is believed to hold, $\mathtt{untell}$ to express that φ is not

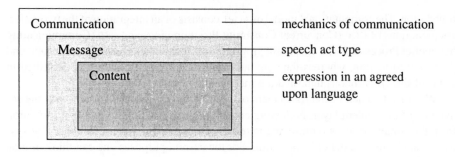

Fig. 1. Layers of the agent communication language KQML

believed to hold or ask to ask whether the content is believed to hold. Finally, the third layer deals with the mechanics of communication, involving aspects like the channel along which the communication takes place and the direction of the communication (that is, sent or received).

An example of a communication action is: c ! $\text{ask}(p)$. The content layer of the action consists of the proposition p, the message layer of the speech act ask and the communication layer of the communication channel c and the operator '!'. As noted, the operator '!' indicates that the message is sent along the communication channel, while the anticipated receipt of messages is indicated by the operator '?'.

For a clear understanding of agent communication we find it important not to consider communication actions in isolation, but to study them in the larger context of the multi-agent system in which they are performed. In this larger context, we can study aspects of conversations and dialogues, such as the specific order in which communication actions are executed, the conditions under which they take place and the effects they have on the (mental) states of the agents that are involved (see also [23]).

Therefore, we add one extra level to the three-layer model of KQML, namely the layer of the *multi-agent system*. We consider multi-agent systems that are defined in terms of a programming language. We assume the programming language to contain basic programming concepts, such as actions to examine and manipulate an agent's mental state, the aforementioned communication actions for interaction between agents, operators to make complex agent programs such as sequential composition '·', non-deterministic choice '+', parallel composition '&' and recursion and finally, operators to combine individual agent programs to form multi-agent programs like parallel composition '||'.

3   Semantic Approaches

One of the most prominent issues in the study of agent communications concerns their semantics. The current situation is that agent communication languages like KQML and FIPA-ACL are not fully understood from a semantical point of view [46].

In this paper, we consider some essential semantic aspects of agent communication. We will do this on the basis of ACPL (Agent Communication Programming Language), which is a formal framework that identifies basic aspects of agent communication [13–17]. In contrast to the languages FIPA-ACL and KQML, ACPL is supported by a semantic foundation. The computational model of ACPL consists of an integration of the two different paradigms of CCP (Concurrent Constraint Programming) and CSP (Communicating Sequential Processes). The constraint programming techniques are used to represent and process information, whereas the communication mechanism of ACPL is described in terms of the synchronous handshaking mechanism of CSP.

We consider each of the four layers of agent communication. We start with the semantics of the content layer. Following constraint programming, in ACPL, information from the content layer is represented in terms of a constraint system. A constraint system is an abstract model of information. For the current purposes one can think of it as a set of basic pieces of information, which can be combined to form complexer constraints by means of a conjunction operator $\wedge$. For instance, constraints can be formulas from propositional logic, like p and $p \rightarrow q$. Constraints are ordered by means of an information-ordering. For instance, q contains less information than $p \wedge (p \rightarrow q)$. Usually, the reverse of the information-ordering is considered, which is called the entailment relation, denoted as $\vdash$. For instance, we have $p \wedge (p \rightarrow q) \vdash q$. The entailment relation defines the semantics of the content layer.

The second layer of agent communication involves speech act types. We assume an extension of the entailment relation of the constraint system that includes speech acts. For instance, given the constraints ψ and φ, we can stipulate:

$$\texttt{untell}(\varphi) \vdash \texttt{untell}(\psi) \iff \psi \vdash \varphi,$$

which expresses the anti-monotonicity of the speech act untell. So, for instance, we have $\texttt{untell}(p) \vdash \texttt{untell}(p \wedge q)$, or in other words $\texttt{untell}(p \wedge q)$ contains less information than $\texttt{untell}(p)$. Other stipulations are for instance:

$$\texttt{tell}(\neg\varphi) \vdash \texttt{untell}(\varphi)$$
$$\texttt{untell}(\varphi) \nvdash \texttt{tell}(\neg\varphi),$$

which express some possible relations between the speech acts tell and untell. The reason why $\texttt{untell}(\varphi)$ does not entail $\texttt{tell}(\neg\varphi)$ is that an agent can believe neither φ nor $\neg\varphi$ to hold.

The third layer involves the communication channel and the direction of communication. There are many sorts of communication channels like one-to-one, one-to-many, many-to-one and many-to-many channels. Usually, we will consider one-to-one channels that have a unique sender and recipient associated with them. At this level, we consider the interplay between sending and anticipating the receipt of communication actions. In ACPL, the basic communication mechanism is synchronous. A synchronous communication step consists of a handshake between an agent that performs a communication action of the form $c\,!\,\texttt{speech\_act}_1(\varphi_1)$ and an agent that performs a matching communication act of the form $c\,?\,\texttt{speech\_act}_2(\varphi_2)$ along the same channel c. For them to match it is required that the sent message $\texttt{speech\_act}_1(\varphi_1)$ contains at least as much information as the message that is anticipated to be received, or in terms of the entailment relation:

$$\texttt{speech\_act}_1(\varphi_1) \vdash \texttt{speech\_act}_2(\varphi_2).$$

For instance, employing the above-mentioned relations between the speech acts tell and untell, we have that $c\,!\,\texttt{tell}(\neg p)$ matches with $c\,?\,\texttt{untell}(p)$, but $c\,!\,\texttt{untell}(p)$ does not match with c ? tell($\neg p$). By means of the synchronous communication mechanism different forms of asynchronous communication can be modelled, such as for instance sending a question without waiting for its answer (see [17] for more details).

Finally, we consider the semantics of the fourth layer. This layer consists of the context in which the communication actions take place: the multi-agent system. We assume multi-agent systems to be developed in terms of a particular programming language. The semantics of programming languages provide a rigorous mathematical description of the meaning of their symbols. An important motive to develop the semantics of a programming languages is that it defines a precise standard for its implementations. Moreover, the semantics allows us to study and understand the interplay between communication acts and the programming constructs.

Before we continue let us consider some simple examples.

Example 3. (Semantic distinctions)
The semantics of an agent communication language among others should allow us to identify in what ways (if at all) the following programs differ:

$$(1)\ c\,!\,\texttt{tell}(p) \cdot c\,!\,\texttt{tell}(q)$$
$$(2)\ c\,!\,\texttt{tell}(q) \cdot c\,!\,\texttt{tell}(p)$$
$$(3)\ c\,!\,\texttt{tell}(p \wedge q)$$
$$(4)\ c\,!\,\texttt{tell}(p \wedge q) + c\,!\,\texttt{tell}(p)$$

In ACPL, (1) and (2) have a different meaning because of the different order in which messages are exchanged. Programs (1) and (3) semantically differ because of the different number of exchanged messages. However, and this may be to some readers' surprise, there are circumstances under which there is no semantic difference between (3) and (4). We will come back to this issue later when we discuss full abstractness.

In the research on semantics of programming languages, there are several different methods to provide a language with a semantics [24, 43]. The most important methods are the axiomatic approach, operational approach and denotational approach.

Axiomatic Semantics. The first approach to the semantics of programming languages is the axiomatic approach, which constitutes an implicit form of giving semantics. In this approach, the meaning of the language is not explicitly defined but given in terms of properties that the language concepts satisfy. Usually these properties are formally derived by means of inference rules from a set of axioms.

The current approaches to the semantics of agent communication languages as KQML and FIPA-ACL belong to this class. In these frameworks, the semantics of a program P is defined by a triple

$$\{pre\}\ P\ \{post\},$$

where *pre* denotes a precondition that holds before the execution of P and *post* constitutes a postcondition that hold afterwards. For instance, in [30], a semantics of KQML is presented in which these conditions are based on *speech act theory*, which is a model of human communication [5, 38]. Additionally, following the approach of [45], the axiomatic semantics of the message tell(φ) communicated from the agent i to the agent j can be defined by:

$$\{\mathbf{B}_i\varphi\}\ \texttt{tell}(\varphi)\ \{\Diamond\mathbf{B}_j\varphi\},$$

which expresses that if before the execution of the action $\texttt{tell}(\varphi)$ the sender i believes the information φ to hold, then afterwards this information is eventually (denoted by the operator $\Diamond$) believed to hold by the recipient j.

The axiomatic approach is not generally thought of as a satisfactory way of giving formal semantics [37]. In general, the knowledge of only its properties is not sufficient for a thorough understanding of the language. The approach is therefore typically used to provide preliminary specifications of programming languages, which give the user insight in the important aspects of the languages. The axiomatic semantics should however be underpinned by other forms of semantics, in particular an *operational* semantics that gives insight in the implementations of the language, and a *denotational* semantics that provides an exact meaning of the language concepts.

Operational Semantics. An intuitive view of the execution of a program is to describe it in terms of the evolution of an abstract machine. The state of this machine is comprised of a control part consisting of the instructions that are to be executed and secondly, a data compartment that collects the data and information structures that are being manipulated. The execution of the program is then a sequence of subsequent transitions of the abstract machine, where the point of control moves along the program instructions. This form of semantics is referred to as *operational semantics* [34]. A major advantage of having an operational semantics is that an implementation of the language can be based upon an implementation of the corresponding abstract machine. To illustrate the approach, we consider the following (simplified version of a) transition from ACPL:

$$\langle c\,!\,\texttt{tell}(\varphi) \cdot P, state\rangle \xrightarrow{c\,!\,\texttt{tell}(\varphi)} \langle P, state\rangle \quad \text{if } state \vdash \varphi.$$

The operational reading of the program $c\,!\,\texttt{tell}(\varphi) \cdot P$ is that provided that φ is true of the agent's current state, which is noted by the condition $state \vdash \varphi$, it amounts to sending the information φ along the communication channel c, which is denoted by the label $c\,!\,\texttt{tell}(\varphi)$, after which the program P denotes the part of the program that will be executed next. The state of the agent remains invariant under the transition. In the semantic framework of ACPL, this action of telling information is just one part of a communication step, the other part is given by the transition of a corresponding agent in the system that anticipates the receipt of a matching message along c.

Denotational Semantics. In this methodology, each syntactic entity of a programming language is assigned a meaning, which is called its denotation. This form of semantics has the advantage that the different parts of a programming language can be studied in isolation; i.e., it gives a precise definition of what each individual language concept really means. To illustrate this approach, we consider the (simplified form of the) denotational semantics of ACPL.

This semantics makes use of *communication histories*. A communication history is a sequence of communication actions that have taken place. There are two kinds of communication histories: local and global. A local communication history consists of the communication actions that an individual agent has performed. It contains actions of the form $c\texttt{!speech\_act}(\varphi)$ and $c\texttt{?speech\_act}(\varphi)$. A global history is comprised of the communication actions that have taken place in a multi-agent system. It contains tuples of the form:

$$(c, \texttt{speech\_act}_1(\varphi_1), \texttt{speech\_act}_2(\varphi_2)).$$

Here, c denotes the channel along which has been communicated, $\texttt{speech\_act}_1(\varphi_1)$ and $\texttt{speech\_act}_2(\varphi_2)$ denote the matching communication actions of the sending and receiving agent, respectively. Matching means $\texttt{speech\_act}_1(\varphi_1) \vdash \texttt{speech\_act}_2(\varphi_2)$.

The semantics $[\![\ ]\!]$ of ACPL maps a program to the set of communication histories that it generates. This is a *set* because programs can give rise to more than one execution due to non-determinism. For instance, we have:

$$[\![c \,!\, \texttt{tell}(\varphi) \cdot P]\!] = \{ c \,!\, \texttt{tell}(\varphi) \cdot h \mid h \in [\![P]\!] \},$$

which says that the meaning of the program $c \,!\, \texttt{tell}(\varphi) \cdot P$ is given by the set of local communication histories h as generated by the program P, which are *prefixed* with the act of telling the information φ along the channel c.

4   Semantic Properties

In defining the denotational semantics of programming languages, the principle of *compositionality* plays a crucial role. This principle states that the meaning of a compound program can be derived from the meaning of its components. For instance, the denotational semantics of the parallel composition of two agent programs P_1 and P_2 can be derived from the denotational semantics of its two programs. That is, the global communication history of the multi-agent program $P_1 \,||\, P_2$ consisting of matching communication actions can be derived from the local communication actions of the individual agent programs P_1 and P_2. Formally, this can be defined as follows:

$$[\![P_1 \,||\, P_2]\!] = \{ h \mid h \!\upharpoonright\! P_1 \in [\![P_1]\!] \text{ and } h \!\upharpoonright\! P_2 \in [\![P_2]\!] \}$$

where $h \!\upharpoonright\! P_i$ denotes the projection of the global communication history h to the communication actions of the agent P_i, for $i = 1, 2$. So, for instance, we have:

$$[\![P_1]\!] = \{ (c \,!\, \texttt{ask}(p)) \cdot (d \,?\, \texttt{untell}(p)) \cup$$
$$(c \,!\, \texttt{ask}(p)) \cdot (d \,?\, \texttt{tell}(p)) \}$$

$$[\![P_2]\!] = \{ (c \,?\, \texttt{ask}(p)) \cdot (d \,!\, \texttt{tell}(\neg p)) \}$$

$$[\![P_1 \,||\, P_2]\!] = \{ (c, \texttt{ask}(p), \texttt{ask}(p)) \cdot (d, \texttt{tell}(\neg p), \texttt{untell}(p)) \}$$

The reason why the global history $(c, \texttt{ask}(p), \texttt{ask}(p)) \cdot (d, \texttt{tell}(\neg p), \texttt{tell}(p))$ is not part of $[\![P_1 \,||\, P_2]\!]$ is that the communication acts $d \,!\, \texttt{tell}(\neg p)$ and $d \,?\, \texttt{tell}(p)$ do not match.

An equivalent formulation of the principle of compositionality is that if one of the components of a program is replaced by a component that has exactly the same meaning, the meaning of the program is preserved. Formally, this is phrased as follows:

If $[\![P_1]\!] = [\![P_2]\!]$ then for all contexts C we have $[\![C[P_1]]\!] = [\![C[P_2]]\!]$.

In the area of concurrency, the semantics of programming languages are usually defined relative to a notion of *observable behaviour*, which exactly captures the aspects of the behaviour of the systems that an external observer is interested in. In reasoning about the behaviour of multi-agent systems, we are typically not interested in all details of the execution of the system. Important aspects are the communication histories and the agents' mental states at some specific points during the execution, such as for instance right before and after a performed communication action.

Furthermore, a semantics is called *correct* if the observable behaviour can be extracted from the semantics. As an example we take as our observable behaviour whether a multi-agent system enters into a deadlock situation or successfully terminates. In order for the above denotational semantics $[\![\ ]\!]$ to be correct, it needs to be refined with deadlocking behaviour. A solution to this is the introduction of *failure sets* [6]. In ACPL, failure sets consist of all communication actions that do not match with the current communication action that an agent wants to execute next. The corresponding form of semantics is referred to as *failure semantics*.

Finally, the semantics of a programming language can make unnecessary distinctions. This is the case if two programs have a different meaning but this difference cannot be observed, that is, there is no context in which they exhibit different observable behaviour. A semantics that does not make such unnecessary distinctions with respect to the observable behaviour is called *fully-abstract*. The failure semantics of ACPL is proven to be fully-abstract [16].

For instance, consider again the programs (3) and (4) of Example 3. It can be formally proven that there does not exist a context in which the programs (3) and (4) exhibit different observable behaviour. As the failure semantics of ACPL is fully-abstract, both programs thus have the same failure semantics. The crucial observation here is that any communication action that matches $c\ !\ \mathtt{tell}(p)$ also matches $c\ !\ \mathtt{tell}(p \wedge q)$. In general, we could say that sending a message includes sending all messages that contain less information. A similar property holds for the anticipated receipt of messages. There is no observable difference between the following programs (5) and (6):

$$(5)\ c\ ?\ \mathtt{tell}(p)$$
$$(6)\ c\ ?\ \mathtt{tell}(p) + c\ ?\ \mathtt{tell}(p \wedge q)$$

Any communication action that matches $c\ ?\ \mathtt{tell}(p \wedge q)$ also matches $c\ ?\ \mathtt{tell}(p)$. In other words, anticipating the receipt of a messages includes anticipating the receipt of all messages that contain more information.

Once the semantics of a programming language has been established, it allows us to consider the *specification* and *verification* of agent communication. Verification amounts to the process of checking whether a program satisfies desired behaviour as expressed by a specification. Specifications are usually defined in what is called an *assertion language*. An example of an assertion in the assertion language of ACPL is the following assertion Ψ:

$$\forall i (h(i) = (c, \mathtt{ask}(p), \mathtt{ask}(p)) \rightarrow \exists j (j > i \wedge$$

$$((h(j) = (d, \mathtt{tell}(p), \mathtt{tell}(p)) \wedge Bel_B(p))) \vee h(j) = (d, \mathtt{untell}(p), \mathtt{untell}(p)))).$$

If we suppose that c and d are one-to-one communication channels that connect the agents A and B, the above assertion expresses that if at some point i in the communication history h agent A asks agent B whether the proposition p holds then at some point j later in history, either agent B tells A that it believes p to hold after which B also believes that φ holds or agent B tells A that it does not believe p to hold.

In the above assertion we find an example of a *conversation policy* [22], namely the policy that if an agent A is asked by an agent B whether a particular proposition holds then A subsequently answers B whether it believes the proposition to hold or not.

Note that both the multi-agent programming language and the assertion language have their own syntax and semantics. They are linked through the underlying computational model: A particular multi-agent program satisfies a particular assertion if the assertion is true for all computations that the multi-agent program gives rise.

In [17], a compositional verification calculus for ACPL is defined. This calculus can be used to verify that a particular multi-agent system satisfies the above assertion Ψ. It is comprised of rules of the form:

$$\frac{P_1 \; sat \; \Phi_1 \cdots P_n \; sat \; \Phi_n}{P \; sat \; \Phi}$$

where P denotes a multi-agent program that is composed of the components $P_1, \ldots, P_n$ and Φ constitutes an assertion that is obtained from the assertions $\Phi_1, \ldots, \Phi_n$. These rules can be used to formally derive the specification of the behaviour of the program P can from the specification of its components. On the basis of this calculus it is possible to implement (semi-)automatic verification procedures. This is a subject of future research.

5   Concluding Remarks

In this paper, we have considered the semantics of agent communication. We have sketched the research on communication in concurrent programming paradigms, starting with communication via shared variables and resulting in communication in multi-agent systems. We have considered the four different layers that play a role in giving semantics to agent communication and the main approaches for developing semantics of programming languages. On the basis of the ACPL framework (Agent Communication Programming Language) we have discussed semantic issues involved in programming agent communication, including communication histories, compositionality, observational behaviour, failure semantics and full abstractness. Finally, we have considered the specification and verification of agent communication. In our view, these issues play an important part in defining a semantic foundation for agent communication languages as KQML and FIPA-ACL, which is a subject of further research.

Acknowledgements

The author would like to thank Mehdi Dastani for his valuable comments on an earlier draft of this paper. The author would also like to express his gratitude to Frank de Boer, Wiebe van der Hoek and John-Jules Meyer for their valuable cooperation on the subject of agent communication over the years.

References

1. G. Agha. Concurrent object-oriented programming. *Communications of the ACM*, 33(9):125–141, 1990.
2. G. Agha, P. Wegner, and Yonezawa. *Research Directions in Concurrent Object-Oriented Programming*. The MIT Press, Cambridge, Massachusetts, 1993.
3. P.H.M. America. Issues in the design of a parallel object-oriented language. *Formal Aspects of Computing*, 1:366–411, 1989.
4. G.R. Andrews. *Concurrent Programming, Principles and Practice*. The Benjamin Cummings Publishing Company, Inc., Redwood City, California, 1991.
5. J.L. Austin. *How to do Things with Words*. Oxford University Press, Oxford, 1962.
6. J.A. Bergstra, J.W. Klop, and E.-R. Olderog. Readies and failures in the algebra of communicating processes. *SIAM Journal on Computing*, 17:1134–1177, 1988.
7. A. D. Birrell and B. J. Nelson. Implementing remote procedure calls. *ACM Transactions on Computer Systems*, 2:39–59, 1984.
8. A.H Bond and L. Gasser. *Readings in Distributed Artificial Intelligence*. Morgan Kaufmann Publishers, San Mateo, CA, 1988.
9. F. Brazier, B. Dunin-Keplicz, N. Jennings, and J. Treur. Formal specification of multi-agent systems: a real-world case. In *Proceedings of International Conference on Multi-Agent Systems (ICMAS'95)*, pages 25–32. MIT Press, 1995.
10. K. Clark and S. Gregory. Parlog: parallel programming in logic. *ACM Transactions on Programming Languages and Systems*, 8(1):1–49, 1986.
11. E.W. Dijkstra. Solution of a problem in concurrent programming control. *Communications of the ACM*, 8(9):569, 1965.
12. E.W. Dijkstra. Cooperating sequential processes. In F. Genuys, editor, *Programming Languages*, pages 43–112. Academic Press, New York, 1968.
13. R.M. van Eijk. *Programming Languages for Agent Communication*. PhD thesis, Utrecht University, Mathematics and Computer Science, 2000.
14. R.M. van Eijk, F.S. de Boer, W. van der Hoek, and J.-J.Ch. Meyer. Information-passing and belief revision in multi-agent systems. In J. P. M. Müller, M. P. Singh, and A. S. Rao, editors, *Intelligent Agents V, Proceedings of 5th International Workshop on Agent Theories, Architectures, and Languages (ATAL'98)*, volume 1555 of *Lecture Notes in Artificial Intelligence*, pages 29–45. Springer-Verlag, Heidelberg, 1999.
15. R.M. van Eijk, F.S. de Boer, W. van der Hoek, and J.-J.Ch. Meyer. On dynamically generated ontology translators in agent communication. *International Journal of Intelligent Systems*, 16(5):587–607, 2001.
16. R.M. van Eijk, F.S. de Boer, W. van der Hoek, and J.-J.Ch. Meyer. Fully-abstract model for the exchange of information in multi-agent systems. *Theoretical Computer Science*. To appear, 2002.
17. R.M. van Eijk, F.S. de Boer, W. van der Hoek, and J.-J.Ch. Meyer. A verification framework for agent communication. *Autonomous Agents and Multi-Agent Systems*. To appear, 2002.
18. T. Finin, D. McKay, R. Fritzson, and R. McEntire. KQML: An Information and Knowledge Exchange Protocol. In Kazuhiro Fuchi and Toshio Yokoi, editors, *Knowledge Building and Knowledge Sharing*. Ohmsha and IOS Press, 1994.
19. Foundation For Intelligent Physical Agents FIPA. Specification part 2 – agent communication language. Version dated 10th October 1997, 1997.
20. M. Fisher. A survey of concurrent METATEM– the language and its applications. In *Proceedings of First International Conference on Temporal Logic (ICTL'94)*, volume 827 of *Lecture Notes in Computer Science*, pages 480–505. Springer-Verlag, 1994.

21. P. Gibbens. *Logic with Prolog*. Oxford Applied Mathematics and Computing Science Series. Oxford University Press, New York, 1988.
22. M. Greaves, H. Holmback, and J. Bradshaw. What is a conversation policy? In F. Dignum and M. Greaves, editors, *Issues in Agent Communication*, volume 1916 of *Lecture Notes in Artificial Intelligence*, pages 118–131. Springer-Verlag, Heidelberg, 2000.
23. F. Guerin and J. Pitt. A semantic framework for specifying agent communication languages. In *Proceedings of fourth International Conference on Multi-Agent Systems (ICMAS-2000)*, pages 395–396, Los Alamitos, California, 2000. IEEE Computer Society.
24. C.A. Gunter. *Semantics of Programming Languages: Structures and Techniques*. Foundations of Computing Series. The MIT Press, Cambridge, Massachusetts, 1992.
25. C. Hewitt. Viewing control as patterns of passing messages. *Artificial Intelligence*, 8(3):323–364, 1977.
26. K.V. Hindriks, F.S. de Boer, W. van der Hoek, and J.-J.Ch Meyer. Agent programming in 3APL. *Autonomous Agents and Multi-Agent Systems*, 2:357–401, 1999.
27. C.A.R. Hoare. Monitors: an operating system structuring concept. *Communications of the ACM*, 17(10):549–557, 1974.
28. C.A.R. Hoare. Communicating sequential processes. *Communications of the ACM*, 21(8):666–677, 1978.
29. G. Jones. *Programming in Occam*. Prentice-Hall International, New York, NY, 1987.
30. Y. Labrou and T. Finin. Semantics for an agent communication language. In M.P. Singh, A. Rao, and M.J. Wooldridge, editors, *Proceedings of Fourth International Workshop on Agent Theories, Architectures and Languages (ATAL'97)*, volume 1365 of *Lecture Notes in Artificial Intelligence*, pages 209–214. Springer-Verlag, 1998.
31. Y. Labrou, T. Finin, and Y. Peng. Agent communication languages: The current landscape. *IEEE Intelligent Systems*, 14(2):45–52, 1999.
32. P. Noriega and C. Sierra, editors. *Agent Mediated Electronic Commerce*, volume 1571 of *Lecture Notes in Computer Science*. Springer Verlag, 1999.
33. J. Pitt and A. Mamdani. Some remarks on the semantics of FIPA's agent communication language. *Autonomous Agents and Multi-Agent Systems*, 2(4):333–356, 1999.
34. G. Plotkin. A structured approach to operational semantics. Technical Report DAIMI FN-19, Computer Science Department, Aarhus University, 1981.
35. A.S. Rao. Agentspeak(L): BDI agents speak out in a logical computable language. In W. van der Velde and J.W. Perram, editors, *Agents Breaking Away*, volume 1038 of *Lecture Notes in Artificial Intelligence*, pages 42–55. Springer-Verlag, 1996.
36. V.A. Saraswat. *Concurrent Constraint Programming*. The MIT Press, Cambridge, Massachusetts, 1993.
37. D.A. Schmidt. *Denotational Semantics: A Methodology for Language Development*. Allyn and Bacon, Inc. Newton, Massachusetts, 1986.
38. J.R. Searle. *Speech acts: An essay in the philosophy of language*. Cambridge University Press, Cambridge, England, 1969.
39. Y. Shoham. Agent-oriented programming. *Artificial Intelligence*, 60:51–92, 1993.
40. M.P. Singh. Agent communication languages: Rethinking the principles. *IEEE Computer*, 31(12):40–47, 1998.
41. G. Smolka. The Oz programming model. In J. van Leeuwen, editor, *Computer Science Today*, volume 1000 of *Lecture Notes in Computer Science*, pages 324–343, Berlin, 1995. Springer-Verlag.
42. L. Sterling and E. Shapiro. *The Art of Prolog*. The MIT Press, Cambridge, Massachusetts, 1986.
43. R.D. Tennent. *Semantics of Programming Languages*. Prentice Hall, Hertfordshire, 1991.
44. S.R. Thomas. *PLACA, an Agent Oriented Programming Language*. PhD thesis, Computer Science Department, Stanford University, Stanford, CA, 1993.

45. M. Wooldridge. Verifying that agents implement a communication language. In *Proceedings of the Sixteenth National Conference on Artificial Intelligence (AAAI-99)*, pages 52–57, 1999.

46. M. Wooldridge. Semantic issues in the verification of agent communication. *Autonomous Agents and Multi-Agent Systems*, 3(1):9–31, 2000.

47. M. Wooldridge and N. Jennings. Intelligent agents: theory and practice. *The Knowledge Engineering Review*, 10(2):115–152, 1995.

Agents with Bounded Temporal Resources

Michael Fisher and Chiara Ghidini

Logic and Computation Group, Department of Computer Science,
University of Liverpool, Liverpool L69 7ZF, United Kingdom,
{M.Fisher,C.Ghidini}@csc.liv.ac.uk

Abstract. In this chapter we introduce a common framework for both the logical specification and execution of agents. This logical framework provides the basis for the specification and execution of agents comprising dynamic (temporal) activity, deliberation concerning goals, and reasoning about belief.

We here focus in particular on the ability of this approach to capture an important aspect of practical agents, notably their resource-bounded nature. We present a logic in which resource-boundedness can be specified both in terms of temporal reasoning, and reasoning about belief. Then we consider how specifications within this logic can be directly executed. The mechanism we use to capture finite resources in reasoning about beliefs is to employ a *multi-context* representation of belief, thus providing tight control over the agent's reasoning capabilities where necessary. The mechanism we use to capture finite resources in temporal reasoning is to use a linear time temporal logic with both finite past and finite future.

1 Introduction

The METATEM [1] and Concurrent METATEM [8] languages were developed in order to provide high-level mechanisms for specifying and executing individual agents and multi-agent systems, respectively. Both are based upon the principle of specifying an agent using temporal logic, and then *directly executing* this specification in order to provide the agent's behaviour. This approach provides a high-level programming notation, while maintaining a close link between the program and its specification.

This approach has provided a useful basis for experimentation with both the logical representation and animation of agents and most of the research work in this area is now devoted to develop more refined versions of the specification language in order to be able to use this framework for 'real world' agents.

First, the basic METATEM system was extended in [9] with mechanisms for representing deliberation within an agent. Deliberation is the process that an agent carries out in order to decide which goal/action/plan to attempt. Inspired by the success of the BDI framework [17] in representing deliberation, METATEM was extended with explicit mechanisms for ordering goals. Goals, corresponding to both desires and intentions in the BDI model were, in turn, represented by temporal eventualities. This then allowed deliberation to be represented using

M. d' Inverno et al. (Eds.): UKMAS 1996–2000, LNAI 2403, pp. 169–184, 2002.

user defined functions providing an ordering on the satisfaction of eventualities. More recently, we have extended the METATEM system in order to capture the key concepts of goals, abilities, beliefs and a more sophisticated notion of *deliberation* between both individual agents and multi-agent systems, using only combination of temporal aspects, agent beliefs and agent abilities [12].

Another stream of work concerns providing METATEM with a simple and concise mechanism for dealing with a further important aspect of 'real' agents, namely their resource-bounded nature [3]. Thus, in [10] we modify the logic used in [9] by replacing the standard KD45 modal logic with a *multi-context* representation of belief [14, 2, 13]. This logic is a modification of KD45 which permits a simple execution mechanism to be employed over belief contexts. Consequently, it allows us to tightly control the use of belief contexts within deliberative agents and so to represent resource-bounded reasoning about belief. In [11], we took a step further examining how the dynamic agents that have resource bounds varying over time can be represented.

In this chapter we continue this stream of work investigating the resource-bounded aspects of *temporal* reasoning. Thus, rather than allowing the agent to reason about an infinite possible future, we will examine how the agent can be restricted so that it has resource bounds on its temporal reasoning process.

The paper is structured as follows. In Section 2, we introduce a running example that will be used throughout the paper. In Section 3, we review the syntax and semantics of the *Temporal Logic of Bounded Belief (TLBB)*. In Section 3.3 we extend TLBB in order to incorporate resource-bounded aspects of temporal reasoning. In Section 4, we outline how implementation can be achieved through direct execution. In Section 5, we provide the logical specification and the execution of the example introduced in Section 2. Finally, we discuss conclusions and future work.

2   An Example

We recall here the "Three Wise Man" (TWM) puzzle, and use it to illustrate how our framework can be used to formalize reasoning about belief within a group of agents. The TWM, first introduced by McCarthy in his well known paper on the formalization of puzzles involving knowledge [15], provides a classical example of the scenario we are addressing:

> *A certain King wishes to test his three wise men. He arranges them in a circle so that they can see and hear each other and tells them that he will put a white or black spot on each of their forehead but that at least one spot will be white. In fact all three spots are white. He then repeatedly asks them "do you know the color of your spot?". What do they answer?*

A group of agents (the three wise men) seek cooperation in order to achieve a particular goal, that is, to answer correctly the question "do you know the color of your spot?". Since agents are not alone, agents may have beliefs about other agent's belief in addition to their knowledge about the world. Moreover, the puzzle involves some temporal aspects given by the fact that the king *repeatedly* asks them the crucial question and they update their beliefs over time as a consequence of the responses from the other agents.

We assume that the wise men answer simultaneously. Under this assumption, did you figure out the answers of the wise men? The first and second time the King asks the question, wise men will answer "I don't know", while the third time the wise men will answer "My spot is white"[1]. Nevertheless, depending on the reasoning capabilities of the men, the puzzle might have different outcomes [5]. In particular, it may be the case that a wise man, say man 3, is not so wise and is not able to reason about more than 2 temporal steps in the time line. In this paper we consider two simple cases. In the first scenario, the wise men have full reasoning capabilities and are able to solve the puzzle. In the second scenario wise man 3 is able to reason about a very short future in time. Therefore, the third time the king repeat the question he won't be able to give the correct answer.

3   Temporal Logic of Bounded Belief

We recall here the syntax and semantics of our base logic, called a *Temporal Logic of Bounded Belief*, or TLBB for short. TLBB combines propositional linear temporal logic [7], with a multi-context belief logic [14]. While temporal reasoning is essentially infinite, reasoning about beliefs can be bounded at a certain depth. In order to review this approach, we first introduce a simple temporal logic based on a linear, discrete model of time (section 3.1), then we combine it with a multi-context belief logic (Section 3.2).

3.1   Representing Temporal Reasoning

The language of the temporal logic used here is formally defined as the smallest set of formulae containing: a set, $\mathcal{P}$, of propositional constants, the symbols **true**, **false**, and **start**, and being closed under propositional connectives $\neg$, $\vee$, $\wedge$, $\Rightarrow$ and temporal operators $\bigcirc$, $\Diamond$, $\square$, $\mathcal{U}$, and $\mathcal{W}$.

As usual, the semantics of this logic is defined via the satisfiability relation on a discrete linear temporal model of time, m, with finite past and infinite future [7]. Thus, m is a sequence of states s_0, s_1, s_2, s_3, ... which can be thought of as 'moments' in time. Associated with each of these moments in time, represented by a temporal index $u \in \mathbb{N}$, is a valuation π for the propositional part of the language.

Intuitively, the temporal formula '$\bigcirc A$' is satisfied at a given moment in time if A is satisfied at the *next* moment in time, '$\Diamond A$' is satisfied if A is satisfied at *some* future moment in time, ' $\square A$' is satisfied if A is satisfied at *all* future moments in time. '$A\,\mathcal{U}\,B$' is satisfied if B is satisfied at some future moment in

---

[1] Generalising to a set of k wise men, there is a "proof" that the first $k-1$ times the King asks the question, the wise men will answer "I don't know", while the k-th time they will answer "My spot is white".

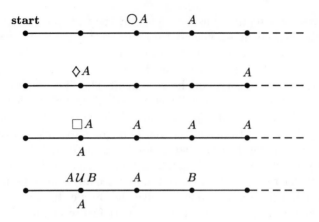

Fig. 1. Pictorial semantics of temporal operators.

time, and A is satisfied in all moments in time *until* B occurs, '$A\,W\,B$' is satisfied if A is always satisfied *unless* B occurs. Notice that B might never occur. In this case A would be always satisfied. The graphical representation of the semantics of '$\bigcirc A$','$\Diamond A$', '$\Box A$', and '$A\mathcal{U}B$' is given in the four different sequences of time in Figure 1. We can graphically represent '$A\,W\,B$' as the combination of '$A\mathcal{U}B$' and '$\Box A$'. In fact either B is satisfied some time in the future, or B is never satisfied. In the first case the representation is similar to the one of '$A\mathcal{U}B$', in the second to '$\Box A$'. Notice also that we use a special propositional constant **start**, which is only true at the initial moment in time.

Formally, the semantics of the temporal language used here is defined in Figure 2. Satisfiability and validity are defined in the usual way.

$$\langle m, 0\rangle \models \textbf{start}$$

$$\langle m, u\rangle \models \textbf{true}$$

$\langle m, u\rangle \models p$ iff $\pi(u, p) = T$ (where $p \in \mathcal{P}$)

$\langle m, u\rangle \models \neg A$ iff $\langle m, u\rangle \not\models A$

$\langle m, u\rangle \models A \vee B$ iff $\langle m, u\rangle \models A$ or $\langle m, u\rangle \models B$

$\langle m, u\rangle \models \bigcirc A$ iff $\langle m, u + 1\rangle \models A$

$\langle m, u\rangle \models \Box A$ iff $\forall u' \in \mathbb{N}.$ if $(u \leq u')$ then $\langle m, u'\rangle \models A$

$\langle m, u\rangle \models \Diamond A$ iff $\exists u' \in \mathbb{N}. (u < u')$ and $\langle m, u'\rangle \models A$

$\langle m, u\rangle \models A\mathcal{U}B$ iff $\exists u' \in \mathbb{N}.$ such that $(u' \geq u)$ and $\langle m, u'\rangle \models B$, and $\forall u'' \in \mathbb{N},$ if $(u \leq u'' < u')$ then $\langle m, u''\rangle \models A$

$\langle m, u\rangle \models A\,W\,B$ iff $\langle m, u\rangle \models A\mathcal{U}B$ or $\langle m, u\rangle \models \Box A$

Fig. 2. Formal semantics of the temporal language.

3.2   Representing Belief-Bounded Reasoning

An extension of the logic presented above is introduced in [10], where the propositional linear temporal logic introduced above is combined with a multi-context belief logic [14, 13]. While temporal reasoning is essentially infinite, this logic, called TLBB, permits a simple execution mechanism to be employed over a finite structure of belief contexts and so to represent resource-bounded reasoning.

The main idea in defining TLBB, is to add to the language a set I of belief predicates, $\{B_1, \ldots, B_n\}$, where formulae of the form '$B_i \phi$' mean "agent i believes that ϕ", and to structure the belief of an agent ϵ about a set $\{1, \ldots, n\}$ of agents, into a structure of *belief contexts* such as that presented in Figure 3. Intuitively, the belief context ϵ represents the knowledge and beliefs of the external agent ϵ, the belief context $3B_1$ represents the beliefs of agent 1 at the third moment in time (from the point of view of ϵ), $3B_1 2B_4$ represents the beliefs of agent 1 at the third moment in time about the beliefs agent 4 at the second moment in time (from the point of view of ϵ), and so on. The set of belief contexts that ϵ is able to build is represented by the set, $I^k \subseteq (\mathbb{N} \times I)^*$, of (possibly empty) strings of the form $u_1 B_{h_1} \ldots u_k B_{h_k}$ with $u_i \in \mathbb{N}$, $B_{h_i} \in I$, and $|u_1 B_{h_1} \ldots u_k B_{h_k}| \leq 2k$. We use α to denote a generic belief context in I^k. Intuitively, each α represents a possible nesting of the belief operators at certain moments in time. The fact that $|\alpha| \leq 2k$, intuitively means that ϵ is able to reason about formulae with a specific bound in the nesting of the belief operators, that is, a bound equal to k.

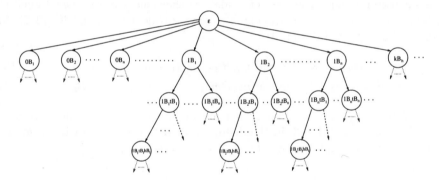

Fig. 3. The structure of belief contexts

The semantics of the TLBB language is based on the semantics for contextual reasoning proposed in [13], and extends the one presented in [10]. Following this approach, a model for the TLBB language is defined over a structure obtained as follows. First we associate to each belief context α a set M_α of discrete linear temporal models of time m. Then, we define a relation R satisfying:

1. $R \subseteq \bigcup_{\alpha \in I^k, u \in \mathbb{N}, B_i \in I} (M_\alpha \times M_{\alpha u B_i})$

2. For each $m_{\alpha u B_i} \in M_{\alpha u B_i}$ there must exist a $m_\alpha \in M_\alpha$ such that $m_\alpha R m_{\alpha u B_i}$.

174 Michael Fisher and Chiara Ghidini

3. For each $m_\alpha \in M_\alpha$ there must exist a $m_{\alpha u B_i} \in M_{\alpha u B_i}$ such that $m_\alpha R m_{\alpha u B_i}$.

A model for the TLBB language is a pair $M = \langle \{M_\alpha\}_{\alpha \in I^k}, R \rangle$. Each $m_\alpha \in M_\alpha$ provides a valuation π_α for the propositional part of the language and for the formulae of the form $B_i \psi$, which are considered atomic formulae. The propositional and temporal part of the language is interpreted in the usual way via the satisfiability relation $\models$ in the appropriate m_α. We say that a model M satisfies a formula ϕ in the belief context α if, and only if, all the $m_\alpha \in M_\alpha$ satisfy ϕ. For the sake of simplicity we use the symbol $M_\alpha \models \phi$ to denote that all the $m_\alpha \in M_\alpha$ satisfy ϕ.

The intended semantics of the belief predicates B_i is defined by introducing appropriate constraints among pairs of belief contexts α and $\alpha u B_i$. Roughly speaking the intended relation between the formula, e.g., $B_i \psi$ at the u-th moment in time in the belief context ϵ and ψ in the (initial moment in time of the) belief context $u B_i$ is that they both mean that ϵ believes that i believes that ψ in the u-th moment in time. In order to ensure that $B_i \psi$ is satisfied in the u-th moment in time in the models for the belief context ϵ if, and only if, ψ is satisfied in the models for belief context $u B_i$ we impose the additional constraints (1) and (2) on the definition of model:

$$\text{if } \langle m_\alpha, u \rangle \models B_i \varphi \text{ and } m_\alpha R m_{\alpha u B_i} \text{ then } m_{\alpha u B_i} \models \varphi \qquad (1)$$
$$\text{if } m_{\alpha u B_i} \models \varphi \text{ for all } m_{\alpha u B_i} \text{ with } m_{\alpha u B_i} R m_\alpha \text{ then } \langle m_\alpha, u \rangle \models B_i \varphi \qquad (2)$$

These constraints force the class of models we consider here to be contained in the class of models for a multi-context logic equivalent to modal K [13, 2]. In addition, constraints (3) and (4)

$$\text{if } \langle m_\alpha, u \rangle \models B_i \varphi \text{ and } m_\alpha R m_{\alpha u B_i} \text{ then } m_{\alpha u B_i} \models B_i \varphi \qquad (3)$$
$$\text{if } \langle m_\alpha, u \rangle \models \neg B_i \varphi \text{ and } m_\alpha R m_{\alpha u B_i} \text{ then } m_{\alpha u B_i} \models \neg B_i \varphi \qquad (4)$$

force M to satisfy a multi-context version of modal axioms **4** and **5** respectively [4], while condition 3. in the definition of R forces M to satisfy a multi-context version of modal axioms **D**.

3.3 Representing Temporal-Bounded Reasoning

Given that we can bound the agent's ability to reason about belief, then can we do the same with temporal reasoning? In this section we describe a variation of the TLBB given above, and we associate to each belief context α a discrete linear *finite* temporal model of time m_α.

In order to do that we modify the definition of the temporal language adding the temporal operator $\odot$ to the set $\bigcirc$, $\Diamond$, $\square$, $\mathcal{U}$, and $\mathcal{W}$. The temporal operators $\odot$ (strong next) and $\bigcirc$ (weak or standard next) have similar meaning. Both $\odot A$ and $\bigcirc A$ are satisfied if A is satisfied at the next moment in time. The difference between them is that $\bigcirc A$ is satisfied also if there is no next moment in time, while $\odot A$ is satisfied *only* if a next moment exists, and satisfies A.

Since the model we are considering is finite, we can easily see that the truth values of $\bigcirc A$ and $\odot A$ coincide in all the moments in time except the last one. At the last moment in time $\bigcirc A$ will always be satisfied, regardless of A. On the contrary $\odot A$ cannot be satisfied for any formula A. Formally,

$$\langle m, u \rangle \models \bigcirc A \quad \text{iff} \quad \forall u + 1 \, \langle m, u + 1 \rangle \models A$$

$$\langle m, u \rangle \models \odot A \quad \text{iff} \, \exists u + 1 \text{ such that } \langle m, u + 1 \rangle \models A$$

As an example of how we can use the weak next $\bigcirc$ operator in order to bound the temporal reasoning let us consider formulae of the form

$$\textbf{start} \Rightarrow \bigcirc^n \textbf{false},$$

where $\bigcirc^n$ is a shorthand for $\underbrace{\bigcirc\bigcirc \ldots \bigcirc}_{n \text{ times}}$.

This formula is only satisfied in temporal models composed of a sequence of (at most) n states. Therefore we can use formulae of this form for bounding the agent's ability to perform temporal reasoning. For instance in the second version of the TWM example, the wise men only can consider two moments in time in their reasoning. This will be done by imposing the formula $\textbf{start} \Rightarrow \bigcirc^2 \textbf{false}$ to hold in the specification of the example.

4 Implementation

We choose to retain a close link between theory and implementation by directly executing each agent specification. The mechanism used to carry out this execution is based upon the work in [9] which is, in turn, a modification or the METATEM approach [1]. Rather than going into detail concerning this approach, we simply outline the key elements below. A detailed description of the execution process, extended to handle formulae in TLBB, can be found in [10]. The only difference here is that the argument recording the depth of nesting of the belief operators (contexts) is not fixed but depends on the value of the predicate *bound*.

- Specifications of agent behaviour in TLBB are first translated to a specific normal form, SNF_{BB}, of the form depicted in Figure 4
- The execution essentially forward chains through a set of such rules, gradually constructing a model for the specification.
- If a contradiction is generated, backtracking occurs.
- Eventualities, such as '$\Diamond move$' are satisfied as soon as possible; in the case of conflicting eventualities, the oldest outstanding ones are attempted first. The choice mechanism takes into account a combination of the outstanding eventualities, and the deliberation ordering functions [9].
- As each B_i operator is expanded, a record of the depth of nesting of such operators is kept. Once the current bound is reached, exploration of the current belief context ceases.

- As in [10], the idea is that, if the original specification is satisfiable, then the execution algorithm will eventually build a model for the specification. Note that, as execution is not the focus of this paper, we will not consider such correctness here.
- If we consider the finite future case, we need to modify the step rule so that it deals both with $\bigcirc$ and $\odot$ formulae. Also, during execution the step rule is are applied and a next temporal state is created if and only if the current temporal state does not satisfy the formula $\bigcirc$**false**.

$$\text{\bf start} \Rightarrow \bigvee_{b=1}^{r} l_b \qquad \text{(an \emph{initial} rule)}$$

$$\bigwedge_{a=1}^{g} k_a \Rightarrow \bigcirc \left[\bigvee_{b=1}^{r} l_b \right] \qquad \text{(a \emph{step} rule)}$$

$$\bigwedge_{a=1}^{g} k_a \Rightarrow \Diamond l \qquad \text{(a \emph{sometime} rule)}$$

$$\bigwedge_{a=1}^{g} k_a \Rightarrow B_i \left[\bigvee_{b=1}^{r} l_b \right] \qquad \text{(a \emph{belief} rule)}$$

$$\bigwedge_{a=1}^{g} k_a \Rightarrow \neg B_i \left[\bigvee_{b=1}^{r} l_b \right] \qquad \text{(a \emph{belief} rule)}$$

Fig. 4. The normal form SNF_{BB}

5 Executing the Example

In the following we present the logical specification of the three wise men described in Section 2, and the executions of the specification. We focus here on wise man 3 trying to answer the third utterance of the crucial question.

The Specification. Let us start with the specific knowledge and beliefs of the system, that is the knowledge and beliefs that must be satisfied in the belief context labelled by ϵ. We use the propositional constants W_1, W_2, and W_3 to express statements about the spots, W_i meaning that the spot of wise man i is white. We provide a specification similar to the one given in [6] for the similar muddy children problem.

1) We take the case where all wise men have white spots

$$\text{\bf start} \Rightarrow W_1 \qquad\qquad\qquad (A)$$
$$\text{\bf start} \Rightarrow W_2 \qquad\qquad\qquad (B)$$
$$\text{\bf start} \Rightarrow W_3 \qquad\qquad\qquad (C)$$

2) We use the variables x, y, and z to denote times 0, 1, and 2.

$$\textbf{start} \Rightarrow x \tag{D}$$

$$x \Rightarrow \bigcirc y \tag{E}$$

$$y \Rightarrow \bigcirc z \tag{F}$$

Let us now turn to the facts that all the wise men know, that they know that they know, and so on. In other words, the information that must be satisfied in every belief context.

1) The colors of the spots never change. That is, if wise man i has a white spot, then the spot remains white, if it is not white then it remains not white:

$$W_i \Rightarrow \bigcirc W_i \tag{G}$$

$$\neg W_i \Rightarrow \bigcirc \neg W_i \tag{H}$$

2) each wise man can see the spot of his colleagues:

$$W_j \Rightarrow B_i W_j \qquad i \neq j \tag{I}$$

$$\neg W_j \Rightarrow B_i \neg W_j \qquad i \neq j \tag{J}$$

3) the king announces that at least one of the spots is white:

$$W_1 \vee W_2 \vee W_3 \tag{K}$$

4) At time 1 wise men do not know the color of their spot, and at time 2 wise men do not know the color of their spot:

$$y \Rightarrow \neg B_i W_i \tag{L}$$

$$z \Rightarrow \neg B_i W_i \tag{M}$$

5) At moment in time x wise men know it is time x. The same for y and z:

$$x \Rightarrow B_i x \tag{N}$$

$$y \Rightarrow B_i y \tag{O}$$

$$z \Rightarrow B_i z \tag{P}$$

The SNF$_{BB}$ rules used in the execution process are shown in Figure 5. They are obtained by translating Equations (A)–(P) into the specific normal form outlined in Section 4.

First Scenario. The execution process begins by examining the initial rules at the initial state and ensuring that all the formulae entailed by **start** are true in the initial temporal state in the context ϵ representing the knowledge of the system about the situation. This process leads to the construction of the initial state of a temporal model in context ϵ, with the formulae x, W_1, W_2, and W_3 all being true. Then execution uses rule K to make $W_1 \vee W_2 \vee W_3$ true, rule I to make $B_2 W_1, B_3 W_1, B_1 W_3, B_2 W_3, B_1 W_2, B_3 W_2$ true, and rule N to make $B_1 x$, $B_2 x$, $B_3 x$ true.

A. **start** $\Rightarrow W_1$	I. $W_j \Rightarrow B_i W_j$
B. **start** $\Rightarrow W_2$	J. $\neg W_j \Rightarrow B_i \neg W_j$
C. **start** $\Rightarrow W_3$	K. **true** $\Rightarrow W_1 \vee W_2 \vee W_3$
D. **start** $\Rightarrow x$	L. $y \Rightarrow \neg B_i W_i$
E. $x \Rightarrow \bigcirc y$	M. $z \Rightarrow \neg B_i W_i$
F. $y \Rightarrow \bigcirc z$	N. $x \Rightarrow B_i x$
G. $W_i \Rightarrow \bigcirc W_i$	O. $y \Rightarrow B_i y$
H. $\neg W_i \Rightarrow \bigcirc \neg W_i$	P. $z \Rightarrow B_i z$

Fig. 5. The SNF$_{BB}$ rules.

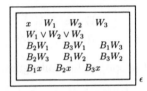

Then the execution process explores the belief contexts B_1, B_2 and B_3 making the appropriate formulae true. As we said previously, we focus on B_3 as we are interested in the reasoning process of wise man 3. Since there are no constraints on the truth value of $B_3 W_3$ the execution continues creating two models in the $\epsilon 0 B_3$ belief context. One where W_3 is true, and one where $\neg W_3$ is true.

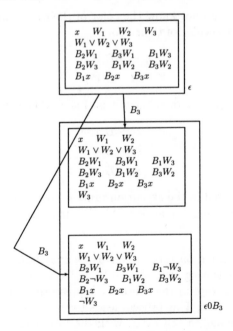

Execution explores all the belief contexts "below" $\epsilon 0 B_3$ until the depth bound is reached. Then execution uses rule E to create a next step for one of the two temporal models in the belief context $\epsilon 0 B_3$. This new temporal state satisfies y.

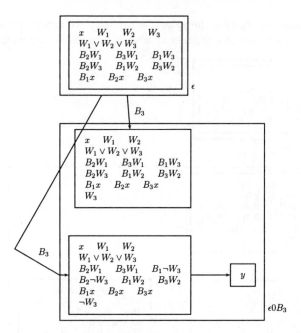

Then execution uses rule L to make $\neg B_1W_1$, $\neg B_2W_2$, $\neg B_3W_3$ true, rules G and H to make W_1, W_2, $\neg W_3$ true, rule O to make B_1y, B_2y and B_3y true, and rules I, J and K as in the previous steps. This process leads to:

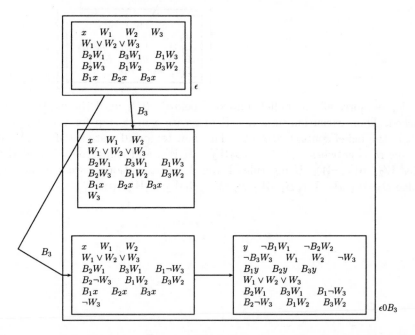

Then execution expands creates the belief contexts B_1, B_2 and B_3 related to the current moment in time and makes the appropriate formulae true. Let us explore belief contexts B_1 (for the sake of simplicity we ignore formulae which are irrelevant to the reasoning process of wise man 3 we are interested in).

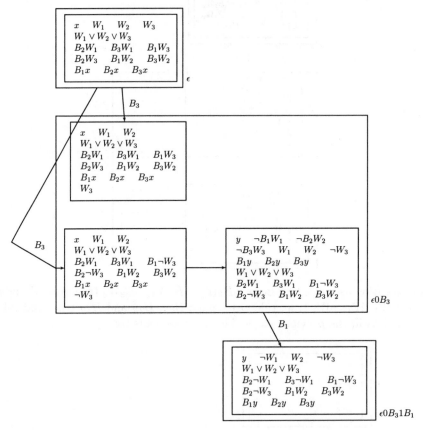

Execution explores all the belief contexts "below" $\epsilon 0 B_3$ until the depth bound is reached. Then execution uses rule F to create a next step for the temporal models in the belief context $\epsilon 0 B_3 1 B_1$. This new temporal state satisfies z. Also, using rule M is satisfies $\neg B_1 W_1$, $\neg B_2 W_2$, $\neg B_3 W_3$, and using rules G and H is satisfies $W_2, \neg W_1, \neg W_3$. Using rules I and J the execution process makes the formulae $B_2 \neg W_1, B_3 \neg W_1, B_1 \neg W_3, B_2 \neg W_3, B_1 W_2, B_3 W_2$ true.

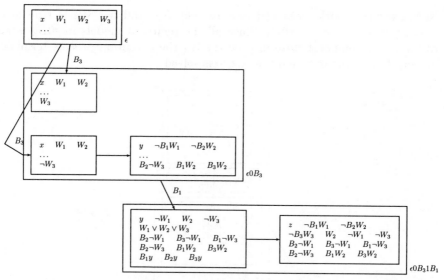

Then execution continues. This time we concentrate on wise man 3 continues in its reasoning process trying to examine the beliefs of wise man 2 in the moment in time labelled by z. That is, we focus on the creation of the belief contexts B_2. It is easy to see that this belief context satisfies $\neg W_1$, $\neg W_2$, and $\neg W_3$. This contradict with the formula $W_1 \vee W_2 \vee W_3$ obtained with the application of rule K:

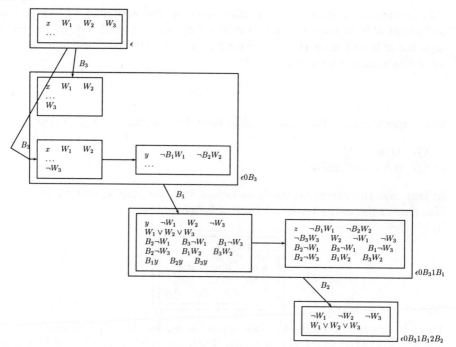

Now, execution backtracks and ensures that W_3, and not W_3 is true in the initial temporal state in $\epsilon 0 B_3$. Since all the temporal models in $\epsilon 0 B_3$ related to the initial temporal state in ϵ satisfy W_3 the execution process terminates making $B_3 W_3$ true in ϵ, and the puzzle is solved.

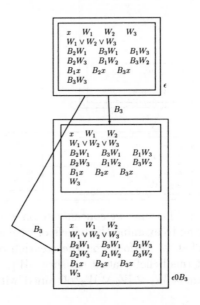

The Execution – Second Scenario. Suppose now that wise man 3 is not so wise and is not able to reason about time in a very sophisticated way. In particular he is not able to reason about the future at all but only about the first one (i.e., x) In this scenario we add a formula

$$B_3(x \Rightarrow \bigcirc \textbf{false}) \tag{Q}$$

to the specification. This translated to the following rules SNF$_{BB}$ rules:

Q1. $\textbf{true} \Rightarrow B_3 a$
Q2. $a \wedge x \Rightarrow \bigcirc \textbf{false}$

In this case the execution starts as before with the only exception of making $B_3 a$ true in the initial temporal state of belief context ϵ.

$$
\boxed{
\begin{array}{llll}
x & W_1 & W_2 & W_3 \\
W_1 \vee W_2 \vee W_3 & & & \\
B_2 W_1 & B_3 W_1 & B_1 W_3 & \\
B_2 W_3 & B_1 W_2 & B_3 W_2 & \\
B_1 x & B_2 x & B_3 x & B_3 a
\end{array}
}
$$

Then, it proceeds creating the two temporal models in belief context $\epsilon 0 B_3$. a and x are satisfied in these new states. Therefore rule Q1 can be used to make $\bigcirc \textbf{false}$ true.

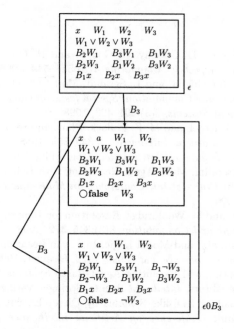

Differently from the first scenario, execution cannot create the moment in time labelled by y in the belief context $\epsilon 0 B 3$. Therefore the execution process is not able to make $B_3 W_3$ true as the contradiction is not reached.

5.1 Summary

As the example above shows, constraints on the amount of temporal reasoning that an agent can carry out can significantly alter the outcome of the execution process. Similar modifications on the execution process may be due to constraints on the amount of reasoning about belief allowed (see [11] for an example). These examples show how our formalism is able to capture an important aspect of complex, rational, practical agents, notably their resource-bounded nature.

6   Conclusions and Future Work

In this chapter we have considered the logical characterisation of agents that have resource bounds on the amount of reasoning that they can carry out. In particular we have considered the extension of basic executable temporal logic (of the METATEM style) with bounded reasoning about belief and time.

The logic proposed in this chapter can provide a practical basis for the high-level logic-based programming of resource-bounded agents. Our future work in this area centres around the full implementation of this approach, in particular the direct execution of TLBB specifications, and the evaluation of this formalism in larger, more practical, examples of resource-bounded rational agents, for example [16].

References

1. H. Barringer, M. Fisher, D. Gabbay, G. Gough, and R. Owens. METATEM: An Introduction. *Formal Aspects of Computing*, 7(5):533–549, 1995.
2. M. Benerecetti, F. Giunchiglia, and L. Serafini. Model Checking Multiagent Systems. *Journal of Logic and Computation, Special Issue on Computational & Logical Aspects of Multi-Agent Systems*, 8(3):401–423, 1998.
3. M. E. Bratman, D. J. Israel, and M. E. Pollack. Plans and resource-bounded practical reasoning. *Computational Intelligence*, 4:349–355, 1988.
4. B. F. Chellas. *Modal Logic – an Introduction*. Cambridge University Press, 1980.
5. A. Cimatti and L. Serafini. Multi-Agent Reasoning with Belief Contexts II: Elaboration Tolerance. In *Proc. 1st Int. Conference on Multi-Agent Systems (ICMAS-95)*, pages 57–64, 1996.
6. C. Dixon, M. Fisher, and M. Wooldridge. Resolution for Temporal Logics of Knowledge. *Journal of Logic and Computation*, 8(3):345–372, 1998.
7. E. A. Emerson. Temporal and Modal Logic. In J. van Leeuwen, editor, *Handbook of Theoretical Computer Science*, pages 996–1072. Elsevier, 1990.
8. M. Fisher. Representing and Executing Agent-Based Systems. In M. Wooldridge and N. R. Jennings, editors, *Intelligent Agents*. Springer-Verlag, 1995.
9. M. Fisher. Implementing BDI-like Systems by Direct Execution. In *Proceedings of International Joint Conference on Artificial Intelligence (IJCAI)*. Morgan-Kaufmann, 1997.
10. M. Fisher and C. Ghidini. Programming Resource-Bounded Deliberative Agents. In *Proceedings of the Sixteenth International Joint Conference on Artificial Intelligence (IJCAI'99)*, pages 200–206. Morgan Kaufmann Publ., Inc, 1999.
11. M. Fisher and C. Ghidini. Specifying and implementing agents with dynamic resource bounds. In *working notes of the 2nd International Cognitive Robotics Workshop*, 2000.
12. M. Fisher and C. Ghidini. The abc of rational agent modelling. In *Proceedings of the first international joint conference on autonomous agents and multiagent systems (AAMAS'02)*, Bologna, Italy, July 2002.
13. C. Ghidini and F. Giunchiglia. Local models semantics, or contextual reasoning = locality + compatibility. *Artificial Intelligence*, 127(2):221–259, April 2001.
14. F. Giunchiglia and L. Serafini. Multilanguage hierarchical logics, or: how we can do without modal logics. *Artificial Intelligence*, 65(1):29–70, 1994.
15. J. McCarthy. Formalization of Two Puzzles Involving Knowledge. In V. Lifschitz, editor, *Formalizing Common Sense - Papers by John McCarthy*, pages 158–166. Ablex Publishing Corporation, 1990.
16. N. Muscettola, P. Pandurang Nayak, Barney Pell, and Brian Williams. Remote agent: To boldly go where no ai system has gone before. *Artificial Intelligence*, 103(1-2):5–48, 1998.
17. A. S. Rao and M. P. Georgeff. Modeling Agents within a BDI-Architecture. In R. Fikes and E. Sandewall, editors, *International Conference on Principles of Knowledge Representation and Reasoning (KR)*, Cambridge, Massachusetts, April 1991. Morgan Kaufmann.

A Model of Delegation for Multi-agent Systems

Timothy J. Norman[1] and Chris Reed[2]

[1] Department of Computing Science, University of Aberdeen,
Aberdeen, AB24 3UE, Scotland, U.K.,
tnorman@csd.abdn.ac.uk
[2] Department of Applied Computing, University of Dundee,
Dundee, DD1 4HN, Scotland, U.K.,
chris@computing.dundee.ac.uk

Abstract. An agent may decide to delegate tasks to others. The act of delegating a task by one autonomous agent to another can be carried out by the performance of one or more imperative communication acts. In this paper, the semantics of imperatives are specified using a language of actions and states. It is further shown how the model can be used to distinguish between whole-hearted and mere extensional satisfaction of an imperative, and how this may be used to specify the semantics of imperatives in agent communication languages. The act of delegating a task from one agent to another can be carried out through the performance of one or more imperative communication acts. In this paper, the semantics of such imperatives are specified using a language of actions and states. The logical system that is developed then supports a notion of responsibility. An agent may not only be issued an imperative to directly carry out an event, or achieve some state, but also to be responsible for an event being carried out or state achieved - and these latter commitments might then be serviced through a subsequent act of delegation. The model thus clearly distinguishes between different classes of responsibility and different forms of delegation, and it is shown how this sound theoretical foundation can then be applied in specifying the semantics of imperatives in agent communication languages.

1   Introduction

To delegate is to entrust a representative to act on your behalf. This is an important issue for agents that may be forced to rely on others. Although autonomous agents have a high degree of self-determination, they may be required to achieve a goal that is made easier, satisfied more completely or only possible with the aid of other, similarly autonomous, agents. For delegation to be successful, there must be a relationship between the agent delegating the goal or task and the agent to whom it is delegated. Furthermore, after successful delegation, responsibility for the task concerned is now shared. For example, the manager of a business unit, in delegating a task, will no longer be solely responsible for that task. The manager must, however, ensure that the employee to whom the task has been delegated acts appropriately (e.g. by completing the task, asking for help or further delegating the task).

This is, according to Castelfranchi and Falcone [5], *strong delegation*; i.e. where there is mutual awareness and social commitment. In particular, Castelfranchi and Falcone [5,

M. d' Inverno et al. (Eds.): UKMAS 1996–2000, LNAI 2403, pp. 185–204, 2002.

4], amongst others [24], address the question: What is the nature of the relationship on which the ability to delegate is predicated? Here, however, we focus on the specification of communicative acts that can be used to delegate tasks, and on a number of the dimensions that characterise what is being delegated and what are the conditions under which it can be said that delegation was successful. We focus on two key dimensions:

1. the distinction between the delegation of *actions to be performed* and *states of affairs to be achieved*; and
2. the restrictions on the further delegation of the activity concerned (i.e. whether further delegation is *permitted, forbidden* or *required.*

There are, of course, many more issues that must be considered in the development of a complete theory of delegation; for example, the discussion is restricted to individuals rather than groups of agents [19, 23]. However, considering these two issues alone does mean that a number of distinct situations must be considered:

(a) "I don't care who achieves (state of affairs) A, but it must be achieved."
(b) "I don't care who does (action) α, but it must be done."
(c) "You must, through your own, direct, intervention achieve A."
(d) "You must, through your own, direct, intervention do α."
(e) "You must ensure that A is achieved by someone other than yourself."
(f) "You must ensure that α is done by someone other than yourself."

Possibly the most common mechanism employed in the delegation of activity (especially in multi-agent systems) is through direct communication. Knowledge level [22] communication between agents through speech act based [2, 28] agent communication languages (ACLs) is both an active area of research [31, 26] and of standardisation [11, 10]. These languages typically include *indicatives* (or assertions) such as 'tell' (KQML) and 'inform' (FIPA); for example, "It's raining". Queries or questions are also common (i.e. *interrogatives*) such as 'ask-if' (KQML) and 'query-if' (FIPA); for example, "Is it raining?". In addition to these, *imperatives* are used to issue commands, give advice or request action; for example, "bring the umbrella". Examples of imperative message types in ACLs are 'achieve' (KQML) and 'request' (FIPA). An intuitive explanation of these message types is that the sender is attempting to influence the recipient to act in some way. In fact, an attempt to influence the mental state of the hearer (or recipient of a message) is common to all knowledge level communication. For example, an agent utters an indicative such as "It's raining" with the intention of inducing a belief by means of the recognition of this intention [12]. In other words, the speaker is attempting to influence the hearer to adopt a belief about the weather.

Similarly, the imperative "bring the umbrella" is an attempt to influence the hearer's future actions by means of the hearer recognising that this is the intention of the speaker. Following Searle's [28] description of the types of illocutionary (or communicative) act, Cohen and Levesque [8] provide a model in which such acts are construed as attempts by the speaker to change the mental state of the hearer. For example, a request for the hearer to do some action, α, is an attempt to change the hearer's mental state in such a way that it becomes an intention of the hearer to do α. The hearer, being an autonomous agent, may refuse. This is, of course, different from misunderstanding the speaker.

With this in mind, Cohen and Levesque [8] distinguish between a speaker's goal of performing an act, and the speaker's intention behind the act. The goal, in the case of an imperative, is that the hearer believes that the speaker intends the hearer to act and the hearer acts accordingly. The intention, by contrast, is only that the hearer believes that the speaker had that communicative goal. If the intention of the speaker is not understood by the hearer, then the communicative act is unsuccessful. A communicative act is then an attempt to achieve the goal, but at least to satisfy the intention that the hearer believes that this is what the speaker wants. Through this definition of 'attempts', Cohen *et al.* [8, 31] provide a concrete characterisation of the communicative acts that are common in ACLs, and go on to specify conversations. For example, one agent offers a service to another, which may be responded to with acceptance, rejection or silence (cf. Barbuceanu and Fox [3]). This extension of an agent communication language to capture typical conversations between agents is the approach taken by the FIPA specification [11], and it is the specification of imperatives within FIPA that is returned to in section 6, where we return to the dimensions introduced above to discuss to what extent existing standards of agent communication are able to express them.

The grounding of agent communication languages in such formal models is essential to ensure that the meaning of communicative acts are clear to those designing agents for practical applications. Without such a grounding, agent communication languages can suffer from inherent ambiguity which, when implemented, can lead to unexpected, undesirable and counter-intuitive results. Although we do require that specifications are unambiguous, it is essential that ACLs support rich dialogues between agents, and so analyses of the possible dimensions of the semantics of communication are important [27]. The work presented in this paper focuses on imperatives, aims to present an account of delegation, and show how this may be better understood by considering both existing models of imperatives [13, 33] and normative positions [20, 29]. Before presenting a formal model of agentative action (sections 3 and 4) upon which the model of delegation proposed in this paper is built, it is important to discuss imperatives in more detail.

2   Imperatives

Numerous proposals have been laid out in both philosophical and computational literature for classification of utterance types, or, more specifically, of illocutionary acts. Austin [2, p. 150] and Searle [28, pp. 66–67] are perhaps the two most prominent.

Though there are a range of similarities and dissimilarities, these schemes have at least one thing in common: not all utterances are indicative. This is not in itself remarkable, until it is considered that the logics employed to handle and manipulate utterances are almost always exclusively based upon the predominant formal tradition of treating only the indicative. The interrogative and imperative utterances (which figure amongst Austin's Exercitives and Expositives, and include Searle's Request, Question, Advise and Warn) rarely benefit from the luxury of a logic designed to handle them.

Interrogative logics for handling questions have been proposed by Åqvist [1] and Hintikka *et al.* [15] among others, and these form an interesting avenue for future exploration. The focus of the current work, however, is on imperative logic. Hamblin's [13] book *Imperatives* represents the first thorough treatment of the subject, providing a systematic analysis not only of linguistic examples, but also of grammatical structure, semantics and the role imperatives play in dialogue.

His classification goes into some detail, but one key distinction is drawn between imperatives which are *wilful*, and those which are not. The former class are characterised by advantage to the utterer, the latter by advantage to the hearer. Thus commands, requests, and demands are all classed as wilful; advice, instructions, suggestions, recipes and warnings are all classed as non-wilful.

The distinction is useful because it highlights the importance of the contextual environment of the utterance: commands would fail to have an effect if the utterer was not in a position of authority over the hearer; advice would fail if the hearer did not trust the utterer, and so on. Any logic of imperatives must both be able to cope with this wide range of locutionary acts, but also be insensitive to any of the extralinguistic (and thereby extralogical) factors affecting the subsequent effect of issuing imperatives.

Hamblin states [13, p. 137] that to handle imperatives there are several features, "usually regarded as specialised", which are indispensable for a formal model: (1) a time-scale; (2) a distinction between actions and states; (3) physical and mental causation; (4) agency and action-reduction; and (5) intensionality. Following the second feature listed above, both events and states of affairs are explicitly represented in the Action State Semantics: a world is a series of states connected by events. The states can be seen as collections of propositions. Events are of two types: deeds, which are performed by specific agents, and happenings, which are world effects. This distinction gives the model an unusual richness: most other formal systems have explicit representation of one or the other, defining either states in terms of the sequences of events (true of most action and temporal logics), or else events in terms of a succession of states such as in classical AI planning.

The situation calculus [21] allows both states and events to be represented, but the commonly adopted "axioms of arboreality" [30] restrict the flexibility so that a given sequence of events is associated with a single, unique situation. Even if all the fluents in two situations have identical values, under the axioms of arboreality, those two situations are only the same if the events leading to them have also been the same. In Hamblin's work, however, there can be several different histories up to a given state and the histories are not themselves a part of those states.

This rich underlying model is important in several respects. First, it allows, at a syntactic level, the expression of demands both that agents bring about states of affairs, and that they perform actions. Secondly, it avoids both ontological and practical problems of having to interrelate states and events — practical problems often become manifest in having to keep track of 'Done events' in every state [9]. Finally, this construction of a world as a chain of states connected by deeds and happenings makes it possible to distinguish those worlds in which a given imperative i is satisfied (in some set of states). Thus the imperative "Shut the door" is satisfied in those worlds in which the door is shut (given appropriate deixis). This 'extensional' satisfaction, however, is contrasted with a stronger notion, of 'whole-hearted' satisfaction, which characterises an agent's involvement and responsibility in fulfilling an imperative. Whole-hearted satisfaction is based upon the notion of a strategy. A strategy for a particular agent is the assignment of a deed to each time point. A partial i-strategy is then a set of incompletely specified strategies, all of which involve worlds in which i is extensionally satisfied. The whole-hearted satisfaction of an imperative i by an agent x is then defined as being x's adoption of a partial strategy and the execution of a deed from that strategy at every time point after the imperative is issued.

A Hamlinian world $w \in W$ is defined such that for every time point in T there is:

1. a state from the set of states S,
2. a member of the set H of 'big happenings' (each of which collect together all happenings from one state to the next), and
3. a deed (in D) for every agent (in X), i.e. an element from D^X.

The set W of worlds is, therefore, defined as $(S \times H \times D^X)^T$. The states, happenings and deed-agent assignments of a given world w are given by $S(w)$, $H(w)$ and $D(w)$.

Let j_t be a history of a world up to time t, including all states, deeds and happenings of the world up to t. Thus j_t is equivalent to a set of worlds which have a common history up to (at least) time t. J_t is then the set of all possible histories up to t; i.e. all the ways by which the world could have got to where it is. A strategy q_t is then an allocation of a deed to each $j_{t'} \in J_{t'}$ for every $t' \geq t$.[1]

Let the possible worlds in which the deeds of agent x are those specified by strategy q_t be $W_{strat}(x, q_t)$, and the worlds in which an imperative, i, is extensionally satisfied be W_i. A strategy for the satisfaction of an imperative i (i.e. an i-strategy) can, therefore, be defined as follows: A strategy $q_t \in Q_t$ is an i-strategy for agent x if and only if the worlds in which x does the deeds specified by q_t are also worlds in which i is extensionally satisfied: $W_{strat}(x, q_t) \subseteq W_i$.

In practice, however, it is not feasible for an agent to select a particular strategy in Q_t at time t that specifies every deed for every time t' after t. For this reason, an agent will adopt a *partial i-strategy*. A partial i-strategy is a disjunction of i-strategies, $Q'_t \subseteq Q_t$, and the world set for x adopting this partial i-strategy is $W_{strat}(x, Q'_t)$.

With this grounding, the whole-hearted satisfaction of an imperative, i, can now be defined. An agent x may be said to whole-heartedly satisfy an imperative i issued at t if and only if for every $t' \geq t$:

1. x has a partial i-strategy, $Q'_{t'}$; and
2. x does a deed from the set of deeds specified by that $Q'_{t'}$.

In addition to Hamblin's monograph [13], more detail on the role of such a model in the wider context of dialogue and a more complete set-theoretic précis is given by Walton and Krabbe [33]. Here, motivated by the work outlined in this section, we present a theory of agentative activity that is appropriate for modelling imperatives. First, an axiomatisation of the two action modalities S and T is presented. Secondly, we develop a possible worlds semantics for these operators as an approximation to the Action State Semantics. Finally, we go on to show how this theory can be used to model imperatives in agent communication.

---

[1] This notion of a strategy has an intensional component, since it prescribes over a set of possible w, rather than picking out, at this stage, the actual world.

3   Axiomatisation of S and T

With the intuitive grounding in Hamblin's Action State Semantics provided by the previous section, we present a syntax that may be used to explicitly refer to agents performing actions and achieving goals. We refer to actions (or deeds) by the symbols $\alpha, \beta, \ldots \in D$, states by $A, B, \ldots \in S$ and agents by $x, y, \ldots \in \mathcal{X}$. World effects, or happenings, are not considered explicitly here; we assume that there is a special agent that models world effects.

In the following discussion, a number of rules of inference and axiom schemas are considered. Those that are included in the logic of the modality S are summarised in figure 1 (these axioms are analogous for T, but do not represent a minimal set — they are listed exhaustively in the interests of clarity). A few others are given in figure 2 for the purposes of discussion, but are rejected for modality S (similarly, they are rejected for T).

The logic of the operators S and T is a regular modal logic [6]. As with other classical modal logics, both are closed under equivalence by the rules RE (see figure 1 for RES). Furthermore, following Jones and Sergot's exposition of their modality E_x, both S_x and T_x use the axiom schema T. The adoption of schema T can be justified on intuitive grounds by reading it as follows for modality S: if an agent sees to it that a state of affairs holds, then that state of affairs does, in fact, hold. Following Jones and Sergot, then, the

RES	$\dfrac{A \leftrightarrow B}{S_x A \leftrightarrow S_x B}$
TS	$S_x A \rightarrow A$
CS	$(S_x A \wedge S_x B) \rightarrow S_x(A \wedge B)$
MS	$S_x(A \wedge B) \rightarrow (S_x A \wedge S_x B)$
RS	$S_x(A \wedge B) \leftrightarrow S_x A \wedge S_x B$
KS	$S_x(A \rightarrow B) \rightarrow (S_x A \rightarrow S_x B)$
DS	$S_x A \rightarrow \neg S_x \neg A$

Fig. 1. Rules of inference & axiom schemas of S.

R¬NS	$\dfrac{A}{\neg S_x A}$
RNS	$\dfrac{A}{S_x A}$
RMS	$\dfrac{A \rightarrow B}{S_x A \rightarrow S_x B}$
5S	$\neg S_x A \rightarrow S_x \neg S_x A$
4S	$S_x A \rightarrow S_x S_x A$

Fig. 2. Further candidate rules of inference and axiom schemas discussed.

current work develops a logic of *successful* action.[2] A similar gloss can be constructed for T_x — if an agent sees to it that an action is performed then that action is performed — but this implicitly requires stretching a possible-worlds interpretation as far as, and perhaps further, than is reasonable, as explained below.

One of the most fundamental disagreements between theories of agency concerns the rule of necessitation (RN for modality S is given in figure 2). This arises from a deep intuitive dilemma. The argument for adopting the reverse R¬N proposed by Jones and Sergot is simply stated: "Whatever else we may have in mind ... on no account could we accept that an agent brings about what is logically true" [17, p. 435]. Thus Jones and Sergot, like Belnap and Perloff (whose *negative condition* entails R¬N) are trying to capture some notion of responsibility, such that no agent can be said to be 'responsible' for a tautology. Chellas' intuitions, by contrast run rather differently. He is happy to accept RN, a much more conventional rule of a normal modal logic, and his argument too is tabled very briefly: "Can it ever be the case that someone sees to it that something logically true is so? I believe the answer is yes. When one sees to something, one sees to anything that logically follows, including the easiest such things, such as those represented by $\top$. One should think of seeing to it that, for example, $0 = 0$ as a sort of trivial pursuit, attendant upon seeing to anything at all." [7, p. 508]. Chellas' decision, in particular, is motivated by the logical consequences of the rule, and in particular on the availability of schemata C and M.

The *outward* distributivity of an action modality is adopted in the axiom schema C. Schema C is adopted by Chellas, Jones and Sergot, Belnap and Perloff, and, similarly, in the work presented here (see figure 1 for CS); it is difficult to argue from an intuitive basis how C might fail.

The *inward* distributivity axiom schema, M, however, is more troublesome. M, like C, seems intuitively appealing, but, for Jones and Sergot (and other systems adopting R¬N), it is pathological, since, with RE, it yields the rule RM (RMS is shown in figure 2). Taking the tautology $A \to \top$, RM gives $S_x A \to S_x \top$. Since R¬N gives $\neg S_x \top$, any $S_x A$ is thus a contradiction. Jones and Sergot, therefore, reject M because they are committed to the notion of responsibility captured by R¬N; Chellas on the other hand, accepts RN and, thereby, the loss of agentative responsibility, but does, as a result, maintain M.

The solution proposed for the modalities S and T represents a half-way house, eschewing both the restrictive nature of a (smallest) classical modal logic, and the counterintuitive results of a normal modal logic, in favour of a (smallest) regular modal logic. We also defer the issue of necessitation (versus "anti-necessitation") to the semantics. Both modalities thus include the rule RE and the axiom schema R (and, consequently, M, C and K), but they require neither the rule of necessitation (RN), nor the rule of anti-necessitation (R¬N).

The preceding discussion has already mentioned the intuitive appeal of M and C; it is also worth digressing to offer an intuitive gloss on the schema K to demonstrate its role, particularly as Jones and Sergot implicitly reject K. An imperative with the form

---

[2] This notion of "successful action" may be better viewed as "successful interaction with the world" considering our distinction between S and T. This alternative reading more clearly indicates that the formula to which the modality is applied is not in any way equivalent or *logically* related to the actions that an agent may carry out.

of an implication is, linguistically, quite straightforward: "Make sure that if you go out then you lock the door". If an agent brings it about that the implication holds then K states that if the agent brings about the antecedent then it is logically responsible also for bringing about the consequent. This does not impinge upon the autonomy of an agent to decide not to fulfil some imperative; rather, it states only that if the agent brought about the antecedent, then it can only also be said to have brought about the implication if it is responsible for the consequent.

The axioms 4 and 5 are commonly employed in mentalistic modalities, and, less frequently, in agentative modalities. First, consider schema 5S (figure 2). This is explicitly rejected for several reasons, not least of which is that with T, it would yield RN, which we wish to avoid. We return to the problems that 5 would throw up in the context of forbearance, section 5.1. Schema 5 is also rejected across the board by Jones and Sergot, Belnap and Perloff, and Chellas. Axiom schema 4, however, is accepted by Belnap and Perloff. Consider schema 4S (figure 2). With TS, this yields the following equivalence, which we reject: $S_x A \leftrightarrow S_x S_x A$. The importance of avoiding this equivalence and the problems that 5 would present with respect to forbearance are discussed in section 5.1.

Finally, the adoption of T in the models of Jones and Sergot, of Belnap and Perloff, and of Chellas entails the inclusion of axiom schema D (see figure 1 for DS).

To summarise then, the logics of S_x and T_x are relativised classical regular modal logics of type RT [6, p. 237].

4   Semantic Model

As the axiomatisation indicates, the proposed logic is considerably smaller than a normal modal logic, and as a result, a standard model is inappropriate. To provide a possible worlds semantics, we therefore use a minimal model [6].

The simplest approach is to define S_x (and T_x analogously) in the same style as a conventional modal logic. Thus with a model $\mathcal{M} = \langle \mathcal{W}, \mathcal{N}, \mathcal{P} \rangle$ with worlds $\mathcal{W}$, "necessitation function" $\mathcal{N}$, and interpretation functions abbreviated by $\mathcal{P}$, we can define the truth conditions of the unrelativised modality S. To characterise the *relativised* modality S_x, we introduce multiple necessitation functions, one for each agent $x \in \mathcal{X}$, thus $\mathcal{M} = \langle \mathcal{W}, \mathcal{N}^x, \mathcal{P} \rangle$. $\mathcal{N}^x$ maps from a given world ω, to a collection of sets of worlds (i.e. $\mathcal{N}^x \subseteq \wp(W)$), picking out those propositions which are brought about (by x) at ω. The standard truth conditions for propositional logic are captured in 1–8, and for the modality S_x in 9. (Note that, $\mathcal{P}$ abbreviates an infinite sequence, $\mathcal{P}_0, \mathcal{P}_1, \mathcal{P}_2, \ldots$, of subsets of $\mathcal{W}$, where, for each n, $\mathcal{P}_n$ represents those possible worlds in which the corresponding atomic sentence P_n holds — this is condition 1.)

$$\models_\omega^\mathcal{M} P_n \quad \text{iff} \quad \omega \in \mathcal{P}_n \text{ for } n = 1, 2, 3, \ldots \tag{1}$$

$$\models_\omega^\mathcal{M} \top \tag{2}$$

$$\not\models_\omega^\mathcal{M} \bot \tag{3}$$

$$\models_\omega^\mathcal{M} \neg A \quad \text{iff} \quad \not\models_\omega^\mathcal{M} A \tag{4}$$

$$\models_\omega^\mathcal{M} A \wedge B \quad \text{iff} \quad \models_\omega^\mathcal{M} A \text{ and } \models_\omega^\mathcal{M} B \tag{5}$$

$$\models_\omega^\mathcal{M} A \vee B \quad \text{iff} \quad \models_\omega^\mathcal{M} A \text{ or } \models_\omega^\mathcal{M} B \text{ or both} \tag{6}$$

$$\models_\omega^{\mathcal{M}} A \rightarrow B \quad \text{iff} \quad \text{if } \models_\omega^{\mathcal{M}} A \text{ then } \models_\omega^{\mathcal{M}} B \tag{7}$$

$$\models_\omega^{\mathcal{M}} A \leftrightarrow B \quad \text{iff} \quad \models_\omega^{\mathcal{M}} A \text{ if and only if } \models_\omega^{\mathcal{M}} B \tag{8}$$

$$\models_\omega^{\mathcal{M}} \mathsf{S}_x A \quad \text{iff} \quad \|A\|^{\mathcal{M}} \in \mathcal{N}_\omega^x \tag{9}$$

Unfortunately, quite apart from practical difficulties in using such a model as the basis for implementation of a multi-agent system [34] the approach fails to provide a good foundation upon which to develop an account of not just static states of affairs but of dynamic states, and of not just individual actions but of series of actions. These extensions are vital to any account of real agentative action, which has motivated works such as those of Chellas [7], Horty and Belnap [16] and others to adopt a much richer "metaphysical backdrop", substantially extending the Leibnizian model.

The development of a full semantics based on Action State Semantics is the subject of current research and is beyond the scope of this paper. A compromise between familiarity and accuracy can be achieved though enriching the possible-worlds approach by building in structure to each world that approximates the Action State Semantics (an analogous approach is adopted by many works founded on branching time logics [34]). Such a compromise serves as a sufficient foundation upon which to explore a rich characterisation of delegation. Thus, we can say that $j\angle_t v$ can be read as a history, j, of the Hamblinian world v up to t; j is an initial segment of v and v is a completion of j (following Walton and Krabbe [33, p. 191]). This is defined recursively as follows:

$$j\angle_0 v = \langle \emptyset, s_0 \in S(v), \delta_0^x \in D(v) \rangle$$
$$j\angle_t v = \langle j\angle_{t-1} v, s_t \in S(v), \delta_t^x \in D(v) \rangle$$

where the functions S and D map from a Hamblinian world, v, to a set of propositions corresponding to the state of the world, $S(v)$, and to a set of deed assignments (agent-action pairs), $D(v)$.

In simplifying the semantics, it is possible to provide an interpretation of the S_x and T_x modalities that is irrespective of time (this simplification constitutes one of the major restrictions by comparison to the full Action State Semantics model under development). This timelessness is achieved through building an entire Kripke structure for a single time point, t. Thus each possible world in the Kripke structure can be seen as containing one particular $j\angle_t v$ for each Hamblinian world v. So a model $\mathcal{M}$, is defined as $\langle \mathcal{W}, \mathcal{X}, \mathcal{I}, S^x, T^x \rangle$ for a set of possible worlds $\mathcal{W}$, a set of agents $\mathcal{X}$, an interpretation function $\mathcal{I}$, and sets of functions S^x and T^x for each $x \in \mathcal{X}$. Following Chellas [6], S_ω^x is the relativised necessitation function S^x at world ω, that gives a subset of the power set of worlds (i.e. $S^x : \mathcal{W} \rightarrow \wp(\wp(\mathcal{W}))$).

Given that a Kripkean possible world encapsulates a Hamblinian history of the form $\langle j\angle v, s, \delta^x \rangle$, we need two components to the interpretation function to return either the current state of Hamblinian history (namely, the set s), or the deeds which are about to be (or are being, instantaneously) carried out by agent x (namely, the set δ^x). Let us use the functions $\mathcal{I}_S$ to map from a possible world ω and a specified state of affairs A to an element of the set $\{\top, \bot\}$ according to whether or not A is in the set s of ω. Similarly, $\mathcal{I}_D$ maps from a possible world ω and a deed-assignment α^x to an element of the set $\{\top, \bot\}$ according to whether or not α^x is in the set δ^x of ω. The interpretation function

$$QS \qquad S_x S_y A \rightarrow S_x A$$
$$QT \qquad S_x T_y \alpha \rightarrow T_x \alpha$$

Fig. 3. Axioms of delegation.

is thus constituted from $\mathcal{I}_S$ and $\mathcal{I}_D$, to refer to the appropriate parts of the Hamblinian history.

We are now in a position to be able to describe the semantics of S_x and T_x in a straightforward manner:

$$\models_\omega^\mathcal{M} A \quad \text{iff} \quad \mathcal{I}_S(\omega, A) = \top$$
$$\models_\omega^\mathcal{M} \alpha^x \quad \text{iff} \quad \mathcal{I}_D(\omega, \alpha^x) = \top$$
$$\models_\omega^\mathcal{M} \alpha \quad \text{iff} \quad \exists x \text{ such that } \models_\omega^\mathcal{M} \alpha^x$$
$$\models_\omega^\mathcal{M} S_x A \quad \text{iff} \quad \|A\|^\mathcal{M} \in \mathcal{S}_\omega^x$$
$$\models_\omega^\mathcal{M} T_x \alpha \quad \text{iff} \quad \|\alpha\|^\mathcal{M} \in \mathcal{T}_\omega^x$$

Bearing in mind that the truth set is simply $\|\phi\|^\mathcal{M} = \{\omega \in \mathcal{M}$ s.t. $\models_\omega^\mathcal{M} \phi\}$, this cleanly propagates the action/state distinction from the Hamblinian core to the desired modalities. This semantics thus offers a simple, if restrictive, interpretation of the two modalities, sufficient to explicate interesting interactions in a range of delegation scenarios.

5   Delegation

Here we propose further axioms and theorems of our logic of agentative action that are relevant to delegation, discuss the issue of forbearance in some detail and then focus on the application of the theory to delegation in multi-agent systems.

5.1   Further Axioms and Theorems

Like the approaches of Chellas and Belnap *et al.*, (but contrary to von Wright's characterisation), the theory offers scope for nesting the two modalities in building a rich notion of responsibility. In contrast to the clean, minimalist account developed by Jones and Sergot, the current work is employed in characterising realistic exchanges in agent systems, and as such the precise nature of the action modality needs to be pinned down. Thus following Chellas *inter alia*, we accept the axiom schemas QS and QT (figure 3).

Schema QT is worthy of particular note: if agent x sees to it that agent y sees to it that action α is done, then x can be said to be responsible for seeing to it that α is done. The adoption of this schema is intuitively appealing: agent x, through seeing to it that y is responsible for α, is itself, by delegating, responsible for its performance.

We further accept the specialisations of the TS schema, TSS and TST (figure 4). These schemata lay the foundation for characterising acts of delegation, but before looking at that in more detail, a second type of nested modality must be addressed that relates to the non-adoption of the axiom schema 5 for S and T (see section 3).

$$\text{TSS} \qquad S_x S_y A \to S_y A$$
$$\text{TST} \qquad S_x T_y \alpha \to T_y \alpha$$

Fig. 4. Further theorems of delegation.

5.2 Forbearance

Pörn [25] claims that, "The proposition *i forbears to bring it about that p* is not synonymous with *it is not the case that i brings it about that p*", basing his notion of forbearance upon an agent's ability to, but restraint from, bringing about the state of affairs. The same idea is presented by von Wright [32], but in Pörn's [25] account, the ability to nest operators supports rendering forbearance simply as: $S_x \neg S_x A$.

As Pörn discusses, forbearance and its associated causal responsibility is intuitively a stronger notion than simply not-bringing-it-about, and the former entails the latter. It is appropriate therefore that by T, $S_x \neg S_x A$ does indeed entail $\neg S_x A$. This account of forbearance is the same as that of refraining discussed by Horty and Belnap [16], where it is also demonstrated to be equivalent to von Wright's original formulation.

Forbearing from action (as opposed to forbearing from responsibility for a state of affairs) is constructed in an analogous way, so that not being responsible for action is captured by $\neg T_x \alpha$, but forbearing from action is the stronger notion expressed by $S_x \neg T_x \alpha$.

There are several points of note in this stronger notion of forbearance. The first is to recall that the modal statements themselves are — just as in standard ontic logics — part of the state of the world, and can thus form the parameter to the S_x modality (but not the T_x modality, which is not referring to the contents of the state of a world at all). The second is to emphasise that $S_x \neg T_x \alpha$ is not equivalent to the statement "x forbears from performing action α". The T_x modality expresses responsibility for the execution of an action, not the agent of the action, so this notion of forbearance should more accurately be read as "x forbears from having action α carried out". With the S_x modality, it is easy to separate the notion of responsibility from a given agent's action; with the T_x modality it is easy to forget that it is responsibility for, rather than direct participation in, action that is being expressed. The symmetry between S_x and T_x, and the focus upon responsibility rather than direct participation in both cases is crucial for the development of notions of delegation.

5.3 Imperatives in Multi-agent Systems

The use of this theory of agentative action as a model for imperatives in agent communication is predicated on the idea that imperatives can be constructed using a deontic action logic. Note that this is not the same as claiming that a deontic logic can be reduced to imperatives or vice versa (cf. Hamblin [13, 113–127]). It is however, claimed that normative positions where both normative (obligation, permission, etc.) and action components are involved can be seen as imperatives.

In this way, the statement $S_x \bigcirc T_y \alpha$, can be read as "x sees to it that the state of affairs holds in which it is obligatory for y to see to it that α is performed". Further, the statement might be issued as an imperative by some third party to x. A linguistic example of such an imperative might be: "Make sure your sister cleans her teeth!" There may be a range of means by which x might bring about this state of affairs (as with any other) but one obvious alternative is for x to issue an imperative to y of the form $T_y \alpha$ (e.g. "Clean your teeth, sis!").

Thus, in general, the act of uttering an imperative can, in the right situation, bring about a normative state of affairs. Clearly, both the form and type of locutionary act employed, and the imperative's overall success, will be partly dependent upon a variety of contextual factors, including in particular the relationship between the utterer and hearer, and existing normative positions both personal and societal. The general form of the interaction, though, is that the utterer attempts to introduce a new norm (and it is this act which counts as the utterer working towards whole-hearted satisfaction at this point); this attempt, if combined successfully with contextual parameters will generate a new normative position (or a modification of an existing position).

$$\text{utter}(s, h, i) \wedge \langle \text{context} \rangle \rightarrow \bigcirc i$$

Here, 'utter' is an appropriate communicative primitive, such as 'request'. s is the speaker, h the hearer and i an imperative formed using the S and T action modalities. The consequent is the normative positionin which the addressee is obliged with respect to the content of the imperative i.

As mentioned above, the imperatives $S_x A$ and $T_x \alpha$ implicitly admit the possibility that x further delegates the activity. This implicit assumption is based on the simple deontic inter-definition between obligation and permission: $P p \leftrightarrow \neg \bigcirc \neg p$. This, combined with some notion of negation as failure, licenses any agent to bring about normative states of affairs (in the right context), unless expressly prohibited from so doing. Suppose that an agent x is obliged to see to it that the state of affairs A is achieved as a result of y issuing the imperative $S_x A$ to x. As long as it is not the case that x is forbidden from seeing to it that some other agent, say z, sees to it that A, x is permitted to do so by further delegating the activity. This represents something of a simplification of Lindahl's [20] theory of normative position (see also Sergot [29]). In fact, there are seven distinct normative positions of an individual with respect to a state of affairs: an agent may have the freedom (or not) to bring about p, the freedom (or not) to bring about $\neg p$ and the freedom (or not) to remain passive towards p. The work presented in this paper does not address the range of freedoms described by Lindahl, but is consistent with it. The focus is on the distinction between an agent being free to act and being free to delegate a task. See Reed et al. [27] for an analysis of the semantics of various communicative acts where the full range of individual agent normative positions (among other dimensions of the semantics of agent communication languages) is considered.

It can further be seen that, from axioms QS and QT (figure 3) and theorems TSS and TST (figure 4), that the further delegation of the activity will mean that the agent, x in this case, will be successful in fulfilling its responsibility for the completion of the activity. For example, from axiom QS and theorem TSS, if agent x sees to it that some other agent y brings about the state of affairs A, then y brings about A (TSS) and x brings about A (QS).

It may be necessary to restrict the freedom of an agent to delegate, and to ensure that it carries out some action or brings about a state by his own, direct, intervention. Equally, there are, rarer, cases in which delegation is demanded. Taking this second and simpler case first, the imperatives $S_x T_y \alpha$ and $S_x S_y A$ capture this enforced delegation. $S_x T_y \alpha$ states that x brings it about that the state of affairs holds in which y is responsible for ensuring that the action α is performed. Similarly, $S_x S_y A$ states that x brings it about that the state of affairs holds in which y is responsible for ensuring that the state of affairs A is achieved.

The first case is slightly more complex. The implicit freedom of T_x (and identically for S_x) must be restricted by ensuring that x does not delegate. There are three important problems with an interpretation of this restriction:

1. Delegation is not a specified action. There are many ways of delegating, and most logics of action are not built around such template actions, in which placeholders such as 'delegate' can then subsequently be instantiated by some real action which constitutes delegation. It is certainly not a feature of the logic of S and T, and is not supported in the underlying semantics either, for good philosophical reasons [13]. It has been argued that delegation might be captured as a single, distinct communicative action [18]. The problem with this approach is that within any single given theory, definitions of other communicative acts already cover all the ground that constitutes delegation. In other words, delegation might be achieved through the application of any number of other primitives. To build on the approach by then predicating such action, and, in particular, abrogating the use of such delegation action, is doomed to failure, since on purely rational grounds, agents would simply employ these other means to their ends. It is thus indefensible to specify the prohibition of a delegation action.

2. As explained above, the distinction between states and events is a key component of action state semantics and to tie states to event postconditions would conflate this distinction, loosing much of the power of the semantics. Therefore, it is also undesirable to prohibit a state of affairs which can be uniquely identified with the postcondition of delegation.

3. An agent, say y, may be subject to a number of imperatives including, for example, the obligation to bring about that α is done, the status of which should not be impinged upon by restrictions on x's power to delegate responsibility for the performance of α. All that we wish to do is to restrict x's licence to delegate.

The solution lies in the notion of forbearance discussed in section 5.2. Intuitively, we wish to ensure that agent x forbears from seeing to it that some other agent becomes reponsible for the activity. Suppose that the imperative concerned is $T_x \alpha$. We wish to ensure that x forbears from bringing it about that another agent, say y, sees to it that α is done: $S_x \neg S_x T_y \alpha$. Thus, the following imperative can be used to ensure that agent x carries out action α by its own, direct, intervention:

$$T_x \alpha \wedge S_x \neg S_x T_y \alpha$$

A simple linguistic gloss on this imperative runs, "x, do α and forbear from delegating responsibility for doing α!" — our adapted version of Pörn's [25] forbearance is thus being reconstructed in the imperative. Similarly, the following imperative may be used to ensure that agent x forbears from bringing it about that another agent, say y, sees to it that A is achieved:

$$S_x A \wedge S_x \neg S_x S_y A$$

These are simply special cases of forbearance from bringing about some state of affairs — $S_x \neg S_x A$, section 5.2 — where the state of affairs concerned is that some other agent becomes responsible for some activity.

So far in this discussion, the operator $\bigcirc$ representing the concept of deontic necessity is introduced with little discussion regarding its logic. Though the properties of deontic logic in general are not a focus of this paper, it is worth bearing in mind the following axiom schemas:

$$\begin{aligned} \text{M} \bigcirc \quad & \bigcirc(\phi \wedge \psi) \rightarrow \bigcirc\phi \wedge \bigcirc\psi \\ \text{C} \bigcirc \quad & \bigcirc\phi \wedge \bigcirc\psi \rightarrow \bigcirc(\phi \wedge \psi) \end{aligned}$$

If both are accepted, as they are in a standard deontic logic (the smallest normal system containing the axiom D$\bigcirc$ [6]), uttering the imperative $T_x\alpha \wedge S_x \neg S_x T_y\alpha$, if successful, will produce the normative state of affairs: $\bigcirc (T_x\alpha \wedge S_x \neg S_x T_y\alpha)$. The inward distributivity of M$\bigcirc$ then yields: $\bigcirc T_x\alpha \wedge \bigcirc S_x \neg S_x T_y\alpha$. The second conjunct is precisely what is required to restrict x's licence to further delegate the activity: x must refrain from establishing the state of affairs in which y is responsible for the performance of action α. This not only avoids problems (1) and (2) by referring to the imperative $T_y\alpha$, but also circumvents (3) by leaving open the possibility that $P\,T_y\alpha$, or even $\bigcirc T_y\alpha$, is (or will) in fact be the case — but not as a result of anything x has done (this, after all, is the definition of extensional satisfaction).

5.4 Examples

A couple of examples will serve to demonstrate not only the syntax of imperatives, the normative positions they engender, and the means by which whole-hearted satisfaction can be determined, but also to show clearly that the formalisation is intuitive and uncluttered.

Example 1. A lecturer is told by her head of department to prepare copies of her lecture notes for her class. She may, for example, copy the notes herself or request that the departmental secretary copy the notes.

The initial instruction refers to the action of copying the lecture notes; the Head of Department's locution is captured in L1, figure 5. This, because of the nature of the relationship between the Head of Department and the Lecturer, results in the normative state of affairs: $\bigcirc T_{\text{Lecturer}} \text{copy\_notes}$.

This imperative may be whole-heartedly satisfied if the lecturer copies the notes herself; i.e. a world in which the deed-agent assignment $\text{copy\_notes}^{\text{Lecturer}}$ is present. This is, however, only one possibility for the Lecturer. The Lecturer could issue the imperative represented by locution L2, figure 5. This should, in the given context, lead to a normative state of affairs: $\bigcirc T_{\text{secretary}} \text{copy\_notes}$; i.e. the state of affairs in which the secretary is obliged to see to it that the copy_notes action is carried out. The action of the secretary carrying out copy_notes would fulfil the definition of extensional satisfaction

L1 Head of Department to Lecturer
    $T_{Lecturer}$ copy_notes
L2 Lectuer to Secretary
    $T_{Secretary}$ copy_notes
L3 Course Director to Lecturer
    $T_{Lecturer}$ write_exam $\land \forall y \in \{\mathcal{X} \setminus \{Lecturer\}\}$ $S_{Lecturer} \neg S_{Lecturer} T_y$ write_exam
L4 Course Director to Lecturer
    $S_{Lecturer} T_{Senior\ Secretary}$ print_exam
L5 Lecturer to Student
    $S_{Student}$ has_paper
L6 Student to Librarian
    $S_{Librarian}$ has_paper
L7 Student to Librarian
    $T_{Librarian}$ complete_ILL

Fig. 5. Locutions in the University examples.

not only of L2, but also of L1 in figure 5 (of course, the worlds of extensional satisfaction of L2 are identical to those of L1 in this case). Notice also that the secretary could further delegate the task to the tea-boy, etc.

Example 2. A lecturer is told by the Course Director that she must, herself, write an exam paper.

The initial request again concerns action, so the positive part of the imperative is captured by the first conjunct of locution L3 in figure 5. There is, however, the non delegation component, captured by the second conjunct. This states that the Lecturer is obligued to forbear from bringing about the state of affairs in which any agent (in the set of agents $\mathcal{X}$) with the exclusion of itself brings it about that the exam is written.

Thus the Lecturer may not be responsible for bringing about that any other agent is permitted to write her exam for her. Of course, it is conceivable that if, for example, she were to fall ill, her head of department might grant exam-writing permission to someone else in her place. Or, at a stretch of the imagination, there might be a role in a higher echelon of exam administration in which someone has the authority to write any exam paper they choose. Thus the normative position $P\,T_y$ write_exam may either exist or come into existence for some agent y — this is extensional satisfaction. It may not, however, come about as the result of whole hearted satisfaction on the part of the lecturer.

Example 3. The Lecturer is told by the Course Director to ensure that the senior secretary prints the exam.

This is an example in which further delegation is demanded — the Senior Secretary is the only person in the department who should print exam papers, so the Lecturer must delegate this action to the Senior Secretary. The locution L4 captures this imperative, and will, if successful, produce the following normative state of affairs:

$$\bigcirc S_{Lecturer} T_{Senior\ Secretary} \text{print\_exam}$$

The Lecturer will then, with a view to whole-heartedly satisfying this imperative, issue the imperative that is captured by the locution $T_{\text{Senior Secretary}}$ print_exam to the Senior Secretary.

Example 4. The Lecturer asks her PhD student to get hold of a paper for her. The student may be able to download the paper right away, or, if it is not available online, to delegate the task of getting hold of the paper via an Inter-Library Loan request to the Librarian.

The imperative issued to the lecturer concerns a state of affairs, having a copy of the paper, and can be captured by locution L5 in figure 5. If the paper is on-line, the deed-agent assignment download_paper^{Student} is sufficient to introduce has_paper into the state of the world, thereby extensionally (and whole-heartedly) satisfying the imperative.

The alternative is to delegate the task to the Librarian (if possible), perhaps by issuing the imperative captured by locution L6 in figure 5. The Librarian would then be responsible (through the new normative position $\bigcirc S_{\text{Librarian}}$ has_paper) for getting hold of the paper by whatever means she might see fit — by filling in an inter-library loan form, by ringing the British Library or whatever. It is of no concern to the PhD Student how the Librarian finds the paper; the Student's task is (in this case) done on creating the obligation on the Librarian.

Alternatively, the Student may decide to specify not the state of affairs that is desired, but rather the means by which they might be achieved. There are two key reasons why she might do this: (i) to avoid informing the Librarian of her goal (not relevant in this example); or (ii) to provide the Librarian with more detailed instructions (as might be appropriate if the PhD Student has already established that the library doesn't have a subscription to the journal in which the paper appears). Delegating the action is formulated, as can be seen from the locution L7 in figure 5, in as natural a way as delegating states of affairs.

6   Discussion

It now remains to discuss the consequences of using the model described in this paper in the practical task of specifying the primitives of an agent communication language. Following the distinction between actions and states, which has proven so useful in this discussion of imperatives, it is proposed that the primitives of an agent communication language should reflect this distinction. The FIPA ACL [11] provides three primitives that can be clearly understood as imperatives: 'request', 'request-when' and 'request-whenever'. A further primitive was included in earlier versions of this specification, but does not appear in the latest version: 'request-whomever'. Each of these primitives refer to actions to be performed. The rationale for this choice being that they may refer to other communication primitives. For example, the primitive 'query-if' is defined in terms of the imperative 'request' and the indicative 'inform' — 'query-if' is a request that the recipient either inform the sender that some proposition is true (according to the beliefs of the recipient of the request) or that it is false.

The communicative act 'request-whomever' was given an informal description in earlier versions of the FIPA specification; it does not appear within the 2000 FIPA specification [11], but it is worth discussing here because of its clear relation to the theory of delegation presented in this paper. The primitive 'request-whomever' was described as "The sender wants an action performed by some agent other than itself. The receiving agent should either perform the action or pass it on to some other agent." This may be interpretated as an attempt (following Cohen and Levesque's [8] terminology) to delegate an action where the freedom to further delegate the action is unrestricted. This means that the recipient can: (1) not understand the message; (2) refuse the request;[3] (3) accept the request and perform the action itself; (4) accept the request and 'request' some other agent to perform it; or (5) accept the request and 'request-whomever' some other agent to perform it. This is, essentially, the same as case (b) mentioned in section 1 — "I don't care who does (action) α, but it must be done" — and is, therefore, the imperative $T_x\alpha$, where x is the recipient and α is the action that is the message content.

A formal specification of the communicative act 'request' is provided. This is, in fact, a primitive communicative act in the FIPA specification, and the other imperatives (mentioned above) are specialisations. In common with the majority of action languages, the formal specification of the primitive 'request', and all other communicative acts within the FIPA specification, provides a set of 'feasibility preconditions' (FP) and a set of 'rational effects' (RE). The definition of request is reproduced in figure 6.[4]

$$\langle i, \text{Request}(j, a)\rangle$$
$$FP : B_i\, \text{Agent}(j, a) \land \neg B_i\, I_j\, \text{Done}(a)$$
$$RE : \text{Done}(a)$$

Fig. 6. The FIPA request communicative act.

There are two issues in this definition that are important to this discussion. First, the model relies on 'pseudo-states': the state of some action a having been done. As discussed, the model presented in this paper avoids this problem: it provides a means through which the primitives of an agent communication language can refer to the delegation of both *actions* and *goals*.

Second, and more importantly, to capture the notion of responsibility for satisfying the request, the preconditions include the belief of the message sender that the recipient is the agent of the action a. This is stated in the FIPA specification as follows [11, p. 32]: "Agent(i, a) means that i denotes the only agent that ever performs (in the past, present or future) the actions which appear in action expression a". This means that the semantics of this communicative act imposes a significant restriction on the action language that may be used as content to a FIPA message — all actions must be exclusive to the agent that performs the act. This is not a problem if the content is another FIPA message because the specification would include reference to the sender of the message, but the action used to illustrate the use of request in the FIPA specification [11, p. 25] is "open \"db.txt\" for input"! Leaving aside this difficulty, the request communicative act is close to case (d) mentioned in section 1: "You must, through your

---

[3] (1) and (2) are appropriate responses for all FIPA messages.
[4] There is a further feasibility condition defined in the FIPA specification [11], but this refers to the feasibility conditions of the action a. Although this is itself problematic, it is not relevant to this discussion, and is therefore omitted.

own, direct, intervention do α". An example of this case has been discussed in section 5.4: locution L5 in figure 5, where the Lecturer is instructed by the Course Director to write an exam paper and forbear from delegating responsibility for writing the paper.

Although this discussion has been restricted to the FIPA agent communication language, similar limitations can be identified in other ACLs such as KQML; see Reed *et al.* [27] for a more detailed analysis. This does, however, illustrate the fact that delegation cannot be captured as a single, distinct communicative act. There is a real need to develop flexible agent communication languages to support the complex dialogues that are required by agents interacting at the knowledge level.

In the discussion on delegation, it is assumed that getting someone else to act on your behalf is a valid means to the satisfaction of a commitment. This avoids the need to restrict the action component, and hence tie ends to sets of means. The restriction that delegation is forbidden (it is forbidden because the agent is obliged not to delegate) must then be explicitly stated within an agreement. This has some parallel with the notion of the protective perimeter of rights [14, 20]. The protective perimeter contains those actions that can be used to fulfil an obligation. This requires that the action component is extended to indicate that set of acceptable methods of achieving the goal. However, in parallel with Jones and Sergot [17], it is essential that an account of delegation is not dependent upon the detailed choices for the logic of the underlying action component.

7 Conclusion

There are several key advantages that can be gained through adopting the model presented in this paper. First, it becomes possible, in a single formalism, to distinguish an agent doing something, being responsible for getting something done, and being responsible for bringing about a state of affairs. This model provides a clear semantic interpretation for each. Second, it becomes possible to consider an agent's actions with regard to its commitment to a future obligation, and to determine whether or not it is behaving reasonably with respect to that commitment. Suppose that x accepts the task of doing α; i.e. it receives the imperative $T_x\alpha$ under the right context. Under this agreement, x is at all times obliged to perform deeds which ensure that it can carry out α, or at least it is forbidden from performing deeds which will remove the extensional satisfaction of $T_x\alpha$ from the bounds of possibility.

Thirdly, the language used for describing states of affairs in which agents have responsibilities and commitments can be used by those agents in ascribing such responsibilities through imperative- (rather than indicative-) based communicative acts of delegation. Finally, the intuitive simplicity of the approach has been demonstrated to be easily applied to real world examples, and to capture cleanly our intuitive understanding of reponsibility and delegation.

References

1. L. Åqvist. *A new approach to the logical theory of interrogatives*. Tubingen, TBL Verlag Gunter Barr, 1975.
2. J.L. Austin. *How to do things with words*. Oxford University Press, 1962.

3. M. Barbuceanu and M. S. Fox. Integrating communicative action, conversations and decision theory to coordinate agents. In *Proceedings of the Second International Conference on Autonomous Agents*, pages 47–58, 1997.
4. C. Castelfranchi. Modelling social action for AI agents. *Artificial Intelligence*, 103:157–182, 1998.
5. C. Castelfranchi and R. Falcone. Principles of trust for MAS: Cognitive anatomy, social importance, and quantification. In *Proceedings of the Third International Conference on Multi-Agent Systems*, pages 72–79, 1998.
6. B. F. Chellas. *Modal logic: An introduction*. Cambridge University Press, 1980.
7. B. F. Chellas. Time and modality in the logic of agency. *Studia Logica*, 51(3/4):485–517, 1992.
8. P. R. Cohen and H. J. Levesque. Communicative actions for artificial agents. In *Proceedings of the First International Conference on Multi-Agent Systems*, pages 65–72, 1995.
9. F. Dignum. Using transactions in integrity constraints: Looking forward or backwards, what is the difference? In *Proceedings of the Workshop on Applied Logics*, 1992.
10. T. Finin, D. McKay, R. Fritzson, and R. McEntire. KQML: An information and knowledge exchange protocol. In K. Funchi and T. Yokoi, editors, *Knowledge Building and Knowledge Sharing*. Ohmsha and IOS Press, 1994.
11. Foundation for Intelligent Physical Agents. *FIPA communicative act library specification: XC00037H*, 2000. http://www.fipa.org/.
12. H. P. Grice. Meaning. *Philosophical review*, 66:377–388, 1957.
13. C. L. Hamblin. *Imperatives*. Basil Blackwell, 1987.
14. H. L. A. Hart. Bentham on legal rights. In A. W. B. Simpson, editor, *Oxford Essays in Jurisprudence*, 2, pages 171–201. Oxford University Press, 1973.
15. J. Hintikka, I. Halonen, and A. Mutanen. Interrogative logic as a general theory of reasoning. unpublished manuscript, 1996.
16. J. F. Horty and N. Belnap. The deliberative stit: A study of action, omission, ability, and obligation. *Journal of Philosophical Logic*, 24:583–644, 1995.
17. A. I. J. Jones and M. J. Sergot. A formal characterisation of institutionalised power. *Journal of the IGPL*, 4(3):429–445, 1996.
18. L. Kagal, T. Finin, and Y. Peng. A delegation based model for distributed trust. In *Proceedings of the IJCAI 2001 Workshop on Autonomy, Delegation and Control: Interacting with Agents*, 2001.
19. S. Kumar, M. J. Huber, D. R. McGee, P. R. Cohen, and H. J. Levesque. Semantics of agent communication languages for group interaction. In *Proceedings of the Seventeenth National Conference on Artificial Intelligence*, pages 42–47, 2000.
20. L. Lindahl. *Position and change: A study in law and logic*. D. Reidel Publishing Company, Dordrecht, 1977.
21. J. McCarthy and P. Hayes. Some philosophical problems from the standpoint of artificial intelligence. In D. Michie and B. Meltzer, editors, *Machine Intelligence*, volume 4, pages 463–502. Edinburgh University Press, 1969.
22. A. Newell. The knowledge level. *Artificial Intelligence*, 18:87–127, 1982.
23. T. J. Norman and C. A. Reed. Group delegation and responsibility. In *Proceedings of the First International Joint Conference on Autonomous Agents and Multi-Agent Systems*, 2002.
24. P. Panzarasa, N. R. Jennings, and T. J. Norman. Formalising collaborative decision making and practical reasoning in multi-agent systems. *Journal of Logic and Computation*, 12(1):55–117, 2002.
25. I. Pörn. *The logic of power*. Basil Blackwell, 1970.
26. C. A. Reed. Dialogue frames in agent communication. In *Proceedings of the Third International Conference on Multi-Agent Systems*, pages 246–253, 1998.

27. C. A. Reed, T. J. Norman, and N. R. Jennings. Negotiating the semantics of agent communication languages. *Computational Intelligence*, to appear.
28. J. R. Searle. *Speech acts: An essay in the philosophy of language*. Cambridge University Press, 1969.
29. M. J. Sergot. Normative positions. In P. McNamara and H. Prakken, editors, *Norms, Logics and Information Systems*. ISO Press, 1998.
30. M. Shanahan. *Solving the Frame Problem: A Mathematical Investigation of the Common Sense Law of Inertia*. MIT Press, Cambridge, MA, 1997.
31. I. A. Smith, P. R. Cohen, J. M. Bradshaw, M. Greaves, and H. Holmback. Designing conversation policies using joint intention theory. In *Proceedings of the Third International Conference on Multi-Agent Systems*, pages 269–276, 1998.
32. G. H. von Wright. *An essay in deontic logic and the general theory of action*, volume 21 of *Acta philosophica Fennica*. North-Holland, Amsterdam, 1968.
33. D. N. Walton and E. C. W. Krabbe. *Commitment in dialogue: Basic concepts of interpersonal reasoning*. SUNY, New York, 1995.
34. M. J. Wooldridge. *Reasoning about rational agents*. MIT Press, 2000.

Agent Specification Using Multi-context Systems

Simon Parsons[1], Nicholas R. Jennings[2], Jordi Sabater[3], and Carles Sierra[3]

[1] Center for Coordination Science, Sloan School of Management,
Massachusetts Institute of Technology, 3 Cambridge Center, Cambridge, MA 02142, USA,
sparsons@mit.edu
[2] Department of Electronics and Computer Science,
University of Southampton, Highfield, Southampton SO17 1BJ, UK,
nrj@ecs.soton.ac.uk
[3] IIIA – Artificial Intelligence Research Institute,
CSIC – Spanish Council for Scientific Research,
Campus UAB, 08193 Bellaterra, Catalonia, Spain,
{jsabater,sierra}, @iiia.csic.es

Abstract. In the area of agent-based computing there are many proposals for specific system architectures, and a number of proposals for general approaches to building agents. As yet, however, there are comparatively few attempts to relate these together, and even fewer attempts to provide methodologies which relate designs to architectures and then to executable agents. This paper discusses an attempt we have made to address this shortcoming, describing a general method of defining architectures for logic-based agents which can be directly executed. Our approach is based upon the use of multi-context systems and we illustrate its use through examples of the specification of some simple agents.

1 Introduction

Agent-based computing is fast emerging as a new paradigm for engineering complex, distributed systems [18, 36]. An important aspect of this trend is the use of agent architectures as a means of delivering agent-based functionality (as opposed to work on agent programming languages [19, 31, 34]). In this context, an architecture can be viewed as a separation of concerns – it identifies the main functions that ultimately give rise to the agent's behaviour and defines the interdependencies that exist between them. As agent architectures become more widely used, there is an increasing demand for unambiguous specifications of them and there is a greater need to verify implementations of them. To this end, a range of techniques have been used to formally specify agent architectures (including Concurrent MetateM [12, 35], DESIRE [3, 32] and Z [8]). However, these techniques typically fall short in at least one of the following ways: (i) they enforce a particular view of architecture upon the specification; (ii) they offer no explicit structures for modelling the components of an architecture or the relationships between them; (iii) they leave a gap between the specification of an architecture and its implementation.

To rectify these shortcomings, we have proposed the use of *multi-context systems* [15] as a means of specifying and implementing agent architectures. Multi-context systems provide an overarching framework that allows distinct theoretical components to be defined and interrelated. Such systems consist of a set of contexts – each of which can

M. d' Inverno et al. (Eds.): UKMAS 1996–2000, LNAI 2403, pp. 205–226, 2002.

informally be considered to be a logic and a set of formulae written in that logic – and a set of bridge rules for transferring information between contexts. Thus, different contexts can be used to represent different components of the architecture and the interactions between these components can be specified by means of the bridge rules between the contexts. We believe multi-context systems are well suited to specifying and modelling agent architectures for two main types of reason: (i) from a *software engineering perspective* they support modular decomposition and encapsulation; and (ii) from a *logical modelling perspective* they provide an efficient means of specifying and executing complex logics.

From a software engineering perspective, multi-context systems support the development of modular architectures. Each architectural component – be it a functional component (responsible for assessing the agent's current situation, say) or a data structure component (the agent's beliefs, say) – can be represented as a separate context. The links between the components can then be made explicit by writing bridge rules to link the contexts. This ability to directly support component decomposition offers a clean route from the high level specification of the architecture through to its detailed design. Moreover, this basic philosophy can be applied no matter how the architectural components are decomposed or how many architectural components exist.

Moving onto the logical modelling perspective, there are four main advantages of adopting a multi-context approach. The first is an extension of the software engineering advantages which specifically applies to logical systems. By breaking the logical description of an agent into a set of contexts, each of which holds a set of related formulae, we effectively get a form of many-sorted logic (all the formulae in one context are a single sort) with the concomitant advantages of scalability and efficiency. The second advantage follows on from this. Using multi-context systems makes it possible to build agents which use several different logics in a way that keeps the logics neatly separated (all the formulae in one logic are gathered together in one context). This either makes it possible to increase the representational power of logical agents (compared with those which use a single logic) or simplify agents conceptually (compared with those which use several logics in one global context). This latter advantage is illustrated below where we use multi-context systems to simplify the construction of a BDI agent.

Both of the above advantages apply to any logical agent built using multi-context systems. The remaining two advantages apply to specific types of logical agent – those which reason about their beliefs and those of other agents. The first is that multi-context systems make it possible [15] to build agents which reason in a way which conforms to the use of modal logics like KD45 (the standard modal logic for handling belief) but which obviates the difficulties usually inherent in theorem proving in such logics. Again this is illustrated in [23]. Thus the use of multi-context systems makes it easy to directly execute agent specifications where those specifications deal with modal notions. The final advantage is related to this. Agents which reason about beliefs are often confronted with the problem of modelling the beliefs of other agents, and this can be hard, especially when those other agents reason about beliefs in a different way (because, for instance, they use a different logic). Multi-context systems provide a neat solution to this problem [1, 6].

When the software engineering and the logical modelling perspectives are combined, it can be seen that the multi-context approach offers a clear path from specification through to implementation. By providing a clear set of mappings from concept to design, and from design to implementation, the multi-context approach offers a way of tackling the gap that currently exists between the theory and the practice of agent-based systems.

2 Multi-context Agents

As discussed above, we believe that the use of multi-context systems offers a number of advantages when engineering agent architectures. However, multi-context systems are not a panacea. We believe that they are most appropriate when building agents which are logic-based and are therefore largely deliberative[1].

2.1 The Basic Model

Using a multi-context approach, an agent architecture consists of four basic types of component. These components were first identified in the context of building theorem provers for modal logic [15], before being identified as a methodology for constructing agent architectures [20]. The components are[2] :

- *Units*: Structural entities representing the main components of the architecture.
- *Logics*: Declarative languages, each with a set of axioms and a number of rules of inference. Each unit has a single logic associated with it.
- *Theories*: Sets of formulae written in the logic associated with a unit.
- *Bridge rules*: Rules of inference which relate formulae in different units.

Units represent the various components of the architecture. They contain the bulk of an agent's problem solving knowledge, and this knowledge is encoded in the specific theory that the unit encapsulates. In general, the nature of the units will vary between architectures. For example, a BDI agent may have units which represent theories of beliefs, desires and intentions (see Section 3), whereas an architecture based on a functional separation of concerns may have units which encode theories of cooperation, situation assessment and plan execution (see Section 4). In either case, each unit has a suitable logic associated with it. Thus the belief unit of a BDI agent has a logic of belief associated with it, and the intention unit has a logic of intention. The logic associated with each unit provides the language in which the information in that unit is encoded, and the bridge rules provide the mechanism by which information is transferred between units.

Bridge rules can be understood as rules of inference with premises and conclusions in different units. For instance:

$$\frac{u_1 : \psi, u_2 : \varphi}{u_3 : \theta}$$

means that formula θ may be deduced in unit u_3 if formulae ψ and φ are deduced in units u_1 and u_2 respectively.

---

[1] See [38] for a discussion of the relative merits of logic-based and non logic-based approaches to specifying and building agent architectures.

[2] For more detail see [20].

When used as a means of specifying agent architectures, all the elements of the model, both units and bridge rules, are taken to work concurrently. In practice this means that the execution of each unit is a non-terminating, deductive process[3]. The bridge rules continuously examine the theories of the units that appear in their premises for new sets of formulae that match them. This means that all the components of the architecture are always ready to react to any change (external or internal) and that there are no central control elements.

2.2   The Extended Model

The model as outlined above is that introduced in [20] and used in [23]. However, this model has proved deficient in a couple of ways, both connected to the dynamics of reasoning. In particular we found it useful [29] to extend the basic idea of multi-context systems by associating two control elements with the bridge rules: *consumption* and *time-outs*. A consuming condition means the bridge rule removes the formula from the theory which contains the premise (remember that a theory is considered to be a set of formulae). Thus in bridge rules with consuming conditions, formulae "move" between units. To distinguish between a consuming condition and a non-consuming condition, we will use the notation $u_i > \psi$ for consuming and $u_i : \psi$ for non-consuming conditions. Thus:

$$\frac{u_1 > \psi, u_2 : \varphi}{u_3 : \theta}$$

means that when the bridge rule is executed, ψ is removed from u_1 but φ is not removed from u_2.

Consuming conditions increase expressiveness in the communication between units. With this facility, we can model the movement of a formula from one theory to another (from one unit to another), changes in the theory of one unit that cause the removal of a formula from another one, and so on. This mechanism also makes it possible to model the concept of state since having a concrete formula in one unit or another might represent a different agent state. For example, later in the paper we use the presence of a formula in a particular unit to indicate the availability of a resource.

A time-out in a bridge rule means there is a delay between the instant in time at which the conditions of the bridge rule are satisfied and the effective activation of the rule. A time-out is denoted by a label on the right of the rule; for instance:

$$\frac{u_1 : \psi}{u_2 : \varphi}[t]$$

means that t units of time after the theory in unit u_1 gets formula ψ, the theory in unit u_2 will be extended by formula φ. If during this time period formula ψ is removed from the theory in unit u_1, this rule will not be applied. In a similar way to consuming conditions, time-outs increase expressiveness in the communication between units. This is important when actions performed by bridge rules need to be retracted if a specific event does not happen after a given period of time. In particular, it enables us to represent situations

---

[3] For more detail on exactly how this is achieved, see [29].

where silence during a period of time may mean failure (in this case the bridge rules can then be used to re-establish a previous state)[4].

2.3 Modular Agents

Using units and bridge rules as the only structural elements can be cumbersome when building complex agents (as can be seen from the model we develop below in Section 3). As the complexity of the agent increases, it rapidly becomes very difficult to deal with the necessary number of units and their interconnections using bridge rules alone. Adding new capabilities to the agent becomes a complex task in itself. To solve this problem we suggest adding another level of abstraction to the model – the *module*.

A module is a set of units and bridge rules that together model a particular capability or facet of an agent. For example, planning agents must be capable of managing resources, and such an agent might have a module modeling this ability. Similarly, such an agent might have a module for generating plans, a module for handling communication, and so on. Thus modules capture exactly the same idea as the "capabilities" discussed by Busetta *et al.* [4]. Unlike Busetta *et al.*, we do not currently allow modules to be nested inside one another, largely because we have not yet found it necessary to do so. However, it seems likely that we will need to develop a means of handling nested hierachies of modules in order to build more complex agents than we are currently constructing.

Each module must have a communication unit. This unit is the module's unique point of contact with the other modules and it knows what kind of messages its module can deal with. All of an agent's communication units are inter-connected with the others using *multicast bridge rules* (*MBRs*) as in Figure 1. This figure shows three MBRs (the rectangles in the middle of the diagram) each of which has a single premise in module a and a single conclusion in each of the modules n_i.

Since the MBRs send messages to more than one module, a single message can provoke more than one answer and, hence, contradictory information may appear. There are many possible ways of dealing with this problem, however here we consider just one of them as an example. We associate a weight with each message. This value is assigned to the message by the communication unit of the module that sends it out. Weights belong to $[0, 1]$ (maximum importance is 1 and minimum is 0), and their meaning is the strength of the opinion given in the message, and this can be used to resolve contradictory messages. For instance, the message with highest weight might be preferred, or the different weights of incoming messages could be combined by a communication unit receiving them to take a final decision (for instance using the belief revision mechanism described in [21]). Note that weights are used only in *inter-module* messages.

---

[4] Both of these extensions to the standard multi-context system incur a cost. This is that including them in the model means that the model departs somewhat from first order predicate calculus, and so does not have a fully-defined semantics. We are currently looking at using linear logic, in which individual propositions can only be used once in any given proof, as a means of giving a semantics to consuming conditions, and various temporal logics as a means of giving a semantics to time-outs.

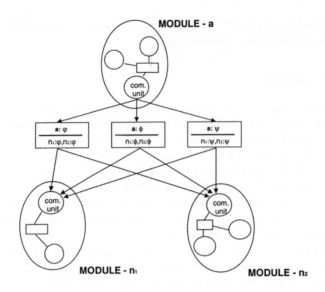

Fig. 1. The inter-connection of modules (from a's perspective only)

2.4 Messages between Modules

Given a set AN of agent names and a set MN of module names, an inter-module message has the form:

$$I(S, R, \varphi, G, \psi)$$

where

- I is an illocutionary particle that specifies the kind of message.
- S and R both have the form $A[/m]^{*5}$ where $A \in AN$ or $A = Self$ (*Self* refers to the agent that owns the module) and $m \in MN$, or $m = all$ (*all* denotes all the modules within that agent). S reflects who is sending the message and R indicates to whom it is directed.
- φ is the content of the message.
- G is a record of the derivation of φ. It has the form: $\{\{\Gamma_1 \vdash \varphi_1\} \ldots \{\Gamma_n \vdash \varphi_n\}\}$ where Γ is a set of formulae and φ_i is a formula with $\varphi_n = \varphi^6$.
- $\psi \in [0, 1]$ is the weight associated with the message.

To see how this works in practice, consider the following. Suppose that an agent (named B) has four modules (a, b, c, d). Module a sends the message:

$$Ask(Self/a, Self/all, Give(B, A, Nail), \psi_1, 0.5)$$

---

[5] As elsewhere we use BNF syntax, so that $A[/m]^*$ means A followed by one or more occurrences of $/m$.

[6] In other words, G is exactly the set of grounds of the argument for φ [23]. Where the agent does not need to be able to justify its statements, this component of the message can be discarded. Note that, as argued by Gabbay [13] this approach is a generalisation of classical logic – there is nothing to stop the same approach being used when messages are just formulae in classical logic.

This means that module a of agent B is asking all its modules whether B should give A a nail. The reason for doing this is ψ_1 and the weight a puts on this request is 0.5. Assume modules c and d send the answer

$$Answer(Self/c, Self/a, not(Give(B, A, Nail)), \psi_2, 0.6)$$

and

$$Answer(Self/d, Self/a, not(Give(B, A, Nail)), \psi_3, 0.7)$$

while module b sends

$$Answer(Self/b, Self/a, Give(B, A, Nail), \psi_4, 0.3)$$

Currently we treat the weights of the messages as possibility measures [9], and so combine the disjunctive support for $not(Give(B, A, Nail))$ using max. As this combined weight is higher than the weight of the positive literal, the communication unit of module a will accept the opinion $not(Give(B, A, Nail))$.

The messages we have discussed so far are those which are passed around the agent itself in order to exchange information between the modules which compose it. Our approach also admits the more common idea of messages between agents. Such inter-agent messages have the same basic form, but they have two minor differences:

- S and R are agent names (i.e. $S, R \in AN$), no modules are specified.
- there is no degree of importance (because it is internal to a particular agent – however inter-agent messages could be augmented with a degree of belief [21] which could be based upon the weight of the relevant intra-agent messages.)

With this machinery in place, we are in a position to specify realistic agent architectures.

2.5 Examples of Multi-context Agents

This remainder of this paper contains two examples of agent specification using multi-context systems, each illustrating one of the uses of units introduced in Section 2.1 – the first of these (based on the model in [23]) is that for a BDI agent, the second (based on the model in [29]), is that for an agent in which the architectural units are based on a functional separation of concerns. The first illustrates how the multi-context approach can be used to handle the kind of "mental attitudes" agent architectures which have become common. The second shows how modules can help to simplify the multi-context model.

Both of these examples are based around the example of home improvement agents introduced in [22], and sketched below[7]. In order to save space (and also to save the sanity of the authors and readers familiar with the example), neither treatment does any more than specify the agents – fuller versions can be found in the papers cited above.

For those unfamiliar with the example, it is as follows. Two agents, A and B have, respectively, the tasks of hanging a picture and hanging a mirror. A knows one way of hanging a picture and one of hanging a mirror. B just knows how to hang a mirror (using

---

[7] Initially unnamed, this example seems to have become known as "The Nail Problem" (TNP); despite being simple to express it turns out to be rather hard to handle.

a different technique from A). A has the means to hang a mirror using its technique, B has the means to hang either its mirror, using its own technique, or A's picture. The full solution to the problem involves A convincing B to use A's approach and resources to hang the mirror so that A can use B's resources to hang the picture.

3   Agents with Mental Attitudes

Our first example examines how a particular class of agent architecture – BDI agents – can be modelled and then describes how particular individuals of that class can be specified in order to solve the example. This seems an appropriate choice because BDI agents are currently of wide interest within the multi-agent system community [37].

3.1   A High-Level Description

The first step in specifying the agent is to choose the units and the logics that they contain. In this example, the choice is driven by the fact that we are modelling BDI agents. The particular theory of BDI on which the architecture is based is that of Rao and Georgeff. This model has evolved over time (as can be seen by comparing [25] and [26]) and in this section we account for the most recent approach [26] where three modalities are distinguished: B for beliefs – used to represent the state of the environment, D for desires – used to represent the motivations of the agent, and I for intentions – used to represent the ends (or goals) of the agent. In order to fit this kind of model into our multi-context framework, we associate a separate unit for each of the modalities[8]

As dicussed in [23], we could then equip each of these units with exactly the same logic as is used in Rao and Georgeff's model, taking the logic of the belief unit to be modal logic KD45 and the logics of the desire and intention units to both be modal logic KD, and to take all these modal logics to be combined with the temporal logic CTL [10]. However, it is more in the spirit of multi-context systems [15] to take B, D and I as predicates. Such systems again have separate B, D and I units along with a communication unit, and use first order logic. The necessary interaction between the predicates is established using bridge rules (as discussed below) and the axioms of the relevant modal logics are modelled by adding formulae to the theories in each unit (again this is discussed below).

3.2   Specification of Bridge Rules

Having decided on the units and the logics that they contain, the next step in the specification is to write down the bridge rules which connect the units. Here we have two distinct sets of such rules. The first model the relationships between beliefs, desires and intentions. These are domain independent and would hold for any BDI agent specified in this way. The second model some domain specific knowledge.

---

[8] In fact the general approach allows more than one unit for beliefs (as in [5]), desires or intentions if deemed appropriate. In the examples presented, however, this is not necessary.

BDI Bridge Rules. As stated above, the set of bridge rules determine the relationship between the modalities and hence the behaviour of the agent. Three well established sets of relationships for BDI agents have been identified [26]:

- *Strong realism.* The set of intentions is a subset of the set of desires which in turn is a subset of the beliefs. That is, if an agent does not believe something, it will neither desire nor intend it [25].
- *Realism.* The set of beliefs is a subset of the set of desires which in turn is a subset of the set of intentions. That is, if an agent believes something, it both desires and intends it [7].
- *Weak realism.* A case in between strong realism and realism. Agents do not desire propositions the negation of which are believed, do not intend propositions the negations of which are desired, and do not intend propositions the negations of which are believed [24].

Figure 2 gives a suitable set of bridge rules for each of these interpretations. In [23], we only considered strong realist agents. In addition to this set of rules, we found that we needed a couple of additional rules which relate intentions to beliefs:

$$\text{AWARENESS\_OF\_INTENTION}(1) = \frac{I : I_i(\alpha)}{B : B_i(I_i(\alpha))}$$

$$\text{AWARENESS\_OF\_INTENTION}(2) = \frac{I : \neg I_i(\alpha)}{B : B_i(\neg I_i(\alpha))}$$

Agents are aware of their intentions, so if an agent has an intention it also believes that it has that intention. We also have:

$$\text{IMPLUSIVENESS} = \frac{B : B_i(I_i(\alpha))}{I : I_i(\alpha)}$$

When an agent believes it has an intention, it adopts that intention.

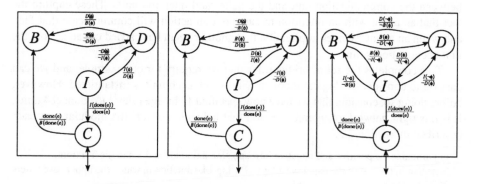

Fig. 2. Different types of BDI agent. From left to right, the relations between modalities correspond to strong realism, realism and weak realism.

These last two are similar in some ways to the basic rules of modal logic[9], except that in standard modal logic they don't apply across modalities in the way that they do here.

Domain Dependent Bridge Rules. The bridge rules for the appropriate form of realism will be required for the specification of any such agent whatever domain it is operating in. Without them, the agent will not conform to Rao and Georgeff's idea of what a BDI agent is. In addition we believe that the awareness of intentions and implusiveness rules (or something like them) will be required in practice by any BDI agent.

In addition to these domain independent rules, any agent will require a set of bridge rules which define how it interacts with other agents. In the domain of this example, these relate the mental state to what an agent says (and what it hears to its mental state). These are as follows[10]:

$$\text{REQUEST} = \frac{I : I_i(Give(X, i, Z))}{C : Ask(i, X, Give(X, i, Z))}$$

When an agent (i) needs something (Z) from another agent (X), it asks for it

$$\text{OFFER} = \frac{I : I_i(Give(i, X, Z))}{C : Tell(i, X, Give(i, X, Z))}$$

When an agent (i) has the intention of offering something (Z) to another agent (X), it informs the recipient of this fact.

$$\text{TRUST} = \frac{C : Tell(X, i, B_X(\varphi))}{B : B_i(\varphi)}$$

When an agent (i) is told of a belief of another agent (X), it accepts that belief.

$$\text{AWARENESS\_OF\_ILLOCUTIONS} = \frac{C : \alpha}{B : B_i(\alpha)}$$

In addition, Figure 2 includes some bridge rules which allow the transfer of information between the communication unit and the belief and intention units. These capture the fact that an agent with an intention to carry out an action will communicate that fact, and when an agent receives notification that another agent has carried out an action, the first agent believes this.

This completes the set of bridge rules that we require for our example, and we can pass on to consider the logical theories with which each unit is instantiated. However, before doing so, consider that we have now specified 13 bridge rules[11] to connect 4 units. It is this tight network of interconnection that led us to conside the modular approach described in Section 2.3.

---

[9] In particular the positive and negative introspection axioms 4 and 5 and the T axiom.

[10] Note that in the rest of the paper we adopt a Prolog-like notation in which the upper case letters X, Y, Z, P are taken to be variables.

[11] That is we require 13 in order to specify a strong realist agent. A weak realist agent would require 15.

3.3   Instantiating the Contexts

Having specified the contexts, logics and bridge rules we have to consider what formulae will appear in each unit. Some of these will be specific to an individual agent (the desires with which it is programmed for example), but others will be more generic and be common between a number of agents. It is these more generic formulae that we consider here. In the case of the home improvement agents, both agents need a simple theory of action that integrates a model of the available resources with their planning mechanism. This theory needs to model the following ideas (where i is an index identifying the agent):

Ownership.   When an agent (X) is the owner of an artifact (Z) and it gives Z to another agent (Y), Y becomes its new owner:

$$B : B_i(Have(X,Z) \wedge Give(X,Y,Z) \rightarrow Have(Y,Z))$$

Unicity.   When an agent (X) gives an artifact (Z) away, it no longer owns it[12]:

$$B : B_i(Have(X,Z) \wedge Give(X,Y,Z) \rightarrow \neg Have(X,Z))$$

Benevolence.   When an agent i has something (Z) that it does not intend to use and is asked to give it to another agent (X), i adopts the intention of giving Z to X. Naturally more complex cooperative strategies can be defined if desired:

$$B : B_i(Have(i,Z) \wedge \neg I_i(Have(i,Z)) \wedge Ask(X,i,Give(i,X,Z)) \rightarrow$$
$$I_i(Give(i,X,Z)))$$

The following axioms represent a similarly simplistic theory of planning (but again one which suffices for our example). In crude terms, when an agent believes that it has the intention of doing something and has a rule for achieving that intention then the preconditions of the rule become new intentions. Recall that the $\rightarrow$ between the P_i and Q is not material implication.

Parsimony.   If an agent believes that it does not intend something, it does not believe that it will intend the means to achieve it.

$$B : B_i(\neg I_i(Q)) \wedge B_i(P_1 \wedge \ldots \wedge P_j \wedge \ldots \wedge P_n \rightarrow Q) \rightarrow \neg B_i(I_i(P_j))$$

Reduction.   If there is only one way of achieving an intention, an agent adopts the intention of achieving its preconditions.

$$B : B_i(I_i(Q)) \wedge B_i(P_1 \wedge \ldots \wedge P_j \wedge \ldots \wedge P_n \rightarrow Q)$$
$$\wedge \neg B_i(R_1 \wedge \ldots \wedge R_m \rightarrow Q) \rightarrow B_i(I_i(P_j))$$

where $R_1 \wedge \ldots \wedge R_m$ is not a permutation of $P_1 \wedge \ldots \wedge P_n$.

---

[12] As it stands this formula appears contradictory. This is because we have, for simplicity, ignored the treatment of time. Of course, the complete specification of this example (which is not our main focus) would need time to be handled. We could do this by including time as an additional argument to each predicate, in which case the unicity formula would read $B : B_i(Have(X,Z,t) \wedge Give(X,Y,Z,t) \rightarrow \neg Have(X,Z,t+1))$. Doing this would involve making the base logic for each unit "time capable", for instance by using the system introduced by Vila [33].

Unique Choice. If there are two or more ways of achieving an intention, only one is intended. Note that we use $\triangledown$ to denote exclusive or.

$$B : B_i(I_i(Q)) \wedge B_i(P_1 \wedge \ldots \wedge P_j \wedge \ldots \wedge P_n \rightarrow Q)$$
$$\wedge B_i(R_1 \wedge \ldots \wedge R_m \rightarrow Q) \rightarrow$$
$$B_i(I_i(P_1 \wedge \ldots \wedge P_n)) \triangledown B_i(I_i(R_1 \wedge \ldots \wedge R_m))$$

where $R_1 \wedge \ldots \wedge R_m$ is not a permutation of $P_1 \wedge \ldots \wedge P_n$. As mentioned above, we acknowledge that both the theory of action and the theory of planning are rather naive. The interested reader is encouraged to substitute their own such theories if desired.

So far, we have identified the contexts and the logics they will contain, decided on the bridge rules between them, and identified the bits of the theories expressed in each logic that are common to both agents in our example. It remains to add to the model those bits of the theories that are unique to each agent.

3.4   Instantiating the Individual Agents

Agent a has the intention of hanging a picture, it has various beliefs about resources and how they can be used to hang mirrors and pictures:

$I : I_a(Can(a, hang\_picture))$

$B : B_a(Have(a, picture))$

$B : B_a(Have(a, screw))$

$B : B_a(Have(a, hammer))$

$B : B_a(Have(a, screwdriver))$

$B : B_a(Have(b, nail))$

$B : B_a(Have(X, hammer) \wedge Have(X, nail) \wedge Have(X, picture) \rightarrow$
$\quad Can(X, hang\_picture))$

$B : B_a(Have(X, screw) \wedge Have(X, screwdriver) \wedge Have(X, mirror) \rightarrow$
$\quad Can(X, hang\_mirror))$

Now, agent b wants to hang a mirror (and has this as an intention) and has various beliefs about its resources and the action of hanging mirrors:

$I : I_b(Can(b, hang\_mirror))$

$B : B_b(Have(b, mirror))$

$B : B_b(Have(b, nail))$

$B : B_b(Have(X, hammer) \wedge Have(X, nail) \wedge Have(X, mirror) \rightarrow$
$\quad Can(X, hang\_mirror))$

We have now demonstrated how the multi-context approach can be used to specify BDI agents. As mentioned above, [23] shows how this specification can be used to solve the example.

4 A Functional Agent

This section gives a specification of an agent which is capable of solving a simplified version of the home-improvement example. The simplification is to reduce the problem to one in which a single agent has all the resources necessary to hang a picture. As a result, compared with the more complex versions of the home improvement agents described above, the agent is not quite solipsistic (since it has some awareness of its environment) but it is certainly autistic (since it has no mechanisms for interacting with other agents). For an example of the specification of further agents in the context of this example, see [27–29][13].

4.1 A High-Level Description

The basic structure of the agent is that of Figure 3. There are three modules connected by multicast bridge rules. These are the plan library (**PL**), the resource manager (**RM**), and the goal manager (**GM**). Broadly speaking, the plan library stores plans for the tasks that the agent knows how to complete, the resource manager keeps track of the resources available to the agent, and the goal manager relates the goals of the agent to the selection of appropriate plans.

There are two types of message which get passed along the multicast bridge rules. These are the following:

- **Ask:** a request to another module.
- **Answer:** an answer to an inter-module request.

Thus all the modules can do is to make requests on one another and answer those requests. We also need to define the predicates which form the content of such messages. Given a set of agent names AN, and with $AN' = AN \cup \{Self\}$.

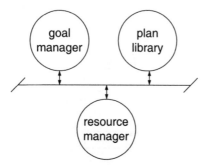

Fig. 3. The modules in the agent

---

[13] Note that [27] is distinct from [28]. The former is the version in the workshop preproceedings, whereas the latter is the version available in the published proceedings and the examples they contain are substantially different.

- *Goal(X)*: *X* is a string describing an action. This denotes the fact that the agent has the goal *X*.
- *Have(X, Z)*: *X* ∈ *AN'* is the name of an agent (here always instantiated to *Self*, the agent's name for itself, but a variable since the agent is aware that other agents may own things), and *Z* is the name of an object. This denotes Agent *X* has possession of *Z*.

As can be seen from the above, the content of the messages is relatively simple, referring to goals that the agent has, and resources it possesses. Thus a typical message would be a request from the goal manager as to whether the agent possesses a hammer:

$$ask(Self/GM, Self/all, goal(have(Self, hammer)), \{\})$$

Note that in this message, as in all messages in the remainder of this paper, we ignore the weight in the interests of clarity. Such a request might be generated when the goal manager is trying to ascertain if the agent can fulfill a possible plan which involves using a hammer.

4.2   Specifications of the Modules

Having identified the structure of the agent in terms of modules, the next stage in the specification is to detail the internal structure of the modules in terms of the units they contain, and the bridge rules connecting those units. The structure of the plan library module is given in Figure 4. In this diagram, units are represented as circles, and bridge rules as rectangles. Arrows into bridge rules indicate units which hold the antecedents of the bridge rules, and arrows out indicate the units which hold the consequents. The two units in the plan library module are:

- The communication unit (CU): the unit which handles communication with other units.

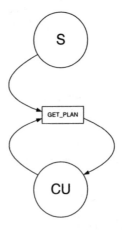

Fig. 4. The plan library module

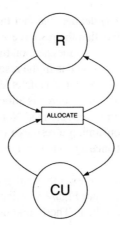

Fig. 5. The resource manager module

– The plan repository (S): a unit which holds a set of plans.

The bridge rule connecting these units is:

$$\text{GET\_PLAN} = \frac{\begin{array}{c} CU > ask(Self/Sender, Self/all, goal(Z), \{\}), \\ S : plan(Z, P) \end{array}}{CU : answer(Self/PL, (Self/Sender, goal(Z), \{P\})}$$

where the predicate $plan(Z, P)$ denotes the fact that P, taken to be a conjunction of terms, is a plan to achieve the goal Z[14].

When the communication unit sees a message on the inter-module bus asking about the feasibility of the agent achieving a goal, then, if there is a plan to achieve that goal in the plan repository, that plan is sent to the module which asked the original question. Note that the bridge rule has a consuming condition – this is to ensure that the question is only answered once.

The structure of the resource manager module is given in Figure 5. The two units in this module are:

– The communication unit (CU).
– The resource respository (R): a unit which holds the set of resources available to the agent.

The bridge rule connecting the two units is the following:

$$\text{ALLOCATE} = \frac{\begin{array}{c} CU > ask(Self/Sender, Self/Receiver, goal(have(X, Z)), \{\}), \\ R > resource(Z, free) \end{array}}{\begin{array}{c} CU : answer(Self/RM, Self/Sender, have(X, Z), \{\}), \\ R : resource(Z, allocated) \end{array}}$$

---

[14] Though here we take a rather relaxed view of what constitutes a plan – our "plans" are little more than a set of pre-conditions for achieving the goal.

where the $resource(Z, allocated)$ denotes the fact that the resource Z is in use, and $resource(Z, free)$ denotes the fact that the resource Z is not in use.

When the communication unit sees a message on the inter-module bus asking if the agent has a resource, then, if that resource is in the resource repository and is currently free, the formula recording the free resource is deleted by the consuming condition, a new formula recording the fact that the resource is allocated is written to the repository, and a response is posted on the inter-module bus. Note that designating a resource as "allocated" is not the same as consuming a resource (which would be denoted by the deletion of the resource), and that once again the bridge rule deletes the original message from the communication unit.

The goal manager is rather more complex than either of the previous modules we have discussed, as is immediately clear from Figure 6 which shows the modules it contains, and the bridge rules which connect them. These modules are:

- The communication unit (CU).
- The plan list unit (P): this contains a list of plans the execution of which is currently being monitored.
- The goal manager unit (G): this is the heart of the module, and ensures that the necessary sub-goaling is carried out.

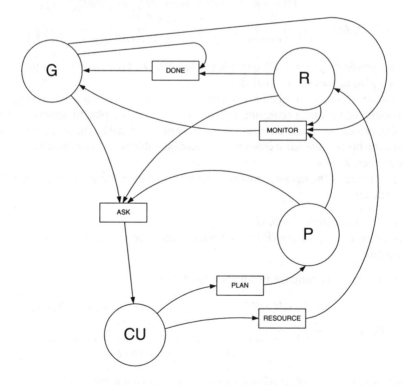

Fig. 6. The goal manager module

– The resource list module (R): this contains a list of the resources being used as part of plans which are currently being executed.

The bridge rules relating these units are as follows. The first two bridge rules handle incoming information from the communication unit:

$$\mathsf{RESOURCE} = \frac{CU > answer(Self/RM, Self/GM, have(Self, Z), \{\})}{R:Z}$$

$$\mathsf{PLAN} = \frac{CU > answer(Self/PL, Self/GM, goal(Z), \{P\})}{P:plan(Z, P)}$$

The first of these, **RESOURCE**, looks for messages from the resource manager reporting that the agent has possession of some resource. When such a message arrives, the goal manager adds a formula representing the resource to its resource list module. The second bridge rule **PLAN** does much the same for messages from the plan library reporting the existence of a plan – such plans are written to the plan library. There is also a bridge rule **ASK** which generates messages for other modules:

$$\mathsf{ASK} = \frac{\begin{array}{c} G:goal(X), \\ G:not(done(X)), \\ R:not(X), \\ P:not(plan(X, Z)) \\ G:not(done(ask(X))), \end{array}}{\begin{array}{c} CU:ask(Self/G, Self/all, goal(X), \{\}), \\ G:done(ask(X)) \end{array}}$$

If the agent has the goal to achieve X, and X has not been achieved, nor is X an available resource (and therefore in the R unit), nor is there a plan to achieve X, and X has not already been requested from other modules, then X is requested from other modules and this request is recorded. The remaining bridge rules are:

$$\mathsf{MONITOR} = \frac{\begin{array}{c} G:goal(X), \\ R:not(X), \\ P:plan(X, P) \end{array}}{G:monitor(X, P)}$$

$$\mathsf{DONE} = \frac{\begin{array}{c} G:goal(X), \\ R:X \end{array}}{G:done(X)}$$

The **MONITOR** bridge rule takes a goal X and, if there is no resource to achieve X but there is a plan to obtain the resource, adds the formula $monitor(X, P)$ to the G unit, which has the effect of beginnning the search for the resources to carry out the plan. The **DONE** bridge rule identifies that a goal X has been achieved when a suitable resource has been allocated.

4.3 Specifications of the Units

Having identified the individual units within each module, and the bridge rules which connect the units, the next stage of the specification is to identify the logics present within the various units, and the theories which are written in those logics. For this agent most of the units are simple containers for atomic formulae. In contrast, the G unit contains a theory which controls the execution of plans. The relevant formulae are:

$$monitor(X, P) \rightarrow assert\_subgoals(P)$$
$$monitor(X, P) \rightarrow prove(P)$$
$$monitor(X, P) \wedge proved(P) \rightarrow done(X)$$

$$assert\_subgoals(\bigwedge_i Y_i) \rightarrow \bigwedge_i goal(Y_i)$$

$$prove(X \wedge \bigwedge_i Y_i) \wedge done(X) \rightarrow prove(\bigwedge_i Y_i)$$

$$\bigwedge_i done(Y_i) \rightarrow proved(\bigwedge_i Y_i)$$

The *monitor* predicate forces all the conjuncts which make up its first argument to be goals (which will be monitored in turn), and kicks off the "proof" of the plan which is its second argument[15]. This plan will be a conjunction of actions, and as each is "done" (a state of affairs achieved through the allocation of resources by other bridge rules), the proof of the next conjunct is sought. When all have been "proved", the relevant goal is marked as completed.

The specification as presented so far is generic – it is akin to a class description for a class of autistic home improvement agents. To get a specific agent we have to "program" it by giving it information about its initial state. For our particular example there is little such information, and we only need to add formulae to three units. The plan repository holds a plan for hanging pictures using hammers and nails:

$$S : plan(hangPicture(X),$$
$$have(X, picture) \wedge have(X, nail) \wedge have(X, hammer))$$

The resource repository holds the information that the agent has a picture, nail and a hammer:

$$R : Resource(picture, free)$$
$$R : Resource(nail, free)$$
$$R : Resource(hammer, free)$$

Finally, the goal manager contains the fact that the agent has the goal of hanging a picture:

$$G : goal(hangPicture(Self))$$

With this information, the specification is complete. A full description of the execution of this specification is contained in [28].

---

[15] Given our relaxed view of planning, this "proof" consists of showing the pre-conditions of the plan can be met.

5   Related Work

There are two main strands of work to which ours is related – work on executable agent architectures and work on multi-context systems. As mentioned above, most previous work which has produced formal models of agent architectures, for example dMARS [16], Agent0 [30] and GRATE* [17], has failed to carry forward the clarity of the specification into the implementation – there is a leap of faith required between the two. Our work, on the other hand, maintains a clear link between specification and implementation through the direct execution of the specification as exemplified in our examples. This relation to direct execution also distinguishes our work from that on modelling agents in Z [8], since it is not yet possible to directly execute a Z specification. It is possible to animate specifications, which makes it possible to see what would happen if the specification were executed, but animating agent specifications is some way from providing operational agents. Our work also differs from that which aims to describe the operational semantics of agent architectures using the π-calculus [11], since our models have a declarative rather than an operational semantics.

More directly related to our work is that on DESIRE and Concurrent MetateM. DESIRE [3, 32] is a modelling framework originally conceived as a means of specifying complex knowledge-based systems. DESIRE views both the individual agents and the overall system as a compositional architecture. All functionality is designed as a series of interacting, task-based, hierarchically structured components. Though there are several differences, from the point of view of the proposal advocated in this paper, we can see DESIRE's *tasks* as modules and *information links* as bridge rules. In our approach there is no explicit task control knowledge of the kind found in DESIRE. There are no entities that control which units, bridge rules or modules should be activated nor when and how they are activated. Also, in DESIRE the communication between tasks is carried out by the information links that are wired-in by the design engineer. Our inter-module communication is organized as a bus and the independence between modules means new ones can be added without modifying the existing structures. Finally the communication model in DESIRE is based on a one-to-one connection between *tasks*, in a similar way to that in which we connect units inside a module. In contrast, our communication between modules is based on a multicast model.

Concurrent MetateM defines concurrent semantics at the level of single rules [12, 35]. Thus an agent is basically a set of temporal rules which fire when their antecedents are satisfied. Our approach does not assume concurrency within the components of units, rather the units themselves are the concurrent components of our architectures. This means that our model has an inherent concurrent semantics at the level of the units and has no central control mechanism. Though our exemplar uses what is essentially first order logic (albeit a first order logic labelled with arguments), we could use any logic we choose – we are not restricted to a temporal logic as in MetateM.

There are also differences between our work and previous work on using multi-context systems to model agents' beliefs. In the latter [14], different units, all containing a belief predicate, are used to represent the beliefs of the agent and the beliefs of all the acquaintances of the agent. The nested beliefs of agents may lead to tree-like structures of such units (called *belief contexts*). Such structures have then been used to solve problems like the three wise men [6]. In our case, however, any nested beliefs would typically be included in a single unit or module. Moreover we provide a more comprehensive formalisation of an autonomous agent in that we additionally show how capabilities other than that of reasoning about beliefs can be incorporated into the architecture. In this latter respect this paper extends the work of [23] with the idea of modules which links the approach more strongly with the software engineering tradition.

6 Conclusions

This paper has proposed a general approach to defining agent architectures. It provides a means of structuring logical specifications of agents in a way which makes them directly executable. This approach has a number of advantages. Firstly it bridges the gap between the specification of agents and the programs which implement those specifications. Secondly, the modularity of the approach makes it easier to build agents which are capable of carrying out complex tasks such as distributed planning. From a software engineering point of view, the approach leads to architectures which are easily expandable, and have re-useable components.

From this latter point of view, our approach suggests a methodology for building agents which has similarities with object-oriented design [2]. The notion of inheritance can be applied to groups of units and bridge rules, modules and even complete agents. These elements could have a general design which is specialized to different and more concrete instances by adding units and modules, or by refining the theories inside the units of a generic agent template. However, before we can develop this methodology, there are some issues to resolve. Firstly there is the matter of the semantics of the comsuming conditions and time-outs in bridge rules. Secondly, there is the question of how to handle nested hierachies of modules – something which is essential if we are to develop really complex agents.

Acknowledgments

This work has been supported by the UK EPSRC project Practical Negotiation for Electronic Commerce GR/M07076 and the EU IST project Sustainable Lifecycles for Information Ecosystems IST-1999-10208.

References

1. M. Benerecetti, A. Cimatti, E. Giunchiglia, F. Giunchiglia, and L. Serafini. Formal specification of beliefs in multi-agent systems. In J. P. Müller, M. J. Wooldridge, and N. R. Jennings, editors, *Intelligent Agents III*, pages 117–130. Springer Verlag, Berlin, 1997.
2. G. Booch. *Object-oriented analysis and design with application*. Addison Wesley, Wokingham, UK, 1994.
3. F. M. T. Brazier, B. M. Dunin-Keplicz, N. R. Jennings, and J. Treur. Formal specification of multi-agent systems. In *Proceedings of the 1st International Conference on Multi-Agent Systems*, pages 25–32, 1995.
4. P. Busetta, N. Howden, R. Ronnquist, and A. Hodgson. Structuring BDI agents in functional clusters. In N. R. Jennings and Y Lespérance, editors, *Intelligent Agents VI*. Springer Verlag, Berlin, 1999.

5. A. Cimatti and L. Serafini. Multi-agent reasoning with belief contexts: The approach and a case study. In *Proceedings of the 3rd International Workshop on Agent Theories, Architectures and Languages*, 1994.

6. A. Cimatti and L. Serafini. Multi-agent reasoning with belief contexts: The approach and a case study. In M. J. Wooldridge and N. R. Jennings, editors, *Intelligent Agents*, pages 62–73. Springer Verlag, Berlin, 1995.

7. P. R. Cohen and H. J. Levesque. Intention is choice with commitment. *Artificial Intelligence*, 42:213–261, 1990.

8. M. d'Inverno, D. Kinny, M. Luck, and M. Wooldridge. A formal specification of dMARS. In M. P. Singh, A. S. Rao, and M. Wooldridge, editors, *Intelligent Agents IV*, pages 155–176. Springer Verlag, Berlin, 1998.

9. D. Dubois and H. Prade. *Possibility Theory: An Approach to Computerized Processing of Uncertainty*. Plenum Press, New York, NY, 1988.

10. E. A. Emerson. Temporal and Modal Logic. In J van Leeuwen, editor, *Handbook of Theoretical Computer Science*, pages 996–1071. Elsevier, 1990.

11. J. Ferber and O. Gutknecht. Operational semantics of a role-based agent architecture. In N. R. Jennings and Y Lespérance, editors, *Intelligent Agents VI*. Springer Verlag, Berlin, 1999.

12. M. Fisher. Representing abstract agent architectures. In J. P. Müller, M. P. Singh, and A. S. Rao, editors, *Intelligent Agents V*, pages 227–242. Springer Verlag, Berlin, 1998.

13. D. Gabbay. *Labelled Deductive Systems*. Oxford University Press, Oxford, UK, 1996.

14. F. Giunchiglia. Contextual reasoning. In *Proceedings of the IJCAI Workshop on Using Knowledge in Context*, 1993.

15. F. Giunchiglia and L. Serafini. Multilanguage hierarchical logics (or: How we can do without modal logics). *Artificial Intelligence*, 65:29–70, 1994.

16. F. F. Ingrand, M. P. Georgeff, and A. S. Rao. An architecture for real-time reasoning and system control. *IEEE Expert*, 7(6):34–44, 1992.

17. N. R. Jennings. Controlling cooperative problem solving in industrial multi-agent systems using joint intentions. *Artificial Intelligence*, 75:195–240, 1995.

18. N. R. Jennings. Agent-based computing: Promise and perils. In *Proceedings of the 16th International Joint Conference on Artificial Intelligence*, pages 1429–1436, 1999.

19. J. J. Meyer. Agent languages and their relationship to other programming paradigms. In J. P. Müller, M. P. Singh, and A. S. Rao, editors, *Intelligent Agents V*, pages 309–316. Springer Verlag, Berlin, 1998.

20. P. Noriega and C. Sierra. Towards layered dialogical agents. In J. P. Müller, M. J. Wooldridge, and N. R. Jennings, editors, *Intelligent Agents III*, pages 173–188, Berlin, 1996. Springer Verlag.

21. S. Parsons and P. Giorgini. An approach to using degrees of belief in BDI agents. In B. Bouchon-Meunier, R. R. Yager, and L. A. Zadeh, editors, *Information, Uncertainty, Fusion*. Kluwer, Dordrecht, 1999.

22. S. Parsons and N. R. Jennings. Negotiation through argumentation—a preliminary report. In *Proceedings of the International Conference on Multi Agent Systems*, pages 267–274, 1996.

23. S. Parsons, C. Sierra, and N. R. Jennings. Agents that reason and negotiate by arguing. *Journal of Logic and Computation*, 8(3):261—292, 1998.

24. A. Rao and M. Georgeff. Asymmetry thesis and side-effect problems in linear time and branching time intention logics. In *Proceedings of the 12th International Joint Conference on Artificial Intelligence*, 1991.

25. A. S. Rao and M. P. Georgeff. Modeling Rational Agents within a BDI-Architecture. In *Proceedings of the 2nd International Conference on Principles of Knowledge Representation and Reasoning*, pages 473–484, 1991.

26. A. S. Rao and M. P. Georgeff. Formal Models and Decision Procedures for Multi-Agent Systems. Technical Note 61, Australian Artificial Intelligence Institute, 1995.

27. J. Sabater, C. Sierra, S. Parsons, and N. R. Jennings. Using multi-context agents to engineer executable agents. In *Proceedings of the 6th International Workshop on Agent Theoreies, Archiectures and Languages*, 1999.

28. J. Sabater, C. Sierra, S. Parsons, and N. R. Jennings. Using multi-context agents to engineer executable agents. In N. R. Jennings and Y. Lesperance, editors, *Intelligent Agents IV*, pages 277–294. Springer-Verlag, 2000.

29. J. Sabater, C. Sierra, S. Parsons, and N. R. Jennings. Engineering executable agents using multi-context systems. *Journal of Logic and Computation*, 2002. (to appear).

30. Y. Shoham. Agent-oriented programming. *Artificial Intelligence*, 60:51–92, 1993.

31. S. R. Thomas. The PLACA agent programming language. In M. J. Wooldridge and N. R. Jennings, editors, *Intelligent Agents*, pages 355–370. Springer Verlag, Berlin, 1995.

32. J. Treur. On the use of reflection principles in modelling complex reasoning. *International Journal of Intelligent Systems*, 6:277–294, 1991.

33. L. Vila. *On temporal representation and reasoning in knowledge-based systems*. IIIA Monographies, Barcelona, Spain, 1994.

34. D. Weerasooriya, A. Rao, and K. Rammamohanarao. Design of a concurrent agent-oriented language. In M. J. Wooldridge and N. R. Jennings, editors, *Intelligent Agents*, pages 386–402. Springer Verlag, Berlin, 1995.

35. M. Wooldridge. A knowledge-theoretic semantics for Concurrent MetateM. In J. P. Müller, M. J. Wooldridge, and N. R. Jennings, editors, *Intelligent Agents III*, pages 357–374. Springer Verlag, Berlin, 1996.

36. M. Wooldridge. Agent-based software engineering. *IEE Proceedings on Software Engineering*, 144:26–37, 1997.

37. M. Wooldridge. *Reasoning about rational agents*. MIT Press, Cambridge, MA, 2000.

38. M. J. Wooldridge and N. R. Jennings. Intelligent agents: Theory and practice. *The Knowledge Engineering Review*, 10:115–152, 1995.

An Adaptive Choice of Messaging Protocol
in Multi Agent Systems

Chris Preist and Siani Pearson

Agent Technology Group,
Hewlett-Packard Laboratories Bristol,
Filton Road, Stoke Gifford,
Bristol BS12 6QZ, UK,
cwp@hplb.hpl.hp.com,
siani@hplb.hpl.hp.com

Abstract. There are a variety of choices which need to be made when setting up a multi-agent community. In particular, which agents communicate with which, what protocols they use, and what information flows from one to another. Such design choices will affect the efficiency of the community with respect to several parameters - accuracy, speed of solution, and message load.

In this paper, we consider one class of problem which multi-agent systems engage in - service provision. Using a simple, abstract, form of this problem, we use a mathematical analysis to show that three different messaging protocols result in varying message loads, depending on certain parameters such as number of agents and frequency of request.

If the parameters are fixed, we can conclude that one of these three protocols is better than the others. However, these parameters will usually vary over time, and hence the best of the three protocols will vary. We show that the community can adopt the best protocol if each individual agent makes a local decision based on which protocol will minimise its own message load. Hence, local decisions lead to globally good behaviour. We demonstrate this both mathematically and experimentally.

1 Introduction

The designer of a multi-agent system needs to make various choices as to how the agent community is organised; in particular, how the agents communicate and co-ordinate with each other. A variety of different approaches have been proposed in the literature, such as the contract net [13], the facilitator approach [5], distributed blackboard architectures [7,9] and market-based control [2].

Increasingly, flexible multi-agent toolkits and languages are being developed which do not constrain the developers to any one of these approaches [1,3,8,12]. They must make a choice between the alternatives proposed. Such a choice involves making decisions about:

- How to partition the tasks performed by the system between different agents and what reasoning each agent can perform.

M. d' Inverno et al. (Eds.): UKMAS 1996–2000, LNAI 2403, pp. 227–242, 2002.

- How to partition the information used by the system between different agents, and whether to allow information to be duplicated.
- What messages one agent can send to another, and in what circumstances.

The literature provides examples of such choices (e.g.[4]) and case studies of successful applications (e.g. [10]). However, there is very little comparative analysis of the effect of different design decisions on the capability and efficiency of a multi-agent system to perform its task. If multi-agent systems are to become pervasive in the world of software engineering, it is important that we provide designers with information that will help them make these decisions, based on the characteristics of the application they are working on.

When comparing alternative approaches, it is unlikely that any one will be the 'best'. Instead, the system designer needs to make trade-offs between various criteria for assessing the performance of the system, depending on the characteristics of their application.

These criteria include, amongst others;

- Quality of solution - how well the system task is done, according to some measure.
- Communications efficiency - how much communication takes place to produce a solution.
- Time - how long it takes to produce a solution.

A more extensive list of such criteria is given in [11].

If a designer knows that, for problems similar to their application, one set of design choices leads to a fast system, while another set leads to a system which is communications efficient, they can choose which to adopt, based on what is important in their circumstances. In a time-critical application, the system designer would be prepared to use more communication if it produces a solution more quickly. They may even be prepared to accept a poorer quality solution in less time. In other circumstances, time may not be a major issue.

For this reason, we believe that systematic comparative analysis of how different design choices affect different performance criteria is necessary. In this paper, we present work of this nature.

We present a simple form of the service provision problem in section 2, and three different messaging protocols in section 3. In section 4, we assess the communications efficiency of these protocols with respect to this problem.

As we argue above, other factors must be taken into account when deciding which protocol to use. However, for the purpose of this paper, we will assume that, (providing the protocol produces a quality solution), communications efficiency is the priority. For brevity, we will refer to the most communications efficient protocol in a given circumstance as "optimal".

Given certain parameters of the problem, such as rate of service requests and number of service providers, we determine the number of messages agents would send under each protocol. Hence, for given parameter values we can determine which protocol is optimal.

However, the parameters of the problem are rarely static. New agents may join, increasing the amount of activity in the system. Agents may become increasingly loaded, and so less available to perform tasks. For this reason, the optimal protocol at one time may not be optimal at another. It will change as the environment the system is in changes. It may therefore be better to allow the system to make such choices dynamically, rather than fixing them at design time. As circumstances change, the system can adapt, choosing a new protocol as its current one ceases to be optimal.

In section 5, we demonstrate mathematically that a decentralised adaptive approach can be used by a system carrying out our simple form of service provision. Local decisions, taken by each individual agent, can lead to the agent community adopting a protocol that is optimal. Section 6 presents an overview of experimental results to support this mathematical analysis.

2 The Service Provision Problem

We have chosen to use the service provision problem as the initial focus of our work. In the abstract, service provision consists of matching client agents with certain needs with service provider agents able to meet those needs. The service provider agents may themselves act as clients, and subcontract parts of the service they provide to other agents.

Service provision is similar to task distribution, though the latter term tends to be used to refer to a closed community of agents which are all working towards a collective goal. Service provision is considered to take place in a large scale open system, such as the Internet, where agents can join or leave freely, and have potentially conflicting aims.

Examples of service provision problems could be:
1. Connecting an agent requiring the fax number of a customer with any database able to provide that information.
2. Connecting an agent wishing to purchase a CD with an Internet supplier able to provide it at the best price.
3. Connecting an agent gathering information with a pay-per-use information service that provides a good quality service at a reasonable price.
4. A person has a problem with their computer. Their agent makes an appointment with the agent of a computer technician who is available soon, has the appropriate skills, and is reasonably priced.
5. A nurse's patient has a cardiac arrest. The nurse's agent contacts the first cardiac specialist available in the area, asking for their assistance.

The different characteristics of these examples will have an affect on the choice of protocol (and other design decisions). An efficient protocol for example 3 is not likely to be the most efficient for example 1; it will be too complex for such a simple problem. Hence, we cannot analyse the effect of choosing different protocols with respect to service provision in general. Instead, we must analyse it with respect to various service provision problems with different characteristics.

In this paper, we focus on a relatively simple service provision problem. We use this to demonstrate our approach, as even this case is quite rich. There is no single 'best' protocol choice in it, so we can consider how the agent community can swap protocols in response to changes in the environment.

The characteristics of the problem are;
- All service providers give the same service, with the same quality.
- Service providers get no benefit from providing the service.

- Service providers can be unavailable; they all have a probability p of being unavailable at any given time.

We consider an abstract service provision problem with these characteristics, and analyse the communications efficiency of three different messaging protocols. By performing the analysis in the abstract, it can be applied to any service provision problem with these characteristics. One example would be the routing of a client request to one of a team of people on an information helpline.

3 The Protocols to be Compared

For the purposes of this analysis, we assume that certain design decisions have been made about the system. In particular, we assume that there is a single facilitator with which all service providers must register. It operates in recommend mode [4], giving clients lists of service providers when they request it to.

We consider three alternative protocols, to explore the effect of two design decisions. Firstly, whether to broadcast requests, or to send requests to individual agents one at a time. Secondly, whether to provide the facilitator with updated information on the availability of service providers. We call the three protocols embodying these design decisions naïve broadcast, naïve one-to-one, and informed one-to-one.

3.1 Naïve Broadcast

The recommender contains a list of all service providers offering this service, and no other information. It provides a list of providers to a requesting client. The client contacts all providers on the list by broadcasting a message, which does not require a response. Providers reply if they are currently available, and the client selects one. This can be viewed as a simple variant of the contract net operating in general broadcast mode [13].

3.2 Naïve One-to-One

Again, the recommender simply provides a list of service providers to a client on request. This time, the client contacts one of these[1] with a request for service, using a message which requires a reply. The service provider either replies that it is available, or that it is busy. In the latter case, the client contacts another, repeating the process. This is a variant of the contract net operating in point-to-point mode [13,].

---

[1] Here, and in the informed one-to-one subsequently, we assume that if a client makes a selection of one of a set of alternative providers which appear equivalent, then it makes this choice randomly.

3.3 Informed One-to-One

This time, the recommender contains information about whether each service provider is currently available or busy. The service providers must keep this up to date by sending a message to it whenever their state changes. On request from a client, the recommender gives a list of all service providers currently available. The client contacts one of them.

There is a small chance that this provider has become unavailable in the time taken for the message to travel from recommender to client, and client to provider. In such a case, the client contacts another on its list, and so on. For the purposes of this analysis, we assume that this small chance is negligible.

4 Analysis of the Protocols

Each of these protocols is designed in such a way that, if there is a service provider available, it will be found. However, the number of messages required will vary. To consider in what circumstances each is optimal, we must see what the average message load in each system is, and how it varies as the parameters of the problem vary.

The parameters we consider are:

N - The number of providers of this service.

p - The probability of a service provider being available.

t_u - The average time a service provider is unavailable.

M - The average number of service requests made by clients per second.

We now derive formulae which give the average number of messages used to satisfy one client request, for each of the three protocols.

4.1 Naïve Broadcast

The client sends a message to the recommender and receives a reply. It then broadcasts a message to all N service providers. Each service provider has a probability p of being available and replies only if it is. Hence, the average number of replies is Np.

Therefore, the average number of messages generated by the naive broadcast protocol for the client to get an offer of service, $c(nb)$, is given by;

$$c(nb) = 2 + N + Np$$

Note that, as p can range between 0 and 1, $c(nb)$ can range between $N+2$ and $2N+2$.

4.2 Naïve One-to-One

Again, the client sends a message to the recommender and receives a reply. It then contacts any one of the providers which the recommender proposed. The provider replies that it is able to perform the service, with probability p, or that it is not, with probability $(1 - p)$. In the latter case the client contacts another provider, and so on.

Hence the average number of messages generated by the naive one-to-one protocol, $c(no)$, is a probablistic summation;

$$c(no) = 2 + \sum_{i=1}^{N} 2ip(1-p)^{i-1} + 2N(1-p)^{N}$$

The last term represents the messages generated in the case that no provider is available.

For simplicity of notation, we let

$$E(N,p) = \sum_{i=1}^{N} 2ip(1-p)^{i-1} + 2N(1-p)^{N}$$

Hence the equation becomes:

$$c(no) = 2 + E(N,p)$$

Solving the summation, we can show that, for $p \neq 0$,

$$E(N,p) = \frac{2(1-(1-p)^{N})}{p}$$

As p ranges from 0 to 1, $E(N,p)$ is a monotonically decreasing function which ranges between $2N$ and 2. Hence, $c(no)$ can range between 4 and $2N+2$.

4.3 Informed One-to-One

In the case of informed one-to-one, there are two kinds of message exchange to be considered; messages sent to connect a client with a service provider, and messages sent by the service provider to keep the status information in the recommender up-to-date.

When a client wishes to connect with a service provider, it firstly contacts the recommender and receives a reply listing the service providers currently available. It then contacts one of these and receives a reply. Therefore, 4 messages are generated.

We now consider the number of status updates a provider sends. A provider has a probability $1-p$ of being unavailable at any given time, and is unavailable for t_u seconds on average. Hence it will become available once every $t_u/(1-p)$ seconds, and similarly, will become unavailable once every $t_u/(1-p)$ seconds. Therefore, each service provider sends, on average, $2(1-p)/t_u$ update messages per second to the recommender.

To compare this protocol with the others, we need to calculate the number of update messages sent per client request. There are N service providers sending update messages, and there are M client requests per second. Hence, there are $2N(1-p)/Mt_u$ update messages per client request.

Hence, the average number of messages generated by the informed one-to-one protocol per client request, $c(io)$, is given by;

$$c(io) = 4 + \frac{2N(1-p)}{Mt_u}$$

We now have equations which give the average number of messages to connect a client with a service provider for each protocol. Hence, given specific parameter values, we can determine which protocol is most communications efficient.

Based on these equations, we can make some general observations;

As p tends towards 1, $c(nb)$ will increase, tending towards $2N + 2$. However, $c(no)$ will decrease, tending towards 4. As $4 < 2N+2$ for all $N>1$, we can conclude that, for high values of p, the naïve one-to-one protocol will be more communications efficient than the naïve broadcast strategy in any system with more than one service provider.

As p decreases towards 0, $c(nb)$ will decrease tending towards $N + 2$, $c(no)$ will increase tending towards $2N + 2$. Hence, for low values of p, the naïve broadcast strategy will be more communications efficient than the naïve one-to-one strategy.

$c(io)$ increases as N increases and p decreases, but the most significant factor in $c(io)$ is the size of Mt_u. As Mt_u tends to zero, then $2N(1-p)/ Mt_u$ tends to infinity (provided $p \neq 1$), and therefore $c(io)$ does too. Hence, one of the other strategies will be more communications efficient.

However, if $Mt_u>N$ then $c(io) \leq 4 + 2(1-p)$. Furthermore, as Mt_u increases, $c(io)$ rapidly decreases towards 4. Hence, in almost all circumstances where $Mt_u>N$, informed one-to-one will be the most communications efficient strategy.

Mt_u can be viewed as a measure of the busyness of the system; Busyness increases as the number of requests per second increases, and also as the downtime of service providers increases. Hence, informed one-to-one is most communications efficient when a system is reasonably busy. If a system is not very busy, then another protocol is better.

Note that this protocol is particularly effective, partly because of our initial decision to focus on a set-up which has only one facilitator agent. Hence, the cost of keeping the information up to date is low. However, if we assume there are F facilitator agents which a service provider must keep up-to-date, the equation becomes;

$$c(io) = 4 + \frac{2FN(1-p)}{Mt_u}$$

Clearly, this increases linearly as F increases. For informed one-to-one to be the most communications efficient protocol irrespective of p, it is now necessary that $Mt_u > FN$.

Hence, even with the simplifying assumptions we have chosen, no one protocol is the most efficient in all circumstances. Any one of the three may be most efficient, depending on how many providers there are, how many requests are made, and how often and for how long providers can be unavailable.

For given parameter values, the equations derived above can be used to determine which of the three protocols would be most efficient. However, the parameters that determine this decision may vary with time. New service providers may arrive, or existing ones may leave, resulting in a change of N. The probability, p, of a provider being unavailable is likely to fluctuate dramatically, as client demand varies. Hence, it is not possible to decide which protocol is most efficient at design time. Rather, it is necessary to allow the decision to be made dynamically by the agent community, in response to changing circumstances. We will now consider a possible mechanism for doing this.

5 Dynamic Choice of Messaging Protocol

5.1 Local Choices Lead to an Optimal Global Choice

The decision to change from one protocol to another could be either centralised or decentralised. In a centralised approach, a monitoring agent would make the decision to change protocol on behalf of the entire community, and then inform all the agents. This has the advantage that the monitoring agent could make decisions based on what is best for the community as a whole, but has the disadvantage that it would need to gather vast amounts of data, and would need to handle agents joining and leaving the system. In a decentralised approach, agents alter their protocol in response to what is happening locally to them, and to what task they are performing. This has the advantage that no single agent needs to gather vast amounts of data, and hence the decision process should be simpler. However, it has the disadvantage that no agent takes a global view, and hence their decisions may not be best for the community as a whole. We will consider the latter approach, and show that, in this case, local decisions do lead to an optimal choice globally.

Firstly, we consider the choices available to each agent. A client agent has a choice between adopting a naïve broadcast protocol, or a naïve one-to-one protocol. Once it has sent messages of the given type, the service providers are constrained in how they react. However, the service providers have the choice of whether to provide availability information or not; they control the decision of when to move to an informed one-to-one protocol. (The client, of course, still has the option of using one of the other protocols).

Now we will look at what information is available locally to each agent. We focus on the number of messages an agent sends and receives, and compare this with the total number of messages sent and received in the community. We will show that if each agent chooses the protocol which will result in it minimising the number of messages it sends and receives, then the community overall will adopt the protocol which is most efficient. In section 5.2, we will look at how an agent can determine this.

For the naive broadcast and naive one-to-one protocols, a client agent either sends or receives every message involved in the provision of its service. Hence, if the client chooses the protocol which minimises the number of messages it sends and receives, this choice will be the better for the community as a whole.

The situation is more complex when the third protocol, informed one-to-one, is also considered. We would like the service providers to offer availability information only if the informed one-to-one protocol would be the most efficient for the agent community. Furthermore, we would like the client agents to adopt the informed one-to-one protocol as soon as the providers offer availability information. If the providers are offering the information and it is not being used, then the messages which update this information are wasted. Assume that service providers offer availability information only if the informed one-to-one protocol would result in them sending and receiving less messages, on average, than either of the other two protocols. We now show that, at such a time, the informed one-to-one protocol would be the most efficient for the community to adopt.

We do this by considering the average number of messages a provider sends and receives per client request. We consider this for each protocol;

- Under the naïve broadcast protocol, each service provider agent sends and receives, on average, $1 + p$ messages per client request.
- Under the naïve one-to-one protocol, each service provider agent sends and receives, on average, $E(N,p)/N$ messages per client request. As $2 \le E \le 2N$, this varies from between $2/N$ to a maximum of 2.

- Under the informed one-to-one protocol, each service provider agent sends and receives, on average, $2/N + 2(1-p)/Mt_u$ messages. The first term represents the average number of messages it sends and receives to/from the client, while the second represents the number of update messages it sends to the facilitator.

Firstly, we consider the choice between the informed one-to-one protocol, and the naive one-to-one protocol.

A single service provider agent will choose the informed one-to-one protocol if;

$$\frac{E(N,p)}{N} > \frac{2}{N} + \frac{2(1-p)}{Mt_u}$$

As $E(N,p) \ge 2$, and $N \ge 1$, this is equivalent to;

$$E(N,p) - 2 > \frac{2N(1-p)}{Mt_u} \qquad \text{(Equation 5.1)}$$

We now consider the total number of messages. The informed one-to-one protocol is more communications efficient if $c(no) > c(io)$.

Hence, this gives the inequality;

$$2 + E(N,p) > 4 + \frac{2N(1-p)}{Mt_u}$$

Subtracting 4 from each side gives:

$$E(N,p) - 2 > \frac{2N(1-p)}{Mt_u}$$

This is identical to equation 5.1. Therefore, a service provider will select the informed one-to-one protocol in preference to the naive one-to-one protocol only if it is more efficient for the community as a whole.

We now consider the naïve broadcast, and compare it to the informed one-to-one protocol. A service provider will select the informed one-to-one protocol in preference to the naive broadcast protocol if;

$$1 + p > \frac{2}{N} + \frac{2(1-p)}{Mt_u}$$

Multiplying this by N, $(N \geq 1)$, and adding 2 to each side gives:

$$2 + N + Np > 4 + \frac{2N(1-p)}{Mt_u}$$

Recalling the equations from section 4, this is equivalent to
$$c(nb) > c(io)$$
Hence, a service provider will select the informed one-to-one protocol in preference to the naive broadcast protocol only if it is more efficient for the community as a whole.

Combining this with the previous result, we have shown that a service provider will only provide the information necessary for the informed one-to-one protocol if and only if the informed one-to-one protocol is more communications efficient than the other two protocols.

We must now show that if the service provider agents make the effort to provide the information necessary for the informed one-to-one protocol, then the client agents will use it. We assume that they will do so if and only if it will result in them sending and receiving less messages than either of the two other protocols they could adopt. Recall that, in the other two protocols, all messages are either sent or received by the client.

Hence, the client sends and receives $c(no)$ messages in the naïve one-to-one protocol, and $c(nb)$ messages in the naïve broadcast protocol. In the informed one-to-one protocol, the client sends and receives 4 messages. So we must show that, if the service providers offer the information for informed one-to-one, then $4 < c(no)$ and $4 < c(nb)$.

We have already shown that the service provider agents will offer the information for informed one-to-one if and only if $c(io) < c(no)$ and $c(io) < c(nb)$.

As $c(io) = 4 + 2N(1-p)/Mt_u$, where N, M and t_u are all greater than zero, and $1 \geq p \geq 0$, it follows that $4 \leq c(io)$. Hence $4 < c(no)$ and $4 < c(nb)$, as required.

So we have shown that, if service providers offer availability information when the informed one-to-one protocol is most efficient from their local perspective, then the protocol will also be most efficient from the perspective of the client.

To summarise, we have shown that;
- If a client agent makes a choice between the naïve broadcast and naïve one-to-one strategy based on which minimises the number of messages the agent sends and

receives, this choice will also globally be the more communications efficient of the two alternatives.

- If a service provider agent offers the information needed for the informed one-to-one protocol only if this protocol would result in it sending and receiving, on average, fewer messages than either of the other two protocols, then it will do so only when the adoption of this protocol would globally be the most communication efficient.
- If a service provider agent offers the information needed for the informed one-to-one protocol in the circumstances described above, then a client agent will always make use of it.

From these results, we can draw an important conclusion. If each agent decides which protocol to adopt based simply on which will minimise the average number of messages it sends and receives, then the agent community as a whole will adopt the protocol which is most communications efficient.

5.2   How Agents Choose the Protocol

We have shown that in a simple form of the service provision problem, a local choice of protocol by each agent can lead to a choice which is the best for the community as a whole. Each agent simply needs to choose the protocol that minimises the total number of messages it sends and receives. We now consider how an agent is able to make this decision.

Client agents need to make two decisions; whether to use the informed one-to-one protocol if some service providers are offering the necessary information, and whether to use naïve broadcast or naïve one-to-one otherwise. The first decision is trivial; we showed in section 4.1 that it is always better for a client to use informed one-to-one if it is offered.

Secondly, the client must decide what to do if informed one-to-one cannot be used. This can occur either because no service provider is offering availability information, or because all service providers offering availability information are currently busy.

In this case, the client can use the two equations which give the number of messages it will send and receive under the naïve broadcast and naïve one-to-one protocols;

$$c(nb) = 2 + N + Np$$
$$c(no) = 2 + E(N, p)$$

Given the estimate of N and p, it can use these equations to give an informed guess as to which protocol should be adopted.

N can be known for certain - it is the number of service provider agents on the list given by the recommender agent. If a hybrid protocol is being used, and all service providers providing information are busy, then we remove these agents from the list. (This can be done either by the client, or by the recommender sending the list).

The probability p can be estimated by the agent keeping track of how often a service provider agent is free when it tries to make contact with it. If, as is likely, p is expected to vary with time, more recent experience could be weighted more strongly when calculating the estimate.

Alternatively, a client can adopt a more empirical approach. It can try using the protocol it isn't currently using every now and then, and swap when it finds that the other protocol usually results in less message traffic.

A service provider needs to decide whether to offer availability information or not. It can do this by comparing the number of update messages it would send with the number of messages it would receive and send when busy if it didn't keep this information updated.

For an agent which is not offering availability information, it simply counts how many times it switches from available to unavailable, or vice-versa, in a given time period, and counts how many messages it receives and sends while unavailable. When the number of messages it receives and sends while unavailable is usually above the number of switches it makes, it is worthwhile providing availability information.[2] Hence, the agent will switch protocol at this point.

If an agent is offering availability information, then it needs to determine when it is no longer worth it doing so. i.e. at what time the number of messages it sends to keep the availability information updated is greater than the number of messages it avoids having to send and receive while unavailable.

From the agents perspective, assuming all service provider agents are also using the informed one-to-one protocol, it receives M/N service requests, on average, per second. It can get a value for N from the recommender agent. (Possibly, it would keep a note of N, and whenever N changes, the recommender would inform it). Hence, it can calculate M. It can estimate p by observing what proportion of the time it is unavailable. It can then compare the actual number of messages it currently receives per second, with an estimate of what it would expect to receive under the other protocols.

It would expect to send and receive $M(1+p)$ messages per second under the naïve broadcast. Under the naïve one-to-one, it would expect to send and receive $ME(N,p)/N$. If either of these is consistently lower than the actual number of messages sent and received, then the agent should stop giving availability information.

Hence, in this way, a service provider agent can monitor it's behaviour, and decide when it wishes to swap from providing availability information to not providing it. In an idealised homogenous agent community, all providers will make this decision at the same time, as they will all be receiving and handling the same number of service requests. However, in practice, this will not occur. Some providers may wish to change, while others do not. For the purposes of this paper, we will assume that we wish to ensure that the community as a whole adopts the same protocol.[3]

To ensure this, we add a co-ordination agent, which acts as a vote collector from the service providers. If a provider wants to change strategy, it registers a vote. When enough votes are registered, the co-ordination agent sends a message to all service providers, and they swap protocol. Hence, we can maintain a homogenous protocol among service providers, using a loose form of centralised control.

---

[2] Exactly how to define 'usually above' in this context will require experimentation.

[3] If we do not place this restriction, a hybrid protocol can develop, with some agents providing availability information and others not. This can be more communications efficient than any of the three protocols discussed, but needs careful management to prevent oscillation of behaviour.

6 Experimental Comparison of Protocol Efficiency

We have carried out experiments to provide empirical support for the mathematical analysis provided above. Our methodology is similar to that used in [6]. We have developed a system that can generate a community of agents for given values of the parameters N, p, t_u and M, with a given protocol. The community consists of a single client, a single facilitator, and N service providers, each which are available with a probability of p and have a down time of t_u time units. The client issues 100 task requests, at a rate of M requests per time unit[4]. The system then counts the total number of messages that are generated in the community by these requests.

We present here the results of three series of experiments. In each case, we fix three of the four parameters, and consider a sequence of values of the fourth. For each value, we run the experimental system 100 times, and plot the mean number of messages as a point on a graph. We repeat this for the different protocols, to get graphs of how the efficiency of the different protocols varies as the fourth parameter changes.

In experiment 1, we use the parameter values $N = 5$, $t_u = 2$ and $M = 1$. We allow p to range from 0.05 to 1 in increments of 0.05. Chart 1 gives the resulting graphs for each of the three protocols. These graphs corroborate the mathematical equations of section 4 The average difference between the theoretical predictions and the mean values found by experimentation is 0.22% for naïve broadcast, 1.22% for naïve one-to-one and 1.11% for informed one-to-one.

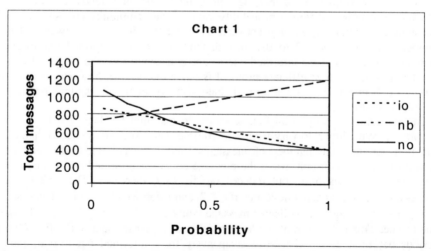

In experiment 2, we use the same parameter values, but introduce a fourth protocol; the vote collector. Service providers vote if they wish the community to swap from informed to naïve or vice-versa, using the techniques described in section 5.2 to make their decision. This vote takes place every 10 time units. The facilitator acts as the vote collector. The initial protocol is informed one-to-one. If a majority of

---

[4] As the rate of requests by all clients is the factor which determines how many messages are generated, rather than the number of clients, we can safely use only one client agent without loss of generality.

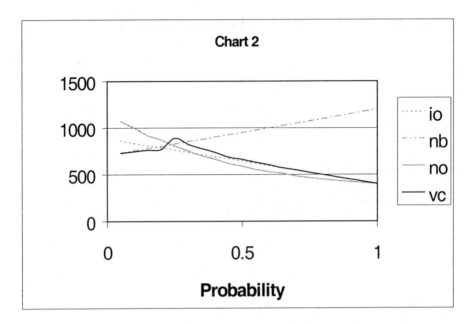

service providers vote for a protocol swap, it sends a message out to indicate that the swap should take place. Chart 2 plots the resulting graphs. Both vote and swap messages are included in the message count.

We can see from chart 2 that the vote collector protocol tends to choose more efficient protocols at different probability values. The community chooses to use the naïve broadcast for values of p between 0.05 and 0.2. It wavers between all three protocols in the range 0.2 to 0.4, though tends to choose informed one-to-one in general. Finally, it choose informed one-to-one consistently for the range 0.4 to 1. In this last range, the most efficient protocol is naïve one-to-one; however, because the difference between this and informed one-to-one is small, the system remains on informed one-to-one.

In experiment 3, we plot all four protocols for parameter values $N = 10$, $p = 0.25$ and $M = 1$. We allow t_u to vary from 1 to 10 time units. We see in chart 3 that, as the equations predict, the number of messages used by naïve one-to-one and naïve broadcast remains constant, while the message count for informed one-to-one is very high for low values of t_u, but reduces rapidly as t_u increases. The vote collector successfully chooses naive one-to-one if $t_u \leq 2$, and informed one-to-one otherwise.

On the graph, the vote collector message count is higher for $t_u \leq 2$ than the naïve one-to-one. This is because of the large number of messages sent in the first 20 time periods before it gets a chance to swap away from informed one-to-one, and the messages used in the vote collection process. If the experiment were run for more tasks (say 1000), we would expect this discrepancy to become less significant.

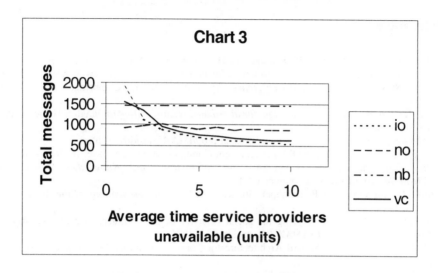

Chart 3

7 Conclusions and Future Work

In this paper, we have demonstrated that mathematical and experimental analysis of multi-agent system protocols can provide useful information to guide design choices when developing such systems. We have shown that some of these choices may best be made at runtime by the system in response to changes in the demands placed on it. Furthermore, we have shown that this decision can be made in a decentralised way, by allowing client agents to swap their protocol freely, and service provider agents to vote on the protocol to be used by their community.

We hope to be able to allow such decision making to be taken in an even more decentralised way, without the use of a vote collector. Such a protocol, the *hybrid protocol*, allows some service providers to provide availability information, while others do not. We believe that such a system will be more efficient than any of the other protocols, though care needs to be taken to ensure it settles in a stable state.

We believe that the approach of allowing an agent community to make architecture decisions dynamically, in a decentralised fashion, can lead to systems which are robust and efficient in the face of change. We hope to extend this approach to other architecture decisions, such as the number of facilitators and the mode in which they operate, and to more complex forms of the service provision problem.

Acknowledgements

Thanks to Martin Merry, Janet Bruten, Miranda Mowbray and Lin Jones for their assistance.

References

1. J. L. Alty, D. Griffiths, N.R. Jennings, E. H. Mamdani, A. Struthers, and M. E. Wiegand. ADEPT - Advanced Decision Environment for Process Tasks: Overview & Architecture. In *Proc. BCS Expert Systems 94 Conference* (Applications Track), Cambridge, UK, 359-371, 1994.
2. *Market-Based Control: A Paradigm for distributed resource allocation.* ed S.H.Clearwater. World Scientific, 1996.
3. dMARS product brief. http://www.aaii.oz.au/proj/dMARS-prod-brief.html
4. T. Finin and R. Fritzson. KQML as an Agent Communication Language. In *Proceedings of the Third International Conference on Information and Knowledge Management (CIKM'94),* ACM Press, November 1994.
5. M.R. Genesereth and S.P. Ketchpel. Software Agents. *Communications of the ACM,* 37:7, 48-53, 1994.
6. C.Gu and T.Ishida. Analyzing the social behavior of the contract net protocol. *Agents Breaking Away, Proc. MAAMAW 96.* pp 116-127, 1996.
7. B.Hayes-Roth. A Blackboard Architecture for Control. *Artificial Intelligence Journal 26,* pp 21-321. 1985
8. H. Jean. JATlite overview. http://java.stanford.edu/java_agent/html/
9. L.V.Leao and S.N.Talukdar. An Environment for rule-based blackboards and distributed problem solving. *International Journal for Artificial Intelligence in Engineering,* 1(2): 70-79, 1986.
10. H.V.D. Parunak. Applications of Distributed Artificial Intelligence to Industry. *In Foundations of Distributed Artificial Intelligence.* Ed G.M.P. O'Hare and N.R.Jennings. Wiley Interscience, 1996.
11. T.Sandholm. Agents in Electronic Markets. *Tutorial notes, Autonomous Agents 97 conference.*
12. A.Sloman. The SIM_AGENT toolkit. http://www.cs.bham.ac.uk/~axs/cog_affect/sim_agent.html
13. R.G. Smith. The contract net protocol: high-level communication and control in a distributed problem solver. *IEEE Trans. Comput.,* 29, 1104-1113, 1980.

On Partially Observable MDPs and BDI Models

Martijn Schut[1], Michael Wooldridge[2], and Simon Parsons[2,3]

[1] Department of Artificial Intelligence, Vrije Universiteit Amsterdam,
1081 HV Amsterdam, The Netherlands,
schut@cs.vu.nl
[2] Department of Computer Science, University of Liverpool,
Liverpool L69 7ZF, United Kingdom,
m.j.wooldridge@csc.liv.ac.uk
[3] Center for Coordination Science, Sloan School of Management, MIT,
Cambridge, MA 02142, USA,
sparsons@csc.liv.ac.uk

Abstract. Decision theoretic planning in AI by means of solving Partially Observable Markov decision processes (POMDPs) has been shown to be both powerful and versatile. However, such approaches are computationally hard and, from a design stance, are not necessarily intuitive for conceptualising many problems. We propose a novel method for solving POMDPs, which provides a designer with a more intuitive means of specifying POMDP planning problems. In particular, we investigate the relationship between POMDP planning theory and belief-desire-intention (BDI) agent theory. The idea is to view a BDI agent as a specification of an POMDP problem. This view is to be supported by a correspondence between an POMDP problem and a BDI agent. In this paper, we outline such a correspondence between POMDP and BDI by explaining how to specify one in terms of the other. Additionally, we illustrate the significance of a correspondence by showing empirically that it yields satisfying results in complex domains.

1 Introduction

Designing autonomous agents that are to operate in uncertain environments has been the focus of substantial research in various sub-areas of AI. These agents have to deal with executing actions that may not have the intended results, with environments that change while the agent is operating, and with making observations that might not be completely accurate. Much research effort has gone into specifying such agents by means of Markovian planning. In this respect, agents are implemented as solutions to Markov Decision Problems: they are, as such solutions, mappings from states to optimal actions. Although theoretically very appealing, the Markov planning framework poses some important problems when put into practice. For example, computing optimal solutions of MDPs is computationally very hard. Fast close-optimal solution algorithms and various abstraction techniques have been proposed to solve this problem. We propose an alternative technique. If we are able to map MDP components to BDI components, we can use the BDI architecture to design a bounded optimal MDP agent. Then we utilise the theoretical rigorousness of the MDP framework, combined with the practical utility of the BDI framework.

M. d' Inverno et al. (Eds.): UKMAS 1996–2000, LNAI 2403, pp. 243–259, 2002.

In this paper, we investigate the correspondence between the theory of Markov decision processes for planning in partially observable stochastic domains (POMDP) and the belief-desire-intention (BDI) architecture for programming situated agents. The motivations for obtaining this correspondence are diverse. Firstly, we show that it is possible to utilise an important characteristic of intentions – the constraint of reasoning – in practice by using it to solve POMDPs. Secondly, because solving POMDPs is inherently intractable, our approach contributes to dealing with this intractability by utilising tractable corresponding BDI models. Thirdly, whereas POMDP models take away part of the burden of explicitly programming agents, the identification of relevant problem structure often proves to be very hard and unintuitive from a design point of view. BDI models seem to be easier to specify, and if we can establish this corespondance and so build POMDP models from BDI models, we may be able to simplify the construction of POMDP models.

This paper does not address all these issues. Here we just point out the correspondence between the BDI and POMDP models and demonstrate empirically that the performance of a BDI model approximates the performance of a discrete MDP model. Although we present a general formulation of the correspondence, the experiments are still for the specific case of MDP problems and we are currently working on POMDP experiments. This paper summarises the prerequisites for the construction of initial formal and empirical correspondences between the two models. Thus the payoff of the work presented here is in the future, but for now we have provided the first detailed comparison between the models.

The paper is structured as follows. In the following Section, we provide some background information on the BDI agent architecture and we show how to specify BDI agent programs. Section 3 presents the Markov decision framework upon which our approach builds. Section 4 explains the correspondence between the BDI architecture and partially observable MDPs. In Section 5 we empirically evaluate our approach with respect to effectiveness and computational leverage. Finally, in Section 7 we present our conclusions and describe related and future work.

2   Belief-Desire-Intention Agents

The idea of applying the concepts of beliefs, desires and intentions to agents originates in the work of [4] and [9]. In this paper, we use the conceptual model of BDI agency as developed by Wooldridge and Parsons [14]. This model is shown in Figure 1. The model distinguishes three main data structures in an agent: a *belief* set, a *desire* set and an *intention* set. An agent's beliefs represent information that the agent has about its environment, and may be partial or incorrect. Desires can be seen as states of affairs that an agent ideally would want to accomplish. Intentions are those desires that an agent has committed to bringing about. The behaviour of the agent is generated by four main components: a *next-state* function, which updates the agent's beliefs on the basis of an observation made of the environment; a *deliberation* function, which constructs a set of appropriate intentions on the basis of the agent's desires, and its current beliefs and intentions; an *action* function, which selects and executes an action that ultimately satisfies one or more of the agent's intentions; and a *meta-level control* function, the

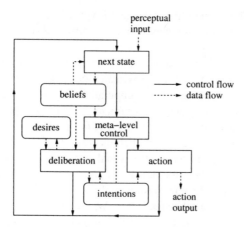

Fig. 1. An abstract BDI agent architecture.

sole purpose of which is to decide whether to pass control to either the deliberation or action subsystems. On any given control cycle, an agent begins by updating its beliefs through its next-state function, and then, on the basis of its current beliefs, the meta-level control function passes control to either the deliberation function (in which case the agent expends computational resources by deliberating over its intentions), or to the action subsystem (in which case the agent acts). As a general rule of thumb, an agent's meta-level control system should pass control to the deliberation function when the agent will change intentions as a result; otherwise, the time spent deliberating is wasted.

We present a simple formal model of BDI agents. First, we have to consider that agents are situated in *environments*; an environment denotes everything that is external to the agent. Let P be a set of *propositions* denoting environment variables. In accordance with similar proposition based vector descriptions of states, we let environment states be built up of such propositions. Then E is a set of *environment states* with members $\{e, e', \ldots\}$, and $e = \{p_1, \ldots, p_n\}$, where $p_i \in P$. Let A denote the set of actions that an agent can execute. A state transition function $\tau : E \times A \rightarrow \Pi(E)$ manages the probabilistic transition of environment states, based on doing some action $a \in A$ in state $e \in E$.

The internal state of an agent consists of beliefs, desires and intentions. Let $Bel : E \rightarrow [0, 1]$, where $\sum_{e \in E} Bel(e) = 1$, denote the agent's *beliefs*: we represent what the agent believes to be true of its environment by defining a probability distribution over the possible environment states. The agent's set of *desires*, Des, is a subset of the set of environment variables: $Des \subseteq P$. Finally, we denote the set of intentions by Int. An intention denotes a number of different means to achieve a certain desire. This is represented here by letting an intention be a stack of partially instantiated plans, i.e., plans in which some variables have been instantiated (as in [9]). We assume that a plan consists of some trigger event, a context and a series of actions. The context is a series of propositions that are evaluated true (for achievement plans) or false (for maintenance plans) after executing the specified series of actions. Let the *head* of a plan be a trigger event and context. Then a plan that is intended typically contains a head that includes some true or false belief that the agent wants to bring about. This belief literal is an environment proposition.

Note that an intention is a sequence of actions in a partially instantiated plan. This is also the key to the way that BDI approximates POMDP: a BDI agent chooses a pre-compiled plan (which is why the online computation is quick) which is nearest to being optimal (which is why we only ever approximate the optimal solution).

An internal state s is then $s = \langle Bel, Des, Int \rangle$, where $Bel : E \rightarrow [0, 1]$ is a probability distribution over the agent's beliefs, $Des \subseteq P$ a set of desires and Int a set of intentions. Let S be the set of all internal states. For a state $s \in S$, we refer to the beliefs in that state as Bel_s, the desires as Des_s and to the intentions as Int_s. We use subscript S to refer to beliefs, desires and intentions for all states; for example, Bel_S refers to the beliefs for all states $s \in S$. We refer to an $i \in Int_s$ as a *background intention* of state $s \in S$. We assume that it is possible to denote values and costs of the outcomes of intentions[1]: an *intention value* $V : Int \rightarrow \mathbb{R}$ represents the value of the outcome of an intention; and *intention cost* $C : Int \rightarrow \mathbb{R}$ represents the cost of achieving the outcome of an intention. The *net value* $V_{net} : Int \rightarrow \mathbb{R}$ represents the net value of the outcome of an intention; $V_{net}(i)$, where $i \in Int$, is typically $V(i) - C(i)$. We denote the *quality* of a state by a function $Q : S \rightarrow \mathbb{R}$, which we assume to be based on the net values of the outcomes of the intentions in a state. Moreover, we assume that if $\forall s, s' \in S, \forall p \in Int_s, \forall p' \in Int_{s'}, V_{net}(p) \geq V_{net}(p')$, then $Q(s) \geq Q(s')$. In the empirical investigation discussed in this paper, we illustrate that a conversion from intention values to state qualities is feasible, though we do not explore the issue here[2]. Finally, A denotes the set of actions the agent is able to perform; with every $\alpha \in A$ we identify a set of propositions $P_\alpha \subseteq P$, which includes the propositions that change value when α is executed. (In the remainder of this paper, we label the various BDI components with label BDI.)

3   Partially Observable Markov Decision Processes

A partially observable Markov Decision Process (POMDP) can be understood as a system that at any point in time can be in any one of a number of distinct states, in which the system's state changes over time resulting from the performance of actions and in which the current state of the system cannot be determined with complete certainty [2]. POMDPs satisfy the Markov assumption in that knowledge of the current state renders information about the past irrelevant to making predictions about the future [2]. In a POMDP, we represent the fact that the knowledge of the agent is not complete by

---

[1] We clearly distinguish intentions from their outcome states and we do not give values to intentions themselves, but rather to their outcomes. For example, when an agent *intends* to deliver coffee, an *outcome* of that intention is the state in which coffee has been delivered.

[2] Notice that this problem is the inverse of the utilitarian *lifting problem*: the problem of how to lift utilities over states to desires over sets of states. Discussing the lifting problem, and its inverse, is beyond the scope of this paper, and therefore we direct the interested reader to the work of Lang et al. [7].

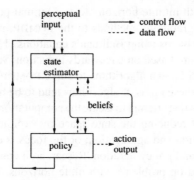

Fig. 2. Components of a POMDP agent.

defining a probability distribution over all possible states. An agent then updates this distribution when it observes its environment.

Let a set of states be denoted by S and a set of actions be denoted by A. An agent might not have complete knowledge of its environment, and must thus *observe* its surroundings in order to acquire knowledge: let Ω be a finite set of observations that the agent can make of the environment. Then an *observation function* $O : S \times A \to \Pi(\Omega)$ defines a probability distribution over the set of observations; this function represents the observations an agent can make resulting from performing an action $a \in A$ in a state $s \in S$. The agent receives rewards for performing actions in certain states: this is represented by a *reward function* $R : S \times A \to \mathbb{R}$. Finally, a *state transition* function $\tau : S \times A \to \Pi(S)$ defines a probability distribution over states resulting from performing an action in a state – this enables us to model non-deterministic actions. (In the remainder of this paper, we label the POMDP components with subscript MKV[3].)

Figure 2 shows the components of a POMDP. Unlike a discrete MDP, a POMDP model includes a *state estimator SE*, which controls the belief state transitions, based on the last action, the current observation and the previous belief state. This component is not necessary in a discrete MDP, since there the agent's policy is based on external states that always accurately reflect the current state of the environment. The state estimator computes a new belief state from basic probability theory, as explained in [5]. The output of the state estimator is used in the agent's state transition function by assigning a probability of 1 to belief state b' resulting from executing action a in belief state b and making observation o if $SE(b, a, o) = b'$ and a probability of 0 otherwise.

Having defined the sets contained in a POMDP, we solve a POMDP by computing an *optimal policy*: an assignment of an action to each possible state such that the expected sum of rewards gained along the possible trajectories in the POMDP is a maximum. An MDP has either an infinite horizon, which renders the policy to be a mapping from states to actions, or a finite horizon, which makes the policy a mapping from states and time to actions. In finite horizon POMDPs it thus matters *when* an action is executed. In this paper,

---

[3] Note that both the discrete MDP and continuous POMDP are Markov processes, hence the acronym MKV.

our concern is mainly with infinite horizon MDPs. Optimal policies can be computed by applying dynamic programming methods to the POMDP, breaking the problem up into one-step decision problems using Bellman's equations [1]. The standard dynamic programming algorithms are based on backwards induction; value iteration and policy iteration are the most well known algorithms to solve POMDPs. A major drawback of applying POMDPs is that these kinds of algorithms tend to be highly intractable.

Traditional approaches that attempt to tackle the computational complexity of solving MDPs are either aimed at reducing the state space by exploiting the space structure, e.g., by means of abstraction and aggregation; or the focus is on designing algorithms that are faster than value and policy iteration. Research on computing optimal policies for POMDPs have focused on problems with finite horizons. For some finite horizon problems, for example, the Tiger problem in [5], the optimal policy turns out to be an infinite horizon policy, i.e., a policy that does not depend on time. Computing infinite horizon policies for POMDPs turns out to be extremely hard[4].

4   Correspondence between BDI and POMDP

The belief-desire-intention model can be used to specify partially observable Markov decision processes. In this Section we show how BDI models correspond to POMDP models and what this means in terms of offline and online computation time and effectiveness.

The objective of our approach is to demonstrate that it is possible to identify a correspondence between the structure of POMDPs and structure of an existing agent model, in this case the BDI model. The main motivation behind our approach is the fact that, viewed at its most abstract, both the POMDP and BDI models ultimately model decision making by mapping perceptual inputs to actions; all other components in the POMDP model and the BDI model are there *in the service* of this abstract decision making function. This can be easily observed by comparing Figures 1 and 2.

In this Section, we first explain what the problem of finding correspondence encompasses, in particular in relation to the BDI agent model. We do this by letting both the POMDP model and BDI model be instantiations of an abstract generic agent function. Secondly, we explain the correspondence in computing agent runs in both models and actually running the models.

Agent Functions

Both the POMDP and BDI model can be represented on some level of abstraction, so that they both correspond to some abstract agent function $ag : S \rightarrow A$ that maps agent states to agent actions. This agent function can then be implemented by either a POMDP or BDI model. As shown above, we define a POMDP as a tuple $\langle S_{MKV}, A_{MKV}, \Omega, R, \tau_{MKV} \rangle$. A BDI model is defined as $\langle S_{BDI}, A_{BDI}, Bel, Des, Int \rangle$ with the BDI control functions as described earlier. Let the implementation of ag by a POMDP be denoted by ag_{MKV} and

---

[4] Algorithms for solving finite horizon POMDPs utilise the fact that in this case the value function is piecewise-linear and convex. However, in an infinite POMDP, the value function is convex, but not necessarily piecewise-linear.

the BDI implementation of ag by ag_{BDI}. We show here how the components of ag_{MKV} and ag_{BDI} map into each other.

Firstly, we identify the following obvious mappings between the BDI and POMDP models:

- *Actions* – The sets of external actions that an agent has at its disposal in the BDI and POMDP model are identical: $A_{MKV} \equiv A_{BDI}$. In the BDI model these actions can be collected and represented more expressively through the concept of plans (or intentions).
- *States* – Because it is assumed that the environment is only partially observable in both the BDI and POMDP model, agent states are belief states rather than environment states. The sets of belief states are identical: $S_{MKV} \equiv Bel_S$, where Bel_S refers to the BDI set of beliefs. Thus the set of POMDP states is identical to the set of BDI states when we exclude the desires and intentions in every BDI state. But because desires and intentions are internal data structures, this issue is not a major obstacle to form state correspondence and thus we let $S_{MKV} \equiv S_{BDI}$.
- *Transition* – The external transition functions, as defined over the environment states and external actions, are identical, because such functions are external to the agent: $\tau_{MKV} \equiv \tau_{BDI}$. The internal transition functions are identical as well: in the BDI model this is the next state function and in the POMDP model the state estimator controls internal transitions: $nextState \equiv SE$. As such, the BDI next state function can be implemented as a POMDP state estimator.

This leaves us with some mappings between components that are somewhat more convoluted: rewards on the POMDP side and desires and intentions on the BDI side. We relate desires to rewards and intentions to a combination of rewards and actions. As mentioned above, *rewards* are received for executing some action in a particular state and are thus defined over action and state combinations. *Desires* are states of affairs that the agent wants to bring about, and thus define some kind of ordering over the set of states. Currently, we are not concerned with how this ordering is exactly realised; in this paper, we define desires simply as a subset of the environment propositions. But, for example in [7], this ordering is based on the individual utilities of the environment propositions. Let $D : S \rightarrow \mathbb{R}$ be a function that represents the ordering of desires over the state space. On the POMDP side, we can distill the rewards in such a way that they are defined only over states[5]. Again, we do not prescribe how this should be done, but merely utilise the fact that it can be done. An example conversion, that works for our experimental testbed as described below, would be to define the *worth* of a state, denoted by $W : S \rightarrow \mathbb{R}$, as the maximum reward of all actions that can be executed in a state $s \in S$:

$$W(s) = \max_{a \in A_s} R(s, a),$$

where $A_s \in A$ denotes the set of all actions that can be executed in s. Then this concept of state worth corresponds to the ordering on desires: $W \equiv D$. From this we conclude that rewards correspond with desires.

---

[5] We claim that this conversion can be done in general without any loss of information, but cannot currently support this claim with conclusive proof. Research is ongoing on this issue.

Finally, we identify the concept of *intentions* with a combination of rewards and actions. An intention is a stack of partially instantiated plans: it specifies a sequence of actions which, when executed, fulfills some desire of the agent. There is thus an action as well as a desire aspect to intentions. First, we explore the desires part of this plan definition of intentions. The set of desires is a subset of the set of environment propositions. As mentioned above, the head of an intended plan contains an environment proposition that the agent wants to be either true or false: this is thus a desire. In terms of a POMDP, this first part of intentions relates to rewards, because desires correspond to POMDP rewards, as described previously.

The second part of intentions concerns the sequence of actions. In terms of a POMDP, this clustering of actions into intentions is some form of *action abstraction*. It is this abstraction which gives BDI approach its computational edge, but also means it may only approximate optimal actions. Because POMDPs generate complicated plans progressively by mere execution of single actions rather than to build and – partially or completely – execute complex plans, we cannot simply utilise this similarity as a proper correspondence. However, these plans are not ordinary plans, but organised in intentions. Intentions have particular characteristics, under which most importantly representing a number of different means to fulfill the same desire. Based on the differences between traditional plans and the characteristics of intentions, we claim a valid correspondence between this part of intentions and actions. We further have to distinguish between deterministic and stochastic actions. An optimal agent decides the stability of its intentions based on the degree of determinism of its actions, the degree of observability of the environment, the rate of change of the environment [12] and the agent's own changing preferences. As for deterministic actions, this leaves intention stability to depend on the other three factors. However, we are concerned with stochastic domains and this renders the agent's actions stochastic. In that case, we have to take this non-determinism into account by expressing it on the level of intentions rather than the level of actions.

To summarise, we have discussed the following correspondences between the BDI and POMDP models. Firstly, the action spaces and transition functions (both internal and external) of the models are identical. Secondly, the POMDP state space and the belief parts of internal BDI states are the same. Thirdly, the BDI desires correspond to the rewards. And finally, BDI intentions correspond to a combination of POMDP rewards and actions.

Agent Runs

Assuming that the above correspondences are valid, we can identify the correspondence between running ag_{MKV} and ag_{BDI}. In both models, a run is a sequence of states connected by the actions executed by the agent. The method of choosing such a run in the POMDP model is based on the policy, as computed when solving the POMDP. In the BDI model, such a run defines the optimality of the agent; an optimal agent generates an optimal run. Computing runs for particular implementations of both models involves an *offline* and *online* component. Offline computation takes place outside of the environment in which the agent is to be situated and thus before executing actions. This computation results in an optimal policy for the POMDP case, or in an agent program in the BDI case. The online computation involves executing the policy or program. In case of a policy, this boils down to looking up the most believed state given the observations in the policy and executing the optimal action for that state. In case of a program, the online computation concerns the whole process that happens between receiving perceptual input and executing action output. Thus ag_{MKV} and ag_{BDI} correspond to each other, though we have to be aware of potential differences in online and offline computation times.

An important issue to keep in mind is the Markov property: it is not necessary to maintain an action history. Obviously, ag_{MKV} obeys this property. However, in the BDI model it often happens that selection of an optimal action is based on the history leading up to the current state. Similar to approaches that turn non-Markovian processes into Markovian ones, we assume for now that the BDI history is contained in the current state. Since we have shown above that the belief states correspond and a belief state in ag_{MKV} is updated using the previous belief state, we can safely state that we can make ag_{BDI} obey the Markov property.

Finally, we mention the role of observability in the correspondence specification. In ag_{MKV}, observations are not only used to contain *physical* types of observations, but *informational* as well. In this way, it is possible to capture notions of resource-bounded information gathering or obtaining the value of information. We can use this correspondence in ag_{BDI}. An important issue when designing situated agents concerns the dynamism of the agent's environment, i.e., the world changes while the agent executes its policy. We can use the concept of observability to represent dynamism. In this way, we move to another type of POMDP in which there is no uncertainty about the current environment state, but there is uncertainty over state transitions and non-determinism of actions. We return to this issue in Section 7.

5   Empirical Validation

In this Section we apply our model in the TILEWORLD testbed [8]. The results of our experiments support the suggested benefit of our model in two ways. Firstly, we demonstrate that the increase in effectiveness of a MDP agent over a BDI agent is small. Secondly, we show that when the problem size grows, one cannot compute an MDP solution any more. This is mainly due to the intractability of solving complex MDPs. This issue is discussed and illustrated below by indications of some offline computation times for solving an MDP representing the TILEWORLD.

The TILEWORLD [8] is a grid environment on which there are agents and holes. An agent can move up, down, left, right and diagonally. Holes have to be visited by the agent in order for it to gain rewards. The TILEWORLD starts in some randomly generated world state and changes over time with the appearance and disappearance of holes according to some fixed probability distributions. An agent moves about the grid one step at a time.

The TILEWORLD testbed is easily represented as an MDP. Let L denote the set of locations, i.e., $L = \{i : 1 \le i \le n\}$ represents the mutually disjoint locations, where n denotes the size of the grid. A proposition p_i then denotes the presence ($p_i = 1$) or absence ($p_i = 0$) of a hole at location i. An environment state is a pair $\langle \{p_i, \ldots, p_n\}, m \rangle$, where $\{p_i, \ldots, p_n\}$ are the propositions representing the holes in the grid, and $m \in L$ is the current location of the agent.

Table 1. Offline computation times of running a value iteration algorithm for an MDP specification of the TILEWORLD with discount rate = 0.9 (measured performance of JAVA2 on PentiumIII-500Mhz, 128MB RAM).

Tileworld size (length × width)	$\|S_{\mathrm{MKV}}\|$	# Iterations before optimal	Iteration duration (msec)
3 × 3	81	5	84
4 × 4	256	7	840
5 × 5	625	9	5,200
6 × 6	1296	11	23,750
7 × 7	2401	13	92,700
8 × 8	4096	15	250,000

We computed the optimal infinite horizon MDP policy, using value iteration, for an agent situated in a TILEWORLD. An environment state in this MDP is a combination of the current location of the agent and the locations of present holes; the possible actions are up, right, down, left and stay; an action succeeds with probability 0.9 – failure means that another action is chosen with equiprobability. Because the TILEWORLD is dynamic, we have to take into account that every cell is either occupied by a hole or not. Combining this fact with the current location of the agent, makes the state space of size $2^n \times n$. In order to render the necessary computations in some degree feasible, we *abstracted* the TILEWORLD state space. In the TILEWORLD domain, we abstract the state space by letting an environment state e be a pair $\langle p_1, p_2 \rangle$, where p_1 refers to the location of the hole which is currently closest to the agent, and p_2 refers to the current location of the agent. We deem this knowledge sufficient for the agent to choose an appropriate action. This abstraction means that the size of the state space is now reduced to n^4.

We plotted some statistics of these MDP solution computations for a number of TILEWORLDs of different size in Table 1 by means of value iteration. The results merely illustrate that even for a simplistic application such as the TILEWORLD, the offline computation times are exorbitant[6]. Although this approach renders the online computation times negligible, it is clearly not a realistic method for the design of agents in more complex settings. Moreover, as we keep increasing the size of the TILEWORLD, at some point it becomes impossible to compute MDP solutions (simply because of the intractability of solving MDPs). From this point onwards, it pays off for certain to use a BDI approach – even if it only gives marginal results. (Currently, research is ongoing on exactly where this point is for the TILEWORLD testbed and how well the BDI approach performs from that point onwards.)

Whereas obtaining an optimal MDP policy in the TILEWORLD is computationally hard, we observe that this optimal policy is a simple fixed control strategy: the agent

---

[6] We mention explicitly that these results have *only* been inserted for illustrative purposes. We are aware that performance can be increased dramatically by choosing a more efficient algorithm or even a faster programming language or machine. However, this does not refute our claim that computation times are unacceptable for such a simple domain as the TILEWORLD and will become impossibly long for sufficiently large TILEWORLD scenarios.

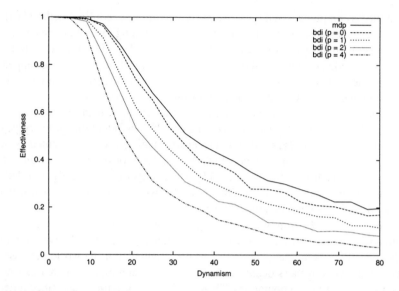

Fig. 3. Overall effectiveness of an MDP and BDI agent. Effectiveness is measured as the result of a varying degree of dynamism of the world. The four curves show the effectiveness for the BDI agent at planning costs (denoted by p) from 0 to 4.

executes the action with highest success probability that brings it closer to the nearest hole. This strategy is easily implemented and we have done so. The effectiveness of this strategy is shown in Figure 3.

In the experiments, the TILEWORLD has dimensions 20×20, thus there are 400 unique locations ($n = 400$). Environments were varied by changing the degree of dynamism (γ). Dynamism is denoted by an integer in the range 1 to 80, representing the ratio between the world clock rate and the agent clock rate. If $\gamma = 1$, then the world executes one cycle for every cycle executed by the agent and the agent's information is guaranteed to be up to date; if $\gamma > 1$ then the information the agent has about its environment may not necessarily be up to date when it carries out an action. (In the experiments in this paper we assume the environment is fully observable, i.e., the agent can update its information at every cycle of its own clock.) The *planning cost* p represents the time cost of planning, i.e., the number of time-steps required to form a plan. The *effectiveness* ϵ of an agent is the ratio of the actual score achieved by the agent to the score that could in principle have been achieved.

We conducted a similar series of experiments with the BDI agent, based on the conceptual BDI architecture as explained in Section 2. The implemented BDI architecture is described in [12]. This BDI agent adopts single intentions to visit a particular hole, constructs a plan, consisting of move actions, to achieve that intention – a path to the hole – and sequentially executes actions of the adopted plan. An intention value corresponds to the reward received by the agent for reaching a hole, and an intention cost is the distance between the current location of the agent and the location that the agent intends to reach. The meta-level control function determines the *stability* of an adopted plan.

The stability is computed based on a discrete deliberation scheduling method [10]. This method determines the efficient trade off between continuing to execute the current plan or to spend computational resources on adopting a new plan[7]. Deciding this trade off is based on knowledge of the probability distributions controlling when holes appear and disappear. The results of the series of experiments with a BDI agent are shown in Figure 3 (for planning cost $p = 0, 1, 2, 4$) in comparison with an MDP agent.

In Figure 4 the results of the BDI experiments are shown in comparison with a cautious and bold agent. A *cautious* agent reconsiders its intentions at every possible opportunity whereas a *bold* agent does not reconsider until it has fully executed its current plan. We have investigated the relationship between the reconsideration rate and various properties of an agent's environment in [11]. The results of this investigation led us to undertake further research on the problem of adaptive reconsideration, hence the BDI agent based on discrete deliberation scheduling.

We conclude this Section with a short analysis of the demonstrated results. A more in depth analysis of the BDI experiments are described in [12]. Firstly, we observe that the effectiveness of both agents decreases as the dynamism of the world increases and the BDI agent's effectiveness decreases as the cost of planning cost increases (the cost of the online part of the computation). The planning cost is a time cost, since it denotes the number of time-steps required to construct a plan.

Secondly, the most important observation we make from comparing the graphs in Figure 3 to each other is that the BDI effectiveness curve clearly approximates the MDP effectiveness curve, assuming that the planning cost is small enough. We base this conclusion on matching the MDP agent's effectiveness curve to the BDI agent's effectiveness curve for $p = 0$. This suggests that the BDI approach might be viewed as an approximation to the MDP approach, and one which is tractable, but shifts the computational burden from offline to online. As this burden increases (p gets larger), the quality of the approximation decreases.

Thirdly, the BDI approach can handle TILEWORLD examples which are beyond the scope of the MDP approach, e.g., a 40×40 TILEWORLD. As the size of the TILEWORLD increases, Table 1 shows that MDP computation times increase rapidly. One may safely assume that from some point onwards, computing an optimal MDP policy becomes unfeasible and even impossible. As mentioned above, it is necessary to investigate where this point is and how the BDI approach performs from that point onwards. For this, we need to know how well BDI methods scale and this issue is currently under investigation.

Finally, we comment on the performance of the MDP agent in this real-time domain. We observe that although every action is chosen optimally by the MDP agent, the overall effectiveness of the agent is not a maximum. For example, in the TILEWORLD domain, we observe that for environments with a dynamism that is more than 6 ($\gamma > 6$), the effectiveness of the MDP agent is less than 1 ($\epsilon < 1$). The reason for this is that the frequency with which holes appear and disappear is too high for the agent to get to one of those that appear even when choosing the decision-theoretically optimal actions. Additionally, the fact that an agent cannot precisely *anticipate* future events – the appearance and disappearance of holes – lowers the effectiveness of the agent. One example

---

[7] In BDI terminology this decision making function is better known as an *intention reconsideration* function.

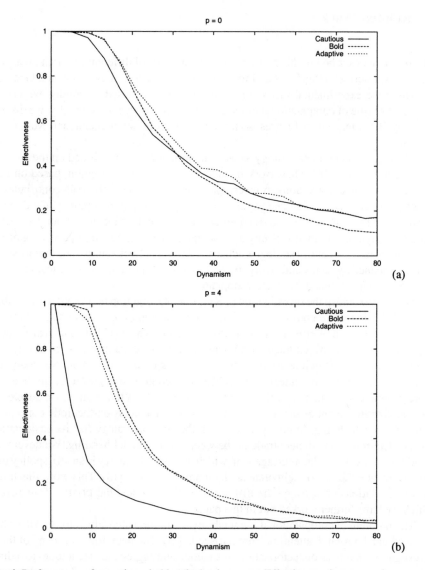

Fig. 4. Performance of a cautious, bold and adaptive agent. Effectiveness is measured as a result of a varying degree of dynamism of the world at planning costs (denoted by *p*) p = 0 in (a) and p = 4 in (b). The adaptive agent is a BDI agent based on discrete deliberation scheduling. (From [12])

of this is the appearance of an hole exactly at the same time that the agent moves away from that location. With the benefit of hindsight, the agent would have done better to have stayed there instead of moving away. However, from the viewpoint of the agent, these are merely unlucky situations from which it is hard to escape in realistic domains. These two issues illustrate that choosing optimal actions individually does not guarantee overall optimal performance.

6   Related Work

The research described in this paper relates to a number of different research areas that we briefly describe in this Section. Firstly, we describe research by Kinny and Georgeff on which the experimental methodology in this paper is based. Secondly, we briefly discuss the issue of computational intractability in solving POMDPs. Finally, we discuss work by Boutilier, which focuses on the relationship between agents and Markovian planning.

The experimental methodology as used in our investigation is based on the work of Kinny and Georgeff [6]. Their work includes an experimental program, based on Pollack's TILEWORLD, that aims to investigate how commitment to goals contributes to the effective behaviour of situated agents. This research is part of a more general investigation into the reactive meta-level control of deliberation for resource-bounded agents situated in dynamic domains. Kinny and Georgeff show that in dynamic environments different meta-level control strategies achieve a different effectiveness. The empirical results as obtained by Kinny and Georgeff emphasise the importance of meta-level control, but closely relate to the TILEWORLD domain.

We have extended the investigation of Kinny and Georgeff in two ways[8] as described in [11, 12]. Firstly, we considered partially observable and non-deterministic domains for the investigation of effectiveness of situated agents. This enabled us to clearly identify a relationship between the environment (in terms of dynamism, observability and determinism) and the deliberation control strategy as used by the agent. Secondly, we aimed to develop domain independent deliberation control strategies to be applied in a more general context then only the TILEWORLD testbed. As to the latter, we developed the adaptive BDI agent as described above, based on the decision-theoretic concept of deliberation scheduling. In this type of agent, the control strategy (or: reconsideration policy) determines an efficient trade off between acting and deliberating. We developed an additional decision-theoretic agent, in which the control strategy is an MDP policy that lets the agent either act or deliberate at any moment in time[9] [13]. This work illustrates the close relationship between the BDI agent architecture and the POMDP framework, which we have further worked out in this paper.

The problem of computational intractability of solution algorithms for POMDPs has received much research attention (summarised in [2]). The main focus of many of these investigations has been on factorisation, abstraction and aggregation techniques to reduce the state space or action space. Probabilistic STRIPS operators and influence diagrams are such techniques that can be used to factor the state space of Markov problems. Although these methods have been developed without the POMDP framework directly in mind, they have proven successful in factoring POMDP state spaces and consequently rendering computation times feasible. As such, our proposal for using the BDI agent architecture to solve POMDPs can be considered a similar effort. However, more than solely reducing the state space or action space, the BDI architecture includes techniques

---

[8] This work has been presented at the UKMAS workshops 2000 and 2001, respectively.

[9] Since this agent suffers from the same intractability of solving POMDPs, as mentioned above, we decided to compare this paper's MDP agent with the deliberation scheduling agent.

to direct reasoning while solving a POMDP. This is a potential important benefit over other methods.

The POMDP planning framework has for long been brought into relation with agent based architectures. As mentioned in the paragraph above, several techniques from planning under uncertainty have been successfully applied in a POMDP setting as well as in the agent based research. Recently, the POMDP planning framework is being applied in multi-agent settings[10], in which either a POMDP problem is distributed among several agents or every agent is represented as a POMDP. This new development brings, as any, novel problems with it, but the multi-agent research area can contribute much to better solve existing POMDP problems. Work in this area is relevant to the research described in this paper, since it illustrates the importance and suggested benefit of combining POMDP planning and agent-based systems.

Finally, we point out research by Boutilier et al. [3] which integrates Markov decision processes with Golog, a high level programming language with a situation calculus semantics. Our model distinguishes from this work in the way that our method views the programming and planning approaches as distinctive alternatives for each other, whereas the work in [3] views them as complementary processes. Golog can be understood as an agent specification language and as such can replace the BDI part of our approach. This replacement is an interesting further extension in order to investigate the behaviour of our model with respect to other correspondence specifications.

7   Discussion

In this paper we presented a preliminary analysis of the correspondence between the theory of Markov decision processes for planning in partially observable domains and the belief-desire-intention agent architecture. The main contributions of integrating these two models are as follows: it would explain the existence of a correspondence between the POMDP and BDI models, it would demonstrate how intentions contribute to efficiently solving POMDPs, and it would provide an intuitive method to specify POMDPs by using BDI models. We have not addressed all these issues in this paper, and, as described below, leave further elaboration of non-addressed issues to future work.

Our research is centered around the hypothesis that BDI can still be used when MDP is intractable. The results in this paper give reasonable support to suppose that this hypothesis is true. Further support must be gathered through more rigorous theoretical and empirical investigation as initiated above. Supposing the hypothesis is correct, one concrete issue to address is to find the point at which it becomes impossible to compute MDP solutions, but where BDI models still give reasonable performance.

The main contributions of this paper are to point out the correspondence between the BDI and POMDP model and to demonstrate empirically that the performance of a BDI model approximates the effectiveness of a POMDP model. Exactly how good this approximation is depends on the time cost of planning in the BDI model, as we have shown in this paper. Although the analysis and formalisation of our approach in this

---

[10] The application of the POMDP framework in multi-agent systems was addressed by Boutilier in the keynote talk of UKMAS 2000.

paper are preliminary, the results of our experimental validation are promising as such that further research is necessary to explore our findings in more detail.

The conclusions we derived from the TILEWORLD experiments are as follows. Firstly, our findings confirm results as obtained earlier in similar experiments. Secondly, the BDI model approximates the MDP model in terms of effectiveness. Thirdly, we claim that on the basis of our results, BDI can deal with problems that are beyond the MDP approach. Finally, we remark that the optimality of MDP solutions is only relevant with respect to individual actions, not necessarily regarding overall optimal performance. To this extent, the BDI approach might approximate the POMDP approach, where the computational burden has been shifted from offline to online. In the testbed used in this paper, the BDI approach can handle problems which are beyond the scope of an MDP approach. We propose future research to investigate the behaviour of performance with respect to balancing offline and online computation.

Our method is to be used for the design of autonomous agents that will operate in uncertain environments. We express this uncertainty by measurements of: *dynamism*, the rate of change of the environment, independent of the activities of the agent; *observability*, the extent to which the agent has access to the current state of the environment; and *determinism*, the degree of predictability of the system behaviour for identical system have inputs.

Exploration of future research paths from here is interesting from a number of different viewpoints. Firstly, as mentioned above, we intend to conduct further investigation of the formal analysis of our approach. Such research will give more insight into the computational efficiency of our method compared to traditional POMDP solution algorithms. The issue of balancing offline and online computation is a serious consideration for design. Through research on how these two different types of computation contribute to the computational cost of our model and under which circumstances, we hope to eventually automate balancing offline and online computation.

Secondly, we have undertaken preliminary research into the potential benefit of using the notion of intentions in solving POMDPs. Previously, POMDP researchers have combined single actions into plans (called options or macro-actions) as a type of action abstraction. We have used intentions to cover this notion of plans. The added benefit of intentions over options is that, by definition, intentions direct and constrain future reasoning. As such, intentions are a very natural way for abstracting the action space.

Finally, our experimental validation can be extended in different ways. We are currently working on the implementation of our model in a more realistic type of testbed, robot navigation, to demonstrate wider model applicability. Besides this, we are investigating the implementation of observability as means of resource-bounded information gathering, i.e., acquiring value of information, in the TILEWORLD. For this, it is necessary to have solution algorithms for infinite horizon POMDPs, and these algorithms are currently, to our best knowledge, not available.

References

1. R. Bellman. *Dynamic Programming*. Princeton University Press, Princeton, NJ, 1957.
2. C. Boutilier, T. Dean, and S. Hanks. Decision-theoretic planning: Structural assumptions and computational leverage. *Journal of AI Research*, pages 1–94, 1999.

3. C. Boutilier, R. Reiter, M. Soutchanski, and S. Thrun. Decision-theoretic, high-level agent programming in the situation calculus. In *Proceedings of the 7th Conference on Artificial Intelligence (AAAI-00)*, pages 355–362, Menlo Park, CA, 2000.
4. M. E. Bratman, D. J. Israel, and M. E. Pollack. Plans and resource-bounded practical reasoning. *Computational Intelligence*, 4:349–355, 1988.
5. L. P. Kaelbling, M. L. Littman, and A. R. Cassandra. Planning and acting in partially observable stochastic domains. *Artificial Intelligence*, 101:99–134, 1998.
6. D. Kinny and M. Georgeff. Commitment and effectiveness of situated agents. In *Proceedings of the Twelfth International Joint Conference on Artificial Intelligence (IJCAI-91)*, pages 82–88, Sydney, Australia, 1991.
7. J. Lang, L. v. d. Torre, and E. Weydert. Utilitarian desires. *Journal of Autonomous Agents and Multi-Agent Systems*, 2002. To appear.
8. M. E. Pollack and M. Ringuette. Introducing the Tileworld: Experimentally evaluating agent architectures. In *Proceedings of the Eighth National Conference on Artificial Intelligence (AAAI-90)*, pages 183–189, Boston, MA, 1990.
9. A. S. Rao and M. P. Georgeff. An abstract architecture for rational agents. In C. Rich, W. Swartout, and B. Nebel, editors, *Proceedings of Knowledge Representation and Reasoning (KR&R-92)*, pages 439–449, 1992.
10. S. Russell and E. Wefald. Principles of metareasoning. *Artificial Intelligence*, 49(1-3):361–395, 1991.
11. M. C. Schut and M. Wooldridge. Intention reconsideration in complex environments. In M. Gini and J. Rosenschein, editors, *Proceedings of the Fourth International Conference on Autonomous Agents (Agents 2000)*, pages 209–216, Barcelona, Spain, 2000.
12. M. C. Schut and M. Wooldridge. Principles of intention reconsideration. In E. Andre and S. Sen, editors, *Proceedings of the Fifth International Conference on Autonomous Agents (Agents 2001)*, Montreal, Canada, 2001.
13. M. C. Schut, M. Wooldridge, and S. Parsons. Reasoning about intentions in uncertain domains. In D. Dubois and H. Prade, editors, *Proceedings of European Conference on Symbolic and Quantitative Approaches to Reasoning with Uncertainty*, Toulouse, France, 2001.
14. M. Wooldridge and S. D. Parsons. Intention reconsideration reconsidered. In J. P. Müller, M. P. Singh, and A. S. Rao, editors, *Intelligent Agents V (LNAI Volume 1555)*, pages 63–80. Springer-Verlag: Berlin, Germany, 1999.

Author Index

Lecture Notes in Artificial Intelligence (LNAI)

Lecture Notes in Computer Science